Bermuda
FIVE CENTURIES

Rosemary Jones

Published by Panatel VDS Ltd.

Produced by Brimstone Media Ltd.

A Project of the Bermuda Millennium Committee

Sponsored by

Bank of Bermuda
FOUNDATION

Cover images courtesy of: Luciano Aicardi, Bermuda
Archives, Bermuda Industrial Union, Bermuda Maritime
Museum, Bermuda Media, *The Bermudian*, Brimstone
Media, Patricia Ferguson, Government House,
Department of Communication and Information,
Sandra Rouja, the Watlington Family

Pages 8–9: Sea Venture *in a Storm*, painting by William
Harrington, 1959, Bermuda Maritime Museum;
Pages 50–51: painting by Thomas Driver, 1823, Bermuda
Archives; Pages 98–99: painting by Lt. H. S. Clive, RE,
Bermuda National Trust Collection; Pages 146–47:
Bermuda Volunteer Engineers on the Bermuda Railway,
Bermuda Archives; Pages 190–91: Dr. E. F. Gordon,
Bermuda Industrial Union

Bermuda: Five Centuries, by Rosemary Jones
Book and cover designed by Paul Shapiro,
Brimstone Media Ltd.
Copyright © 2004 Panatel VDS Ltd.
Text copyright © 2004 Rosemary Jones
Published by Panatel VDS Ltd., Bermuda
No part of this book may be reproduced in any form
without the publisher's written permission
Printed in China
ISBN 0-921560-13-3
First Edition 2004
Second printing 2005

Contents

Bank of Bermuda
FOUNDATION

This project has been made possible by a generous grant from the
Bank of Bermuda Foundation to the Bermuda Millennium Committee,
Department of Cultural Affairs.

Introduction

History, they say, is yesterday's news. A valid truism, perhaps, but one that deceives by omission. Portraying the past as a static recital of facts and figures neglects the far more dynamic truth about time gone by: that history is the story of real people. Individual courage, personal triumph, gut-wrenching tragedy—our past is an organic skein shaped and shared by generations, a living, breathing story-in-motion which belongs not locked away in the vaults of archives, but in the hearts and minds of contemporary lives.

Born of a six-part film series conceived and produced by Panatel VDS Ltd. for the government's Millennium Committee in 1999, this book, *Bermuda: Five Centuries*, completes the project, capturing the sights, sounds and human emotions of the island's past, through the eyes of the people who lived it. The concept for the book grew from the realisation that while Bermuda counts many commendable niche publications in its libraries, there existed no popular compilation history of the island that both tantalised readers with eye-catching design and colour images, and also brought together so many disparate elements—the first settlers with the suffragettes, the privateers with the insurance titans, Second World War veterans with civil-rights activists and 9/11 survivors.

Thanks to a generous grant from the Bank of Bermuda Foundation, made possible through the Millennium Committee, the dream for such a publication has become a reality, and with it, we hope, a reason to celebrate our heritage. The goal, above all else, was to make the book accessible to everyone, from the curious school student to the adult history buff, to dip into at leisure, or read cover to cover. The approach we chose was largely journalistic, relying on the directness of compelling reportage to make history relevant in human terms. Eye-witness story-telling evokes the excitement, the fear, the intense emotion of a moment when history is being made. Sometimes the subject realises the greater context while they're living it—when he was covering the December 1977 riots, for example, television reporter Rick Richardson was struck by the social implications of the anger he was encountering. Others are simply trying to survive.

How did it feel to be dragged through the sea by a roaring whale on the end of a harpoon? Or be shot down by enemy gunfire over war-torn France? What was it like to frantically search ghost-town streets for friends and family during a yellow-fever epidemic? Or dodge a maelstrom of splintering glass as the World Trade Center began to implode? We hear the torment of a 12-year-old girl as she is sold as a slave in front of her weeping mother, and feel the boredom of a Boer War prisoner with nothing to do during a year's internment on the Great Sound except carve trinkets and learn French. We witness the pride of an Azorean farmer who spends exhausted evenings learning to write so he may sign status papers with his name instead of an "X." We sense the icy fear of a renowned scientist, who, locked in a bathysphere 300 feet below the sea, happens to glance at the steel door…and notices a trickle of water creeping beneath. The stories of these and others throughout the narrative bring history to life and serve as a vital testimony to Bermuda's past.

The book is an overview of 500 years, from 1505—the year Spaniard Juan de Bermúdez caught sight of the "Isle of Devils"—to the present day, as Bermuda prepares to honour its quincentennial anniversary. Covering such a wide timespan made it necessary to be highly selective in our focus. The book's organisation is chronological, divided into five major eras, each made up of four chapters. We could not include a date-by-date reckoning of the years, nor profile all the newsmakers or every achievement or failure. Instead, we attempted to paint the broad brushstrokes of history that had the largest human impact; rather than presenting a strictly linear narrative, we tried to expose the mood, trends and social themes of periods which engaged and inspired us, which irrevocably changed us, which shaped how Bermudians see themselves today.

Uncovering both the human drama of well-known events and the routine minutiae of lives often overlooked by history books was our mission. While many key Bermudians are featured, the book's focus has tried not to be too heavy on the famous and influential; just as relevant, we considered, were the lives of everyday people, the general public through whose eyes, ears and mouths history was felt and told.

To improve accessibility and add to the book's educational value, we used timelines throughout the major sections to trace Bermuda's evolution to a modern society along with that of the wider world. Throughout the chapters, we included features such as *In Their Own Words*, based on diaries, letters and interview testimonials; *How They Lived*, describing the daily challenges of life during particular eras; sidebars to detail a noteworthy personality or event; margin excerpts to illustrate how others saw us; and select commentaries by noted Bermuda historians. Liberal use of photography, artwork and illustration puts faces to the many stories.

Most of the factual content of the main narrative is drawn from already-published works on Bermuda history, which are listed in the bibliography. However, some primary sources such as newspapers, periodicals and film, as well as material collected in contemporary interviews, was also used, along with my own personal recollections and experiences in some of the later chapters—one of the advantages, perhaps, of being both a journalist and a born-and-bred islander.

The book strives to be even-handed, especially when treating some of the more contentious periods of the island's past, particularly those rooted in racial prejudice and social friction. We did not shy away from presenting a "warts-and-all" scrutiny of Bermuda's collective memory; while highlighting the feel-good times of high achievement and community triumph, we included the uglier growing pains that marked the country's path to the modern era. Even more importantly, we felt an edition of the 21st Century should be a seamlessly inclusive story, bringing together the whole fabric of backgrounds, races and cultures that make up Bermuda society.

Bermudians have perennially pondered the question, "Who Are We?" That is perhaps best answered not with proof of genealogical lineages or arguments about our cultural differences, but by examining, instead, what we have in common. This is the story of what shaped our collective identity, a story of an unlikely community's adaptability, innovation and courage against all odds. It is not without ignoble episodes, but its central theme is a fierce sense of pride, self-sufficiency and survival.

Moreover, it is an opportunity, we hope, for all Bermudians to learn about or re-experience our past, to celebrate it, and to protect our heritage and identity for the sake of generations to come.

ABOUT THE AUTHOR

Born in Bermuda, Rosemary Jones is a writer and editor with 20 years' journalistic experience. She has been a news and features reporter at the *Toronto Star*, *Toronto Sun* and Broadcast News, Toronto, and was managing editor of *The Bermudian* magazine from 1994 to 1999. She is a correspondent for *People* magazine, and is president and editorial director of Brimstone Media Ltd., a Bermuda-based consultancy for publications, public relations and museum exhibit production.

ABOUT THE PUBLISHER

Panatel VDS Ltd., established in 1982, is a leading producer of television documentaries interpreting themes of cultural and social value to Bermudians. Creator of *Treasures* and *The LearnaLots*, its six-part film series, *Bermuda: Five Centuries*, is a definitive visual record of the island's past and the springboard for this book.

Acknowledgements

This book owes its existence to generosity of all kinds. I am indebted to everyone who gave so graciously of their time, advice and expertise, not to mention their photographs, cherished mementoes and memories; without you, this project could not have happened.

The production of *Bermuda: Five Centuries* would never have left the drawing board without the inspiration of Wendi Fiedler of Panatel VDS Ltd., who conceived the original film series, and helped support the book in partnership with the Millennium Committee, under Culture Minister Terry Lister and chairman Jay Bluck. The generosity of the Bank of Bermuda Foundation, which believed in the project at concept stage, allowed an editorial dream to become published reality. In particular, David Lang and the Foundation deserve recognition for projects that leave a legacy for all Bermudians.

Special thanks goes to interviewees who agreed to re-live fascinating, and sometimes painful experiences, for the *In Their Own Words* series carried throughout the book. While personalities of the past were represented through use of diaries, journals, letters and speeches, contemporary figures were interviewed. Andy Bermingham, Bill Way, Nichole Tatem, Noel Chiappa, Rick Richardson and Shaun Goater all shared detailed moments of their personal lives, which also captured a wider cultural relevance—something we felt helped readers relate to history on human terms.

Much appreciation is also due to the numerous Bermudian families, private individuals and public institutions willing to share their newsworthy stories, artifacts, artworks and photographs. Panatel, the Bermuda Maritime Museum, the Bermuda National Trust, the St. George's Historical Society, the Bermuda Historical Society, Bermuda National Library and the Bermuda Industrial Union opened their archives, and in doing so, provided a pictorial wealth we could not have done without. I would like to extend special thanks to Charles Barclay of Bermuda Media; Howard Cutts of the Bermuda Police Service; Tina Stevenson and Meredith Ebbin, of the Bermudian Publishing Company; Collin Simmons of the BIU; and Karla Hayward, Jane Downing and staff at the Bermuda Archives.

I am extremely grateful to those who agreed to read select chapters and share resources, including parliamentarian and author Dale Butler; Dr. Edward Harris and Charlotte Andrews of the Bermuda Maritime Museum, editors Tony McWilliam, of the *Bermuda Sun*, Bill Zuill of *The Royal Gazette*, and Tim Hodgson, of the *Mid-Ocean News*; Dr. Wolfgang Sterrer and Penny Hill of the Bermuda Aquarium, Museum & Zoo; David Fox of the Bermuda Insurance Institute; film-maker Errol Williams; authors Duncan McDowall, Ira Philip and Sandra Rouja; historians John Cox and Keggie Hallett, Portuguese-Bermudian community activists Trevor Moniz and Robert Pires, and many others.

Absolutely instrumental to the book's progress and outcome was historian Dr. Clarence Maxwell, of the Bermuda Maritime Museum. As chairman of the book's editorial board, he fielded my barrage of historical queries with diligence, insight and always-constructive advice. Thanks also to the other members of the board—Dr. Edward Harris, Wendi Fiedler, Ruth Thomas, Colin Benbow, Heather Whalen, Patricia Marirea Mudd, Peter Smith and David Lang—for their support and suggestions.

This book, as a narrative compilation history, relies heavily on the scholarship of others. I am indebted to the work and expertise of the many researchers, historians and authors of past publications on Bermuda, whose long hours in archives both here and abroad generated a wealth of factual evidence and important commentary on our past. I have cited works I consulted in this book's bibliography.

Lastly, my heartfelt gratitude goes out to the incredibly supportive colleagues, friends, and family who gamely followed the book's progress with interest and much-welcomed encouragement. Not least among them was my son Gabriel, whose embryonic life mirrored the book's own genesis. Born a fortnight after I officially signed on to write the project, he is now two-and-a-half, and has learned to share his mother with a demanding laptop and an archive of fragile tomes. As one of this millennium's first Bermudians, he will, I trust, grow to appreciate the story of his island heritage—a story that will continue to be told, by his generation and the next.

—Rosemary Jones, April 2004

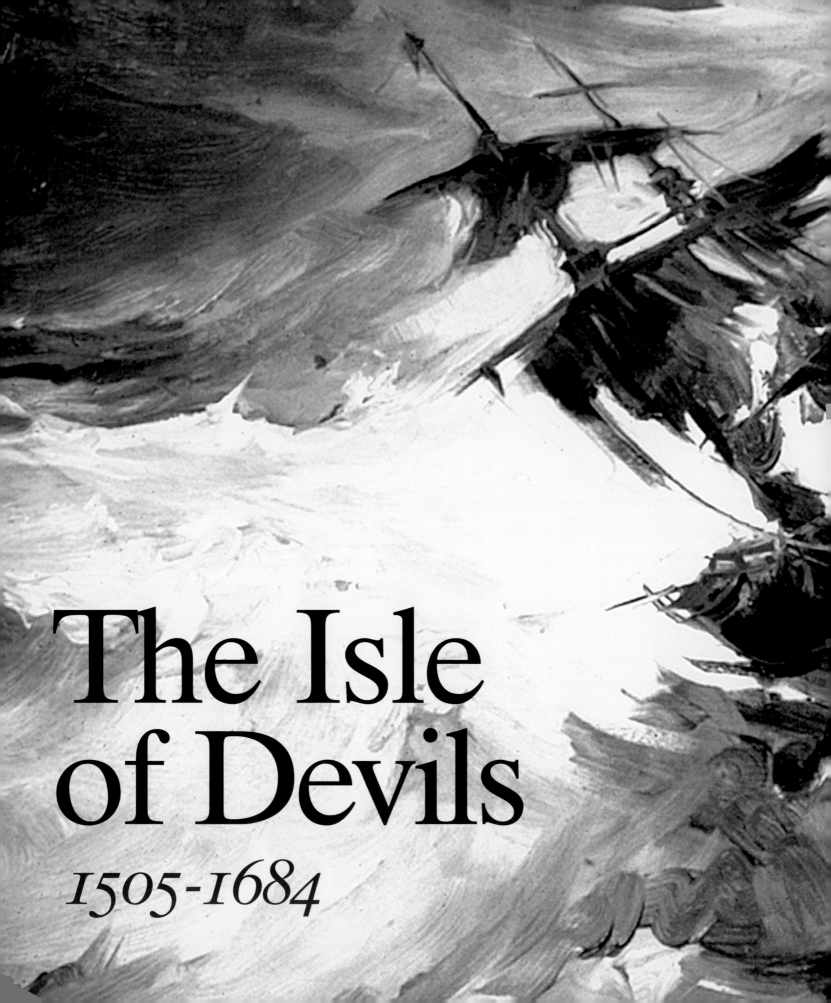

The Isle of Devils

1505-1684

CHAPTER ONE

Age of Discovery

LAND-HO! ISLAND NAMED FOR A MARITIME PIONEER

In October 1603, a Spanish sea captain named Diego Ramirez found himself exploring a deserted half-moon-shaped island in the Atlantic where his galleon had run aground during a storm. Four other ships in the same fleet had been destroyed, but he and his men lost only provisions and were able to hobble into the nearest bay. They anchored and went ashore to scout for fresh supplies. Ramirez would describe his surroundings over the next 22 days in Edenic detail—a reef-guarded oasis blanketed in cedar forests and palmetto palms, where plump pigs roamed wild with herons, sparrow-hawks and web-footed cahows so tame, his crew caught hundreds of the strange birds to eat on their return voyage to Europe. The island's natural harbours swam rich with turtles, parrotfish and red snappers and its shallow inlets were littered with oysters, though when he cracked these open, Ramirez found no pearls.

"The island is very peaceful, it is not high," he wrote of the idyllic but barely-known archipelago called 'Bermuda.' "One can travel all over it on foot or on horseback, good black soil, thinly wooded, very good level country. Very deep on the south side, no shoals from end to end. A vessel can come within a musket shot of land, for the sea breaks on the coast itself."

The captain, who eventually resumed his voyage to Spain from the Americas, sailed around the whole island and drew a rough sketch, a chubby facsimile of the map of Bermuda we recognise today. The drawing, together with his detailed account, provide an engaging snapshot of early Bermuda before its eventual settlement by the English nine years later. His description of a pearl-laden paradise also renewed Spanish interest in the island, which for more than a century had been decried as an "Isle of Devils" or "Isla de Demonios" and shunned by mariners plying trans-Atlantic routes between the New World and Europe.

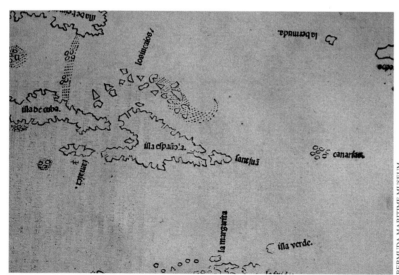

BERMUDA MARITIME MUSEUM

Peter Martyr's map of 1511 offers the first cartographic record of Bermuda, shown upside-down at top right

Treasure island

Bermuda's reefs are strewn with the wrecks of ill-fated treasure ships, many of which have given up glistening examples of Spanish and Portuguese New-World riches

BERMUDA MARITIME MUSEUM

Spanish gold on display at Bermuda Maritime Museum. The so-called Tucker Cross is a replica; the original was stolen in 1975

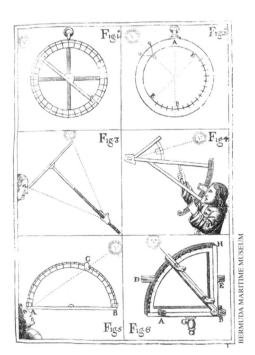

BERMUDA MARITIME MUSEUM

Navigational equipment of the 16th Century. Ships' pilots also used Bermuda as a northern landmark to find their way home to Europe

Bermuda's fearsome label, drawn from tales of ill-fated vessels gored on its treacherous necklace of reefs, was sharply at odds with the bucolic tranquillity experienced by those who actually made it ashore. Ramirez was far from the first to land on the island; he and his men found numerous signs of human presence: a ship's mast, planted tobacco, a cedar cross indicating the location of potable water. Indeed, throughout the 1500s, Bermuda was well-known to merchant vessels, albeit as little more than a landmark which helped them find their way back to Europe. The island appeared on many maps of the time, after 1511.

Generally, mariners of the period made every effort to avoid Bermuda, but several landed there by accident or necessity. They discovered the island's bountiful natural larder, and added to it by offloading hogs, which multiplied on their own. Ramirez's pilot, Hernando Muñiz, told officials of the "many very large cedar trees, on the fruit of which they lived for the time they were there, because they had salvaged no provisions whatever. There are also many palms, resembling dates, which produce a wild berry providing sustenance for a great number of hogs, which it is said had been set ashore by Commander Menéndez [Don Pedro Menéndez de Ávila]"—a Spaniard who, in 1563, apparently landed on Bermuda in search of his shipwrecked son before continuing to Florida.

By the time Ramirez arrived, the archipelago was by all accounts a mid-Atlantic provisions store, a garden of plenty offering refreshment and survival—for those who dared to stop. Like others, the Spanish were "affrighted and dismaied with the frequencie of hurricanes which they ever meet about that place," observed England's maritime hero Sir Walter Raleigh, adding they "durst not adventure [there] but called it 'Demoniorum Insulam.'"

Ironically, it was neither fictitious devils nor elusive spirits that would return to haunt the Spanish, but the cold realisation they had missed the opportunity to make

BERMUDA MEDIA

Italian pioneer Christopher Columbus forged the way to the New World in 1492

Juan de Bermúdez c. *1449–1519*

The Spaniard who gave Bermuda its name is something of an enigma, despite his pioneering maritime exploits. Born around 1449 in the eastern Spanish port of Palos, Juan de Bermúdez hailed from a well-known seafaring family. Indeed, one of his relatives, Diego de Bermúdez, was a teenager aboard the ship *Pinta* during Christopher Columbus's 1492 voyage to the New World.

But it was Juan who was the family's star mariner, and it was he who would be remembered—for the sheer number of consecutive trans-Atlantic voyages he completed in the early 1500s, including his discovery of Bermuda. Had it not been for the latter accomplishment, we may never have known about him. To date, little biographical information has been discovered about Bermúdez other than his impressive maritime reputation. No letters, diaries or other hand-written testimonials have turned up—probably because, like so many mariners of the age, Bermúdez did not know how to read or write.

Yet, Bermúdez was a seasoned navigator who along with a small group of the era's best sailors had pioneered the route west from Europe across the Atlantic—a journey repeated by thousands of later explorers, merchants and sea captains during the Age of Discovery. Although he did not participate in Columbus's celebrated 1492 crossing, he knew him well and in 1496 was chosen by Columbus to captain the ship *Santa Cruz* which accompanied Columbus's *Niña* on a return voyage to Cadiz.

Bermúdez himself was educated solely through maritime pursuits from an early age. Known as a skilled and courageous sailor, a 'king' of the caravel—the fast, sturdy

16th-Century sailing ship—he distinguished himself even among experienced seafarers by crossing the vast span of Atlantic at least 11 times between 1495 and 1519. His impressive record contributed to the confusion over Bermuda's exact date of discovery.

While Bermúdez was always undisputed as the island's discoverer; the year of his achievement was long a puzzle to historians because he made so many voyages between Europe and the New World in the first two decades of the 16th Century. He is named in various expeditions of 1495, 1498, 1502, 1503, 1505, 1507, 1509, 1511, 1512,1513 and 1519, to Jamaica, Puerto Rico, Hispaniola (today, the island of Haiti and the Dominican Republic), and several other parts of the

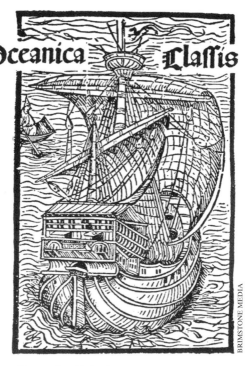

From the 15th Century, European explorers crossed the Atlantic in search of new territories

Indies. More voyages may be undocumented. He died in 1519 in Cuba, where his remains are believed to lie.

Gonzalo Fernández de Oviedo y Valdés, the first person to record the history of the West Indies, named the Spanish captain as the man who first sighted Bermuda, but he neglected to cite a specific year. However, Oviedo called the island "Bermuda" or

This expedition may also have been a milestone, as the first to carry African slaves to the West Indies

"Garza" (Heron), an important clue because it referred to the ship under Bermúdez's command at the time he first encountered the island. Based on maritime records of the period, historians now believe 1505 is almost certainly the date when he encountered Bermuda; it was only during this year that Bermúdez, then 56, served as captain of the ship *La Garza*, owned by a Spaniard named Alfonso Nuñez. It is thought that for unknown reasons, he veered north from the normal Caribbean-Europe route home and spotted the islands on this journey.

The outward-bound leg of this particular expedition may also have been an historic milestone, marking the first to carry African slaves to the West Indies. Records show Bermúdez set sail from Palos for Hispaniola with provisions and 16 slaves aboard *La Garza*. The slaves, natives of the Guinea coast, had been purchased in Lisbon as copper-mine labourers. It was on the return trip, having delivered his human cargo, that Bermúdez would have seen the archipelago to which he gave his name.

This wood called cedar *It is a good wood to work with to make boxes, door and window frames and other workings. It is timber that the shipworm and gnawing creature do no damage. For this reason some say that this wood is so free of disease and that the shipworm does not penetrate it…It is true that a few months ago the pilot Bartolome Carreño brought from the island of Bermuda to the city of Santo Domingo some beautiful pieces or logs of this wood called cedar.*
　　—Spanish courtier Gonzalo Fernández de Oviedo y Valdés, aboard Juan de Bermúdez's ship La Garza *on a stop at Bermuda in 1515*

In their own words

■ Gonzalo Fernández de Oviedo y Valdés, *1515*

I sayled above the island Bermuda, otherwise called Garza, being the furthest of all the islands that are found at this day in the world, and arriving there at the depth of eight yards of water, and distance from the land as far as the shot of a piece of ordnance, I determined to send some of the ship to land, as well as to make search of such things as were there, as also to leave in the island certaine hogs for increase. But the time not serving my purpose by reason of contrarie winde, I could bring my ship no neerer the Island...

While I remayned here, I saw a strife and combat betweene these flying fishes, and the fishes named giltheads, and the fowles called sea mewes, and cormorants, which surely seemed unto me a thing of as great pleasure and solace as could be devised.

While the giltheads swam on the brim of the water, and sometimes lifted their shoulders above the same, to raise the flying fishes out of the water to drive them to flight, and to follow them swimming to the place where they fall, to take and eat them suddenly. Againe on the other side, the sea mewes and cormorants take many of these flying fishes, so that by this means they are neither safe in the aire, nor in the water. In the selfe same perill and danger doe men live in this mortal life, wherein is no certaine securities, neither in high estate, nor in lowe.

—*Gonzalo Fernández de Oviedo y Valdés, author of* La Historia General y Natural de las Indias

Bermuda their own. Ramirez's landing and its repercussions brought into sharp light the fact that Spain could have colonised the island 100 years earlier. For during the opening years of the 1500s, one of Ramirez's countrymen was recorded as the first person to sight Bermuda, and it was he who gave the faraway atoll its name. History would prove Spain's loss was to be England's gain.

Born about 1449 in Palos, a thriving port on Spain's east coast, Juan de Bermúdez was a pioneering captain who made numerous Atlantic crossings between Spain and the West Indies during the 16th Century, the so-called "Age of Discovery." Bermúdez did not participate in Christopher Columbus's 1492 journey to the New World, but he was one of the first mariners to forge a maritime path westward in the years following Columbus's much-hailed "Voyage of Discovery." Like the Italian navigator, Bermúdez's expeditions into the erstwhile geographical abyss helped ignite a golden age of European expansion lasting more than a century.

It was a time of heady possibilities, of ambitious exploration, bold personalities and unbridled hope and imagination. Spain and Portugal were untouchable maritime forces whose early discoveries in the west excited the rest of Europe with the untold possibilities of vast new lands and material wealth. Under a 1493 decree by Pope Alexander VI, and the Treaty of Tordesillas signed by Spain and Portugal a year later, the unknown world was divided between the two Catholic powerhouses: all territories from 100 leagues west of the Cape Verde islands and beyond (a zone that included Bermuda) would be considered Spanish; all lands east would belong to Portugal. The map of the world had been re-drawn and empires had never

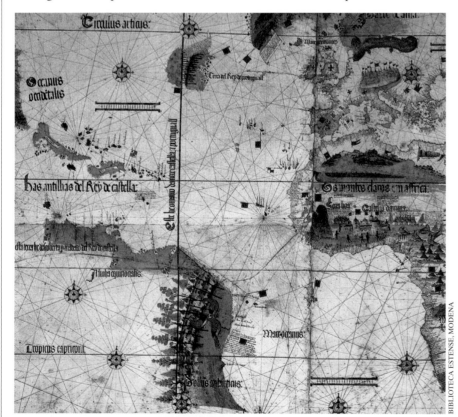

BIBLIOTECA ESTENSE, MODENA

A 16th-Century representation of Europe, Africa and the New World

In their own words

■ Antonio de Herrera y Tordesillas, *1527*

Hernando Camelo of the island of St. Michael, one of the Azores, knowing the wish the king had to people the island of Bermuda, offered to establish a settlement therein of a good number of persons. The conditions the king accepted were: that the people should be settled within four years and no more; that, on account of the difficulty of having a settlement solely of Spanish and Portuguese, leave should be granted to take persons though not belonging to these realms; that for twenty years the settlers should be free of alcavala or any other tax except tithes, which are due to God, and which in all the realms of the Indies belong to the Kings of Castille and Leon by gift of the Holy Apostolic See…

This agreement was entered into very readily, for the island of Bermuda being a thousand leagues to the westward from Castile and two hundred from the island of San Juan of Porto Rico, and being uninhabited, having neither in itself or vicinity any people whatever, and being made for by all the fleets and vessels coming from the Indies, it was desirable it should be inhabited, so that there could be found a road-stead and also assistance for so long a voyage, and to ascertain if, with the peopling of it, a remedy could be found for the tempests there encountered, caused by the great dampness owing to its dense woods. This island was called Bermuda or La Garza after the captain who discovered it and of his vessel.

—*Spanish historian Antonio de Herrera y Tordesillas*

been built so grand or rapaciously. Felipe II (King Philip II of Spain, 1527–98) engineered the Iberian union of Portugal and Spain under his monarchy and saw control of an empire that also encompassed Milan, Naples, Sicily, the Netherlands—and sprawling territories in the New World.

Throughout the 1500s, Portuguese and Spanish explorers such as Fernão de Magalhaes (Magellan), Vasco da Gama, Hernán Cortés, Bartolomeu Dias and Francisco Pizarro led expeditions that conquered thousands of square miles of foreign territories and brutally enslaved American civilisations, including the Aztecs of Mexico and Incas of Peru. Spain eventually held much of North and South America except for Brazil, which remained Portuguese after 1532 due to a geographical error that misjudged its longitudinal location. Otherwise, Spanish rulers considered the entire New World their empire, and enforced a strict monopoly on Spanish goods to supply their far-flung colonists. Lisbon and Seville became boomtowns, hubs from which heavily-armed fleets would depart packed with provisions, and return spilling over with exotic produce such as maize, tobacco, sugar, potatoes and cacao. Often, their cargo contained actual riches: gold, silver and pearls.

Under the consecutive reigns of Carlos I (Holy Roman Emperor Charles V) and Felipe II, the Spanish dominated European adversaries and led New World invasions that multiplied Spain's overseas colonies and its wealth. Later in the century, Dutch, French, and English mariners could only try to snare their share of the wealth through piracy, lying in wait in the Caribbean, for example, until Spanish galleons departed for home, heavy with New-World treasures. This game of maritime cat-and-mouse played out for much of the 16th Century, until England came to hold the sway of European power.

The tale of such epic adventurers launches the story of Bermuda itself, for the island played a pivotal role in their journeys. Lying at 32 degrees north latitude—isolated some 1,000 miles north of the islands of the West Indies—Bermuda came to be a key navigational landmark for homeward-bound ships to Europe. In an age in which longitude position cast on maps could not be accurately measured, mariners travelling the route between the Indies and Europe relied on physically seeing Bermuda to be able to judge their correct northerly boundary; on homeward journeys, they would sail the Gulf Stream north from the Caribbean and Florida until they spotted the island. Heading just past it, to about 34 degrees latitude, they would begin their sweep back to Europe on the south-west prevailing winds.

As a prominent mariner of the time, Bermúdez was a pioneer of this oceanic highway. Though he did not know how to write and left no known record of his life, he is believed to have been the first to sight and name the island in 1505 as he sailed back to Spain from Hispaniola. The voyage was one of at least 11 documented trans-Atlantic crossings Bermúdez made between 1495 and 1519. Historians believe 1505 is the key date, since it was on this return journey that Bermúdez captained *La Garza*, "the Heron," the ship cited in an account of Bermuda by Gonzalo Fernández de Oviedo y Valdés. A Spanish courtier, who would become the official historian of the Indies, Oviedo visited the island with Bermúdez in 1515 and later noted Bermuda was nicknamed Garza after Bermúdez's ship. "I sayled above the island Bermuda, otherwise called Garza," he said, "being the furthest of all the islands that are found at this day in the world."

The island first appeared on a map a short time after Bermúdez's

*Pottery retrieved from a Spanish
vessel wrecked off Bermuda*

Waves like mountains

*On quitting the said channel one
comes in sight of Bermuda, a
mountainous island which it is
difficult to approach on account of
the dangers that surround it. It
almost always rains there, and
thunder is so frequent, that it seems
as if heaven and earth must come
together. The sea is very tempestuous
about the said island, and the waves
as high as mountains.*

—*French explorer Samuel
de Champlain, c. 1600*

A hazard *All shipps bound
from Barbados and the Leewards to
England…pass but a little to the
Eastward of the Island. Ships
bound from Jamaica…and from
Virginia, Carolina, &tc.
Unavoidably pass nigh Bermuda to
and from England…If the Island
was in an Enemies hands, with a
small number of cruisers…it would
hazard all passing ships.*

—*Isaac Richier, Bermuda's fourth
English Royal Governor, in a letter to
the Lords of Trade, July 3, 1691*

Stormes

*Compared to these stormes, death is
but a qualm,
Hell somewhat lightsome, the
Bermudas calm.*

—*English poet John Donne, 1597*

discovery: "La Bermuda" is seen on a woodcut map published in Peter Martyr's book of 1511, *Legatio Bablyonica*. It was the first of numerous cartographic renditions of Bermuda to be published over the next several decades, some of them portraying the island in distorted shapes and inaccurate positions, or as an unnamed island. However, they provide proof Bermuda's existence was at least recognised in world views long before it was settled by the English.

So why did no one claim the strategically vital island before the 17th Century? The answer partly lies in the rampant superstitions of the time, spawned by the common belief in devilry, paganism and the occult. Witchcraft was prevalent in Europe, where practitioners or those believed to be such were burned alive by the thousands. Mass hysteria and ignorance fed Bermuda's supernatural reputation among sea-goers. Many believed the island was haunted or inhabited by enchanted spirits. Ramirez, himself, describes the blood-chilling screeching that filled the night air which he and his men at first believed to be the sound of attacking devils—until they realised it was merely the raucous call of nocturnal seabirds.

Hundreds of shipwrecks helped perpetuate these strange beliefs. Long before the popularity of the Bermuda Triangle myth, seafarers blamed bad luck on malevolent forces surrounding Bermuda. More than 30 wrecks are known to have occurred by 1600; many other vessels, like Ramirez's ship, suffered only minor mishaps in Gulf Stream storms and were able to sail on to Europe or back-track to the Caribbean. Bermuda's seabirds, turtles and fish made a natural larder of provisions. But along with their salted pork and cedar berries, crews would also take home the fabulous tales of Bermuda's evil spirits, dragons and sea monsters.

Other early visitors to Bermuda included a Portuguese surveyor, Estevão Gomez, who in 1525 explored the island under a commission received from Spain. Unfortunately his map has not survived. Two years later, Felipe II sent an Azorean named Hernando Camelo to start a colony on the island. Camelo was promised the island's governorship, as well as the title of 'captain general' for life.

Under a detailed contract signed on December 20, 1527, Camelo was to bring all his own supplies and ensure that at least 20 settlers—all of them Spanish—be living in Bermuda by the end of four years. Spain was even prepared to investigate a 'remedy' for Bermuda's violent storms, suggesting such tempests were caused by dampness that emanated from the island's thickly-wooded areas. Whether Camelo attempted the settlement plan is unclear; no evidence remains to suggest he made any progress.

A group of Portuguese castaways landed on Bermuda in 1543 and is believed responsible for inscribing the so-called 'Spanish Rock' on the island's South Shore. When their vessel, thought to be a slave ship, wrecked on reefs, 32 members of the crew escaped ashore. They managed to salvage wood and other materials with which they built a pinnace and sailed back to Puerto Rico. But they left behind the inscription, "RP 1543," carved into a southern shore cliff face, where the Spittal Pond Nature Reserve stands today. The initials, perhaps for "Rex Portugaliae," are thought to refer to the Portuguese monarch, João III, while a cross inscribed there is believed to be a good-luck symbol and royal emblem known as the Order of Christ.

A half-century later, Bermuda received its first documented visit from

In their own words
■ Diego Ramirez, 1603

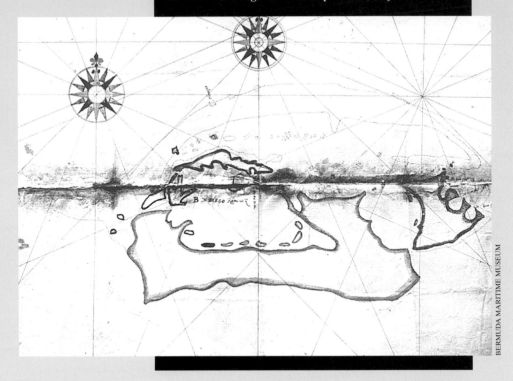

Spaniard Diego Ramirez's rough map of Bermuda, sketched during his 1603 exploration of the island

In these waters and harbours there are great numbers of fish, groupers, parrotfish and especially red snappers, and so stupid we caught them in our hands, with pointed sticks, nooses and with bent nails. Many turtles large and small, although the island has few sandy beaches, the most of it being sharp coral rock.

All the island and keys are covered with cedar forests and tufted palmetto palms and other underbush of various varieties. There is good timber for vessels, many stumps, curved, and lumber of all sorts in abundance. There are great droves of hogs in the island, which have over-run it and trodden wide paths like well-travelled roads to the watering places. Along these trails there are palms worn in two fingers' lengths where they have scratched themselves. Little grass. The hogs free of vermin.

There are many very large dark herons, many very handsome sparrow-hawks, so stupid that we even clubbed them. Great numbers of medium-sized crows, like those in Havana. When we landed, they came to us, perched on our heads, uttering a multitudinous chorus of cries. The headlands are undermined at water level with the haunts of certain nocturnal birds which during the day remain in their caves but at night come out to feed on fish, especially on squid of which there are great numbers. These birds come out from their caves at night-fall with such an outcry and varying clamour that one cannot help being afraid until one realises the reason.

The first night that I anchored in the bay I sent a small boat to an inlet to look for water, but none was found. At dusk, such a shrieking and din filled the air that fear seized us. Only one variety of bird makes this noise, but the concerted yell is terrible, and standing out from it were individual voices shouting, "Diselo! Diselo!" (tell 'em, tell 'em). One seaman said to me: "What is this devil trying to tell me? Out with it! Let's hear what it is!" I replied, "A la! These are the devils reported to be about Bermuda. The sign of the cross at them! We are Christians!"

While we were in this confusion, the men of the small boat rushed up, exclaiming in their alarm: "What devils are these?" The boat's rudder is broken. I ordered another to be made immediately, because in the morning the coast had to be searched for water. One Venturilla, a negro, was sent on shore with lantern and axe to cut a piece of cedar. The moment he landed and entered the bush, he set up such a yell, that I shouted: "The devil's carrying off the negro! Everybody ashore!" The men jumped into a boat and rushed to the spot, where the negro was brandishing his lantern and his fists against the birds, and mingling his yells with theirs. The birds, meanwhile, attracted by the light, dashed against him, so that he could not keep clear of them even with a club. Neither could the men of the relief party.

More than 500 birds were brought off to the ship that night, and having gone through hot water and been plucked, proved to be very fat and fine. Thereafter a capture was made every evening. The birds were so plentiful that 4,000 could be taken in a single bag. The men relished them enough to eat them all the time, and when we left we brought away more than 1,000 well dried and salted for the voyage.

—*Captain Diego Ramirez landed on Bermuda in 1603 after his ship was caught in a storm that destroyed four other galleons in the fleet of Don Luis Fernández de Córdova. Ramirez's ship escaped, losing just its provisions*

In their own words
■ Henry May, *1593*

When we came on shore, being all the day without drink, every man took his way to see if he could find any; but it was long before any was found. At length one of the pilots digging among a company of weeds found fresh water, to all our great comforts being only rain water; and this was all the water we found on shore. But there are in this Island many fine bays wherein if a man did dig, I think there might be found store of fresh water. This Island is divided all into broken Islands; and the greatest part I was upon, which might be some four or five miles long, and two miles and a half over, being all woods, as Cedar and other timber, but Cedar is the chiefest.

Now it pleased God before our ship did split, that we saved our carpenters tools, else I think we had been there to this day; and having recovered the aforesaid tools, we went roundly about the cutting down of trees, and in the end built a small barque of some eighteen tons, for the most part with tronnels and very few nails. As for tackling, we made a voyage aboard the ship before she split; and cut down her shrouds, and so we tackled our barque and rigged her. Instead of pitch we made lime, and mixed it with the oil of tortoises, and as soon as the carpenters had caulked, I and another, with each of us a small stick in our hands, did plaster the mortar into the seams, and being in April, when it was warm and fair weather, we could no sooner lay it on, but it was dry, and as hard as stone.

In this month of April 1594, the weather being very hot, we were afraid our water should faile us; and therefore made the more haste away; and at our departure we were constrained to make two great chests, and caulked them, and stowed them on each side of our mainmast, and so put in our provision of rain water and thirteen live tortoises for our food, with fish and fowl of which there were an abundance, but no pork, because the hogs at that season were so lean.

—*Englishman Henry May, shipwrecked off Bermuda, December 1593*

A bronze copy of the Spanish Rock inscription, believed to have been carved by stranded Portuguese mariners in 1543

BRIMSTONE MEDIA

an Englishman. In 1593, a decade before Ramirez, Henry May was a passenger aboard a French pirate ship commanded by Captain Charles de la Barbotière which left Hispaniola at the end of November. The ship headed north and 17 days later arrived in waters off Bermuda. Following maritime tradition, the captain rewarded his pilots with rations of wine, dubbed "wine of height," for having brought the vessel to a safe enough north latitude to make the eastward journey home to Europe. But the celebration was premature. At midnight, the ship struck reefs, possibly North Rock some nine miles off the North Shore. Twenty men survived, and May was among them.

Like previous castaways, the crew grabbed tools, tackle and sails from their wreck and over the next six months fashioned a new ship of island cedar, resourcefully caulking the hull with lime and turtle oil. May and his comrades eventually set sail the following spring for Newfoundland, where he boarded another ship to return to England. Though a Caribbean detour followed, he did get home later that year and gave the first detailed account in English of a Bermuda misadventure.

Despite 100 years of various encounters such as these, Bermuda remained something of a mystery in the European mind. Its value as a strategic Atlantic outpost in an era when maritime prowess shaped world power seemed undeniable. Its status as an uninhabited territory would also have proved attractive. Yet Bermuda's lack of natural resources such as fresh water or alluring deposits of gold or silver may have diminished its worth in the eyes of money-hungry conquistadors.

And while its safe harbours, easy provisions and lack of indigenous peoples should have made the island an easy acquisition, these advantages were overshadowed, perhaps, by the daunting navigational dangers posed by its reef line. When a group of English did stumble ashore in 1609, paving the way for Bermuda's human habitation, it was thanks only to a profound accident.

CHAPTER TWO

The *Sea Venture*

DISASTER BROADCASTS BERMUDA'S RICHES

Pottery and a candlestick from
the Sea Venture *wreck of 1609*

*Right: an early map of the wild
Atlantic, Bermuda and the North
American coast*

BERMUDA MARITIME MUSEUM

William Strachey and his fellow passengers believed they were forging an illustrious future for themselves and their nation as they set sail from Plymouth, England on June 2, 1609. Their proud fleet of seven ships, plus two smaller attending ships, or pinnaces, was on a mission of mercy, to be sent almost 4,000 miles across the Atlantic to deliver supplies and expertise to James Fort, Virginia, England's struggling two-year-old colony on the James River, off Chesapeake Bay. The settlement, which became known as Jamestown, was facing starvation and the fleet carried England's hope for its survival.

For Strachey, the journey was also a personal quest: having recently

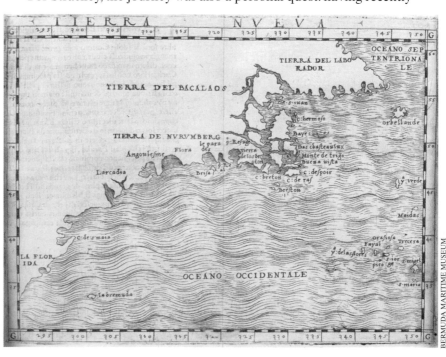

BERMUDA MARITIME MUSEUM

Newes from Virginia

Tis true that eleven monthes and more,
*   these gallant worthy wights*
Was in the shippe **Sea Venture** *nam'd*
*   depriv'd Virginia's sight.*
And bravely did they glyde the maine
*   till Neptune gan to frowne,*
As if a courser prowdly backt
*   would throwe his ryder downe.*

The seas did rage, the windes did blowe,
*   distressed were they then;*
Their ship did leake, her tacklings breake,
*   in daunger were her men.*
But heaven was plyotte in this storme,
*   and to an iland nere,*
Bermoothawes call'd, conducted then,
*   which did abate their fear.*

But yet these worthies forced were,
*   opprest with weather againe,*
To runne their ship betweene two rockes,
*   where she doth still remaine.*
And then on shoare the iland came,
*   inhabited by hogges,*
Some foule and tortoyses there were,
*   they onley had one dogge.*

To kill these swyne, to yield them foode
*   that little had to eate,*
Their store was spent, and all things scant,
*   alas! They wanted meate.*
A thousand hogges that dogge did kill,
*   their hunger to sustaine,*
And with such foode did in that ile
*   two and forty weekes remaine...*

—Newes from Virginia, *originally printed in*
1610, by R. Rich, a "soldier" adventurer who
returned with Captain Newport to England

been appointed the colony's secretary-elect, he was embarking on a challenging new career. For most of the other 150 men, women and children aboard the flagship *Sea Venture*—among the fleet's 600-strong entourage of emigrants from England's West Country who had left behind homes, relatives and friends, presumably forever—the voyage must have symbolised a life-changing journey into the unknown.

Any fears in such circumstances would have been justified, but the group could not have anticipated the sheer terror they were soon to experience before ever reaching Virginia. As helpless victims in the path of a furious hurricane, they would, indeed, make history that summer, though their story would be remembered more for shaping the fate of a small island than that of America.

The journey began promisingly enough, with the 108-foot *Sea Venture* under the command of a respected admiral, Sir George Somers, and his experienced captain, Christopher Newport. Sir Thomas Gates, who was to be the deputy governor of Virginia under Lord de la Warre, was also on board. Somers had chosen a more northerly sea route than the norm; instead of dipping south via the West Indies, he had charted what he thought would be a more direct path to Jamestown. The wind and weather cooperated, and the fleet progressed a leisurely seven weeks into the voyage, the ships sailing together both for companionship and safety. Then, just seven days from reaching Cape Henry, Virginia, disaster struck.

On July 24, a Monday, the wind suddenly began to pick up, whistling through the ships' shrouds as an eerie prelude to the howling attack to follow. As the gale strengthened, the *Sea Venture* was forced to cast loose the pinnace it was towing. Within hours, according to Strachey, "a dread storm and hideous" blowing from the north-east began to hammer the

In their own words
■ William Strachey, *1610*

For foure and twenty houres the storme in a restlesse tumult had blowne so exceedingly, as we could not apprehend in our imaginations any possibility of greater violence, yet did we still find it, not only more terrible, but more constant, fury added to fury, and one storme urging a second more outragious than the former; whether it so wrought upon our feared or indeed met with new forces: sometims striks in our Ship amongst women, and passengers, not used to such hurly and discomforts, made us looke one upon the other with troubled hearts, and panting bosoms: our clamours dround in the winds and the winds in thunders. Prayers might well be in the heart and lips, but drowned in the outcries of the Officers: nothing heard that could give comfort, nothing seen that might encourage hope. Our sailes wound up lay without their use, six and sometimes eight men were not enough to hold the whipstaffe in the steerage, and the tiller below in the Gunner roome, by which may be imagined the strength of the storme: In which, the Sea swelled above the Clouds, and gave battell unto Heaven.

It could not be said to rain, the waters like whole Rivers did flood in the ayre. And this I did still observe, that whereas upon the Land, when a storm hath powred itself forth once in drifts of rain, the wind as beaten down, and vanquished therewith, not long after indureth: here the glut of water (as if throttling the wind ere

while) was no sooner a little emptied and qualified, but instantly the winds (as having gotten their mouths now free, and at liberty) spake more loud, and grew more tumultous, and malignant. What shall I say Winds and Seas were as mad, as fury and rage could make them. There was not a moment in which the sudden splitting, or instant over-setting of the Shippe was not expected.

Howbeit this was not all; it pleased God to bring a greater affliction yet upon us; for in the beginning of the storme we had received a mighty leake. And the Ship in every joint almost, having spued out her Okam, before we were aware (a casualty more desperate then any other that a Voyage by Sea draweth with it) was growne five foote suddenly deepe with

water above her ballast, and we almost drowned within, whilst we sat looking when to perish from above. This imparting no lesse terror then danger, rann through the whole Ship with much fright and amazement, started and turned the blood, and took down the bravest of the most hardy Mariner of them all, insomuch as he

that before happily felt not the sorrow of others, now began to sorrow for himself, when he saw such a pond of water so suddenly broken in, and which he knew could not but instantly sink him. So as joining in the public safety; there might be seen Master, Master's Mate, Boatswaine, Quarter Master, Coopers, Carpenters, and who not, with candles in their hands, creeping along the ribs viewing the sides, searching every corner, and listening in every place, if they could heare the water runne.

Our Governour, upon the Tuesday morning had caused the whole Company, about one hundred and forty, besides women, to be equally divided into three parts, and opening the Ship in three places appointed each man where to attend; and thereunto every man came duly upon his watch, took Bucket, or Pump for one hour, and rested another. Then men might be seen to labour, I may well say, for life, and the better sort, even our Governour, and Admirall themselves, not refusing their turn, and to spell each the other to give example to other. The common sort stripped naked, as men in Gallies, the easier both to hold out, and to shrink from under the salt water, which continually leapt in among them, kept their eyes waking, and their thoughts and hands working, with tired bodies, and wasted spirits, three days and four nights destitute of outward comfort, and desperate of any deliverance, testifying how mutually willing they were, yet by labour to keep each other from drowning, albeit each one drowned whilst he laboured.

Having travailed now from Tuesday till Friday morning, day and night, without either sleep or food; and carefulness, grief,

We found it to be the dangerous and dreaded ilands of Bermuda ... feared and avoided of all sea travellers alive and our turn at the Pump or Bucket, were sufficient to hold sleep from our eyes.

Sir George Summers, when no man dreamed of such happiness, had discovered, and cried Land. Indeed the morning now three quarters spent, had won a little cleereness from the days before, and it being better surveyed, the very trees were seen to move with the wind upon the shore side: whereupon our Governour commanded the Helmesman to bear up, the Boatswaine sounding at the first, found it thirteen fathom, and when we stood a little in seven fatham; and presently heaving his lead the third time, had ground at four fathom, and by this, we had got her within a mile under the South-east point of the land, where we had somewhat smooth water. But having no hope to save her by coming to an anker in the same, we were inforced to run her ashore, as neer the land as we could, which brought us within three quarters of a mile of shore, and by the mercy of God unto us making out our Boats, we had ere night brought all our men, women, and children, about the number of one hundred and fifty, safe into the Iland.

We found it to be the dangerous and dreaded Iland, or rather Ilands of the Bermuda: whereof let me give your Ladyship a brief description, before I proceed to my narration. And that the rather, because they be so terrible to all that ever touched on them, and such tempests, thunders, and other fearful objects are seen and heard about them, that they be called Bermuda commonly, The Devils Isles, and are feared and avoided of all sea travellers alive, above any other place in the world. Yet it pleased our merciful God, to make even this hideous and hated place both the place of our safety and means of our deliverance.

—William Strachey, secretary-elect of Virginia, and a passenger aboard the Sea Venture

vessel, and separated it from the rest of the party. The sky turned black, and real fear gripped the passengers as mountainous waves broke over the *Sea Venture*'s decks while rain and wind lashed the ship.

Strachey, who would later catalogue the "dreadful Tempest" in a detailed account believed to have inspired William Shakespeare's play, *The Tempest*, watched incredulously as the storm intensified over the course of a day. The wind screamed overhead and a deluge of rain fell, swamping the ship as surely as the giant waves which madly rocked it. The *Sea Venture* had suffered a substantial leak when the storm first struck, and now rivers of sea water poured through the hull. Before long, the 300-ton ship had sunk five feet below its waterline, bedraggled passengers flailing below decks in water that rose to their waists. Many were completely without hope, and, believing they were on the verge of death, said farewell to friends and loved ones and prayed for a quick end to their misery.

But Gates was not about to give up and he urged them to fight to save the ship and themselves. He divided the passengers into three groups and allocated a different part of the ship to each. For the next 72 hours, Tuesday to Friday, the colonists battled the influx of water, using buckets, pumps, even kettles, in what seemed a futile attempt to stay alive. The crew resorted to pushing luggage and cargo overboard and stuffed pieces of beef into the leaking timbers to keep the sea at bay. Gates himself and Somers—who spent most waking hours at the helm trying to keep the ship on course—took turns bailing alongside the rest of the company.

At one point during the ordeal, Somers noticed a strange phenomenon, a dancing light, like the sizzle of electricity or a star, zigzagging about in the rigging. It darted around the heaving ship's shrouds for several

'Many were completely without hope'

hours. Was it an omen of good luck or bad? Somers called his crew to witness the bizarre apparition, and the superstitious seamen blamed it on all manner of evil and enchantment, claiming it would portend catastrophe. The cosmic light show was likely nothing more sinister than an appearance of St. Elmo's Fire.

The following day, just in time to boost the sagging spirits of his ship, the unexpected happened: Somers, who had been ensconced for most of the past three days in the poop deck, spotted land. They had arrived—not at Virginia, some 700 miles away, but at the dreaded island of Bermuda. Unable to sail the crippled ship into a natural harbour, Somers instructed his crew to run the *Sea Venture* aground on reefs just three-quarters of a mile from shore. Once the ship was lodged firmly on shoals, he organised the ferrying of all the passengers by skiff to the nearest beach, a procedure that lasted most of the day.

The waterlogged castaways welcomed the feeling of dry land underfoot, but what they found surprised them and overturned a century of preconceived notions about the supposedly bewitched "Bermudas." Instead of devils and witches, they were met by tranquil beauty; in place of spells and spirits, they discovered abundant supplies of fish and meat. Silvanus Jourdan, a passenger from Lyme Regis (also Sir George Somers's birthplace) would later write: "Wherefore my opinion sincerely of this Iland is, that whereas it hath been and is still accounted, the most dangerous, infortunate, and most forlorn place in the world, it is in truth the richest, healthfullest, and pleasing land."

A hellish sea *The channel of Bahama, coming from the West Indies…cannot be passed in the Winter, and it is at its best, it is a perilous and fearful place. The rest of the Indies for calms and diseases very troublesome, and the Bermudas a hellish sea for thunder, lightning, and storms. This very yeare there were seventeen sayle of Spanish ships lost in the channel of Bahama, and the great Philip like to have sunke at Bermuda was put back to Saint Juan de Puerto Rico.*

—*Sir Walter Raleigh, 1596*

Dread time

*When heaven was lost, when not a
    tear-wrak'd eye
Could tell, in all that dread time, if
    they were
Sinking or sailing; till a quickening
    clear
Gave light to save them by the ruth
    of rocks
At the Bermudas.*

—*Poet Laureate
George Chapman, 1612*

Habitation for devils

These islands of the Bermudas have ever been accounted as an enchanted pile of rocks, and a desert habitation for devils; but all the fairies of the rocks were but flocks of birds, and all the devils that haunted the woods were but herds of swine. Our people in the Bermudas found such abundance of hogs that for nine months' space they plentifully sufficed, and yet the number seemed not much diminished.

—A true declaration of the estate of
the colonie in Virginia, *published by
the Virginia Company, November 1610*

S uch positive reports would change Bermuda's destiny forever. Until then, England had never considered colonising the tiny island which seemed to offer nothing of value to a nation intent on claiming its role as the new European superpower. Virginia—named by Sir Walter Raleigh for Elizabeth I (1533–1603), the "Virgin Queen"—was the western focus of English hopes, following Raleigh's 1584 expedition to America and Parliament's confirmation of his right to establish a colony there the following year. Colonists came and went in various attempts, but England's first permanent settlement was finally established at Jamestown in 1607. America's immense expanses, its immeasurable natural resources, riches such as gold, silver and precious minerals—these were the magnets for 17th-Century adventurers, not a seemingly insignificant reef-strewn outpost like Bermuda.

England's power shift had taken place during the reign of Elizabeth, whose imperial ambitions were the lightning rod for a national rebirth in the arts, letters, sciences and commerce. This cultural explosion was largely inspired by England's unprecedented geographical expansion during what would be remembered as a golden epoch: the Elizabethan Age. The climax of England's achievements was its defeat of the Spanish Armada in 1588, marking an ignominious end to a naval behemoth. The once-invincible Spanish fleet had attempted to storm the English Channel with 130 ships and nearly 30,000 men—only to be driven out and annihilated by both a storm and English naval squadrons led by maritime heroes Sir Francis Drake and Sir John Hawkins. Having dealt a lethal blow to Spain, and its long monopoly on New World trade and colonisation, an empowered England turned its attention to similar commercial conquests. Elizabeth put her royal stamp of approval on colonial expeditions to America to enforce the coming era of English supremacy, both political and mercantile. Furthermore, she believed an English colony in Virginia would further diminish Spanish ambitions, particularly in the Newfoundland fisheries and the West Indies.

When King James VI of Scotland ascended the English throne as James I after Elizabeth's death in 1603, this campaign of westernisation continued. James encouraged the creation of the first colonies and paved the way for English nobility and merchants—so-called 'Adventurers'—to form a Council of Virginia, later to become the Virginia Company. He granted them a mandate "to make habitation, plantation and to deduce a colony of sundry of our people into that part of America, commonly called Virginia."

Commercial affluence at home fuelled by imperial bravado overseas stoked the fires of English nationalism. It was a time of greatness, a time for bold dreams to grow. English colonists were widely sought and heavily encouraged to sign up for new lives in foreign lands under the banner of patriotic duty. The Virginia Company's enterprise was promoted in just such a fashion, inviting participation by stakeholders in the new 'plantation' via persuasive pamphlets and proclamations. Colonisation had been conceived in the optimistic glow of commercial ambitions and jingoistic pride, yet the New World reality was clouded by disease, disorganisation, starvation, exploitation of indigenous peoples, and the resulting attacks on settlers. Jamestown struggled through crop failures and illness that ravaged its fledgling community.

It was against this harsh backdrop that the *Sea Venture* and the rest of the fleet had left Plymouth Harbour in 1609, full of manpower, provisions and wide-eyed emigrants looking forward to an American adventure. Little

Shakespeare and *The Tempest*

Like the best Hollywood epic, William Shakespeare's last play, *The Tempest*, was almost certainly inspired by a true story—the *Sea Venture* shipwreck. News of the disaster off Bermuda and the escape by all aboard filtered back to London society, thanks to detailed written accounts by passenger William Strachey and crewman Silvanus Jourdan, along with the safe return of other survivors. The dramatic tale succeeded in firing 17th-Century enthusiasm for colonisation in general, and Bermuda in particular.

Notably, the *Sea Venture* episode would have circulated among Virginia Company members and friends, a group that included Shakespeare. The playwright's patron was Henry Wriothesley, Earl of Southampton, a key member of both Virginia and Bermuda Companies for whom Southampton Parish was later named. Academics therefore believe it is no coincidence *The Tempest* was written in 1611—just a year after the eyewitness narratives by Strachey and Jourdan were published—and performed in court in November the same year.

Indeed, *The Tempest* depicts a fanciful island purported to be in the Mediterranean, but whose physical detail mirrors its very own reference to "the still-vex'd Bermoothes." Included are descriptions of "hogges of force and bignesse," "a pleasant drinke" made of cedarberries, and seabirds whose tongues could "walke as fast as any Englishwoman's."

Inhabited by characters Prospero, his daughter Miranda, a sprite named Ariel and monstrous Caliban, the play is an allegorical romance launched by a spectacular storm. Its "dreadful thunderclaps and sulphurous roaring" parallel Strachey's description of the maelstrom which claimed the *Sea Venture*.

Shakespeare also pays tribute in the play to England's new role as a sea power and a leader in science and arts. And *The Tempest*'s dominant themes—destiny, fortune and the power of chance—could describe Bermuda's own, immortalised in its Latin motto, *Quo Fata Ferunt*, meaning "Whither the Fates Carry Us."

> *The deep nook, where once*
> *Thou call'dst me up at midnight,*
>   *to fetch dew*
> *From the still-vex'd Bermoothes.*
> —*William Shakespeare*, The Tempest,
>   *Act X, Scene X, 1611*

The Bermuda palmetto was an important source of food and materials

did they know it would be almost a year before they would finally reach their destination.

Somers and his shipload of colonists struggled ashore at Bermuda, overcome with exhaustion and relief after their harrowing ordeal. Astonishingly, everyone aboard the *Sea Venture* had survived the ferocious storm. And though they feared the six other ships in their fleet had been lost, the vessels had actually arrived safely in Jamestown.

While the *Sea Venture* sat lodged on reefs within sight of their landing spot, the crew went back to gather all the possessions they could rescue. Tools, rigging, wood, food and water—the castaways took everything they could manage and rowed it to the beach. To their wonder and delight, like Ramirez six years earlier, they stumbled upon a smorgasbord of natural offerings. Far from being a menacing netherland, it was a bucolic place of plenty, providing more than enough for the following nine months they would spend preparing to escape.

The castaways set up camp on a small island near modern-day St. George's, digging wells and building palmetto-roofed huts. Once they recovered some of their strength after the exhausting storm, they converted the *Sea Venture*'s longboat into a pinnace, jury-rigged with sails and oars, and persuaded one of the ship's mates, Henry Ravens, to attempt the relatively short passage to Virginia to alert settlers there of the *Sea Venture*'s demise. Ravens readily agreed to undertake the expedition, and set off with a crew of seven, promising to return by the next new moon. They were never seen again.

In their own words
■ **Silvanus Jourdan,** *1610*

We fell upon the shore of the Barmudas; where after our Generall Sir Thomas Gates, Sir George Sommers, and Captain Newport, had by their provident carefulness landed all their men and so much of the goods and provisions out of the ship as was not utterly spoiled. Sir George Summers, by his careful industry went, and found out sufficient of many kind of fishes, and so plentiful; thereof, that in half an hour he took so many fishes with hooks, as did suffice the whole company one day. And fish is there so abundant, that if a man steppe into the water, they will come round about him: so that men were faine to get out for feare of biting. These fishes are very fat and sweet, and of that proportion and bignesses that three of them will conveniently lade two men: those we called Rockfish. Besides there are such store of mullets that with a seine might be taken at one draught one thousand at the least, and infinite store of Pilchards, with divers kinds of great fishes, the names of them unknown to me: of tray fishes very great ones, and so great store, as that there hath been taken in one night with making lights, even sufficient to feed the whole company a day.

The countrie affordeth great abundance of Hogges, as that there hath been taken by Sir George Sommers, who was the first that hunted for them, to the number of two and thirtie at one time, which he brought to the company in a boate, built by his owne hands. There is fowle in great number upon the Ilands, where they breed, that there hath beene taken in two or three houres, a thousand at the least: the bird being of the bignes of a good Pidgeon, and layeth then dayly, although men sit downe amongst them: that there hath beene taken up in one morning by Sir Thomas Gates men one thousand of Egges: and Sir George Sommers men, coming a little distance of time after them, haue stayed there whilst they came and layed their eggs amongst them, that they brought away as many more with them; with many young birds very fat and sweet.

Another Sea fowle there is that liveth in little holes in the ground, like unto Coney holes, and are in great numbers, exceeding good meate, very fat and sweet (those we had in the winter and their eggs are white, and of that bignesse, that they are not to be knowne from these egges. The other birds egges are speckled and of a different colour: there are also great store and plenty of Herons and those so familiar and tame, that we beat them downe from the trees with stones and staves: but such were young Herons: besides many white Herons, without so much as a blacke or grey feather on them: with other birds so tame and gentle, that a man walking in the woods with a stick, and whistling to them, they will come and gaze on you so neare that you may strike and kill many of them with your sticke, and with singing and hollowing you may do the like.

There are also great store of Tortoises (which some call turtles), and those so great, that I have seene a bushell of egges in one of their bellies, which are sweeter than any Hen egg: and the Tortoise otselfe is all very good meate, and yieldeth great store of oil, which is as sweet as any butter: and one of them will suffice fifty men a meale at least: and of these hath beene taken great store, with two boates at the least forty in one day.

The country yieldeth divers fruits, as prickled peares, great aboundance, which continue green upon the trees all the year: also great plenty of mulberries, white and red: and on the same are great store of silke-wormes, which yield cods of silke, both white and yellow, being some coarse, and some fine. And there is a tree called a Palmito tree, which hath a very sweet berry, upon which the hogs do most feed: but our men finding the sweetness of them, did willingly share with the hogs for them, they being very pleasant and wholesome, which made them careless almost of any bread with their meat.

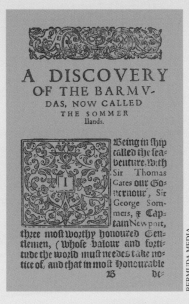

The head of the Palmito tree is verie good meat, either raw or sodden, it yeeldeth a head which weighteth about twentie pound, and is far better meat then any cabbidge. There are infinite number of cedar trees (the fairest I thinke in the world) and those bring forth a verie sweete berrie and wholesome to eat.

The countrey (for as much as I culd finde myself, or heare by others) affords no venimous creature or so much as a Rat or a mouse or any other thing unwholesome. There is great store of Pearls and some of them very fair round and oriental and you shall find at least one hundred seede pearle in one oyster.

There hath beene likewise found some good quantitie of Ambergreece and that of the best sort. There are also great plentie whales which I conceive are very easie to bee killed, for they come so usually and ordinarilie to the shore, that wee heard them oftentimes in the night abed: and have sen many of them near the shore, in the daytime.

—*Sea Venture crewman Silvanus Jourdan,* A Discovery of the Barmudas, now called the Sommer Ilands

Enchanted *For the islands
of the Barmudas, as every man
knoweth that hath heard or read of
them, were never inhabited by a
Christian or heathen people but
were ever esteemed and reputed a
most prodigious and enchanted
place, affording nothing but gusts,
storms and foul weather, which
made every navigator and mariner
to avoid them as Schylla and
Charybdis or as they would shun
the Devil himself.*

—*Reverend Lewis Hughes,* A Plaine
Description of the Barmudas, *1612*

Bitter feud *These dissensions
ripened into a complete schism;
and this handful of shipwrecked
men, thus thrown together on an
uninhabited island, separated into
two parties, and lived asunder in
bitter feud, as men rendered fickle
by prosperity, instead of being
brought into brotherhood by a
common calamity.*

—*Washington Irving on the rivalry
between Somers's and Gates's men,*
The Three Kings of Bermuda, *1864*

'Benficiall' island

*The home-minded company had no
soner reached their destination,
but every man tells abroad, and
everwher rumours his travailes and
adventures; and as travailours were
they heard and not believed, till it
came to be apprehended by some
of the Virginia Company, how
benficiall this island might be for
that colony of thers.*

—*Captain Nathaniel Butler,*
Historye of the Bermudaes or
Summer Islands, c. *1624*

Work began on two new ships to carry the entire company to Virginia. Demonstrating traditional rivalry, Somers, the sailor, and Gates, the soldier, each took a phalanx of men and set about felling and sawing cedars for carving into planks. Gates's team was joined by an experienced shipwright, Richard Frobisher, who started fashioning a pinnace. Somers borrowed the services of two carpenters and 20 men and headed off to build the second ship, a barque, on the main island (probably the area that became known as Buildings Bay).

Unfortunately it was not long before the peace of paradise was broken by squabbles and insurrection. Many of the colonists began to question the wisdom of sailing away from Bermuda's bounty, particularly given Virginia's known hardships. One of the troublemakers, Stephen Hopkins, severely undermined Gates's leadership, claiming the governor's authority ended with the *Sea Venture*'s shipwreck and arguing the island's plentiful food supplies were worth staying for. When word of his arguments leaked out, Hopkins was court-martialled. He immediately apologised and, claiming his family would suffer if he were punished, was forgiven by a compassionate Gates. Despite the incident, the general malcontent persisted. Secret death-threats were made against Gates and others. Guards were put on duty. One man, Henry Paine, refused to serve in such a capacity; he swore at Captain Newport, and physically attacked him. An unrepentant Paine was eventually called before Gates, who ordered him hanged. Paine begged for a gentleman's execution instead; asking that "he might be shot to death," recounts Strachey, "and towards the evening, he had his desire, the sunne and his life setting together."

Busy on the main island, Somers had been absent during this unrest, but he suffered his share of rebellion nonetheless. Some of his own men, incited by Paine's death, left his party and ran off into the woods, where they penned a petition demanding the right to stay in Bermuda and take a large share of the provisions for their own use. Gates wrote back to Somers refusing their request, condemning it as an insult to the King as well as to the London Adventurers.

Gates urged Somers to exert his influence on the breakaway group to bring the men back into the company fold and force them to apologise for their actions so they could be pardoned. Somers did so successfully, convincing all but two to admit they had been foolish, and to give up plans of leaving the group. The intransigent pair, Christopher Carter and Edward Waters (a pardoned murderer who also went by the name of Robert), refused to rejoin the company, and they would stay in Bermuda when the colonists departed for Virginia.

Eventually, the two new vessels were ready for launch. The first, Frobisher's, was 40 feet long and weighed 80 tons. The hull was crafted of cedar, which, Strachey says, was "caulked along the bilge with ocam made from our old cable, a barrel of pitch and a barrel of tar, otherwise wee breamed her with lime made of wilkshels and a hard white stone, slaked with fresh water and tempereed with tortoyses oyle. Our Governor called her *Deliverance*." Somers's barque was smaller, 29 feet and 30 tons. Strachey says the admiral "had laboured from morning unto night as duelie as any workman doth labour for wages, and made her all with cedar without wither pitch or tar and with litle or no yron worke at all; having in her but one boult which was in the kilson. Hee called her the *Patience*."

The *Sea Venture*

The flagship *Sea Venture* was one of a new breed of English galleon that emerged to help defeat the Spanish Armada in 1588. Built during a period of innovation in naval architecture between 1511 and 1628, *Sea Venture* would have been among the first purpose-built ships of war, designed as a versatile vessel able to travel long distances, repel pirates and other enemies, and carry colonists, weapons and provisions to the New World.

The 300-ton, 108-foot *Sea Venture* was newly built when she set sail for the New World. Like other galleons of her kind, she was heavily armed, and extremely fast and manoeuverable. The vessel was of the first generation of warships to be built from detailed plans—a break with previous ship-building tradition in which techniques were passed on through family artisanry.

Partly owned by Admiral Sir George Somers, the *Sea Venture* led a relief fleet of ships collectively known as the "Third Supply." The ships, *Blessing, Diamond, Unitie, Falcon, Lion, Swallow, Virginia* and *Catch*, assembled in Woolwich on May 15, 1609, then sailed to Plymouth, departing for Jamestown on June 2. Unlike the others, *Sea Venture* never reached her destination. Instead she was separated by the huge storm that drove her onto reefs just three-quarters of a mile off St. Catherine's Beach, now called Gates's Bay.

Sea Venture's survivors stripped the galleon of rigging, timbers and possessions to help their escape from Bermuda, and later settlers would continue to salvage materials from the wreck, which remained visible for several years. In 1620, Governor Nathaniel Butler refers to the retrieval of a saker, an anchor and various bits of iron and steel from the ship's hull. But eventually, *Sea Venture* sank from sight and lay undetected beneath the sand for nearly 340 years.

In 1958, American Edmund Downing, an employee of the US Naval Air Station and descendant of *Sea Venture* passenger George Yeardley, rediscovered the wreck. Diving near Sea Venture Flat, off St. David's, he found ballast, timbers and artifacts such as cannon and pottery.

It was not until after 1974 and the establishment of the Bermuda Maritime Museum that underwater archaeology led to a positive identification of the *Sea Venture*. Under the later work of the Sea Venture Trust, hundreds of artifacts were found, including pieces of porcelain, stone jars, clay pipe bowls, a pewter candlestick and an ointment jar—all testament to the lives of the *Sea Venture*'s passengers.

Doomed flagship

Built: *1609*
Displacement: *300 tons*
Length: *108 feet*
Mission: *Flagship, "Third Supply" relief fleet to Virginia*
Admiral: *Sir George Somers*
Captain: *Christopher Newport*
Passengers: *150*

BERMUDA MARITIME MUSEUM

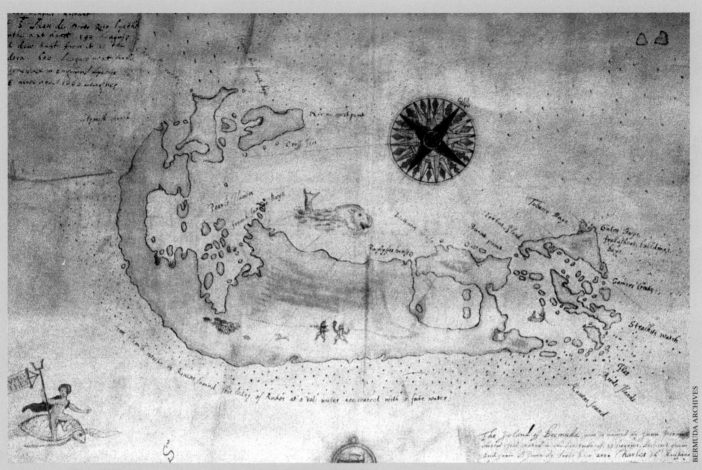

BERMUDA ARCHIVES

Sir George Somers's map of Bermuda, including a representation of two men hunting wild hogs

How they lived
■ Castaway cuisine *1609–10*

As castaways forced to fend for themselves on a desert island, the 150 *Sea Venture* passengers had to use instinct, innovation and teamwork to survive their 10-month ordeal.

For shelter in and around the site where they landed—later called St. George's—they built huts thatched with umbrella-like palm fronds. Because Bermuda lacked fresh water such as streams or lakes, they dug wells to trap the rain.

For food, they were luckier, for the island's wildlife provided plenty of meat, fish and fruit, though the colonists, used to English farms or towns, found their surroundings exotic. "The fish…which being for the most part unknown to us, each man gave them names as they best liked," noted Strachey.

"As one kind they called rock fish, another groopers, others porgy fish, hogge fish, angel fish." Hawks, herons, sparrows and crows made for fresh meat, but the easiest birds to catch were the large, plump cahows, which were attracted to the noise of laughter or shouting that mimicked their own cries.

"The birds would come flocking and settle upon the very arms of him that so cryed," Strachey told, "by which our men would weigh them and which weighest heaviest they tooke, twentie dozen in two hours." The castaways hunted wild hogs using the ship's dog to track them. Some expeditions brought back 30 pigs in a week; the meat was salted to keep it preserved.

Land of plenty *The Bermooda is the most plentiful place that ever I came to, for ffishe, hogges and fowle.*
—*Sir George Somers, June 1610*

The seasons saw a changing menu of natural treats. Men, women and children harvested cedar and palm berries August to November, fermenting the fruit to make wine. Turtles arrived in February, and were caught for their succulent meat and eggs. The colonists also learned to experiment; they discovered roasting the heart of palms lent a sweet taste, like fried melons, and that prickly pears could be eaten raw or baked.

They also learned what to avoid. Poison ivy was abundant even in those days, and "being touched," reported Strachey, "causeth reddnesse, itchinge and lastly blisters."

Sir George Somers *1554–1610*

Sir George Somers used his prowess at sea to escape a humble family history and become a self-made 'gentleman.'

Born to a poor family of traders in Lyme Regis, Dorset, in 1554, he was the youngest of three sons of John and Alice Somer—a surname spelling indicating the family's meagre social standing (by 1589, Sir George would be using 'Summers' or 'Somers' in his new course as a veritable gentleman). Historians believe Somers's father may have been an archer, and when both his parents died, their legacy amounted to no more than a shared eight-acre plot of land and a total of £8.

His eldest brother Nicholas had died, leaving George and the middle son, John, to share the paltry inheritance. But Somers's later wealth would derive not from the land, but from the sea, where he carved a reputation as a masterful privateering captain, one of Queen Elizabeth's most talented, whose vessels captured many Spanish vessels in the late 1500s. At the age of 33, Somers was already a substantial landowner, the properties likely purchased with prize money and goods won through his career exploits.

Around 1583, Somers married Joan Heywood, the daughter of a Lyme Regis yeoman, another family of lowly means. The couple nevertheless were owners of 106 acres in Whitchurch and Marshwood; a farm of 200 acres at Berne, Whitchurch, and a 1,160-acre manor property at Upway, which included two mills.

Captain Somers dabbled with life as a country gentleman, but it was at sea that his real ambitions lay. By 1595, he had returned to his maritime career and for the next several years was employed on numerous expeditions, including voyages to the West Indies in 1596 and Virginia in 1604. As captain of the *Swiftsure*, a 400-ton ship he sailed to Ireland, he attacked the Spanish at Kinsale in 1601, and also commanded the 600-ton *Warspite*, Sir Walter Raleigh's ship. On July 23, 1603, Somers was knighted at Whitehall.

Somers returned to land after England restored diplomatic relations with Spain, and he was elected the Lyme Regis representative in King James's first

BERMUDA HISTORICAL SOCIETY

Parliament. In 1605, he was elected mayor of Lyme Regis, and in keeping with his new standing, acquired a family crest and coat of arms.

William Strachey calls Somers "a gentleman of approved assuredness and ready knowledge in seafaring actions"—"a lamb on the land," in the words of another contemporary, theologian and historian Dr. Thomas Fuller, "so patient, that few could anger him; and (as if entering a ship he had assumed a new nature) a lion at sea, so passionate that few could please him," but "a good man in all passages."

His biggest maritime exploit, of course, would be the ill-fated 1609 voyage to Virginia that resulted in the *Sea Venture*'s accidental encounter with Bermuda and England's claiming the mysterious island as its own.

Admiral Somers may have cursed the storm that wreaked havoc with his navigation, but his strong leadership helped his shipload of colonists survive, sealing Bermuda's destiny for the next 400 years. Notably, Somers's hand-drawn map of the island, complete with its famous hog-hunting scene, attests to his resourcefulness and curiosity as a navigator. The crude map also provided the world with its first and most realistic look at the previously feared "Isle of Devils."

But Bermuda would cut short Somers's adventurous life, for he died on the island on November 9, 1610 after returning to gather more supplies for the Jamestown colony. One report blamed "a surfeit of pork" for his undoing; contaminated meat could have been the cause. The admiral's embalmed body was sailed home to Dorset and buried with military honours at the Church of St. Candida and Holy Cross in Whitchurch.

His heart remained in the island town that would bear his name: St. George's. The grave, at first marked by a wooden cross, was replaced in 1619 with a marble slab erected by Governor Nathaniel Butler.

Somers's nephew, Matthew Somers—who had ignored his uncle's dying command to take supplies back to Virginia—inherited his English estates. Matthew was also a sea captain, but unlike his accomplished uncle, had a mediocre career and squandered his inheritance, spending his last years in a debtors' prison.

The 'Noble Sir George'

In the Year 1611 Noble Sir George Summers
    went hence to heaven,
Whose well-tried worth that held him still
    imploid,
Gave him the knowledge of the world so wide;
Hence 't was by Heaven's decree that to this
    place
He brought new guests and name to mutual
    grace;
At last his soul and body being to part,
He here bequeathed his entrails and his
    heart.
    —*Grave inscription erected in 1619,*
        to replace a wooden cross

Seal of the Virginia Company, which ran Bermuda's affairs until 1615

Near this spot was interred in the year
1610 the Heart of the Heroic Admiral Sir
George Somers, Kt., who nobly sacrificed
his life to carry succour to the infant and
suffering Plantation now the State of
Virginia. To Preserve his fame to future ages,
Near the scene of his Memorable Shipwreck
of 1609, The Governor and Commander-in-
Chief Of this Colony for the time being,
Caused this tablet to be erected, 1876.
    —*Memorial in public gardens,*
        Kent Street, St. George's

Admiral Sir George Somers, Kt.,
Shipmate of Sir Walter Raleigh,
Coloniser of the Bermudas.
Born near Lyme Regis, 1554.
Owner of Berne Manor, Whitchurch
Canonicorum.
Died in the Bermudas, November, 1610.
Buried beneath the old Cantry, under the
Present Vestry, July 4, 1611.
    —*Erected by public subscription, at the*
        Church of St. Candida and Holy Cross,
        Whitchurch, Dorset, 1908

*D*eliverance and *Patience* set sail from Bermuda on May 10, 1610—nearly 10 months after the *Sea Venture* wreck. To the passengers' relief, the voyage was uneventful this time. Two weeks later, the ships reached Jamestown, where they were met by a sorry group of settlers desperate for provisions and floundering amid "misery and misgovernment." Of the 500 original settlers at James Fort, just 60 had survived famine and disease of the 1609–10 winter. Their prospects were so bleak, the entire company, including the Bermuda survivors, decided their chances would be better if they abandoned the settlement and went to Newfoundland to pick up provisions before returning to England. They boarded two ships and on June 7 sailed partway down the river to make good on this plan, when luck sided with them. Heading for the open sea, they met three incoming ships carrying Lord de la Warre—and a bounty of much-needed supplies.

His relief fleet would finally save Jamestown. But the stories of Bermuda's exotic larder proved too alluring for de la Warre to ignore, and he asked for volunteers to return to the island to collect six months' worth of provisions of pork and fish. Perhaps also intrigued by the possibility of establishing Bermuda as a separate English colony, Somers offered to undertake the mission in the *Patience*, accompanied by another pinnace, *Discovery*. On June 19, he left Jamestown and returned to the "Isle of Devils," once again encountering stormy weather; although he managed to arrive safely, the second ship had to turn back to Virginia. Somers found Carter and Waters "alive and lustye" on the island, according to Strachey. The duo, later joined by a third man, Edward Chard, who also found himself bewitched by the island's charms, would remain to greet Bermuda's first official settlers two years later. For Somers, however, this was to be his last sojourn, for his health began to fail and he died later that year in Bermuda at age 56. His dying wish, that his ship return as requested with supplies to Virginia, was ignored by the crew, who decided to go to England. Following custom, Somers's nephew, Captain Matthew Somers, removed his uncle's heart and entrails and buried them in Bermuda. He put the body in a cedar chest and smuggled it aboard the homeward-bound *Patience* to avoid stirring superstitions among the crew who, like most mariners of the time, felt carrying corpses would bring a ship bad luck.

Back in England, tales of adventures on the Isle of Devils prompted much public gossip. Word of the *Sea Venture* escapade, of the wealth of natural beauty and food supplies, reached members of the Virginia Company, and finally prompted those in authority to consider Bermuda in a new light. Perhaps the Devils' Isle slur was misplaced; perhaps Bermuda—with so many natural and geographical advantages and not a single indigenous inhabitant—was just as worthy of colonisation as Jamestown, and might even facilitate enterprises in America. Before long, the Company decided "to propound a course of experiment," says Strachey, "and so resolved upon a general purpose to send over thither some voluntary men, who were to be entised with hope of gaine." Under the Company's original charter endorsed by King James, the Adventurers held mandate over offshore islands located within just 100 miles of Virginia. A 1612 amendment pushed this boundary to 600 miles, allowing Bermuda to be included within the scope of England's burgeoning colonial ambitions. Pearls? Ambergris? Spanish treasure? What would they find?

CHAPTER THREE

The First Settlers

SPAIN'S LOSS IS ENGLAND'S GAIN AS COLONISTS TAKE ROOT

A good example *As soon as wee had landed all our company, we went all to prayer, and gave thankes unto the Lord for our safe arrivall, and whilst we were at prayer, wee saw our three men come rowinge downe to us, the sight of whom did much revive us. They showed us a good example for they had planted corne, great store of wheate, beanes, peas, pompions, mellons, and tobacco; besides they had wrought upon timber in squaring and sawing of cedar trees, for they intended to build a small pinnace to carry them into Virginia, being almost out of hope and comfort of our coming.*

—*A colonist aboard the* Plough, *1612*

An intriguing flurry of correspondence between Felipe III (King Philip III), his Board of Trade in Seville, and the Council of War in Madrid revealed just how poorly informed Spain was about Bermuda early in the 17th Century. Word about the island had begun to spread throughout Europe. Given Pope Alexander VI's 1493 Line of Demarcation decree that all unknown territory from 100 leagues west of the Cape Verde islands belonged to Spain, news that the English had claimed the mysterious Isle of Devils set off alarm bells in the Iberian peninsula. Afraid that a lucrative source of pearls and ambergris—not to mention a potential strategic naval base— were about to be lost forever to their rival, Spanish officials finally turned their focus to the island they had virtually ignored for a century. It would

BERMUDA MARITIME MUSEUM

Welcome to Virginiola...

When the London-based Virginia Company decided to colonise Bermuda in 1612, it called the new acquisition "Virginiola," since the islands lay off the coast of the first permanent English settlement at Jamestown, Virginia. Later, Bermuda was named the "Somers Islands" or "Summer Islands"—a salute to Admiral Sir George and the colony's balmy climate. The first Bermuda settlement was named "New London" by the colonists, but eventually became St. George's.

From thatched huts to a stone town

Bermuda's settlers learned new building methods by trial and error. At first, desperate for basic shelter, they crafted thatched roofs over their rudimentary cabins using palm fronds, which also covered the ground inside. Eventually, they replaced palmetto thatch with cedar shingles. In time, the frames of homes and public buildings were constructed with plastered brick rather than cedar timber, which became scarce and also posed a fire risk. By the end of the 1600s, settlers were encouraged to build with limestone—and if they did so, were awarded land to call their own.

Invasion plan *The English confirm that there are about 200 there and in shacks. Delay will make it more difficult. If the secret is half kept…little money will be required. I propose to remove these people without doing them harm and send them off to England.*
—*Suggestion by the Spanish Duke of Medina Sidonia to send an invading squadron to Bermuda headed by Captain Diego Ramirez*

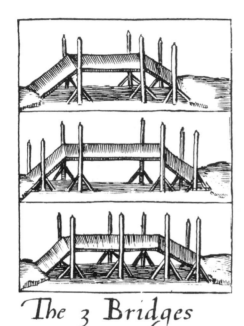

The 3 Bridges

Bridges and fortifications as detailed in the 1624 John Smith map of Bermuda

prove to be a vain attempt to turn back history.

Eight years had passed since Ramirez accidentally landed on Bermuda and wrote his descriptive account, but a May 24, 1611 letter between Seville and Madrid appeared to take note of the captain's observations for the first time. The president of the Board of Trade, Don Francisco de Varte Ceron, included the reports of Ramirez and his pilot with a letter of reply to the War Council query about Bermuda pearls.

"An Englishman who came to Cadiz said that the flagship of an English squadron had been lost at Bermuda," wrote Don Francisco of the *Sea Venture* debacle, "that her survivors had built a pinnace there, and on returning to England, had talked much of the great wealth of pearls at that island, with the result that many people were minded to go and settle there, and a number had banded together for that very purpose."

The story would unleash a volley of letters that continued for the next four years between various Spanish government ministers, noblemen and the lackadaisical monarch, to whom the Council of War persistently urged a rapid naval and military response—but to no avail. Spain's inaction would give the English all the time they needed to firmly establish their colony in Bermuda.

The first group of English settlers in Bermuda was laying the physical and cultural foundations for the next 400 years. Sixty men, women and children had spent 11 weeks sailing to the "Summer Islands" aboard a ship named the *Plough*, under the command of Captain Robert Davis, a member of Somers's 1609 fleet. Among them was Richard Moore, a carpenter chosen by the Virginia Company for a three-year term as Bermuda's first governor. Arriving on July 11, 1612 at St. George's, Moore quickly set up camp at what is now Smith's Island in the natural east-end harbour, and began the business of building a colony.

Previously employed by a large London shipping company, Moore was known to be an energetic, careful and industrious man. He had been sent to the island with explicit instructions to plant corn and other crops that would free the colony from total dependency on shipped supplies. The Company Adventurers, or investors, also wanted proof of Bermuda's riches: they instructed Moore to send back samples of ambergris, silk, tobacco, pearls, whale oil, or any other treasures he might find, along with specimens of curiosities like "fair birds" or "beasts" with which they could impress friends and colleagues as gifts.

Smith's Island, so named for the Company's governor in London, Sir Thomas Smith, became the settlers' first home in this exotic setting, though after a few days Moore moved the company across the bay to the larger island now called St. George's. Everything had to be learned through experiment: planting crops that would thrive in a new soil and climate; building homes with subtropical materials; hunting for food and locating fresh water—each task demanded determination, labour and innovation. Survival depended on their efforts being successful, something even the larger Jamestown settlement was finding a difficult challenge.

The settlers fashioned huts thatched with palmetto leaves and dug wells deep into the earth to tap natural water supplies when they found to their dismay the island had no lakes, streams or rivers. The little community, at first dubbed "New London," would slowly grow up around a market square

The Three Kings

American novelist Washington Irving's 1864 tale *The Three Kings of Bermuda* is based on the adventures of three fugitive colonists who chose to stay on the island rather than sail to Virginia or back to England. Christopher Carter, Edward (also known as Robert) Waters and Edward Chard—along with the *Sea Venture*'s dog—lived alone on Bermuda until the first settlers arrived aboard the *Plough*.

Carter and Waters, a pardoned murderer, fled into self-imposed exile when Somers and the rest of the 1609 castaways continued their voyage to James Fort. Somers found them "alive and lustye" when he returned in 1610. Chard, one of Somers's crew, had opted to join the pair instead of sailing home with Matthew Somers aboard the *Patience*. The trio built huts, fished and farmed, and when Moore's party arrived in the summer of 1612, they had cleared and cultivated Smith's Island with tobacco and other crops.

The Three Kings' renown is mostly due to their discovery of a large pile of ambergris, which played a key part in Moore's first year as governor. The coveted commodity, valued at £3 an ounce in London, legally belonged to the Adventurers, but the three men decided to keep it a secret. They planned to sail to Newfoundland and return to England, but just as they were to set off, the *Plough* sailed into St. George's. Word leaked out about the treasure and Carter confessed everything. Chard was sentenced to death, but later won a reprieve—three years' imprisonment.

Moore used the ambergris to entice more supplies and settlers from London. He finally sent it back in small increments to the investors, who mistakenly believed they would continue to profit from a constant harvest of the rare substance for years to come.

into the town of St. George, the first capital of Bermuda and the oldest surviving English town in the Americas after Jamestown fell into ruin.

Following the Adventurers' orders, the settlers cleared land, planted corn and tobacco, and became proficient at fishing with nets and hunting hogs, wild birds and turtles to feed themselves. They had to swear loyalty to the King and behave as they would be expected to do in any "well-governed commonwealth." They also had to uphold the values of the Church of England, which included observing the Sabbath. One of their first public buildings was a frame church, St. Peter's. Moore also had them build a wharf and a watchtower, and he constructed a house for himself. Later buildings would be constructed with stone carved from the island's porous limestone base, but this did not become common practice for another half-century. Moore's settlers also made bridges to connect nearby islands, and a town began to take shape, complete with trappings of 17th-Century justice: stocks and gallows to punish wrongdoers and 'witches.'

Bermuda remained under the Virginia Company umbrella until November 25, 1612, when a corporate restructuring saw a new, but connected company, composed of members of the former, instituted in London. The aim was to put responsibility for the island on the entire Company, and it would remain as such until the Somers Island Company was formed three years later. The latter entity comprised a distinguished group made up of 19 Adventurers, including members of the pioneering East India Company, which under Queen Elizabeth and King James had been pushing out the boundaries of England's eastern colonies in tandem with the western expansion. Despite the alluring fables of pearls and other natural riches, the Adventurers viewed Bermuda less as a treasure trove in its own right, than as a convenient provisioning larder for their colony at Jamestown. Yet they hoped the Bermuda settlement would turn self-sufficient and, more importantly, profitable.

Moore, under pressure to achieve both goals, played a cheeky game of leverage with his London bosses. Using an amount of ambergris he had managed to confiscate from the "Three Kings"—the trio who had stayed in Bermuda and lived on Smith's Island since 1610—Moore tantalised the Adventurers with the prospect of easy wealth. In effect, he used the ambergris as a 'carrot' to entice them to direct more supplies and settlers to his colony. Ordered to send the entire stockpile of ambergris back to London aboard the ship *Elizabeth*, which arrived at the island in March 1613 with 60 passengers, Moore instead divided up the valuable stash and handed over only a small portion. *Elizabeth* returned with more people and provisions, and Moore finally had to deliver the remainder, but he had got what he wanted.

So had the investors. In London, the ambergris sold for more than £3 an ounce, for a total of £10,000. The sum made up for their expenses in establishing the colony to that point—and whetted their appetites for more.

Defence was Moore's obsession in Bermuda. As soon as basic housing had been built, he started organising the construction of towers and forts to protect the strengthening English interest in the island. Having rescued two guns from the *Sea Venture* shipwreck, the settlers began building Paget and Smith's batteries (on Paget and Governor's Islands), Pembroke Fort on Cooper's Island, Charles Fort on Charles Island, St.

The legacy of Bermuda's forts

Dr. EDWARD CECIL HARRIS

In late 1612, the first colonial English town was founded at Bermuda's east end and named for Saint George. More than half of Bermuda's 90 fortifications were erected here, and have survived the centuries largely intact. They are the earliest English masonry forts of the New World—a milestone recognised in 2000 by UNESCO when it designated St. George's a "World Heritage Site," along with fortifications of the entire parish.

In the period prior to the American Revolutionary War, Bermuda's forts were small structures, tiny replicas of their European counterparts. Built in stone, not timber as in most other parts of the Americas, and mostly located on isolated islets within the archipelago, they served the island purely for local defence, since Bermuda was in many senses a 'company town,' rather than an imperial enterprise.

Indeed, the fate of Bermuda was of little concern to the British government until the breakaway of America's rebellious continental colonies in 1783. At that time, Bermuda's geography suddenly made the island a key possession. Located midway between British colonies in Canada and the West Indies, Bermuda took on a new role as a strategic stronghold in the international defence of its overseas territories.

The 'enemy,' up to the first decade of the 1900s, was the United States. With the exception of the last British work, built at Warwick Camp at the start of the Second World War, all the great forts built in the 19th Century were intended to hold Bermuda from an American conquest. That the Americans ended up assuming the coastal defence of Bermuda from 1941–45 is perhaps the greatest military irony of our history.

All of Bermuda's surviving fortifications could be classed World Heritage Sites, for it is unlikely the island has any peers with which to compete as far as sheer number and types of forts. As a group, Bermuda's forts span the evolution of the whole British Empire until its demise in the 1950s. At that time, coincidentally, coastal defence had also become obsolete, its

Pagets forte

death knell sounded by the buzz of V2 rockets over Britain in the Second World War—harbingers of the intercontinental ballistic missiles and "smart bombs" to come.

The forts on Castle and Southampton Islands in Castle Harbour were the first structures to be built in Bermuda stone, the soft, but durable limestone which forms a cap of white gold atop the volcano of Mount Bermuda. To this day, limestone is Bermuda's sole mineral resource and was also an export like tobacco and later, the Bermuda sloop. Built from this stone, houses, churches, stores and warehouses of historic St. George's Town lay claim to their historical status. Other forts, all except one in timber, were to follow in limestone and many of these colonial

works survive throughout Bermuda.

With Bermuda's rise in status as Britain's "Gibraltar of the West," new and much bigger forts were erected on the island, from the largest at the western Dockyard to the extraordinary Fort Cunningham in the east. The former was built of very hard limestone, while Fort Cunningham was remodelled in the 1870s with experimental wrought-iron frontages, prompting one member of Parliament to question if it was built of gold, such was the cost to Queen Victoria's Exchequer.

The fortifications of Bermuda may be said to have served their purpose, though but a few shots were ever fired in anger and only one fort was ever invaded (Wreck Hill Fort, by two privateers, for six days in June 1777). When the Americans became independent, the island became the oldest element of the overseas British empire. Bermuda remains one of the last 13 such settlements—all islands, except Gibraltar. Surpassing even the continental lands, it was the islands which contributed most to the new wealth of Britain during the Industrial Revolution. Indeed, without the all-important sugar income from the British West Indies, world history as we know it would probably be very different.

From the Industrial Revolution came the 20th-Century's arms race, and the historic artillery that survives in Bermuda also demonstrates the evolution of guns for which forts here were built. It is an international legacy evoking, in the range of forts and cannon, from 1612 to 1957, Bermuda's place in the worldwide emigration of peoples and the military necessities that accompanied European colonisation of the globe from the 15th Century onwards.

■ *Dr. Edward Harris is Executive Director of the Bermuda Maritime Museum and author of* Bermuda Forts, 1612–1957

'That the Americans ended up assuming the coastal defence of Bermuda ... is perhaps the greatest military irony of our history'

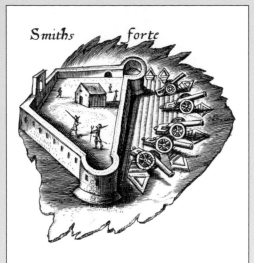

Smiths forte

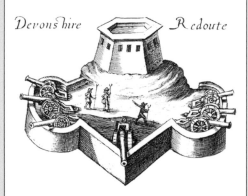

Classic depictions of Bermuda's early forts, drawn by John Smith and published in 1624

Devonshire   Redoute

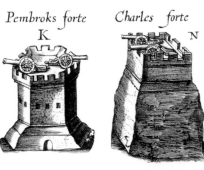

Pembroks forte
K

Charles forte
N

St Catherins forte
F

Penistons Redoute
G

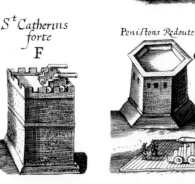

BRIMSTONE MEDIA

Catherine's fort in St. George's, and the King's Castle and other fortification on Castle Island leading into Castle Harbour. Warwick Castle, just north of St. George's, guarded the colony's fresh water supply.

So single-minded was Moore in his mission to build forts and docks that his rallying efforts began to annoy the other colonists. All their time was now consumed by fort-building, leaving them unable to tend their crops or cattle, properly feed their families or significantly develop the colony beyond the area of St. George's. Yet Moore's dogged efforts were somewhat vindicated in March 1614 when settlers posted at Castle Island spotted two ships approaching along the South Shore. One of the *Sea Venture*'s guns had been stationed here; the other was mounted at Smith's Fort. Following naval custom, the lookouts jumped in a couple of rowboats and went out to meet the visitors, assuming they were English. Still, they remained cautiously within firing range of their own cannon to the ships and, as they drew close, they shouted a greeting. The only response was a voice telling them to come aboard one of the ships to talk.

Suspicious, the settlers returned to Castle Island, where Moore had arrived with more men and correctly concluded the ships were Spanish. What happened next amounted to a farcical chronicle of mishaps by the English that in time could have opened the door for a Spanish invasion— had serendipity not favoured the settlers.

Moore again went out in a small boat to hail the ships, but this time there was no answer. Returning to the fort, he fired a cannon shot at the first ship, and then another, this time sending the shot through its rigging. Both ships turned and sailed away. What the Spanish strangers didn't realise was that despite the show of bravado, the settlers' position was precarious. True, they had four guns ready—but only one cannon shot remained. Worse, during the confusion as the ships approached, the settlers accidentally knocked over and spilled the single remaining barrel of gunpowder. Sheer luck prevented the powder igniting and blowing up their fort and themselves.

"These direct demonstrations of heavenly assistance exceedinge wrought upon most of them, and especially it moved the Governour," according to one account. "So callinge his men together like a good Christian and a soldier, he publickly gave thancks to God for this his so protecting a preservation."

The interloping ships were later identified as those belonging to Captain Domingo de Ulivari, a Spanish mariner sailing home from San Domingo who spotted smoke signals and decided to investigate. "They thought the land peaceful, and saw that the plantings were very green," noted a Spanish report on the incident and Ulivari's observations. "The launches that put out to them were newly built and, they judged, of native wood, because it was very red…cedar abounds in that island."

Ulivari's scouting mission for his king confirmed Spain's worst suspicions. The English had landed on the island for a purpose—and drastic measures would be needed to get rid of them.

Indeed, Bermuda's strategic importance—and the benefits of colonisation —were becoming uncomfortably apparent to Spain during these years. Letters suggesting possible plans of attack to oust the English had been ricocheting since 1611 between various players in Spanish officialdom.

"It would appear that the English who were in Virginia are seeking to

In their own words

■ The Royal Society, *1610*

Here follows a Relation, somewhat more divertifying, than the precedent Accounts; which is about the new Whale-fishing in the West Indies about the Bermudas, as it was delivered by an understanding and hardy Sea-man, who affirmed he had been at the killing work himself. His account, as far as remembered, was this; that though hitherto all Attempts of mastering the Whales of those Seas had been unsuccessful, by reason of the extraordinary fierceness and swiftness of these monsterous Animals; yet the enterprise being lately renewed, and such persons chosen and sent thither for the work, as were resolved not to be baffled by a Sea-monster, they did prosper so far in this undertaking, that, having been out at Sea, near the said Isle of Bermudas, seventeen times, and fastned their Weapons a dozen times, they killed in these expeditions 2 old Female Whales, and 3 Cubs, whereof one of the old ones, from the head to the extremity of the Tayl, was 88 Foot in length, by measure; its Tayl being 23 Foot broad, the swimming Finn 26 Foot long, and the Gills three Foot long: having great

BERMUDA MARITIME MUSEUM

bends underneath from the Nose to the Navil; upon her after-part, a Finn on the back; being within paved (this was the Sea-man's phrase) with fat, like the Cawl of a Hog…

Their celerity and force he affirmed to be wonderful, insomuch that one of those Creatures, which he struck himself, towed the boat wherein he was, after him, for the space of six or seven Leagues, in three quarters of an hours time. Being wounded, he saith, they make a hideous roaring, at which, all of that kind that are within hearing, come towards that place, where the Animal is, yet without striking, or doing any harm to the wary. He observed, that the Oyl of the Blubber is as clear and fair as any Whey: but that which is boyled out of the Lean, interlarded, becomes as hard as Tallow, spattering in the burning and that which is made of the Cawl, resembleth Hoggs-grease.

The same Person, that communicated the particulars about the new Whale-fishing near the Bermudas, gives this further Information; that there have been since taken by order of the Bermudas Company, sixteen of those Whales, the Oyle wherof, to the quantity of 50 or 60 Tuns arrived in Ireland at Limrick, some few months agoe.

—*The Philosophical Transactions of the Royal Society, London, c. 1660*

Ambergris

Literally "grey amber," ambergris is a by-product of the sperm whale's digestive tract, and has been a highly-prized substance over the centuries. Solid and waxy, it is soft and black when found in the intestines of dead whales, but over time, becomes hard, grey and fragrant. Ambergris is used in the manufacture of perfume and as a spice in the Far East.

About six days ago a ship came in from [Bermuda]. It brings seventy four pounds of ambergris which is sold in this city at fourteen ducats the ounce. It also brings some wheat, grown there. They tell men their wheat plantings do not produce very well.

—Letter to Felipe III from Ambassador Don Diego Sarmiento de Acuña, London, October 5, 1613

settle and fortify that island for obvious purposes," Spain's Council of War noted to Felipe III on July 6, 1613. Spanish spies and ships had relayed the information about Moore and his developing Bermuda colony to Madrid, which was under the assumption that lands to the west, colonised or not, were Spanish by right.

"If they were to attain these, it might occasion serious worry, since not only is it detrimental to our reputation that they do so in a quarter so much Your Majesty's own—and in such plain view of all—but also," wrote the Council, "the day they establish a footing and fortify themselves there, being to windward of all the Indies, they can do very great damage in proportion to the strength they may possess, even if this be not a fleet, but only four or six ships, even on the high seas, without a fixed rendezvous wherein to await the silver galleons and fleets, since these, not sighting land, endeavouring to keep far out, nevertheless approach the altitude of Bermuda. Knowing the season when they must pass, the English will be able to lie in wait to do what damage they can, at least to vessels that straggle or fall behind."

Moreover, the Council was worried an English Bermuda would severely impinge on Spain's West Indian commercial interests. "They will let no ship pass without capturing it and they can raid and infest all those coasts in such a manner that they will make it necessary to increase the garrisons and soldiery there, and compel us to augment the size of the Armada on the Indies course, which is so costly to Your Majesty's treasury," it wrote, proposing Spain immediately send five ships plus a caravel to Bermuda, led by none other

A princess bride

One of the colonists wrecked at Bermuda with Sir George Somers is better known for marrying the storied daughter of a powerful North American Indian. Widower John Rolfe married Pocahontas in Jamestown, Virginia, where she had become a folk heroine for befriending the English settlers. Notably, she was said to have saved the life of Captain John Smith, the settlers' leader, when he was captured by her father, Powhatan during the colony's first months.

Rolfe had endured much hardship as a colonist. His infant daughter—christened Bermuda—was one of five deaths recorded during the castaways' 10 months on the island in 1609–10. Later, the child's mother, Rolfe's first wife, had died in Virginia.

By the time Rolfe and his fellow colonists finally reached their destination, Smith had left Jamestown and relations between settlers and Indians were fuelled by distrust. Rolfe met Pocahontas, whose name means "playful one," when the settlers took her captive in a bid to force the Indians to stay peaceful and supply them with food such as fish and corn. Pocahontas was held prisoner for several months, as negotiations took place between Indians

and settlers. Rolfe was one of those sent to talk with representatives for her father, who ruled over 40 area tribes.

Pocahontas learned English, converted to Christianity and married Rolfe, becoming 'Rebecca Rolfe' in April 1614. The wedding was blessed by both her father and Jamestown's governor, and peace between natives and settlers was restored.

The couple had one child, Thomas, and in 1616 they travelled to England, where Pocahontas was the toast of the upper classes. She was invited to special parties, painted by celebrity portraitists and officially received by the King and Queen. Tragically, Rolfe and Pocahontas were about to return to Virginia in March 1617 when she contracted smallpox and died, at age 21. She is buried in a parish church in the southern port of Gravesend, England.

Back in Virginia, Rolfe was instrumental in developing the tobacco crop at Jamestown. Their son Thomas was educated in England before moving back to the colonies to live.

Pocahontas, the Native American princess who married a Bermuda widower. Below, Captain John Smith, whose life she supposedly saved

BRIMSTONE MEDIA

A feast of birds *Every cabin had pots and kettles full of birds boiling, and others roasting on spits while the living wild birds walked among the people in the cabins, making their strange noises as though begging to be taken.*

—Reverend Lewis Hughes, a Welsh Puritan, describing the community at Cooper's Island, St. George's, where Governor Butler sent hungry settlers to feast on cahows during a famine caused by rats

than Captain Diego Ramirez, with the support of 1,000 soldiers and crew.

When Felipe III wrote back, he was clearly disgruntled: "It does surprise me that in all the years since the Indies have been discovered, no one should have thought to make certain of this island," he said. "And that now so much importance is ascribed to it without even knowing for sure what enemies are there."

The king quashed the idea of a full Spanish assault on Bermuda, suggesting instead that Ramirez sail to Cuba with an information-gathering stop-off at Bermuda en route. If what the Council believed was still true, Ramirez could then launch an expedition from Havana to drive the English out of Bermuda, the king said.

Whether Ramirez ever made a return journey, however, is doubtful. Numerous delays documented in the back-and-forth campaign of letters, and the lack of funding made available for such an invasion, ultimately resulted in inaction. Complacent after a century as a world power, the Spanish had missed their opportunity and their flimsy intentions soon fell into history's wastebin of what might have been.

How they lived

A bill for tools and housewares, also used for barter, from Simon Parker to colonist Robert Rich, 1617–18

Imprimis: for 6 sea hookes att 18d

Item: 2 other hookes att 4d

Item: 3 wegges [wedges] and 2 ringes of a bitte [boring tool] att 6s

Item: for 2 axxes att 5s

Item: for 4 sea hookes 4d

Item: for one axe att 2s 6d

Item: for a phisgig [spear] 3s 4d

Item: for a lamp att 2s

Item: for a pesell [pestle] for a mortar 5s

Item: for a wrest [rest] for a sawe 6d

Item: for stilling [steeling] of an axe 12d

Item: for a new axe 2s 6d

Item: for 4 sea hookes 12d

Item: for a sea knife 12d

Item: for 12 bream hookes 12d

Item: for stilling of an axe 12d

Item: for a new axe att 2s 6d

Item: for six sea hookes att 18d

Item: for stilling 5 axes 5s

Item: for a knife and howe [hoe] 3d

Item: for mending of pesell [pestle] 12d

Item: for a payer of irons 3s

Item: for 2 axxes att 5s

Item: for a new ligge [leg] for a baking paine [pan] 6d

Item: for 3 irons for to sett Corne [plant grain] 6d

Item: for stilling of an axe 12d

Item: for a new legg for a treivt [trivet] 6d

Item: for 3 axxes 7s 6d

Item: for 6 sea hookes 12d

Item: for 4 bills [pickaxe] att 5s

Palmetto

It keeps their houses thatch'd with 't
and its mats
For Bedding makes, with baskets,
brooms and hats.
—*Poem extolling Bermuda's palmetto*
by English visitor John Hardy, c. 1669

The Spanish may have coveted Bermuda, but the island wasn't exactly the paradise it might have appeared. Governor Moore's focus on fortifications at the expense of agriculture left the first settlers facing famine, just as their Jamestown counterparts had done. Many also suffered a strange feverish sickness during those early years. Turtles, fish and stocks of birds like the cahows had vastly diminished since the settlers' arrival, and the meagre crops the inhabitants did manage to harvest were destroyed by an infestation of rats that ravaged the island for several years.

Ironically, the rodents arrived aboard a ship which the settlers first considered a stroke of luck. An English mariner, Daniel Ellffryth, sailed to the island aboard a captured Spanish vessel that happened to be full of grain. But as the community unloaded the cargo, scores of rats ran out of the hold and soon began to multiply. Their scourge would outlast Moore and several subsequent governors.

More worrying for the London-based investors was that Bermuda's supposed natural riches had not materialised. Ambergris was found to be very rare, pearls and silk non-existent. Tobacco, which later would be employed as a barter currency on the island, was not generating expected profits. The more than 500 settlers by now living in Bermuda were dependent on shiploads of supplies the Company was obliged to send regularly from London. From the settlers' point of view, their new life was full of hardship. The lack of ready food left them scrabbling to feed themselves, often by foraging for remaining wildlife. Furthermore, taxes levied by the Virginia Company investors were punitive—leading to bitterness, rancour and low morale.

Exasperated and losing money, the Adventurers finally decided on a new business strategy that would separate Bermuda from the Virginia Company. As a result, they handed over Bermuda to the Crown on November 23, 1614, so that England could help pay for Bermuda's defence. The following year, on June 29, James I granted a new charter to 118 Bermuda investors, incorporating them under "the Governor and Company of the City of London for the Plantacon of the Somer Islands." Under the new entity's rules, investors would hold a monopoly on all trade from Bermuda; island residents were allowed to trade only with Company ships and prohibited from doing business with the American colonies. As reward, they would be freed from taxation for seven years. And for the next 14 years, their products would be dealt a mere five-per-cent duty upon entering English ports. Bermuda settlers were also forbidden to build ships, and denied the right to go whaling. Tobacco would become the only medium of exchange.

Blamed for all the failures despite his efforts, Moore felt he had suffered enough. He returned to England, but continued to take part in maritime adventures; in 1617, he sailed to Guiana aboard Walter Raleigh's flagship, *Destiny*, but died later that year when fever swept the ship. Moore left Bermuda in the hands of six commissioners, who were supposed to rule for a month each as governor. Plagued by laziness and competing self-interests, though, the system disintegrated into several years of administrative chaos.

The investors, realising the island needed a tough leader, yet one they could control, elected a Virginia planter named Daniel Tucker in 1616 to become the first resident governor under the Bermuda Company. His administration, and that of his successor, Nathaniel Butler, would pave the way for the Somers Island Company—or "Bermuda Company"—to operate the island for the next 68 years.

In their own words
■ Richard Norwood, *1616*

Master Moore spent three years of the government for the most part in fortifying the Country, and training the people in martial exercises, which custom hath been continued by his successors; he built some nine or ten Forts, placing Ordnance and Munition in them. In this time, the Lord sent upon the Country a very grievous scourge and punishment, threatening the utter ruin and desolation of it: That it came from God I need not strive to prove, especially considering it was generally so acknowledged by us at that time: The causes and occasions of it I need not name, being very well known to us all that then lived there, which were about 600 persons, though shortly after much diminished. I will only shew the thing itself, which was a wonderful annoyance by silly Rattes: These Rattes coming at the first out of a Ship, few in number, increased in the space of two year, or less, so exceedingly, that they filled not only those places where they were first landed: But swimming from place to place, spread themselves into all parts of the Country. In so much, that there was no Iland, though severed by the Sea from all other Lands, and many miles distant from the Iles where the Rats had their original but was pestered with them.

They had their nests almost in every tree, and in all places their Burrowes in the ground (like Connies) to harbour in. They spared not the fruits of plants of Trees, neither the Plants themselves, but eat them up. When we had set our Corne, they would commonly come by troupes the night following, or so soon as it began to grow, and dig it up again. If by diligent watching any of it were preserved till it came to earing, it should then very hardly scrape them. Yea, it was a difficult matter after we had it in our houses, to save it from them, for they became noysome even to the persons of men. We used all diligence for the destroying of them, nourishing many Cats, wild and tame, for that purpose; we used Rats-bane, and many times set fire on the woods, so as the fire might run half a mile or more before it were extinct: Every man in the Country was enjoyned to set twelve Traps, and some of their own accord set near a hundred,

BRIMSTONE MEDIA

which they visited twice or thrice in a night. We trained up our Dogges to hunt them, wherein they grew so expert, that a good Dogge in two or three hours space, would kill forty or fifty Rattes, and other means we used to destroy them, but could not prevail, finding them still to increase against us.

And this was the principal cause of that great distress whereunto we were driven in the first planting of the Country, for these, devouring the fruits of the earth, kept us destitute of bread a year, or two; so that, when we had it afterwards again, we were so weaned from it, that we should easily neglect and forget to eat it with our meat. We were also destitute at that time of Boats, and other provision for Fishing …All these jointly (but principally the Rats) were the causes of our distress: for being destitute of food, many died, and we all became very feeble and weak, whereof some being so, would not; others could not stir abroad to seek relief, but died in their houses: such as went abroad were subject, through weakness, to be suddenly surprised with a disease we called the Feages, which was neither pain nor sickness, but as it were the highest degree of weakness, depriving us of power and ability for the execution of any bodily exercise, whether it were working, walking or what else. Being thus taken, if there were any in company that could minister any relief, they would straightways recover, otherwise they died there: Yet many after a little rest would be able to walk again, and then if they found any succour were saved.

The extremity of our distress began to abate a little before Master Moore's time of Government was expired, partlly by supplies out of England, of victual and provision for fishing, and partly by that rest and liberty we then obtained, the Country being fortified.

—The Description of the Sommer Islands, once called the Bermudas, *surveyor Richard Norwood, 1616*

Being destitute of food, many died, and we all became very feeble and weak

CHAPTER FOUR

The Company Island

LAND, LAWS AND THE BIRTH OF SLAVERY

The Bermuda Company seal

The Bermuda that faced Governor Daniel Tucker on his arrival in 1616 was an island rapidly degenerating into an idle, rat-infested place. Continual neglect by the six interim commissioners appointed by Governor Moore before his departure had left a fractious community lacking authority, industry or healthy crops. Work on the forts had fallen off since the first settlers' industrious efforts, and the island's future was now threatened by a community complacent amid debauchery and petty crime.

Drastic changes were called for if the colony was ever to sustain itself, let alone turn a profit for the Adventurers. Captain Tucker, an energetic authoritarian who had spent five years running a plantation in Virginia, was known for his self-styled brand of dictatorial discipline—a quality the Bermuda Company felt was sorely needed to shake the island out of its

How they lived

Many of Bermuda's 17th-Century settlers brought conservative middle-class English values and ways of life to their new home, making the island in many ways a miniature replica of the motherland.

Social and religious mores, justice and legislative systems—all were modelled on well-known traditions, creating a paradigm of English life in the New World. England's courts, militia, Westminster govern-ment and church, with all their respective bureaucracy and ceremony, were duplicated, along with England's sharply defined social class system, which in Bermuda ran from the governor down to the lowliest labourer and slaves.

Yet, Bermuda's basic conditions and subtropical surroundings also forced the island's first residents to adapt what they knew and learn new skills to suit their environment. Any previous experience the settlers had with English farming, for example, had to be tailored to the island's very different climate, soil and seasons. They had to learn about new plants and agriculture. Successful plantations of the Spanish Caribbean may have provided a good model. When Bermuda's tobacco crop failed, the colonists sent ships to the West Indies to bring back more appropriate plants such as figs, sweet potatoes, plantains, pineapples, cassava and paw-paw. And while fish, corn and potatoes made up the bulk of their diet, the population remained very dependent on the Company's magazine ships and visiting vessels to bring in food supplies when starvation threatened. Clothing and liquor were also imported.

Shopping list *40 dozens of shoes; 40 hundred hard soap; 12 barrels of powder; one tun of wine; 30 dozen of stockings; 5 dozen of hats* —From a 1630s magazine ship bill of lading

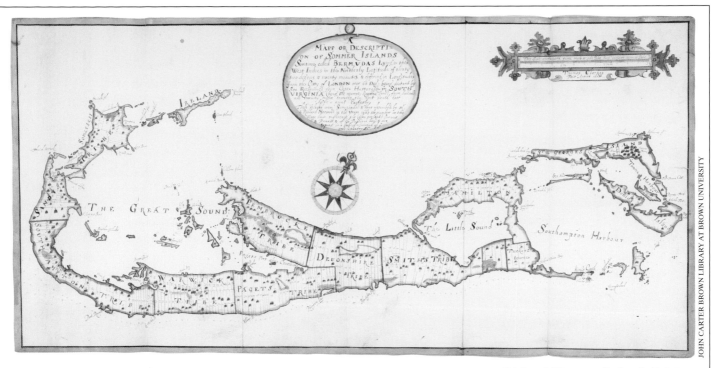

The business of tribes

Richard Norwood's land-division of Bermuda and a detail, below

English shareholders in Bermuda wasted no time carving up the 20-square-mile island to reflect their various investments. The Bermuda Company divided most of the island into eight "tribes," or privately-owned parishes. The word tribe has its roots in the Latin word *tribus*, meaning a political divide, and in English refers to a carving up of land among members of a family or company. Although these continued to be called tribes on some maps through the 1700s, 'parish' became the popular term after the Bermuda Company dissolved in 1684.

Each was named for an Adventurer, usually the investor who had purchased the most shares in a particular tribe. Excluded were St. George's Island, St. David's Island, Longbird, Smith's, Cooper's, Coney and Nonsuch Islands, along with smaller islets, which were kept as public land to pay salaries and other costs. Each tribe, in turn, was split into 50 shares—making a total of 400 shares of 25 acres apiece, which were allotted for development. The tribes or parishes were named for the Adventurers:

■ Bedford's (Hamilton Parish), after Lady Lucy Harrington, Countess of Bedford, who received shares upon the death of her brother Lord Harrington, and later sold them to James Hamilton, second Marquis of Hamilton

■ Smith's, after Sir Thomas Smith
■ Cavendish (Devonshire), after William Cavendish, first Earl of Devonshire
■ Pembroke, after William Herbert, third Earl of Pembroke

■ Paget, after William Paget, fourth Lord Paget
■ Mansil's (Warwick), after Robert Mansfield (or Mansell), who sold his shares to Robert Rich, second Earl of Warwick
■ Southampton, after Henry Wriothesley, third Earl of Southampton
■ Sandys, after Sir Edwin Sandys.

The lowest sort *Last year there were 100 people there, men and women; 300 more are going now—250 men and some women, many of them of the lowest sort, prisoners accused of vagabondage who are being shipped to reside in Bermuda.*
—Dispatches sent to Felipe III of Spain by the Council of War, Madrid, May 14, 1614

Crime and punishment

Colonists were kept on a tight rein and punished for all manner of offences, large and small.

- **Grace Guy, wife of Whitley Guy, on suspicion of incontinency.**
- **Thomas Fosbrooke, goldsmith of Smith's, for melting coin to make bodkins and ear wires.**
- **William Pollard, gent, for irreverent behaviour in church.**
- **William Pollard, gent, for refusing and neglecting to receive Holy Communion ever since he came to the Island, i.e. For two years.**
- **Judith Bailey, wife of Roger Bailey, for disturbing the congregation in Pembroke church**
- **Churchwardens for Smith's for not providing communion wine.**
- **Captain Stokes to clear the path from Tuckers Town to the King's Castle as the Grand Inquest did order at the last summer assizes.**
- **Thomas Pye and Ellen his wife for keeping a common tippling house on the Sabbath and other days.**
- **Peter Lunn and Margery his wife for refusing to live together as man and wife.**
- **Alexander Smith, barber, and Roger Dobbs for playing unlawful games such as dice, cards, nine-pins, etc.**
- **John Edmunds of Devonshire for being an idle and drunk man.**
- **John Ward indicted for stealing, on 26 Sep last, one barrow hog, the property of George Wells, carpenter, value 10s.**
- **John Ditch indicted for participating with Ward in the theft of a hog.**
- **Richard Towell indicted for stealing one potato, weighing 2 or 3 lbs, value 3d. Verdict not guilty.**

—Bermuda Company court records of October 1618

---

downward spiral. He sailed into St. George's aboard the *Edwin* and actually took the islanders by surprise. They had been expecting the return of a frigate the interim governors had sent on a treasure-seeking voyage to the Caribbean, so when Tucker's ship appeared on the horizon, the colonists joyfully thought it might be pay day. Instead, Tucker stepped ashore, and armed with a tough to-do list, wasted no time launching a crackdown.

Tucker carried the king's commission and a list of detailed orders from the Company. These included general administrative plans to improve the governing of the colony as it developed, along with precise rules the settlers were to obey in their daily lives: edicts such as, "Gunpowder shall be carefully stored and not wasted on unnecessary ceremonials" and "All nets and lines shall be carefully dried before being stored." The Company included a hopeful "lesson about whales, spermacetti, ambergris and pearl-fishing," and it had also made numerous provisions for the settlers' health and wellbeing: a surgeon was sent on the ship; rat poison was to be distributed, and fresh water was to be made available to everyone. The investors sent cuttings and seedlings to stimulate the cultivation of "vines" (grapes), aniseed, fennel, marjoram, basil, onions, sugarcane and mulberry trees.

The first steps towards creating a functioning, accountable government were also laid out in the Company's plans. Tucker was to confer with the colony's two religious ministers, Reverends Lewis Hughes and George Keith, and the three were to choose a body of 40 men, who would, in turn, elect a man from each of the eight tribes to act as bailiffs for the colony. The bailiffs would sit with the Governor and two ministers on a General Council that would deal with important colonial matters, including justice.

The Adventurers asked Tucker to take charge of Bermuda's land distribution. He was to split each tribe into shares and allocate these to individual investors. Tenants were then to be assigned to work on the Adventurers' land, with the remaining 200 men kept busy whaling, pearl-diving, fishing, ambergris hunting, and farming. Should the whaling industry not prove productive—as, indeed, turned out to be the case in these years—the Company instructed the whaling ship it had provided to be loaded up instead with "the best and straightest cedar trees from St. David's which must be squared before being loaded" and shipped to England.

With a three-year mandate, Tucker had his work cut out, and no time to lose. But first he had to win the settlers' strict obedience. When one man dared to challenge his authority with comments he felt were "saucy" and "arrogant," Tucker immediately made an example of him, making sure the offender was judged guilty of mutiny and hanged. The so-called "perpetual Christmas" enjoyed by the wayward settlers was over; it was time to get serious about nation-building.

Tucker began to attack the lethargic state of the island's agriculture by ordering widespread planting. He sent his ship *Edwin* to the West Indies to bring back an assortment of suitable southern plants and seeds to supplement those the investors had already sent, and the vessel returned with figs, cassava, pawpaws, plantains, sugarcane and pines. Rats were still rampant, so Tucker had the colonists hunt them with dogs, as well as set traps and poison. He ordered large tracts of infested land to be burned—twice—to kill the vermin. While the destruction of valuable cedar irritated some of the Adventurers, the tactic worked: by May 1617, the

BERMUDA MONETARY AUTHORITY

A Bermuda hog threepence

Hog money

Before coins became widely used in Bermuda, tobacco was popular currency. Settlers used the crop to pay for supplies brought in by Bermuda Company ships. Workers were paid in tobacco. And tobacco was also used as a black-market currency among ships, because Bermuda's first coins, hog money, could not be exported.

Named for the wild boars found roaming Bermuda by the first settlers, "hog money" was among the island's earliest currency and holds the distinction of being the very first of English colonial coins.

Also called "Sommer Islands" coins, the currency arrived from England in 1616 to pay workers employed by the Bermuda Company. Export of the coins was prohibited. Minted in shilling (twelvepence), sixpence, threepence and twopence pieces, the coins bore the image of a hog on one side, and a sailing ship on the other.

Made of copper, some were silver-plated to make them more appealing to the settlers, who preferred English and Spanish gold and silver, or even tobacco and other bartered goods, as a medium for exchange, and dubbed the coins "hogge" money "in a scoff," according to Governor Nathaniel Butler.

As a result, the unpopular coins, redeemable at the Bermuda Company store, did not remain in circulation for many years, vanishing around 1650.

rodent population was shrinking. Farming, in turn, began to flourish, though the Company narrow-mindedly insisted on pushing production of tobacco as a cash crop to the detriment of other products and livestock. The following year, Tucker dispatched a cargo of 30,000 pounds of tobacco to England, the most successful harvest in the settlement's brief history.

He then turned his attention to the division of tribes. The man charged with carrying out the land survey was Richard Norwood, a scholar, inventor, teacher and author who originally had been hired by the Adventurers to search for pearls. When no pearls were found, Tucker's predecessor, Governor Moore, asked Norwood to complete a rough survey of the island, a precursor to the mammoth project he would undertake in Tucker's administration. At that time, he would spend two years drawing up minute details of the land division, finishing his famous map in 1618.

Tucker had a keen interest in the issue of property, because he was entitled to receive a bonus—three shares of land, or 75 acres—and he was determined these would be located in a choice area. He asked Norwood to alert him when he found a particularly good piece of open land, but he was hardly prepared for what the survey would reveal. When he reached the island's west end, Norwood not only discovered an inland valley of "fatte and lustye soil" but also calculated that previous estimates of Bermuda's land mass had fallen short by 200 acres—an "overplus" which, conveniently enough, covered the valley in question, sprawling over the boundary of Southampton and Sandys parishes.

In a calculated move that would ultimately prove to be his undoing, Tucker quickly informed the Bermuda Company the surplus would satisfy his promised share, though he failed to mention how large it was. He staked his claim to it by building an imposing home on the land, using colonists' labour and cedar hauled all the way from the east end. By the time it was finished, Tucker's house was so large, it dwarfed the colony's meagre array of public buildings in St. George's, including the thatch-roofed church, St. Peter's, which was leaking badly. Reverend Hughes, along with many other inhabitants, was alarmed and resentful over Tucker's audacity and complained bitterly to the Company. The Governor had also made enemies among the Adventurers, after feuding with Robert Rich over the wholesale burning of land to kill rats. Rich was one of the original settlers who also happened to be the younger brother of Sir Nathaniel Rich and a cousin of Sir Robert Rich, the Earl of Warwick, both Company heavyweights.

Tucker stoked more back-biting among the people in Bermuda with his ill-fated plan to relocate the capital of St. George's. He wanted to move it across Castle Harbour to an area he named "Tucker's Town." But few colonists left to live there, and the peninsula with its few streets and a dozen or so cottages was used only by guards posted to the Castle Island forts.

To the delight of many of the Bermuda colonists, Tucker finally chose to return to London to defend his controversial actions to members of the Company. At any rate, his three-year term of office was up, though Tucker's ties to Bermuda were far from over; he was eventually given 75 acres of the overplus, and returned to the island where he died in 1623. In the meantime, Captain Miles Kendall took over briefly as acting governor until, in 1619, the Adventurers elected their next candidate—Captain Nathaniel Butler.

Butler was considered the most progressive of the Bermuda Company governors. He organised the construction of bridges between Bermuda's

Who were the Adventurers?

Original investors, or Adventurers, in the Somers Island Company were the 'A-type' personalities of their time, who hoped to combine the excitement of travel and exploration with substantial commercial profits.

Of the 188 initial shareholders, most were businessmen. There were also politicians, knights, courtiers, soldiers, privateers, noblemen and gentlemen, of whom many were connected through family ties. The majority were also share-holders in the Virginia and East India Companies.

The group's key figures were England's power-brokers—luminaries of London society. Shipping magnate Sir Thomas Smith, an MP who served on various House of Commons committees and catalyst for most of England's colonial business ventures, was chosen governor of the Bermuda company—a role he held in the East India Company, the Russia Company and the North West Passage Company. Sir Edwin Sandys, an Oxford-educated Parliamentarian and orator, had drafted the last Virginia charter. Henry Wriothesley, third Earl of Southampton and William Shakespeare's patron, had a large interest in shipping and colonial development. William Herbert, third Earl of Pembroke, was chancellor of Oxford University.

While the Adventurers lived far from their Bermuda colony, they sent friends, relatives and others to look after their interests. In the 1600s, social status in Bermuda was determined by a person's connection to particular Adventurers—the more influential the Adventurer, the more esteemed his island representative.

Devonshire

Sandys

Pembroke

Warwick

Smith

Southampton

BERMUDA HISTORICAL SOCIETY

Who were the Settlers?

Bermuda's first residents were mainly middle-class Englishmen and women from London or its surrounding counties. But the island's early colonists were also pardoned criminals, children sold into bondage, and poor, indentured servants seeking a better life.

Investors of the Virginia and Bermuda Companies reportedly rounded up people from slums and jails, Scottish and Irish prisoners of war, and political and religious outcasts to help boost the workforce in their New World colonies. Petty criminals were often chosen for shipment abroad to relieve overcrowding in English prisons. Even children were recruited. One report of the time described how "many poor boyes and girls [were] taken up out of the streets and hospitals" and shipped to the island. Some emigrants paid their own way, but the average £20 cost of the voyage was prohibitive for many lower-class English. As a result, these would sign on as indentured servants, agreeing to work for a master for five years or more in return for a passage overseas.

Bermuda and other colonies offered a new beginning, or at the very least, a chance for a more prosperous future than these people would have enjoyed in 17th-Century England. Those sent out as planters were given goods and clothes and were also able to share profits with the Adventurers.

Even some members of the English nobility considered Bermuda an enticing prospect. Under English laws of inheritance in that era, younger sons were forced to establish a career, and an adventure in the colonies sometimes offered a fast way to make a fortune. Early colonists included numerous "gentlemen," though some proved less industrious than others due to their lack of experience in farming or other manual labour.

Executive posts on the island were given to hand-picked individuals—East India Company officials, respected sea captains, members of the clergy or military, or relatives and friends of the London-based Adventurers, whose descendants can be found in Bermudian families today.

TIMELINE 1505–1684

BERMUDA

1505 Spaniard Juan de Bermúdez discovers island on a homeward journey from New World	**1511** Bermuda makes its world debut on woodcut map in Peter Martyr's *Legatio Babylonica*	**1525** Spain sends Estevão Gomez to survey island; no map survives	**1603** Spaniard Diego Ramirez lands on Bermuda, detailing a land of plenty	**1609** England claims Bermuda after *Sea Venture* wrecks en route to Jamestown	**1612** The first English settlers, with Governor Richard Moore, arrive aboard the *Plough*

WORLD

1505 Spanish carrying slaves from Africa to the West Indies	**1515** Ottoman Turks build Empire, to include Egypt, North Africa and most of Middle East	**1520** Coffee and chocolate become key New-World exports to Europe	**1607** Captain John Smith founds the first colony at James Fort, Virginia	**1610** Astronomer Galileo publishes his telescope discoveries about Venus	**1611** King James Bible is published in England

main islands, namely at Somerset, Flatts and Coney Island. He recognised the need for environmental conservation, and instituted laws to protect turtles and cedar. He created a grand jury system and rebuilt St. Peter's Church in stone. And he was responsible for establishing the first General Assembly under the Company's instructions, laying the foundations for Bermuda's democratic parliament, the second such assembly in England's colonies, after Virginia's.

The first gathering of the legislative assembly took place in St. Peter's Church on August 1, 1620. Comprising Butler, his Council, bailiffs, a secretary, a clerk and two burgesses who were sworn in that day, the first session passed 15 laws, including a ban on the Company's "stuffinge of the plantation with idle and unprofitable persons," a measure to keep chickens fenced in during planting season, and a ban on the slaughter of turtles. The Assembly had limited powers as all acts had to be ratified by the Company, but it represented the first semi-autonomy allowed the colonists in Bermuda.

BERMUDA MARITIME MUSEUM

Sir Robert Rich, Earl of Warwick, one of Bermuda's first slave-owners

While Butler was known for many positive achievements, the years of his governorship saw the emergence of a sinister institution which would have a lasting, tragic impact on the island. Beginning in the third decade of the 17th Century, Bermudian society would witness an insidious shift from the use of indentured servants to that of outright slavery. For the next 200 years, until abolition in 1834, slaves would be used by Bermuda's colonists as cheap labour —on their land, aboard their ships and in their homes.

The first record of slavery in Bermuda occurred under Daniel Tucker's administration, when the governor sent a ship in 1616 to the West Indies to find "an Indian and a Negar" to dive for pearls in Bermuda—making the island the first English colony to import blacks. Over the ensuing years, more blacks would come to the island in greater numbers, brought on ships from America and the Caribbean, However, during these early years of settlement, blacks typically worked either as slaves, indentured servants or apprentices who, like many of the white English settlers, were bound to a single master for a number of years. Apprentices did so to learn a trade; indentured servants, by contrast, were often working off payment for something, such as their fare to the New World. Most of the island's blacks worked as skilled sugarcane and tobacco farmers in these years. As their terms of servant labour expired, some blacks were freed; for the most part they did the same work, but earned wages.

1616 Bermudian expedition to West Indies collects slaves to replace English labourers	**1617** Mathematician Richard Norwood surveys the island for shareholders	**1620** House of Assembly holds first session, a step towards self-government	**1650** Scores of English immigrants cross the Atlantic to Bermuda and America	**1668** Bermuda captain discovers Turks Islands; colonists to make fortunes from salt	**1684** Rigid trading laws end as Bermuda becomes an English Crown Colony	**BERMUDA**
1616 European powers open trading posts along West Africa's Gold Coast	**1618** The Thirty Years' War, between Catholics and Protestants, embroils Europe	**1620** Pilgrims set sail from Plymouth, England for Massachusetts on the *Mayflower*	**1625** The Dutch establish New Amsterdam (site of New York today)	**1654** First sugarcane plantations develop in the Caribbean, to be worked by slave labour	**1690** The Mogul Empire reaches its zenith, controlling Afghanistan and parts of India	**WORLD**

Evil events *We the General Assembly experimentally finding the evil events of Negroes, Mulattoes, and Mustees walking abroad on nights and meeting together notwithstanding many proclamations made for restraint, yet execution, which is the life of the law, being too often omitted and a continuance of the said misdemeanours: Be it enacted etc. that all and every such person so offending, not having a ticket from their master or mistress shall be well whipped and all magistrates and inferior officers that after complaint made shall neglect the execution of the same shall forfeit each time so neglecting 10s for public uses.*

—*General Assembly's report to the Bermuda Company, 1662–63*

Walking abroad *If any negroe shall hereafter weare any weapon in the day tyme, or knowne to walk abroad at any undue houre in the night tyme or any other tyme or tymes go out of the way into any lands in the occupation of any other person than the land of his Master that then the Master or owner of such negroe shall from tyme to tyme make full recompense to the person grieved for the value of all such things as the Negroes or any of them shall purloyne steale or grable, or any other hurt or damage by them done.*

—*The Act to Restrayne the Insolencies of the Negroes, 1623*

'Procure mee a neger' *I intreat you to procure mee a neger whose name is Francisco. Hee is one [of] the general; his judgement in the cureing of tobackoe is such that I had rather have him than all the other negers that bee here.*

—*Robert Rich, in a letter to his brother Sir Nathanial Rich, 1618*

These slaves are the most proper and cheape instruments for this plantation that can be —*Governor Nathaniel Butler*

Increasingly, blacks living in Bermuda were imported as slaves, from the West Indies or, very rarely, directly from Africa. As Europe's western expansion unfolded, the trans-Atlantic slave trade was exploding, shipping millions of West Africans to the Americas where men, women and children supplied labour for mines on the mainland or the sugar plantations of the Caribbean. Slave ships, laden with tobacco, sugar and gold on return journeys to Europe, were known to have wrecked on Bermuda reefs; at least one shipwreck has been found with telltale artefacts of iron shackles and collars —tools to subdue a human cargo.

The move from servitude to slavery in Bermuda happened gradually. Over time, landowners, like their counterparts in Europe, the West Indies

Slaves were used as divers in a futile search for pearls

and America, chose cheap labour provided by the slave trade. One of the Bermuda Company's founding members, Sir Robert Rich (Earl of Warwick) was one of the first landlords to own slaves in Bermuda and Virginia. He and his Bermuda relatives purchased blacks to farm tobacco on their 600 acres of land in Bermuda. Sir Robert sent his ship, *Treasurer*, under Captain Daniel Ellffryth, to raid Spanish American colonies under a special 'commission.' In 1619, Ellffryth returned to the island with a boatload of black captives, who were put to work on the Rich family's holdings. He left slaves in Virginia on the same journey.

As early as 1623, Bermuda enforced tough measures to discriminate against black slaves and servants. The fledgling Assembly which Butler had proudly convened at St. Peter's Church three years earlier now passed a law against the "insolencies of Negroes," effectively stopping blacks from freely travelling around the island without their masters' permission, or conducting their own commerce. It was the first step aimed at controlling the cheap new labour force. A slew of legal restrictions on black rights and freedoms would follow in the 1650s and '60s, including measures to ban blacks from buying and selling tobacco, and to banish from the island those deemed "insolent" or "mutinous." Many free blacks were expelled from the island in 1656. Toward the century's end, when the Bermuda Company was finally disbanded, most of Bermuda's remaining black residents were bought and sold as chattel.

Blacks fought back by resisting work and by plotting to escape and

Native people as slaves

American, Mexican and Caribbean Indians were shipped to Bermuda and sold as slaves during the 17th Century. Public records indicate Indians from various tribes, including Mohicans, Wamponogs, Narragansetts, Pequots, Caribes, Cherokees and Arawaks were brought to the island throughout the 1600s from New York, Louisiana, New England, Hispaniola, Montserrat and Mexico. By the century's end, they comprised an estimated 10 percent of the slave population.

Bermudian Captain William Jackson, among others, trawled the Caribbean for years to supply the island with Indian and black slaves, many captured from the Spanish. In 1644, Jackson illegally brought in a group of Indian women taken in raids on Spanish villages. However, the London-based Somers Island Company later ordered them released because they were not slaves but freeborn people.

The same year, William Kieft, the Dutch governor of New York, sent a Mohican man as a gift to Bermuda Governor William Sayle. East Coast traders likely brought numerous Indian slaves to the island.

More Indian slaves arrived after the defeat of Pokanoket leader Metacomet during the so-called "King Philip's War" (1675–76). Many worked in sea-related trades such as fishing, whaling, ship-building and net-making.

As Indians married Bermudians, their racial characteristics were added to the island's ethnic mix. Descendants of Native Americans can still be found, particularly among families such as the Minors, Foxes, Lambs, Burchalls and Pitchers of St. David's, where scores of Indians were known to have lived and worked over the centuries.

---

even harm their white masters. A 1656 conspiracy by a group of more than a dozen blacks attempted to take control of the island from the English, but the rebels were found out and two of them hanged. In 1661, blacks and Irish indentured servants allied in a plan to murder all Englishmen. Again, news of the planned revolt leaked out, and Governor William Sayle immediately declared a new system of nightly watches throughout the parishes. More than 15 blacks held secret meetings in the fall of 1673, in which they devised an involved plot to kill their masters and to alert other slaves to do the same by sending messengers on horseback through the island. But the conspirators were all discovered and jailed; some also were branded, whipped and had their noses slit. Free blacks were blamed for stirring such sentiments among Bermuda's slave population and the Assembly immediately passed laws to banish all free blacks from the island unless they gave up their freedom and agreed to a life of servitude.

Harsh retribution such as branding, disfigurements and executions were levelled at blacks who dared to protest what was becoming the status quo in Bermuda by the century's end. And a volley of restrictive laws was unleashed on the black population to strip them of basic human rights. Within two generations, the transformation of Bermuda's social structure was complete. As all trace of freedom evaporated, the island's blacks found themselves trapped in a lifetime of slavery—a nightmare that would last almost 200 years.

England's political and religious sentiments, as well as social mores, crossed the ocean to its colonies. It was a time of volatile politics and religious upheaval throughout Europe in the wake of the Protestant Reformation. In England, the monarchy had rejected Roman Catholicism in the 16th Century, and made the Protestant Church of England autonomous, in a bid to increase its own power. The country's various religious groups quarrelled constantly, but it was not until the mid-17th Century, that a major power struggle erupted. This time, Royalists were pitted against mostly Puritan Parliamentarians—Protestant extremists who had opposed the policies of the Roman Catholic king, Charles I, and in turn, had been victimised by the king's allies. The standoff escalated into civil war (1642–51) and led to the defeat and execution of Charles I. He was replaced by Parliament-arian Oliver Cromwell, who with his Puritan supporters established a period of rule known as the "Commonwealth of England, Scotland and Ireland" that lasted just five years before the monarchy was restored.

Since Bermuda was largely monarchist, local royal supporters rose up in horrified defiance at news of the execution. Snubbing Cromwell, they swore allegiance to the Prince of Wales, the future Charles II, and called out the militia. Headed by John Trimingham, this self-styled 'army' marched on St. George's to confront Governor Thomas Turner and forced him and the Council to declare loyalty to Charles II. In a full-scale coup, the anti-Puritans then replaced Turner with Trimingham in 1649, and attempted to banish the island's Puritans—an oppressive but powerful group who called themselves Independents. Some Puritans fled to Eleutheria (the Bahamas), the southern islands settled in 1646 by Bermuda colonists under Captain William Sayle, who envisioned there an Utopian republic free of religious persecution.

When news of Turner's overthrow was received, the English Parliament declared Bermuda in a state of rebellion, but did nothing to discipline the colony. By 1660, Cromwell was dead and Charles II had returned from exile

In their own words

■ Joan de Rivera y Saabedra, *1639*

Our little boat continued on to the shore and we landed at a peaceful spot where a hill covered with wild palms in green fields looked so beautiful it seemed we were entering some pleasant and delightful gardens where young trees grew among golden flowers. It all seemed to our eyes like Elysian fields.

The harbour and settlement of this island is named St. George. It has only six badly built timber houses, one of them the residence of the Governor, and another that of the Captain of the King's Castle; a third is the minister's house, and another is occupied by the Sheriff; there is a very small jail, and a church; and at a stone's throw is a not very strong little fort; offshore, on a tiny islet, is a building where they keep the gunpowder. The inhabitants of Bermuda have settled the whole of it, sub-dividing the land into tracts (parishes) of one and two miles. They live in cabins made of wooden posts roofed with palm branches. Other houses are good examples of the mason's art. There seem to be about 290 households and each has its portion of land allotted to it and marked out; on this the planter sows tobacco, corn and potatoes, and yucca for making "cazabe" (cassava flour) according to his circumstances; the least competent is able to produce enough to live on, for as they have no expenses and no pretensions to pomp and authority, a little store of anything keeps each one independent of the other in time of need; the poorest is not without his patch of land for raising a crop of tobacco, which is the staple crop; by shipping it to England at the right season they live and maintain themselves. There is great abundance of potatoes and corn, which is the ordinary food of the working people. The potatoes are large, I have seen and eaten many (sweet potatoes), that weighed more than 2 lbs each; they are good in taste and flavour, though the smallest are the best, like those in Spain.

There are some cattle; everyone breeds them and kills them to provide salt beef; he keeps what he needs for himself and distributes the remainder among his neighbours, who in due time will repay him in kind. They also raise pigs, for the same purpose. They make a very rich and delicious fresh butter; and have large quantities of cow's milk.

In most of these farms there are orange trees and lemon trees, which bear very beautiful large fruit, in some places better than the Andalusian. There are many vineyards and rose trees and countless groves of fig trees. We were able to pick fruit from the trees; the figs are small and all the more delicious because not cultivated. Numerous palms and junipers make the entire island a pleasant wooded retreat. There are also many flowers, plants and sweet-smelling herbs of the kind found in Spain; everyone has these growing in a little garden next to his home, so that man is not deprived of the beauties and diversions which the Author of creation intended him to enjoy. Considerable quantities of fish, usually abundant, are caught by the Islanders.

There is very little water, although, for drinking purposes, no one has to go without. On some farms there are wells, but as a rule water is collected and used for the essential needs of the household. This water is employed to make a mixture which they call 'Berberis'; this is somewhat bitter, though to their taste it is delicious.

Labour in the fields and in the farmhouses is performed by boys, who are either orphans or have been abandoned, and most of them, expecting betterment, have been brought to the Island in the ships that call here. They serve for ten years at a very miserable wage, which is paid in tobacco at the end of this term. They are clothed on the same mean scale, and thus live poorly and practically in a state of slavery. On completion of their time, however, they are freed; no force or violence is employed, a point to which much attention is given.

There are also a few negroes; some of them have been left here by the Dutch who captured them. Most of the people have come from very humble and lowly conditions in England, some of them have been sent here as punishment, to colonise the island. For the proceeds of their tobacco, the ships bring them cloth and linen and the other things they need to clothe themselves, for no buying and selling is done among the islanders. Thus they do not use money at all, although occasionally they have some Spanish coin or rather coin of the Indies, from ships which have been lost here. The wreck of a ship is a most happy event for the islanders, but it makes them covetous and over greedy to possess the things which their deprivation has made them desire. When such occasions occur, their rapacity knows no limit, and is indulged even at the cost of the shipwrecked men.

—Joan de Rivera y Saabedra, scrivener to Felipe IV, who was aboard the store ship La Viga *when it ran ashore while sailing with the Spanish Royal Fleet, October 1639*

Everyone plant cedar *The Company has issued a command to prohibit the shipment of any timber out of the Island, for England or any other place. I am myself concerned that there is a great want of timber here now, and that future generations will be severely disadvantaged if the felling of trees, burning of brush, burning for fuel continues. It is ordered that everyone is to plant young cedars every year and to use cedars to fence their grounds. The penalties for non-compliance will be severe.*

—Proclamation by Governor William Sayle, March 1659–60

BRIMSTONE MEDIA

The State House

Commanding a bird's-eye view from its hilltop over King's Square, the State House was the colony's first stone building, and is the only remaining landmark from the era of the Somers Island Company other than archaeological sites. Built in 1622 during Governor Nathaniel Butler's tenure, the sturdy structure was used as a courthouse and General Assembly headquarters. At a time when all the island's other buildings were cedar-framed, the State House comprised limestone blocks set in a mortar of turtle oil and lime. It is possible West Indian slaves worked on the building, introducing new construction methods suited to hurricane-threatened environments. Butler hoped the handsome House would encourage a popularity in stone buildings, but this did not become commonplace until late in the century.

The State House originally incorporated a main floor and two shortened upper levels where gunpowder was stored for many years. But after rain leaked through the roof and damaged the building extensively, it was renovated in the 1730s to remove the upper section. Among other official uses, the State House was also the venue for nearly two-dozen witch trials held over the colony's first 40 years.

to succeed his father on the throne. In Bermuda, the Company replaced Trimingham with Josias Forster in 1650, islanders pledged allegiance to the monarchy once more, and the pattern of rapid gubernatorial turnover on the island continued for a further 33 years.

As the 1600s wore on, Company rule was not working well for Bermuda. The monopoly system was proving to have a strangling effect on the island's economy and morale, aggravated by poor communications, absentee landlords, punitive taxes and the fact the colony still was not generating profit for the investors.

Tenants living on the Adventurers' land cultivated tobacco, using half of it to pay the rent. But in time, many were able to buy the land they had previously rented, as original investors lost interest. Many of the new landowners were defiant in the face of oppressive Company orders and argued for more commercial freedom. Finally, in 1684, the Court of King's Bench in London dissolved the Bermuda Company, and the island became a colony of the Crown.

After more than 70 years of rigid government which had paralysed their economy and stifled entrepreneurial zeal, the colonists were ready to take their destiny into their own hands. With trade restrictions lifted, they abandoned fruitless agriculture efforts and turned their energies to the sea to seek their fortunes. A new era of maritime enterprise, inter-colony trade and commercial independence was about to begin, one that would forever shape the Bermudian identity and way of life.

Witch hunts

Persecution was not limited to the island's blacks during the 17th Century. Witch-hunting, already epidemic in Europe, became prevalent in England under Puritan rule following the Royalists' defeat in the English Civil War (1642–51) and the execution of Roman Catholic king, Charles I. Strict moral codes and rampant superstition created a new social environment in England and the colonies, where petty crime was punishable by death and the innocent were victimised at witch trials and tortured, hanged or even burned.

A chief proponent of this new paranoia was the Earl of Warwick, Sir Robert Rich, responsible for condemning as witches 18 residents of his English county. From the 1650s to nearly the close of the century, witch trials were held at Bermuda's State House.

Those accused of sorcery or "consulting with the devil" were often guilty of nothing more than having a birthmark or mole. But in the eyes of their accusers, these were deemed sinister signs and the victims found themselves at the arbitrary mercy of an intolerant jury.

On January 3, 1654, Elizabeth Page and Jane Hopkins, both passengers aboard the *Mayflower*, were accused of being witches by the ship's captain, who asked Governor Josias Forster for a trial. Witnesses told of seeing Page put her finger on the ship's compass "which went from North to South and back again. She said that any woman with child could do it." Hopkins was discovered to have a "suspicious mark in her mouth, a teat or dugg under her arm, a wart on her shoulder and another on her neck."

The jury acquitted Page, but decided Hopkins "did wickedly consult with the devil" and found her guilty. She was hanged two days later.

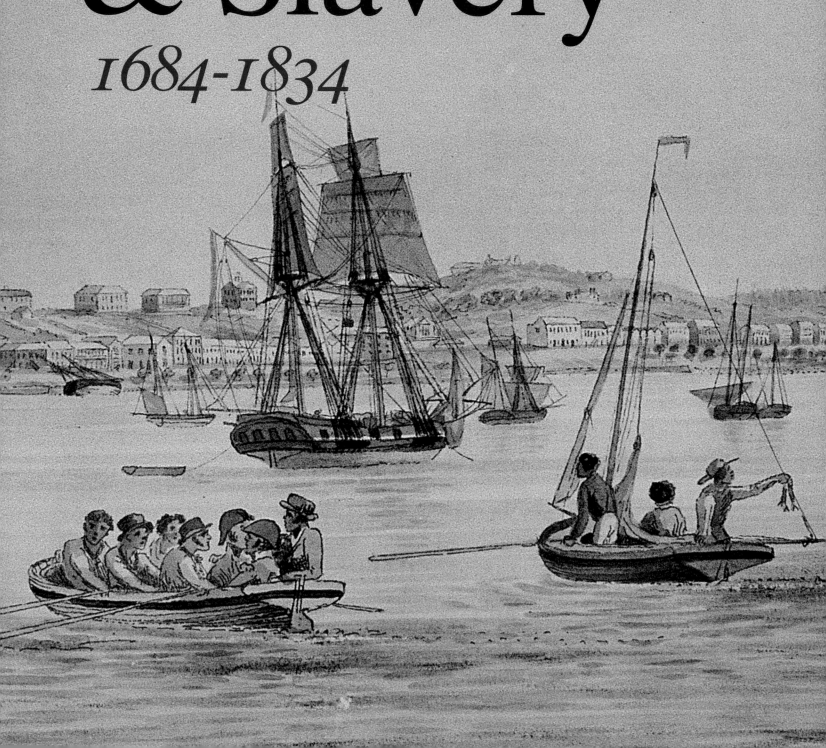

Sea, Salt
& Slavery

1684-1834

CHAPTER FIVE

Call of the Sea

A MIGHTY MARITIME TRADITION IS BORN

Superior *The superiority of our ships and sailors has long been universally known.*
—*Governor William Browne, 1782*

I n 1722, a dashing Scottish soldier in his late 30s arrived in Bermuda to take up the post of Governor. Colonel John Bruce Hope was a pragmatic and enthusiastic personality, who launched into his new duties with vigour and humour, but he is perhaps best remembered for his descriptive accounts to Whitehall about the habits and hardships of island life of the period.

"Thirty to forty years ago," he noted, "these islands abounded with oranges, lemons, dates, mulberries, pawpaws, plantains and pineapples in particular, in such quantities that they loaded their sloops with them. But the trees and plants which remain, after blasts and mildews, seldom bear any fruit and the tobacco has gone, having for successive years been eaten, while still green, by a worm in spite of all efforts.

"The inhabitants live chiefly on fish which they are very dextrous in catching," he wrote, adding of Bermuda's population: "They generally reckon three women for one man on the islands, since vast numbers of men are carried away by shipwreck. In fair weather, the whole inhabitants are almost all out at fishing."

Bermuda had entered a new era in the wake of the Somers Island Company's 1684 collapse, one focussed not on the land, but on everything maritime. England, pre-occupied with military concerns and the management of its larger, more profitable sugar-producing colonies in the West Indies and America, continued to send out governors but otherwise left Bermuda to its own devices—a situation the locals preferred to the decades of long-distance, monopolistic meddling by Company Adventurers. With the long-time ban on colonial trade and shipbuilding lifted, Bermuda's inhabitants

The Bermuda sloop: fast, rot-resistant and in great demand by mariners

BRIMSTONE MEDIA

BERMUDA MARITIME MUSEUM

*A Bermudian privateer
off Martinique*

Parish names

By the 18th Century, Bermudians had their own substitutes for parish names, some of which stand today:

- Somerset for Sandys
- Port Royal for Southampton
- Hern Bay for Warwick (or Heron Bay)
- Crow Lane for Paget
- Spanish Point for Pembroke
- Brackish Pond for Devonshire
- Harris Bay for Smith's
- Bailey's Bay for Hamilton Parish

St. George's kept its original name.

---

were finally free to do as they pleased. They wasted no time in abandoning the failing tobacco industry and other agricultural pursuits in favour of the sea.

Whaling, shipbuilding, maritime commerce, privateering and plunder—the administrative autonomy of the 18th Century offered Bermudians a world of ways to earn a living, and they embraced the myriad opportunities with an entrepreneurial zeal. Bermudians had been slow to embrace land-based industry such as farming, yet at sea they became profit-hungry hustlers adept at rising to tough challenges with innovation and unbridled energy. For the first time, the island's inhabitants began to look beyond Bermuda's shores for ways to foster their fortune and future, developing a network of mercantile ties with the colonies of the Caribbean and the Americas.

Commercial ventures were not the only windows of opportunity. Bermudians' new focus on the sea happened to coincide with an era of perpetual wars among European nations, creating a lucrative environment for merchants-turned-privateers, who prowled Atlantic shipping lanes in search of enemy vessels to plunder. Hostilities throughout the 18th Century provided licence for such nefarious activities, and Bermudian sailors, armed with a seal of approval from the island's royal governors, took full advantage of such political turmoil to line their own pockets.

Bermuda's insularity was over. The result came not without immense social hardships, as Hope and subsequent governors observed, but as the island adapted to a maritime economy, the colony finally began to thrive.

Sea Pudding Soup

When the Tripang comes fresh from the Sea, let lie in a dish for an hour to drain off the Salt Water. Wash them. Put to six Tripangs, two Quarts of Cold Water: let them boil for 10 minutes. Throw the water away. Put to these same fish two Quarts of fresh cold water, about three pounds of Veal or Beef, some Onion and Spice, but no Salt. Let it boil, then take care that the Soup only simmers, which it should be allowed to do, for six hours, as it keeps thickening. Strain it through a Cullender and add one tablespoonful of Cathcup or Worcester Sauce and a tumbler full of White Wine.

—The Royal Gazette, *1846*

A wealth of trees *The*

Juniperus Bermudiensis [sic] *called by the natives "cedar" is the only forest tree on the islands and with it they are covered; it is this tree which in mass from the distance gives them a sad and dark appearance. The wood is used to build boats (sloops) and this has been for all time the principal branch of industry of the Bermudians. The* **Juniperus Bermudiensis** *is the only wealth of the inhabitants and one estimates the wealth of each person by the number of trees which he possesses; they sell them for a guinea apiece.*

—*François Michaux,* Notes on Bermuda, *1806*

Two tons apiece *It is a*

circumstance unprecedented and unparalleled in any age or country that the tonnage of shipping owned in Bermuda, and which is in constant trade, amounts to nearly two tons for each white inhabitant of the Colony, man, woman and child.

—The Bermuda Gazette,
July 26, 1817

No other period in the island's history would shape the idiosyncratic Bermudian character as deeply as these years. Although industries like ship-building, salt-raking and the carrying trade, as well as privateering, would eventually decline and vanish, islanders would emerge from this century an enterprising, stubbornly independent people who would continue to find unique ways to overcome adversity—and in doing so, survive and prosper.

The call of the sea may have galvanised Bermudian imaginations throughout the 1700s, but it was the sturdy cedar tree which actually represented the root of the island's economy. Since the first settlement, the endemic cedar, *Juniperus bermudiana*, had proven a natural survival tool for the colonists, providing a harvest of berries to sustain them, and ample lumber for boats, bridges, cabin frames and furniture. To protect supplies, the island's Assembly had moved to bar exportation of cedar wood later in the 1600s—a prudent decision, for now cedar became central to the shipbuilding industry as the key material used to manufacture the innovatively-designed Bermuda sloop.

Bermuda cedar was coveted by mariners for its fine-grained timber, requiring little caulking to stay dry afloat. The wood also made for light, fast ships, which were nevertheless strong enough to withstand heavy weather as well as marine worm infestation. Before long, Bermuda became renowned throughout the maritime world for its ships and foreign demand for the agile sloop soared, with two-thirds of all Bermuda-made boats being sold overseas. Even before the 17th Century ended, the island's shipbuilders had crafted 400 two-masted fishing boats and 76 ocean-going vessels. During the 1700s, an average of six-dozen ships were built annually, with 100 ships alone produced during one bumper year. At an average 30 tons, Bermuda's sloops, brigs and brigantines were tiny by comparison with those of other nations, but they were considered the best in the world and widely admired as they plied the waters of the North Atlantic and Caribbean.

Of the island's 8,000-strong population in the early 18th Century, a third of Bermudian men were always at sea during these years, and those ashore were primarily involved in shipbuilding. St. George's, where the first settlement had evolved into the first capital, began to thrive as demand for shipping, storehouses and wharves grew, and the number of mariners and merchants increased. Craftsmen, carpenters and shipwrights were sorely needed by visiting ships, and the town's boatyards were kept constantly busy completing refits for the privateering ships that hobbled into port suffering damaged hulls and rigging following their violent forays.

Life at sea was not easy; shipwrecks, piracy and natural disasters such as hurricanes claimed many lives and left a society full of widows and orphans. Yet it also offered the allure of easy riches through privateering and "marooning" (the term Bermudians used to describe the practice of "turtling" and "wrecking"—salvaging the contents of shipwrecks—in the Caribbean). Venturing from Newfoundland to the Spanish Main, and all points between, Bermudian boats and crews covered a vast area, becoming expert in the diverse ports and politics of every region.

Depending on the politics of the time, a mariner who attacked another vessel was considered either a privateer or a pirate. Privateering, the legal and therefore more respectable manifestation of the two, was allowed by a special commission, or 'letter of marque,' granted during wartime. Armed

Bermuda's pirates

Bermudian seafarers of the late 17th Century made hardy, skilled privateers, but at least two became bonafide buccaneers. Both John Bowen and Nathaniel North were born in Bermuda, but spent most of their lives embroiled in maritime pursuits much further afield. Like so many pirates of the age, they were ultimately lured to Far East oceans, where local kings and merchant ships bursting with exotic cargoes like silks and spices made tempting prey.

Bowen, the well-educated son-in-law of surveyor-schoolmaster Richard Norwood, first left the island on a trade voyage to the Carolinas. He so impressed merchants there, they gave him a ship and sent him to the Caribbean, where he spent several years engaged in legitimate business. But when his vessel was captured by French pirates, who kept Bowen aboard for his navigational prowess, his life changed forever. He sailed with his captors around the Cape of Good Hope to Mauritius, escaping a shipwreck to pursue his own ventures. In 1701, Bowen had made enough money to buy his citizenship from the region's governor.

Later, Bowen sailed to Madagascar, another notorious pirates' den, and took part in escapades that earned him a reputation as a savvy and successful pirate aboard his ship, *Speedy Return*. He spent several years in the early 18th Century attacking Moorish vessels, sometimes working with other pirate gangs. Laden with treasures, he eventually returned to Mauritius with his crew, but died a few months later of "dry colic," better known as yellow fever.

Bowen's successor as captain was Nathaniel North, who had served as his quartermaster. A veteran sailor, North had left Bermuda for the Caribbean as a teenage cook, and spent much of his 20s in the islands, press-ganged into Royal Navy service several times, though he always escaped. Like Bowen, he journeyed to the

A pirate with his native consort on the island of Madagascar

BRIMSTONE MEDIA

Indian Ocean in the late 1600s and before long, his ship *Pelican* had engineered a string of ship seizures and kidnappings. North settled in Madagascar, where he ran coffee plantations and tried to settle skirmishes among local warlords. But after forays into the island's civil war, North himself was murdered by rebels—ironically, not at sea, where he had spent so many dangerous years, but at home where he had hoped for a peaceful retirement.

Pirates' lives ashore were as legendary as their oceanic hijinks. While individuals such as Blackbeard and Captain Kidd were

infamous villains who lived by the blood on their cutlasses, most pirates prided themselves on their closeknit brotherhood and strict code of conduct. Indeed, though the Royal Navy pursued pirates as outlaws, others viewed them in a far more benign light. Author Daniel Defoe, who based his character Captain Singleton, of *The Pyrates*, on North, described buccanners as "gentlemen adventurers."

"It may shame not a few," noted Defoe, "who carry a face of religion and act with greater barbarity than those whom we hunt and destroy as nuisances to the world."

In their own words
■ Philip Freneau, *1778*

The great plenty of fish, which constitutes the chief food of the people of the island, according to the opinion of naturalists, renders them very prolific. The great salubrity of the air may also have some share in this quality, which is so remarkable here, that it is no uncommon thing to see 14 or 15 children in every house you come to: These from the time of their birth, are familarised to the water to such a degree, that by the time they are five, six or seven years of age, all the boys, and many of the girls can live under the water and in it, pretty near as well as the fish, to which they seem to be of a congenial nature. Had these people the means of education, in proportion to their genius and abilities, they would certainly produce men whose attainments would be an honour to human nature; but at present they chiefly employ their mental qualities in quibbling and over-reaching each other. The thick population of the island also makes much ill-blood, so that there are few near neighbours who are good friends, and scarcely one man who is not upon such bad terms with 20 or 30 others, as never to speak to them.

Amidst the storms and tempests of the surrounding ocean, these happy people live cheerful and contented. Wars and bloodshed are strangers to this little paradise; the cruel Briton keeps his fleets and armies at a distance; each one here enjoys his own, and lives contented and secure, when havoc and murder are depopulating the rest of the globe.

—*Philip Freneau, May 10, 1778, after a five-week stay on the island*

with such a letter from the king or governor, a captain had *carte blanche* to overpower enemy ships, confiscate the vessels and their cargo, and take crews prisoner. In times of peace, such behaviour was considered piracy, but due to the frequency of England's conflicts with France, Spain and later America, and the murky definition of 'peace' generally, privateers found themselves virtually unrestricted in their quest for easy, illicit rewards.

Bermudian privateers set out in force during the 18th Century and the prizes they won on the high seas often furnished family fortunes. Crews were awarded a share of the capture, be it treasure, slaves, guns and ammunition, a cargo of foodstuffs, or the ship itself. Privateering was an artful game of hide-and-seek, with rival ships lying in wait for each other throughout the Caribbean and Atlantic sealanes. As the Spanish had feared a century earlier, their vessels carrying gold and other riches from New World were favourite victims of English and Bermudian privateers. French vessels were also targets; indeed, so many French prisoners were brought back to Bermuda at one stage, they began to be a burden to the small colony.

Many well-known Bermudian families engaged in privateering, among them names such as Trimingham, Cox, Raynor, Gilbert, Durham, Middleton, Burch, Jennings, Joell and Jones. In some cases, their attacks on foreign ships were simply efforts to defend their own shipping interests. Foreign pirates would lurk near Bermuda in the hope of seizing vessels or storming the island, and local mariners took action to fend them off. Fitted with guns, the speedy Bermuda sloops were particularly suited to these stealthy encounters. Not only were they able to evade ships in pursuit, but they also made perfect 'getaway' vessels after attacking an enemy vessel. As such, they were highly sought, and often captured as prizes in their own right.

The dramatic adventures of these private men-of-war was the stuff of maritime legend and island folklore, and their ships received a hero's welcome when they returned to port. Booming guns from Castle Island's forts heralded their arrival, especially if they brought a prize in tow. On one outing, Captain Lewis Middleton, sailing into St. George's Harbour with several prizes, was heralded with an eight-gun salute—a greeting that would have rivalled the pomp and protocol bestowed on royalty.

The swashbuckling romance of privateering was a magnet for some Bermudians, but most made a living at sea through far more pedestrian means. By 1789, a fleet of more than 175 vessels was engaged in the carrying trade, exporting cabbages and onions, palmetto goods and whale oil to the West Indies, and returning with cotton, rum, molasses and dry goods. Soon Bermudians, secure in the nautical superiority of their sloops, carved out a niche for themselves as the principal carriers between the Caribbean and North American coast.

Some of the main trading ports were those which had been established by adventurous Bermudian colonists at the close of the 17th Century. Bermudians had settled the Carolinas in a 1669 expedition led by Governor William Sayle, and the region now provided trading posts offering beef and grain in exchange for West Indian goods such as rum. Sayle had been the ringleader pushing Bermuda's Puritans to settle Eleutheria in the Bahamas during Cromwell's Commonwealth. Some Bermudians remained there, and when Captain John Darrell later sailed south with emigrants to another Bahamian island, New Providence, survivors were eking out a living from

BERMUDA SLOOP FOUNDATION

A Bermuda-rigged schooner painted by John Lynn and dated August 1, 1834, Emancipation Day. Two newly-free blacks catch a turtle in the foreground

In quest of gain...

The Sturdy craftsman, with laborious
    Hand,
Fells the tall Tree, and drags it to the
    Strand
Resounding Shores return the
    Hammer's Blows
Beneath the Stroke the gaudy
    Pinnace grows
Launch'd and completely mann'd in
    Quest of Gain...
—The Bermudian, *Nathaniel Tucker, 1774*

tobacco and sugarcane. Bermudian planters had also travelled to Providence Island off Nicaragua, as well as to Trinidad, St. Lucia and Barbados in efforts to colonise new areas where tobacco might thrive. Most of these early settlements failed due to disease, Spanish attack or economic reasons. However, former Bermuda governor Philip Bell became the first governor of Barbados in the mid-1600s and held the post for eight years.

At home, Bermudians were known for their keen piloting skills, learned through necessity by navigating the island's treacherous reefline. Most ships arriving at Bermuda required help manoeuvring through the necklace of shoals and into harbour. As they approached, they would sound a gun to alert the local pilots, who would venture out in small cedar gigs manned by six to eight oarsmen. Competitive in their prowess, the various pilots would race each other in a bid to reach an incoming ship first and secure for themselves the job of escorting it safely into port. Often, they travelled up to 50 miles offshore to scout for arriving ships.

Some of the most respected Bermudian pilots were slaves, who, like black crew members on the travelling sloops, sometimes won their freedom through their talents. One such case was Jemmy Darrell, who guided the

The Bermuda sloop

Born in a period of maritime innovation, the Bermuda sloop's enormous popularity was shaped by both the island's geography and economic opportunities of the 18th Century. Bermudians were not the first to build such a vessel; the design originated in Holland and spread throughout the Caribbean. But it was in Bermuda where the sloop was finessed, becoming one of the most sought-after sailing ships in the world.

What differentiated the Bermuda sloop from other vessels was not only its long, narrow design that made it extremely fast, but its materials—namely, Bermuda cedar, which was light, durable and seemingly immune to

Woodcut of an early Dutch design, possibly a forerunner of the Bermuda sloop

BRIMSTONE MEDIA

the ravages of the sea and its parasites. The sloop had a single, raked mast, fore and aft rigging, and weighed between 10 and 30 tons. It was smaller than many other sailing ships of the time; although that meant it could carry less cargo, it also made the sloop more versatile. The sloop could be manned by a crew of four to six men, and due to its speed, could make faster, more frequent journeys.

Built without plans, the Bermuda sloop

evolved from the 'Bermuda rig'—smaller boats dubbed " 'Mudians," which were used for fishing and coastal travel around the island. As more Bermudians turned to the sea for their livelihoods in the 1700s, the Bermuda fleet grew, and with it, the need for larger, open-ocean vessels. By 1700, the fleet counted 70 cedar boats, four of 100 tons. Local shipbuilders experimented with rigging and adapted the sloop's design; its hallmark became a long bowsprit and boom and distinctively long proportions.

Faced with the constant threat of pirates, speed was of the essence—a necessity which shaped the narrow hull. Before long, Bermuda sloops had turned the tables on their attackers, pursuing or fleeing pirate vessels with ease, as well as enemy nations' ships. By the mid-1770s, sloops were the vessels of choice for privateers and merchants throughout the Atlantic—feeding a thriving shipbuilding industry on the island. By the American Revolution in 1776, at the height of the sloop's popularity, the island was producing as many as 100 ships a year.

Sloops were exported worldwide, and also fuelled the busy carrying trade, their speed allowing merchants to ship fresh produce to distant markets. Shipbuilding (along with the need for wharves and warehouses) provided work for blacksmiths, caulkers, carpenters, masons, shipwrights, as well as sailors themselves, most of whom were slaves or free blacks. Bermuda law decreed ship crews have a maximum of six white sailors (including the master), but as many blacks as necessary. The provision was to guard against the depletion of the island's white population at home, but it also saved owners salary expenses, making the sloop business even more profitable.

Excellent builders

There are in Bermuda excellent builders of [sloops]. They ordinarily use only cedar, which…makes their work more light and in a sort indestructible. Other than these ships, which are capable of making very long voyages, they make a sort of boat which they only use in the enclosures of their tranquil sea to go from one place to another. One must be accustomed to their use and without fear, for when they have hoisted their sails, the boats put themselves on their sides and in that situation are apt to upset with a rapidity unequalled anywhere else. It must be said that the English have a large quantity of cedars in that country in view of the prodigious number of ships which they are now building every day. Perhaps they are wiser and more farsighted than the French and are cultivating these trees and planting new ones in measure as they cut down the old ones.

—*Père Labat, 1704*

The most agreeable and least expensive mode of travelling in the Bermudas is by means of boats, which are very safe and are managed with the utmost skill by the daring Islanders, They have in general but one mast, the mainsail like the jib running up to a point; so that the moment the sail is lowered a foot or two in a squall, the boat is greatly relieved and it passes harmlessly over the little vessel. But in navigating about these islands, a person is required who understands the intricate channel.

The Bermudian sloop Devonshire *in West Indian waters*, c. 1720

In their own words

■ Edmund Ward, *1809–16*

Whenever the boat approaches one of these, the pilot takes his station forward, and the transparency of the water enables him to detect any lurking danger. Were it not for this, and the ready manner in which the boats answer their helm, sailing among the coral reefs would be almost impracticable.

These boats—like the larger vessels constructed at Bermuda—are built of cedar, an expensive but very durable wood which never shrinks, so close is its texture; and may be used immediately after the tree is cut down. They are consequently very buoyant, requiring much ballast; and as they draw much more water aft than forward, fly round on their heel as soon as the helm is put down. In beating to windward they more than hold their own; and as a sailor would say, eat up in the wind's eye.

Their having on board a quantity of iron ballast renders them wet in rough weather, as they do not rise in a lively manner on the sea, but throw the spray over the deck, the lee gunwhale when it blows fresh, being under water. Boats that are sent out fishing have what is called a well in the centre, and open at the bottom, with the exception of strips of board, within which the fish that are taken are placed, and in this way brought in alive to replenish the fish ponds from which the families supply themselves when they wish one for dinner, just as they would from a poultry yard.

—*Government printer Edmund Ward,* Seven Years' Residence in Bermuda 1809–1816

Whaling was tough but profitable. A catch provided oil from blubber, "sea beef" for slaves and, sometimes, ambergris

'Turtle in the net' *If a vessel is on the rocks, all the fishing boats make to her, weather permitting, to see what they can purloin. They rejoice at such misfortunes, and call her a "turtle in the net" and all they try is to cause a confusion in the ship, so as to get a load and off. This they do under the pretence of lightening the vessel. But if it should be a 'mudian vessel on the rocks, they are then compelled to work for salvage, because the crew would know the men and boats. To find an honest 'mudian, I think the country would need sifting. They pretend to shudder at the thought of stealing, but would rob a vessel of its compass that was on the rocks, and boast of what they had got out of "the turtle in the net" next day.*

—William Sydes, alias Jones, a prisoner serving time aboard the Dockyard hulks from 1838–45

flagship *Resolution* carrying Sir George Murray into St. George's (to what is now known as Murray's Anchorage). Darrell so impressed the Vice Admiral, that Murray requested the pilot be made a free man. His wish was granted on March 1, 1796, when Darrell was 47. Murray would later establish the King's Pilots, and Darrell was among the first to be appointed.

Jacob Minors, a St. David's descendant of Native American slaves, was another well-known pilot who plied his trade well into old age, dying in 1875 at 84.

Jacob Minors

Black pilots were coveted by foreign mariners, including pirates, who sometimes captured and kept them aboard roaming vessels. "There are now several Negroes borne into these islands aboard their ships who are excellent pilots and know every creek and bay belonging to it," Governor John Pitt warned in a 1731 letter to London.

Still, unwary vessels often found themselves wrecked on Bermuda's reefs, especially if they attempted to sail into port without the help of a knowledgeable pilot.

Bermudians referred to ships in distress as "turtles in the net," and many a crippled ship ended up being 'salvaged' by locals, who always kept an eye on the horizon for injured vessels which needed relieving of their valuable cargoes. According to accounts, some Bermudians were dubbed "wreckers" because they took the greedy practice a step further, actually luring ships into disaster with bonfires on hills or deceiving lights placed on treacherous reefs.

Whaling also demanded the skills of Bermudian seamanship, and it was a worthwhile, though small-scale industry in the 1700s, after a ban on building whaling boats was finally lifted. Whales were taken to Smith's Island, Paget Island and St. David's, where the blubber was boiled in pots to extract oil used to light the island's lamps. No part of the whale was wasted: bone was made into tools, flesh provided meat or "sea beef" for slaves, and occasionally lucky whalers even found the valuable ambergris so coveted by the London market. Between five and 14 whales would be harpooned a year, though costly licences and a tax on whaling profits in 1733 saw the industry dwindle until late in the century when restrictions were lifted.

While harvests of the sea were bountiful, farming suffered heavily during these years. Aside from onions and cabbages, Bermuda's agriculture was subsistence-level only, and the island found itself dependent on America for food supplies. Some years, up to half the colony's food was imported, a precarious situation in the face of looming English-American conflicts that constantly threatened to cut off shipments to the colony. But blinded by the profits and lifestyle offered by the sea and its related industries, islanders neglected the shortfall until they were faced with near-starvation and had to take drastic measures.

Ironically, Bermuda's biggest foray into maritime trade took place nearly 1,000 miles away, at the Turks Islands (a group on the south-east edge of the Bahamas, now called the Turks & Caicos). In 1678, a Bermudian captain found the uninhabited Turks, which, half the size of Bermuda, offered

In their own words

■ Pilot James E. Forbes, *1825*

Seeing a ship and brig signalled for, and not doubting but it was the admiral, I thought it my duty (seeing two other King's pilots go out) to go also. The breeze being very light, I took my gig with me, and intended to stop with the Brig *Harrington* (which was lying off and on), in order that I may be in readiness to proceed after the vessels in the morning. However, not falling in with the *Harrington*, I steered out to the SE about 15 or 20 miles, and then hove to my boat's head SE but unfortunately my light went out, and the night being very dark, I could not see the pointer on the compass, and in consequence of which, the boat must have shifted her course to the NE. In the morning, judging myself to the SE, I made sail, and steered NW about 10 or 15 miles, and not discovering land, I tacked and steered SE, but that proving unsuccessful, I again steered NW and, in five days, found myself in the Gulf.

By this time, one of my men had given up and on the fifth day of my being out, the provisions were all consumed, and (in the place of water) we were obliged to suck lead. On this day, we fortunately discovered a Brig which proved to be the *Charles*, Capt. JB Hotchkiss, from New Haven, bound to Trinidad, in lat. 33, 30, N. long. 64, W. who gave me a supply of provisions and treated me with every possible kindness. Captain H. directed me to steer 75 miles S. 60 W. which I did to the best of my knowledge. I could not discover any land, and the provisions I procured from Capt. Hotchkiss, being nearly consumed, I altered my course to N.W. in hopes to fall in with some vessel, and on the second day after steering W. I fell in with the Brig *Commodore Porter*, Captain Shankland, from Philadelphia, bound to Antigua, who supplied me with provisions and gave me his only log line: he directed me to steer N. 74 miles, E. 153 miles or ENE 185 miles.

Agreeable to his directions I did so, and on Sunday afternoon, at 5 o'clock, I hove to (allowing myself to drift about 10 miles) and at 2 o'clock, on the morning after, my boat struck on the rocks a little to the westward of the North Rock, and remained there about 15 minutes, when I unhung my rudder. The wind at the time was blowing very hard, which caused the boat to float into a hole; I let go my Kedge Anchor, but the sea running high, it parted immediately and I got on shore a second time but did not long remain. Not being able to judge on what side of the Island I was, I drifted, and on the approach of day, found myself in Murray's Anchorage, when I was obliged to steer with two oars. I came into St. Catherine's Bay, where I intended to hang my rudder, but the wind being very high, I could not accomplish it. I then bore up for Fort Cunningham, where I, with my crew, consisting of five men and a boy, safely arrived. All my blocks and running rigging were carried away.

—*Pilot James E. Forbes,*
describing a 21-day ordeal at sea,
The Bermuda Gazette, *January 8, 1825*

This dangerous island

Squalls and storms are not the only things to fear when coming within sight of this dangerous island. It is surrounded by reefs at surface level, which to the north-east extend off shore to a distance of almost six leagues, and many a vessel has come to grief on them. Care must in any case be taken not to sail too close to shore.

—*Nicholas Louis Bourgeois, secretary of the Chamber of Agriculture in San Domingo (now Haiti), in* Voyages intéressants dans différentes colonies françaises, espagnoles, anglaises, etc., *Paris 1788*

the perfect climate and topography for an industry that would dominate Bermuda's economy for the next century—salt-raking.

Hot, barren and impractical for farming, the Turks Islands lent themselves to wreck-salvaging, turtle-hunting, whaling and conch-harvesting, all of which became viable trades. But Bermudians soon developed a much more lucrative summer industry that took advantage of the natural salt pans on the islands of Salt Cay and Grand Turk. Every April, Bermudians and their slaves would sail south to the Turks, where they would spend the next six months producing tons of salt to ship to ports throughout the western Atlantic.

The salt-making process was laborious, but effective. Workers, often in the form of slave gangs, used pumps, canals and waterwheels to fill shallow ponds with seawater, letting it evaporate in the heat and wind over the course of several months. The result was a dense brine which evaporated further to finally form a four-inch-thick 'salt cake.' This coarse crystalline salt was raked into furrows, packaged in cloth bags and carted away for shipping, providing the ballast for homebound voyages.

Typically, Bermudian captains would spend the summer in the Turks, before returning to Bermuda in November for the winter or sailing on to American ports like Boston and Philadelphia to trade their salt for grain, tobacco and meat. The industry was so successful, Bermuda held a salt-trading monopoly in the western Atlantic; at its peak in the 1750s, Bermudians

The price of salt

In their own words

■ Mary Prince, *1831*

When we went ashore at Grand Quay, the captain sent me to the house of my new master, Mr. D., to whom Captain I. had sold me. Grand Quay is a small town upon a sandbank; the houses low and built of wood…My new master was one of the owners or holders of the salt ponds, and he received a certain sum for every slave that worked upon his premises, whether they were young or old. This sum was allowed him out of the profits arising from the salt works. I was immediately sent to work in the salt water with the rest of the slaves. This work was perfectly new to me. I was given a half-barrel and a shovel, and had to stand up to my knees in the water, from four o'clock in the morning till nine, when we were given some Indian corn boiled in water, which we were obliged to swallow as fast as we could for fear the rain should come on and melt the salt. We were then called again to our tasks, and worked through the heat of the day; the sun flaming upon our heads like fire, and raising salt blisters in those parts which were not completely covered. Our feet and legs, from standing in the salt water for so many hours, soon became full of dreadful boils, which eat down in some cases to the very bone, afflicting the sufferers with great torment. We came home at twelve; ate our corn soup, called blawly, as fast as we could, and went back to our employment till dark at night. We then shovelled up the salt in large heaps, and went down to the sea, where we washed the pickle from our limbs, and cleaned the barrows and shovels from the salt. When we returned to the house, our master gave us each our allowance of raw Indian corn, which we pounded in a mortar and boiled in water for our suppers.

We slept in a long shed, divided into narrow slips, like the stalls used for cattle. Boards fixed upon stakes driven into the ground, without mat or covering, were our only beds. On Sundays, after we had washed the salt bags, and done other work required of us, we went into the bush and cut the long soft grass, of which we made trusses for our legs and feet to rest upon, for they were so full of the salt boils that we could get no rest lying upon the bare boards…

When we were ill, let our complaint be what it might, the only medicine given to us was a great bowl of hot salt water, with salt mixed with it, which made us very sick. If we could not keep up with the rest of the gang of slaves, we were put in the stocks, and severely flogged the next morning. Yet, not the less, our master expected, after we had thus been kept from our rest, and our limbs rendered stiff and sore with ill usage, that we still go through the ordinary tasks of the day all the same. Sometimes we had to work all night, measuring salt to load a vessel; or turning a machine to draw water out of the sea for the salt-making. Then we had no sleep—no rest—but were forced to work as fast as we could, and go on again all next day the same as usual. Work, work, work—oh that Turks Island was a horrible place! The people in England, I am sure, have never found out what is carried on there.

—*Mary Prince on salt-raking at Turks Islands*, The History of Mary Prince, A West Indian Slave, *1831*

The Turks Islands, where Bermudian slaves like Mary Prince toiled six months a year in primitive conditions to gather salt

Scorching sands

You industrious salt-rakers, who have torn yourselves from your happy, hospitable climate, from your parents, your wives, your children, from those objects of affection which most irresistibly seize on the hearts of men, to be transported to those scorching and inhospitable sands, to those rude and uncultivated deserts, to those wild and rugged rocks, whose only production depends upon their being washed by the waters of the ocean and then their lighter being exhaled from their grosser particles…

—*Bermudian John Harvey Tucker, a.k.a. Isocrates, in an 1803 letter to the Colonial Assembly about the turf war between Bahamas and Bermuda over the Turks Islands salt trade*

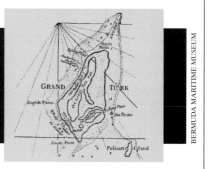

BERMUDA MARITIME MUSEUM

The pretenders *There is such a correspondence betwixt the pyrates and those people that go from hence (as well as from the other Plantations) to those islands where they pretend to rake salt, that except there be some effectual remedy fall'n upon to break off that intercourse these parts will always swarm with those vermin. There is no Law now in force, but one way or other these people will evade with an adroitness that is surprising.*

—*Governor John Hope in a letter to Whitehall about Bermudian wrecking, turtling and illicit trade in the Caribbean, February 21, 1723*

In their own words
■ Hezekiah Frith, *1797*

We were put on board the prison ship of 80 guns in the lower gun deck, in a most filthy place more fit for a hog stye than to put Christians in, with a daily allowance of three wormy cakes of bread and three-quarters of a pound of raw beef per man, which we could not get dressed unless by hiring someone to cook it & even then, not without finding a pot for the purpose, which we often found impracticable to obtain; & we were deprived of all utensils except a 'bullock's horn' to drink water out of without we bribed some of the crew. Some days no fire at all was allowed for cooking…

Had it not been for the kind assistance of some masters of vessels then in Havana, our situation must have been more wretched—particularly Capt. John B. & Capt. Christopher Lusher—their friendly attention we shall ever acknowledge. I hope to have the pleasure yet of taking some of the Spanish prisoners, but am determined to show them the difference of treatment, as it is not the nature of an Englishman to treat his prisoners as we were treated…

—*Captain Hezekiah Frith, whose brig* Hezekiah *was captured by the Spanish on April 5, 1797 and held in Havana, in a letter to* The Bermuda Gazette

Abundant crop *The crop of Salt at Turks Islands has been most abundant this season, surpassing the collection for many years past. A great number of American vessels had been there and loaded.*

—The Royal Gazette, *1832*

Carting salt in the Turks Islands

BERMUDA MARITIME MUSEUM

exchanged up to 130,000 bushels of salt, and more than 1,200 people, or one-tenth of Bermuda's population, earned a living from the trade, either shipping or manufacturing salt.

Salt had long been a substantial commodity, used to preserve fish and meat before refrigeration. But salt was particularly valuable during this combative era of colonisation when the mobilisation of European and North American armies and settlers demanded a ready supply of preserved food. Realising the opportunity they had stumbled upon, Bermudians tenaciously developed it to the extent the Turks became a virtual Bermudian colony and their export as precious as gold.

As the salt trade developed, some 900 Bermudians, both black and white, lived permanently in the Turks, establishing a primitive self-government and sharing revenues among the islands' British subjects. On the annual journey south, Bermuda sloops would carry limestone blocks as ballast which they would use to construct Bermuda-style buildings. Even today, strong family connections and Bermudian architecture, including telltale limestone homes with white roofs, keep the salt-traders' legacy alive.

The success of Bermudians in the Turks excited the envy of nearby foreigners, privateers and pirates, who attacked their ships and sometimes ransacked their settlements. The Bahamas also coveted the islands' commercial importance. Skirmishes between the Bahamas and Bermudian salt-rakers flared throughout the 1700s and Bahamian authorities—led by another Bermudian, Nicholas Trott—tried to regulate and tax the salt trade, claiming the Turks as their own parish. Despite a bitter Bermudian protest, Britain finally gave control of the Turks to the Bahamas in 1803.

FOR TURKS' ISLANDS,
The Schooner GEN. GRANT,
DUNSCOMB, Master,
Will Sail on or about the 3rd Proximo. For FREIGHT or PASSAGE, apply to the CAPTAIN, on Board, or to
HEZEKIAH FRITH, Junr.
Hamilton, 23rd February, 1835.

N. B.—A Lot of Prime *St. Domingo* COFFEE, and *Russia* CORDAGE, by the said Vessel, *on Sale, Cheap for Cash.*

CHAPTER SIX

Scourge of Slavery

A PEOPLE'S FREEDOM DENIED FOR 200 YEARS

*Floggings and punishments on
a West Indian plantation*

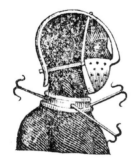

SCHOMBURG CENTER FOR RESEARCH IN BLACK CULTURE

LIBRARY OF CONGRESS

O n an otherwise uneventful day in 1800, a 12-year-old Devonshire girl saw her world disintegrate. Mary Prince, a slave, was sold. Her second owner—a woman who had kept Prince's family as domestic help and companionship for her own daughter Betsey—died, and many of her belongings, including her slaves, were auctioned off. For Prince, it marked the end of childhood comforts and an abrupt farewell to the only home she had ever known. Separated from her grief-stricken mother, three sisters and two brothers at a public market, she was purchased for £57 by a cruel captain and his wife to work at their Spanish Point property—an excruciating experience that would torment her for the rest of her life.

"My mistress set about instructing me in my tasks. She taught me to do all sorts of household work; to wash and bake, pick cotton and wool, and wash floors, and cook," Prince would later recount. "And she taught me more things than these; she caused me to know the exact difference between the smart of the rope, the cart-whip and the cow-skin when applied to my naked body by her own cruel hand. There was scarcely any punishment more dreadful than the blows I received on my face and head from her hard heavy fist…To strip me naked, to hang me up by the wrists and lay my flesh open with the cow-skin, was an ordinary punishment for even a slight offence."

Little did her new owners know that history would record their brutality, and that Prince's catalogue of harsh treatment—in Bermuda, Antigua, London and, perhaps most notably, in the Turks Islands salt pans—would ultimately aid her struggle to become a free woman. At 43, Prince gave a detailed account of her experiences to Britain's Anti-Slavery Society, which published her life story in 1831. Along with many similar slave tales, Prince's graphic narrative was used as ammunition in the Society's lobby which two years later would win abolition of slavery in Britain, followed by Bermuda and other English colonies.

In the 19th Century, Prince's story, like others, created a whole new

A lock-up on North Shore used to hold slaves caught "wandering abroad." Inset, a Bermuda slave register

BERMUDA MEDIA

Slave-owners and slaves on a sugarcane plantation in the Caribbean; a detail from a period map

DR. EDWARD HARRIS

genre of literature: autobiographical slave narratives which represented an indictment of the trans-Atlantic slave trade and the vast suffering it produced. Prince was the first woman to publish a slave narrative, and her detailed account describes in wrenching personal terms the toll of human bondage as experienced by men, women and children in Bermuda and elsewhere. Her story is also noteworthy because it lends a compelling voice to what slaves actually felt and thought about slavery—a far less benign opinion than that which white society would have liked to believe.

"All slaves want to be free—to be free is very sweet," Prince said. "I have been a slave myself—I know what slaves feel. The man that says slaves be quite happy in slavery, that they don't want to be free—that man is either ignorant or a lying person."

Prince was one of nearly 5,000 slaves living in Bermuda in the early 1800s, by which time slavery had evolved from its insidious roots of indentured servitude to become life enslavement enforced by draconian laws. Essentially, slavery was legal ownership of a person,

In their own words
■ Mary Prince, *1831*

The black morning at length came; it came too soon for my poor mother and us. Whilst she was putting on us the new osnaburgs in which we were to be sold, she said, in a sorrowful voice (I shall never forget it!) "See, I am shrouding my poor children; what a task for a mother!" She then called Miss Betsey to take leave of us. "I am going to carry my little chickens to market," (these were her very words) "take your last look of them; may be you will see them no more." "Oh, my poor slaves, my own slaves," said dear Miss Betsey, "you belong to me; and it grieves my heart to part with you." Miss Betsey kissed us all, and, when she left us, my mother called the rest of the slaves to bid us goodbye. One of them, a woman named Moll, came with her infant in her arms. "Ay!" said my mother, seeing her turn away and look at her child with the tears in her eyes, "your turn will come next." The slaves could say nothing to comfort us; they could only weep and lament with us. When I left my dear little brothers and the house in which I had been brought up, I thought my heart would burst.

Our mother, weeping as she went, called me away with the children Hannah and Dinah, and we took the road that led to Hamble Town [Hamilton], which we reached about four o'clock in the afternoon. We followed my mother to the market-place, where she placed us in a row against a large house, with our backs to the wall and our arms folded across our breasts. I, as the eldest, stood first, Hannah next to me, then Dinah; and our mother stood beside, crying over us. My heart throbbed with grief and terror so violently, that I pressed my hands quite tightly across my breast, but could not keep it still, and it continued to leap as though it would burst out of my body. But who cared for that? Did one of the many bystanders, who were looking at us so carelessly, think of the pain that wrung the hearts of the negro woman and her young ones? No, no! They were not all bad, I dare say, but slavery hardens white people's hearts towards the blacks; and many of them were not slow to make their remarks upon us aloud, without regard to our

BERMUDA ARCHIVES

The slave register on display at St. Peter's Church, St. George's

grief—though their light words fell like cayenne on the fresh wounds of our hearts. Oh those white people have small hearts who can only feel for themselves.

At length the vendue master, who was to offer us for sale like sheep or cattle, arrived, and asked my mother which was the eldest. She said nothing, but pointed to me. He took me by the hand, and led me out into the middle of the street, and, turning me slowly round, exposed me to the view of those who attended the vendue. I was soon surrounded by strange men, who examined and handled me in the same manner that a butcher would a calf or lamb he was about to purchase, and who talked about my shape and size in like words—as if I could no more understand their meaning than the dumb beasts. I was then put up to sale.

The bidding commenced at a few pounds, and gradually rose to 57, when I was knocked down to the highest bidder; and the people who stood by said that I had fetched a great sum for so young a slave.

I then saw my sisters led forth, and sold to different owners; so that we had not the sad satisfaction of being partners in bondage. When the sale was over, my mother hugged and kissed us, and mourned over us, begging of us to keep up a good heart, and do our duty to our new masters. It was a sad parting; one went one way, one another, and our poor mammy went home with nothing.

—*Mary Princ*e, The History of Mary Prince, A West Indian Slave, *1831*

Cruel treatment

It is allowed by all who know America and the West Indies, that the slaves are no where so well treated as in Bermuda. But even in Bermuda (such is the condition of servitude) no farther provision is made for the well-being of slaves, than the interest of the owners is concerned…They are neither fully defended against cruel treatment from their owners, if their owners have a mind to inflict it on them.

—*Scottish schoolmaster the Reverend Alexander Ewing, in a letter to the Bishop of London, June 1791*

*Some slaves became skilled pilots.
This boy still bears identification
marks of his clan*

An edifying sight

*The great number of these vessels
[Bermudian sloops] are manned by
negroes, a race of men long since
refined not only by their stay on this
island but by education that they
have received from their masters.
They aid in building ships and afterwards sail them to the islands where
they are preferred above other boats
for navigation and smuggling. Their
ability as sailors and shipbuilders,
their faithfulness as super cargoes,
the punctuality with which they
direct the business of their masters,
and bring home their vessels is
indeed a truly edifying sight. I have
seen several of these black managers
at the tables of the rich Jamaican
planters, treated with all the consideration which their intelligence and
faithfulness merit. There are perhaps
no better swimmers, I have seen
them display enough ability, cool-
ness and audacity to attack sharks
while swimming and to kill them
with their knives.*

—*Jean Crèvecoeur,* Lettres d'un
Cultivateur Americain, *1784*

along with everything—goods, services, children—that person might produce. Slavery was now an integral part of Bermudian society and while the island operated a slave culture that vastly differed from the plantation economies of America and the West Indies, the prejudiced beliefs used to justify the system were the same.

Slavery permeated the island's life, its culture and people, changing forever the face of Bermuda, both figuratively and literally. It was a system of mutual dependence fraught with bitter rebellion and conflicting emotions—hate and hardship co-existing with occasional compassion and camaraderie, however patronising. As owners embraced slavery for their own material wealth, slaves ran away, attempted coups and resisted the odious label of inferiority. In doing so, blacks and whites affected each other's lives profoundly, shaping the look and character of Bermuda as we know it today.

Lifetime slavery was commonplace by the end of the 17th Century as ever-longer contracts of servitude ensured Bermuda's blacks were an available source of cheap labour. White settlers were no longer emigrating in substantial numbers from England to be tenants and servants, leaving a labour shortage in occupations which many of the island's whites felt were beneath them. Bermuda's slaves had to be multi-skilled to serve the island's economy and they adapted to whatever business their owners might be involved in. Typically, most blacks worked as house servants, a status symbol of the time for whites, when personal wealth was reflected often by the number of slaves a person owned.

Female domestic slaves in Bermuda would wash, iron, cook, clean and look after the owner's children and livestock, while their male counterparts worked as house servants or gardeners. Black men were also shoemakers, fishermen, executioners (a post abhorred by whites and difficult to fill), pilots, dockworkers, mechanics, messengers, whale-hunters, sailors and field hands. Farmers were almost exclusively black, since whites had deemed agriculture demeaning.

Many slaves were master artisans and craftsmen, working in highly regarded trades as carpenters, masons, sawyers and boatbuilders. Others did clerical work. Such diversity made them highly prized, and owners would trade and hire slaves between themselves for special services. But being a good wage-earner could be a double-edged sword: when these slaves eventually tried to buy their own freedom, slaveholders were apt to declare them too valuable to lose.

Bermuda's slaves were natives of the West Indies, Central America and Africa, who arrived here in many ways. Some were aboard ships that wrecked at the island or were captured by roving Bermudian privateers; others were purchased in West Indian slave markets. Very few were brought directly from Africa, although a couple of Bermudian captains ventured to the Gold Coast, one of the continent's trading hubs. Sometimes destitute captains would exchange slaves to pay their debts when they came to port in Bermuda. Once here, slaves were sold at auctions held in St. George's, and in Hamilton after 1793 when the capital moved to a deeper harbour. From 1784, advertisements were run in the *Bermuda Gazette & Weekly Advertiser* by landowners and householders seeking to sell or buy slaves. Owners frequently threatened slaves with sale or sold them as punishment or to cover debts; as possessions, slaves were also left in wills, or given as gifts.

In their own words
■ Olaudah Equiano, 1789

ROYAL ALBERT MEMORIAL MUSEUM

A very cruel thing happened on board of our sloop, which filled me with horror, though I found afterward such practices were frequent. There was a very clever and decent free young mulatto man who sailed a long time with us: he had a free woman for his wife, by whom he had a child. Our captain and mate, and other people on board, and several elsewhere, even the natives of Bermudas, then with us, all knew this young man from a child that he was always free, and no one had ever claimed him as their property. However it happened that a Bermudas captain, whose vessel lay there for a few days in [Old Road, Montserrat], came on board of us, and seeing the mulatto man, whose name was Joseph Clipson, he told him he was not free, and that he had orders from his master to bring him to Bermudas. The poor man could not believe the captain to be in earnest; but he was very soon undeceived, his men laying violent hands on him; and although he shewed a certificate of his being born free in St. Kitts, he was forcibly taken from our vessel. The next day, without giving the poor man any hearing ashore, or suffering him even to see his wife or child, he was carried away, and probably doomed never more in this world to see them again.

—Former slave, author and abolitionist Olaudah Equiano, The Interesting Narrative of the Life of Olaudah Equiano, *1789. Equiano spent four years as a crew member aboard a Bermudian sloop in the West Indies*

By the early 18th Century, slaves made up a third of Bermuda's population, their number having tripled in a matter of decades. It was an alarming prospect to colonial authorities, who responded in 1730 by legislating an importation ban on blacks, Indians and so-called mulattoes—those of mixed race. Laws also targeted free blacks, who were blamed for instigating slave uprisings and ordered to leave the island within six months or be sold into slavery. Despite the crackdown, many slaves continued to be smuggled into the island. Kidnappings and seizures of slaves from local properties were also common as Bermudian landlords or ship captains tried to circumvent the law to acquire the slaves they needed.

Throughout the 17th and 18th Centuries, a constant stream of laws was passed by the Colonial Assembly to restrict black freedoms. Historically, these regulations—instituted following crises between slaves and slaveholders such as the conspiracies of the 1600s and the poison plots—prohibited anything from going out at night to carrying sticks, to wearing silk and bracelets. Flogging was the most common punishment for crimes real or imagined; an official post of public whipper was created and its practitioner became known as the "jumper" for the effect his lashes had on victims. Public whipping stations were established in every parish. Treadwheels or treadmills were also used in the 1820s, with victims forced to spend exhausting sessions on the contraption whose speed could be set at whim. Slaves found guilty of more serious crimes such as murder, burglary or witchcraft would be hanged or banished—shipped off the island for sale in overseas slave markets.

WANTED TO PURCHASE, ONE Negro BOY about eighteen years old, One ditto ditto twelve ditto. And at same time to hire a Negro MAN, a Boatman, all for Turk's Island. Enquire at this Office.
December 1, 1810.

As early as 1620, Governor Nathaniel Butler had erected a new pair of gallows, a cage for drunkards, a pillory and a whipping post in St. George's. The hangman's gallows were kept busy throughout the island. Since most transport between the parishes was by boat, gallows around the coastline such as the ones at Gibbet's Island near Flatts Inlet, often faced out to sea and victims' corpses were cut into pieces and left in chains as a warning to other would-be trouble-makers. Corporal punishment of slaves by their owners was also common, as Mary Prince's narrative indicates, and though they were warned by authorities to exercise restraint when disciplining slaves, some slaveholders went as far as setting up stocks on their own properties.

Bermuda's blacks fought infringements on their freedoms through both subtle resistance and dramatic rebellion—poisoning their owners or plotting to overthrow them. On a daily basis, slaves would direct anger and frustration towards their masters and mistresses through theft and sabotage, by running away, holding go-slows or refusing to work altogether. Several intricate conspiracies and uprisings were planned over the years, but all were discovered and leaked to officials.

One of the most serious revolts was an October, 1761 plot by allegedly more than half Bermuda's black population to kill slave owners, along with any slaves who sympathised with them, and seize control of the island. But the plan was uncovered in its early stages by a mariner named John Vickers,

The Middle Passage

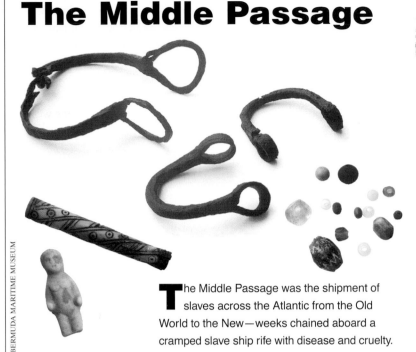

BERMUDA MARITIME MUSEUM

The Middle Passage was the shipment of slaves across the Atlantic from the Old World to the New—weeks chained aboard a cramped slave ship rife with disease and cruelty.

From far left: Items bartered in the slave trade and shackles used on captives during the Middle Passage. Above: slavers often cast overboard the sick or troublesome among their human cargo

Whipping, banishment and death

Draconian laws were enacted and enforced to keep Bermuda's slaves under control:

- *Slaves banished from the island but returning of their own will would suffer death.*
- *Male slaves having bastards by white women would be whipped by the hangman under the gallows.*
- *Cutting or injuring cedar trees would receive 39 lashes.*
- *Clothes, goods, poultry, etc. found in slave cabins would be considered stolen unless proven to the contrary and slaves would suffer death.*
- *For breaking the Sabbath laws, slaves would be publicly whipped.*
- *Found loitering out of a parish without good cause would be whipped by order of the magistrate.*
- *Striking a white person resulted in having both ears cut off and banishment.*

—Bermuda Acts, 1704–94

who overheard those later accused of being involved whispering in a secret meeting one night as he walked home. The plot, which was likely elaborated through the local grapevine, unleashed rampant suspicions and struck terror into Bermuda's white community. Its longterm repercussions would serve to bring more hardship on both slaves and free blacks.

Governor William Popple immediately decreed a period of martial law to soothe fears and take control. As well as further tightening restrictions on black freedoms, the measure allowed authorities to search homes and arrest and jail any black person for as long as was deemed necessary. Under the crackdown, Popple also slapped an embargo on all shipping, in a bid to keep white men on the island, and he ordered every white male over the age of 15 to serve a stint as a parish 'watchman.' Such patrols were doubled throughout the island and slaves found dodging the curfew, even with legitimate excuses, had to kneel when confronted, or face severe whippings.

An expensive commission of inquiry was granted sweeping powers to investigate the whole affair, but despite offers of cash rewards to whites and freedom to slaves in exchange for information, evidence and witnesses were hard to find. Finally, six slaves suspected in the conspiracy were executed; many others were banished to America and other regions.

Winning freedom was the hope and ambition of every slave, but the dream rarely became reality. In scattered cases, manumission—in which owners would free slaves for good behaviour or a brave deed—was the road to a new life as a freeman. Most slaves became free when their owners died and left such requests in their wills. Buying freedom, another possibility, was difficult because slaves could not own land and few earned enough money to buy themselves out of bondage. If they did achieve freedom, blacks had to show a certificate to prove it, a safeguard against bold slaves masquerading as freemen.

Poison plots

Poisoning, inspired by the religion known as 'Obeah,' was common among Bermuda's slaves, born of their African heritage. Skilled in the manipulation of certain herbs, animal substances and deadly plants, many slaves used such knowledge as a form of rebellion against owners and their lives of bondage. Victims would fall into fevers and convulsions, and sometimes die. A crackdown followed a slew of deaths and mysterious illnesses among whites in the 1720s and '30s.

Slaves found guilty of involvement in poisoning plots were banished to the West Indies, or publicly executed, sometimes by burning or beheading. Sarah (also known as "Sally") Bassett is perhaps the best-known of these cases. A mulatto bondwoman owned by a blacksmith in Southampton, she was accused of helping to poison a Sandys couple, Thomas and Sarah Foster, and their slave girl Nancy, using her grand-daughter, Beck, as an accomplice.

According to court records, Bassett gave Beck rags containing two poisons, "rats bane and manchioneel root," one substance red, the other white. The week before Christmas in 1729, she allegedly instructed Beck to put some of the poison over the Fosters' kitchen door, and the rest into their meals, as well as into the food of their slave girl Nancy. The Fosters fell ill, but survived. Nancy's fate remains unclear.

In her trial the following June, Bassett was convicted of the poisoning plot and sentenced to die. "You are to be convey'd to the place of Execution where a pile of wood is to be made & provided," ordered the judge, "and you are thereto to be fasten'd to a sufficient Stake and there to be burnt with fire untill your body be dead."

Bassett was taken to the foot of Crow Lane, where crowds gathered to witness the horrible spectacle. Afterwards, she was remembered in island folklore. A hot day became known as a "Sally Bassett day" and it was said that in her ashes, a small purple flower was found—now the island's national flower, the Bermudiana.

The treadwheel

Lydia (found guilty of stealing a Doubloon) was put on it, and continued for the space of 10 minutes. She evidently suffered considerably from the exertion, and when taken off, could not, without assistance, retain an upright position. Much depends on the person in charge, as to the degree of punishment which the machine inflicts, as the rapidity of it can be increased or diminished at pleasure… It is said to be the terror of indolence, the reformer of vice and the best moral preceptor for those proverbially desolate establishments, gaols. Slaves will not so readily run away from their owners, crimes, we trust, be fewer, indolence overcome, and morality inherit the place of vice. We think, however, this new system of prison discipline ought to be dispensed with in all cases of female delinquency. It is revolting to see women subject to torture and exposure of this nature.

—Description of a treadwheel used to punish slaves, The Royal Gazette, *September 2, 1828*

When Bermuda's tobacco industry failed and islanders abandoned their efforts at serious agriculture, slaves followed their masters into seafaring activities. The shipbuilding boom demanded skilled labour and soon local shipyards were bustling with slaves engaged in building hundreds of Bermuda-rigged sloops and schooners. Blacks adapted to the economic shift quickly, learning to become whalers, pilots and sailors who, with their white captains, would spend months or years at sea. Many slaves were taken to the Turks Islands to labour in the salt industry; others crewed on commercial vessels in the carrying trade between Nova Scotia and the Caribbean, or took part in privateering and wrecking escapades. Some of the best black crews could be found all over the globe, adventuring

BERMUDA MARITIME MUSEUM

The Bermuda-built Sea Pickle *attacking a slaver*

ABSCONDED from the Subscriber, about four weeks past, a Negro Man by the name of **MERCY**; a Mason, Stone-Cutter, and Wall-builder. All Persons are forbid harbouring or employing him, and masters of vessels and others are cautioned against taking him off these Islands, as by so doing they will incur the penalty of the Law, which will be rigidly enforced.

WM. LIGHTBOURN.

Airmont, Pagets, 18th March, 1833.

THE Subscriber cautions all persons from Employing Negro Man *SAM*, a Carpenter, belonging to the Estate of JOSEPH HINSON, Deceased, without application being first made to him, or *Mr. Richard Hayward*, St. Georges; as they may have to pay his wages twice—besides legal expences.

SAM is offered for Sale.

JOS. HINSON,

Executor to Estate of Jos. Hinson, deceased.

Smith's, March 18, 1833.—3.

ABSCONDED,

ON the 9th October last, the Subscriber's Woman *PENNY*, formerly the property of Mrs. GWYNN. All Persons are forbid harboring or employing her, as the Law will be strictly enforced against them.

A Reward of *THREE DOLLARS* will be given to any person who will apprehend and bring her to the Subscriber; and a further Reward of FOUR DOLLARS will be paid to those who will give information of such as harbour or employ her.

ROBERT R. BROWN.

St. Georges, 29th March, 1833.—2§

*Newspaper advertisements
warning against runaway slaves*

in merchant sloops armed for conflict and plunder. The slaves and free blacks aboard even received a share of the captured prize.

The reason blacks came to play such a large part in maritime activities can be traced back to a 1696 ruling that masters of Bermudian vessels longer than 40 feet could have crew made up of four white and three black sailors. Island officials feared that having too many white men away at sea would leave Bermuda unprepared to defend itself should there be attacks by the Spanish, or roaming pirates. Slave labour translated into higher profits for ship owners, because slaves were powerless to demand better wages and could be paid minimally. They were also less likely to desert ship than their white counterparts even in the face of brutality, war or rough living conditions; slaves knew if they angered their masters by fleeing to freedom, their families could be sold off to foreign plantations. Even free blacks were paid less than white sailors. In June 1719, island legislation was further amended to allow Bermudian ships to carry "as many Negroes or other slaves" as they wished.

Closer to home, fishing was a mainstay for the black population, both to feed themselves and to provide fish for sale by their owners at market. Blacks manned commercial boats and whaling vessels, forming fearless crews who ventured out to sea in rowboats to harpoon passing whales. They also worked on boats which operated ferry services around Bermuda's coastline.

Because slaves could not testify in court against a white person, they were commonly used by their owners to help smuggle goods ashore. Merchants would have their slaves unload illicit cargoes into private warehouses at night, evading port customs officials; wreckers and privateers made use of slave crews for the same reason.

BERMUDA ARCHIVES

*Slaves take a break overlooking British warships
anchored in the Great Sound*

Such escapades were not without risk for slaves, who could be seized and sold if their ship was captured by an enemy vessel. However, that was little deterrent for their captains.

Privateering in Bermuda reached its peak during the American Revolutionary War (1775–83), when sloops smuggled arms and munitions through British blockades to George Washington's Continental Army. Blacks played a big role in these dangerous voyages, comprising the majority of the privateering crews. Occasionally, blacks would be offered their freedom in foreign ports, but most declined for, among other reasons, they knew their families in Bermuda would suffer the consequences.

How they lived

With scant income and few personal liberties, slaves had to be resourceful in their daily lives. They made tools and implements such as brooms, baskets and fishpots by weaving palmetto leaves; used sea fans as kitchen whisks, carved buckets, beds and other furniture from cedar, and created culinary staples such as cassava pie, mullet roe, arrowroot pudding and guava jelly, which are still prized as typical Bermudian treats.

During the 18th and 19th Centuries, slaves who worked as domestic and field labourers usually lived in cellar-like quarters in their owner's home, or in separate cottages on the same property, located near the kitchen so they could be quickly called to work. Many Bermudian homes of the period were built with a lower half-storey specifically for use as slave quarters.

Their diet consisted mainly of corn and fish (supplemented with occasional whale meat). Salted cod from Newfoundland was a favourite meal, and barley and bean broths were common staples. Heart of palm, palm berries and cedar berries were also incorporated into homespun recipes. Some slaves were fed from the family kitchen, sharing the owner's fare. They often had small gardens of their own to grow produce in their spare time. Bermuda's laws prohibited slaves from trading or selling, though they did so, often as a form of rebellion. Slaves were also heavily punished for stealing goods such as sugar-cane and citrus fruit. Slaves at sea survived on a diet of codfish, called "poor jack," or, like their white counterparts, ate a mix of flour, water, butter, salt, molasses and dried beef—a typical pudding made of available ingredients.

Slaves wore hand-me-down clothing from the master's family, since most were unable to buy their own wardrobes—though slave crews travelling between ports often traded for cloth. Turbans and palmetto tops were popular. Shoes were a luxury; instead, slaves regularly went barefoot, or used whale skin to fashion a leather-like covering.

Social activities among slaves included attending black weddings, funerals and special 'slave balls.' In church, they were relegated to particular sections or forced to stand outside, and their graves were separated from the tombs of white Bermudians. At Christmas, slaves were allowed several days of holiday, spent dancing, feasting and drinking and visiting family in other parishes—a liberty few enjoyed the rest of the year.

Relationships between blacks and

Many of Bermuda's slaves worked as domestic servants

whites were commonplace despite harsh penalties, and as the races gradually intermingled over the years, families began to share surnames. Children born out of wedlock were a fact of island life. Physical features were also shared. White women sometimes gave birth to black babies, and black women to mixed or white infants—though blacks were severely punished for such relationships. Over time, many Bermudian blacks or "mulattos" had light skin and blue or green eyes—the proof of racial mixing by Bermudians in spite of the slavery's social divisions.

Slave for sale

To Be Sold By the Subscriber
June 12, 1784
A Stout Negro Wench named Beck, about 36 years of age. She is, when minded, an excellent Ground Negro; can also Wash, Starch and Iron, and she is to be sold for no other reason but at times being very impudent to her owners.
Nath. Roberts, St. George's.
—The Bermuda Gazette, *1784*

Education and religion for blacks were frowned on until the 19th Century when Methodist missionaries helped break down racial barriers. One such clergyman was Joshua Marsden, who travelled to Bermuda from Newfoundland with his wife and infant daughter in 1808 and began preaching to blacks from Somerset to Spanish Point. He opened the Zion Chapel at the corner of Church and Queen Streets in Hamilton, and dedicated one side of the church to "black and coloured people." Marsden also started a Sunday school for black children and encouraged blacks to learn reading and writing—long forbidden, as a form of white control over the black population. Slaves and free blacks built their own one-room church in Warwick in 1827, labouring in their spare time to construct the building block by block, using stone from nearby quarries. A Barbadian slave-turned-Methodist minister named Edward Fraser helped push the project, and the Cobb's Hill Wesleyan Church became a symbol of black faith and remains a

Edward Fraser

Sea beef

The whales approach within a mile of the land, and during the season men are stationed on the cliffs to give information when a whale appears. When a whale is killed, the boats tow it as close to the shore as possible; the shore is lined by Black people of both sexes and all ages; the men assist in cutting off the blubber, taking care to help themselves and friends to all the fleshy parts, called 'sea beef.' The noise and confusion is beyond description, women and children calling to the operators, who from time to time throw large pieces of the flesh on shore. In a few hours, a whale approaching sixty feet is reduced to a skeleton, and scarcely a house, whether occupied by whites or Blacks, where a treat of whale beef does not take place that day or the next. The English have a strong prejudice against this food, but the Bermudians have a method of cleansing it, which leaves no fishy flavour, and it is as tender as veal.

—*Richard Cotter,* Sketches of Bermuda or Somers' Islands, *1828*

Expert fishermen

For being not only remarkably fast sailors, but also when it became calm, frequently the case in those months, these Blacks (showing example of attention for good of their Masters' interest worthy of our people) rowed their sloops from two and a half to three miles per hour and in working in and out of narrow harbours excelled the best of our fishing lugger shallops. Also learned from Masters of our Bankers who have been in company with Bermudians on Banks fishing in August that the Black men became as expert in catching fish as old country men and as eager and attentive to catch as any of ours.

—*Jeremiah Coghlan, a St. John's, Newfoundland resident, 1788*

BERMUDA ARCHIVES

Methodist clergyman Joshua Marsden preaches to blacks in Bermuda. He also encouraged them to learn to read and write

place of worship today. Blacks had their own graveyards, and churches such as St. Peter's housed a special gallery for slaves, who had to get their masters' permission to attend. Sometimes blacks could only stand outside and watch the service through the windows. Whites were required by law to go to church every Sunday.

Slaveholders feared educated blacks would no longer serve them, and as a result, schools catering to the black population were not encouraged until the 1800s. While some blacks received religious instruction and basic reading and writing classes at schools run by ladies' and church societies, it was not until 1825 that the Church of England established a system of black schools, but mainly teaching religion. Gradually, day schools and Sunday schools for blacks were opened in every parish, and by the time of Emancipation in 1834, many black people had received a basic education.

CHAPTER SEVEN

Wars and Defence

BERMUDA BECOMES A BASTION OF THE BRITISH EMPIRE

I n a letter to his mother from Bermuda in 1773, Philadelphia Quaker Thomas Coates described an island on the brink of famine. The situation had grown so dire, the government detained the ship on which Coates had sailed and confiscated its cargo of flour and rice, although that was a "mere mouthful" among so many people in need of food, he noted. No other provisions would arrive for more than a month. On January 23, a sloop made port with 200 barrels of flour and 1,500 bushels of corn, rations of less than a quart per family.

"The poor people really bear the marks of hunger in their countenance as many of them cannot muster up more than will buy a peck or two, and in two or three days perhaps could buy more—but it's all sold," Coates remarked. "This is a great disadvantage they labour under. I suppose there's one third of the families here have neither flour, corn or rice to make bread with, obliged to live on fish alone—when they can get it."

When America's 13 colonies went to war with Britain, Bermudians felt the fallout in very physical terms. The American Revolutionary War (1775–83) was essentially a constitutional conflict which forged a new democratic philosophy and created the 'United States.' But the war also proved a milestone in Bermuda's history, not least because it brought home to Bermudians in very serious terms the precarious nature of survival on an island so far removed from mainland food supplies.

The geographical problem was exacerbated by the century's evolving

Fort St. Catherine, an important fortification, was built over one of Bermuda's earliest defences

BERMUDA ARCHIVES

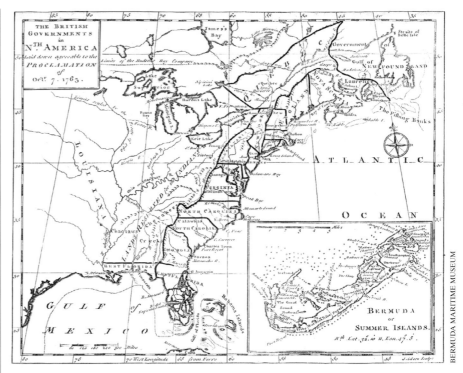

British America in 1763, with Bermuda inset. The North American colonies would soon be lost in the Revolutionary War

Ever-present fear *Our unhappy country feels the severest of ills, thousands have suffered and many have perished for want of bread. We have had several providential but temporary reliefs and our prospect is now as bad as ever. A small quantity of corn and peas brought in on a prize sold at public vendue for upward of 20 shillings a bushel. Fresh meat and poultry are almost a rarity, butter and eggs are equally scarce and there is the ever-present fear of absolute want.*

—Resident Elizabeth Tucker on
Bermuda's food shortage, 1779

Necessities *The main produce is a fine white cabbage, very good eating, which they sell to our colonies whenever its importation is allowed. This is apparently not the only vegetable grown, but the colonists do need other things besides, and New England or the neighbouring states provide them with the necessities of life, beef, butter and other provisions.*

—Nicholas Louis Bourgeois,
secretary of the Chamber of
Agriculture in San Domingo (now
Haiti), in Voyages intéressants dans
différentes colonies françaises,
espagnoles, anglaises, etc., Paris, 1788

political landscape: Bermuda's narrow focus on maritime industry throughout the 1700s had placed its entire economy at the mercy of trade with America. But when America retaliated against Britain's blockade of its ports by stopping exports to British colonies in 1775, this lifeline was cut off. Suddenly the island, which had neglected agriculture and depended on selling salt, rum and other goods to America in exchange for the bulk of its meat, fruit and vegetables, had to fend for itself. Unable to import foodstuffs from Britain because it lacked trading goods the mother country required, Bermuda found itself in a desperate situation.

Not only was its food supply strangled, but Bermuda also saw its ships barred from trading with American ports or engaging **King George III** in any kind of commercial enterprise in American waters. Indeed, America threatened to capture or destroy all trespassing 'foreign' vessels and Bermudian captains now found themselves *personae non gratae* in previously friendly East Coast cities. With their main trading territory off-limits, Bermudians had to venture further afield—to the South Atlantic, to Newfoundland—and their business, and by extension the larger Bermudian economy, suffered sorely.

America's conflict with Britain had been simmering for several years before boiling over into full-scale war. The 13 colonies were thriving and growing more independent and profitable as the years went by. But Britain was loathe to surrender control of its American possessions; it believed the colonies' mandate was to make money for the mother country under the tight control of King George III and Parliament—particularly given the burden of expenses for the Seven Years' War (1756–63). America had a very different notion of its destiny and the colonies began rebelling against the

In their own words
■ George Washington, *1775*

To the inhabitants of Bermuda

Gentlemen,

In the great conflict which agitates the continent, I cannot doubt but the asserters of freedom and the right of the Constitution are possessed of your most favourable regards and wishes for success. As descendants of freemen, and heirs with us of the same glorious inheritance, we flatter ourselves, that, though divided by our situation, we are firmly united in sentiment. The cause of virtue and liberty is confined to no continent or climate. It comprehends, within its capacious limits, the wise and good, however dispersed and separated in space and distance.

You need not be informed, that the violence and rapacity of a tyrranic ministry have forced the citizens of America, your brother colonists into arms. We equally detest and lament the prevalence of those counsels, which have led to the effusion of so much human blood, and left us no alternative but a civil war, or a base submission. The wise Disposer of all events has hitherto smiled upon our virtuous efforts. Those mercenary troops, a few of whom lately boasted of subjugating this vast continent, have been checked in their earliest ravages, and are now actually encircled in a small space, their arms disgraced, and suffering all the calamities of a siege. The virtue, spirit, and union of the provinces leave them nothing to fear, but the want of ammunition. The application of our enemies to foreign states, and their vigilance upon our coasts, are the only efforts they have made against us with success. Under these circumstances, and with these sentiments, we have turned our eyes to you, Gentlemen, for relief.

We are informed that there is a very large magazine in your island under a very feeble guard. We would not wish to involve you in an opposition in which, from your situation, we should be unable to support you; we know not, therefore, what to extent to solicit your assistance, in availing ourselves of this supply; but if your favour and friendship to North America and its liberties have not been misrepresented, I persuade myself you may, consistently with your own safety, promote and further this scheme, so as to give it the fairest prospect of success. Be assured that in this case, the whole power and exertion of my influence will be made with the honourable Continental Congress, that your island may not only be supplied with provisions, but experience every other mark of affection and friendship which the grateful citizens of a free country can bestow on its brethren and benefactors.   —G.W.

—A provisory letter written from Massachusetts, September 6, 1775. It was never delivered, because the gunpowder in question was smuggled to America in the meantime

Brethren *The Inhabitants are a people, who, from their immediate Connection and frequent Intercourse with the Continent, have contracted an affection for this Country. They consider the Americans as Brethren, and their Souls are animated with the same generous Ardor for Liberty that prevails on the Continent; they are most Zealous Friends to the Cause of America, and would readily join with it, in any Measures to secure those inestimable privileges now contending for; in short they consider the Cause as their own, and with pleasure behold every step that has been taken in support of it.*

—Bermudian St. George Tucker, a resident of Williamsburg, Virginia, in a letter to Thomas Jefferson, June 8, 1775

increasing British interference in their affairs. In 1765, Britain levied a stamp tax on the colonies to help pay off its recent war debts against France—a move that drew anger from Americans, whose rallying cry, "No taxation without representation," became the mantra of their struggle.

Anti-British sentiment finally flared as a physical clash at Boston in 1770 when a group of citizens harassed a British soldier to protest troops being sent to the colonies. The incident turned ugly when more soldiers entered the fray and fired at the mob, killing five people. The so-called "Boston Massacre" raised the stakes of the conflict. It escalated further on December 16, 1773, when colonial patriots disguised as Native Americans dumped a cargo of tea from three British ships into the harbour as a demonstration against punitive British import duties, including a tea tax. The repercussions of the "Boston Tea Party," including a siege of Boston Harbour by the British and suspension of other colonial rights, would spiral into war. Enraged colonials created the First Continental Congress in 1774, and fighting between British redcoats and American minutemen followed the next year.

In Bermuda, Governor George James Bruere, a staunch imperialist, considered Americans as enemies, but privately many Bermudians sympathised with the American cause. The island had enjoyed longtime family and commercial ties with America, bonds that would severely test Bermudian loyalty to the Crown. Of course, Bermudians' most immediate concern was

'Horrors of famine'

Self-preservation gave the alarm, and in such an exigency there was no alternative but an application to the American Congress, setting forth the situation of the island and requesting a dispensation of that resolve in favour of a people who without their aid must inevitably perish, or a submission to all the horrors of famine and general distress. When such motives (and such alone) influenced their conduct, the inhabitants of Bermuda assured themselves that the Father of His People would not take umbrage at a measure dictated by the most powerful and irresistible law of nature. The people therefore imprest with those sentiments deputed some persons from the several parishes to make application for that purpose in May, 1775. At that time we scarcely knew of the dawning of civil war and cherished hopes that it might still be prevented from breaking out by an amicable and honourable reconciliation. Altho' this pleasing hope has been blasted by the event, yet we flatter ourselves that your Majesty will regard with a favourable eye a measure which if reprobated by the malevolence of some, or the misinformation and ignorance of others, was yet dictated by necessity, the most urgent of human incentives.

—*Legislature's address to the Crown after Britain banned trade and communication with America on September 10, 1775*

one of self-preservation; they wanted to maintain their very profitable trading ties with America, and also avoid famine. To do that, they could not choke off their connection to America, even at the risk of being disloyal to Britain.

Luckily for the island, Bermuda happened to have something America urgently needed: gunpowder. A delegation of parish representatives led by Colonel Henry Tucker—whose son, Virginia resident St. George, was a vocal champion of the American cause—travelled to Philadelphia in the summer of 1775 to beg the Continental Congress to show mercy towards "a people who without their aid must inevitably perish, or a submission to all the horrors of famine and general distress." Their appeal worked; the Congress indicated it would release food supplies to the island in exchange for a delivery of firearms and ammunition. Indeed, the commander of America's armies, George Washington, wrote a personal request for support to the people of Bermuda. In it, Washington acknowledged the existence of a public gunpowder magazine in St. George's that his sources informed him was weakly guarded. His strong hint came with a promise: that he would use his influence to persuade the Congress to offer food "and friendship" to the island.

But Washington's plea was pre-empted. Before his September 6 letter reached the island, several prominent Bermudians had already taken matters into their own hands, defying the Governor and British authorities in a daring scheme that would cunningly take advantage of the political turmoil to win Bermuda a breathing space of American support in its time of need.

St. George Tucker

Col. Henry Tucker

BERMUDA MARITIME MUSEUM

The night of August 14, 1775 was calm and stifling hot, casting a soporific mood over the island. Governor Bruere, who was not particularly well-liked by the locals, was not surprised when just four assemblymen turned up for the scheduled Parliamentary session that sweltering afternoon. He thought little of it, excused them from coming up the hill to pay their respect to him given the "sultry weather" and later retired for the night. From his official Government Hill residence, he could overlook the entire town of St. George's—as well as the gunpowder magazine just a few hundred yards away. For years, the colony's gunpowder had been kept in the State House, but to prevent an accidental explosion damaging the town, the supply was moved to the new magazine built to explicit specifications on the hill. In 1767, the Assembly and Council agreed the storage spot should be "20 feet long and 10 feet wide from inside to inside with an arch'd roof; the walls to be built of limestone three feet thick. A small Porch to be built adjoining the entrance in such a manner as may best prevent damage to the Powder, which Porch is to be six feet long and 10 feet wide in the clear. The Doors and Locks to be equally secure."

But the best-laid plans were to go dramatically awry. Under a nearly full moon that midsummer night, several dozen men sneaked ashore at Tobacco Bay, crept up the hill to the unguarded magazine and broke in

BERMUDA ARCHIVES

Cannonballs and cannon stacked at the ready in St. George's

In their own words

■ Governor George Bruere, *1775*

In the night of the 14th August when allmost a sufficient Number of Members of Assembly to make an house were come to Town agreeable to Adjournment, I had less suspicion then before that such a daring and Violent Attempt would be made on the Powder Magazine, which in the dead of the Night of the 14th August, was broke into, on Top: just to let a Man down, and the Doors most audaciously, and daringly forc'd open. At the great risk of their Being blown up, they could not force the Powder room door without getting into the Inside on Top. They stole and carried off about 100 Barrels of Gun Powder, and as they left about 10 or 12 Barrels, it may be supposed that those Barrels left would not bear removing.

It must have taken a considerable Number of people, and we may suppose some Negroes to assist, as well as White Persons of Consequence.

On Wednesday 16th, the Legislative Body voted £100 Sterling reward to any Person or persons that shall make any discovery & Legally Convict any

of the Perpetrators of this audacious piece of villany—and I offered his Majesty's most gracious pardon to any one Person that shall make any discovery of any person or persons, so that they be Legally Convicted of this most heinous Crime, and a further reward of £30 out of my own purse, all of which was immediately offered by proclamation. And likeways 30 dollars, or £10, Currency, I have offered to be paid to any Negro or Negroes to inform against any other Negro or Negroes that were aiding and assisting so that they be Legally Convicted.

The next morning, the 15th, one sloop called the *Lady Catherine*, belonging by her Register, to Virginia, George Ord, Master, bound to Philadelphia, was seen under sail, but the Customs house Boat could not overtake her. And likeways a Schooner called the *Charleston & Savannah Pacquet*, belonging to South Carolina, from South Carolina, cleared out at Bermuda the 11th Augt. With 2000 sawed stones for Barbadoes, John

Turner, Master, and was seen under sail the same day at such a distance off that the Customs house Boat could not overtake either of the Vessels.

It may be supposed that neither of the vessels came near the shore to take in the powder, or if they did carry it away, but it is rather to be imagined that it must have been carried out by several Boats, as both these vessels sailed from a harbour at the West End, 20 miles off of the Magazine.

I shall dispatch these by the very first conveyance I can get, which will be extremely difficult, as the minds of the people are very much poison'd, since they chose Delegates and some people from Carolina and Philadelphia have corresponded and visited these Islands.

P.S. I hope some of his Majesty's Sloops of War will arrive soon; I shall contrive all ways and means to convey Intelligence to them of my dismal situation, as I have given hints to your Lordship before, if all the Letters have not been intercepted—your Lordship will receive some—No. 18—by the *Little Porgy*, A. Kirkpatrick Master.

—*Governor George Bruere to Lord Dartmouth, August 17, 1775*

Boston Tea Party

We have by Way of the Leeward Islands a blind Account that the Bostonians have thrown into the Sea three hundred good Chests of Tea—I will not take upon me to determine entirely on the Propriety of their Behaviour—There may be Cause to be assigned for it that I am unacquainted with—but if I form a right Idea of it, the Step they have taken was by no Means necessary—they have exposed themselves to Hazard without Reason & furnished the Enemies to the Liberties of America with Arguments against them—The chief End proposed by the British Ministry appears to be the subjecting the Americans to Taxes imposed by the British Parliament…The Steps adopted by the Bostonians seem rather calculated to aggravate than conciliate Measures—I am as warmly attached to Liberty as any Man, but I cannot say that I like their Proceedings—A Duplicity founded on a Spirit of Puritanism derived from their Ancestors characterises their general Conduct.

—Henry Tucker, March 21, 1774,
writing to his brother-in-law,
St. George Tucker, in Williamsburg,
Virginia about the Boston
Tea Party of December 1773

Lazy, stupid, obstinate

The people of these islands are lazy, stupid, obstinate, small-minded and thoroughly objectionable.

—Governor Bruere, 1763

through the roof. One man was lowered in to unbolt the door and the team began carrying more than 100 casks of gunpowder down the hill to the North Shore. The operation was carried out silently and without a hitch—except for the sudden appearance of a man in uniform. Unwilling to risk discovery, the powder thieves killed him on the spot and buried his body on the grounds of the governor's residence. A century later, the victim was discovered to have been a visiting French soldier simply out for a walk.

Hidden on the shoreline, a fleet of whaleboats was waiting. The men quickly loaded the boats with powder kegs and rowed several miles offshore. The intricate plan saw two American ships—the sloop *Lady Catherine* commanded by Philadelphia Captain George Ord, and the schooner *Charleston & Savannah Pacquet*, with John Turner of Charleston as Master—lying ready to carry away the barrels. Before long, these were safely in the hands of George Washington's Continental Army.

Back in St. George's, the bold theft was discovered at daybreak and the news threw the island into turmoil. Governor Bruere was aghast. "Save your country from ruin which may hereafter happen!" he declared in a public announcement. "The powder stole out of the magazine late last night cannot be carried far as the wind is so light. A great reward will be given to any person that can make a proper discovery before the magistrates."

Bruere offered a £100 reward for information leading to the culprits' capture, but none was forthcoming despite the fact that numerous well-known Bermudians, including assemblymen, were implicated in the heist. An impromptu meeting of the Council asked the Assembly to help it devise the best way to capture "the perpetrators of this most audacious piece of villany." Ironically, the House appointed Colonel Tucker, along with several others, to a special committee to investigate. Later the suspected mastermind of the theft, his name would figure conspicuously in the whole affair: the August 26, 1775 records of the Pennsylvania Committee of Safety cite an invoice received in the amount of £161.14s.8d for "1,182 pounds of gunpowder." The signature on the invoice was none other than Henry Tucker, "chairman of the Deputies of the several parishes of Bermuda." Ironically, his son, Henry Tucker, was married to Governor Bruere's daughter, Frances.

Meantime, Bruere had no luck in getting to the bottom of the embarrassing episode. He was road-blocked by Bermudians at every turn, especially when he tried to get word to British forces in America about the gunpowder seizure. Having written a letter of warning to General Thomas Gage, Commander-in-Chief of the British troops in Boston, Bruere's efforts to find a ship that would agree to carry it to Boston failed. It was not until September 3 that he finally managed to hire a boat. Taking no chances, Bruere entrusted one of his own slaves to hide the secret correspondence on board—a prescient move, since a group of Bermudians, presumably loyal to American revolutionaries, boarded the vessel shortly after it had set sail and tried to find and steal the letter. They were unsuccessful. The message eventually reached Gage, but no one on the island was ever charged or convicted for their part in the gunpowder scandal.

For a while, at least, the treachery achieved what it had intended: the Congress, as promised, lifted sanctions, allowing Bermudians to receive food supplies, lumber, candles and soap in exchange for salt, and despite efforts by British ships to stop such illegal trade, Bermudians were grateful for it. Throughout the war, however, food remained scarce on the island, particularly

In their own words
■ Edmund Ward, *1775*

The occurrence of hostilities with the United States created quite an excitement and stir at Bermuda—but it was not till prizes were arriving that the inhabitants believed the event had happened; the fleets of England having so completely cleared the ocean before this new enemy appeared, that with the exception of a French frigate which sometimes eluded the vigilance of the blockading squadron on the coast of France. Or a solitary merchantman under similar circumstances, who had escaped one danger only to meet another, the arrival of an enemy's vessel was a rare occurrence.

No sooner was the declaration of hostilities by the United States known in England, than ships of war bound for the American Coast crowded the anchorage and harbour of St. George, troops were continually arriving and departing and at one time there were from 90 to 100 prizes lying there. Speculators from the West Indies, England and even from the United States, although the two countries were at war, were there to purchase prize goods; and American vessels with supplies were continually arriving, which were protected by a licence from the Admiral on the Station.

These had permission to import cargoes; but as they were enemies' vessels, they could not reload. To obviate this difficulty on their arrival in Bermuda, they would procure a set of surreptitious Swedish papers, with which and the licence they had obtained, the Captain would proceed to the custom-house, and to load as such. The greatest trouble they experienced, was when they met a cruiser at sea, about whose national character they were uncertain, when the exhibition of the licence would be attended with peril; for if she should happen to be an American ship, the discovery of the licence would lead to the seizure and forfeiture of the vessel and cargo and crime of treason. The consequence was, the document had to be concealed where it could not readily be found; and as the vessel was bound for a British port, if taken by a British cruiser, she would be released on her arrival; and this of course was preferred.

It was no uncommon occurrence, therefore, for ships loaded with cotton from New Orleans, to be carried to Bermuda. In one instance, where the

Bermuda-built frigate HMS Sylph, *1812, engages a French warship*

BERMUDA MARITIME MUSEUM

licence could not be reached without discharging a considerable portion of the cargo, and when it was of importance owing to the high state of the market in England, that a vessel should arrive at her destination before an unfavourable change took place in the price of cotton, a legal gentleman in St. George received a fee of a thousand dollars for procuring her release, there being other evidence as to the character of the vessel.

There were a number of Americans doing business in St. George's, who came on for the purpose of purchasing prizes and prize goods; most of whom wore green spectacles, that they might not easily be recognised by those of their countrymen who came there in a more honourable way by capture. An author whose work I have read remarks that he has known many honest men who wore spectacles, but he never knew a rogue who did not. And the latter part of this observation will apply to those unprincipled men, who thus for the purpose of gain, violated their allegiance to their country and placed themselves in open correspondence with its avowed enemies.

The influx of strangers led to a scarcity of provisions in an island, which, however fertile and calculated to yield a sufficient supply of food for its inhabitants, is still indebted to other countries; and living was accordingly expensive at St. George… But money thus profusely thrown into a community is as prodigally spent; a corresponding extravagance is produced among all classes of society and when this unnatural state of things ceases, but few have been enabled to lay up wealth.

—*Government printer Edmund Ward,*
Seven Years' Residence in Bermuda
1809–1816

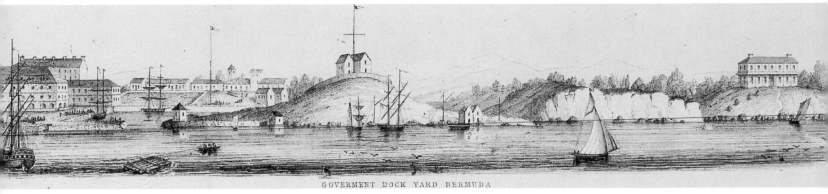

GOVERMENT DOCK YARD BERMUDA

*The new Dockyard was built
after the loss of the American
colonies in the Revolutionary War*

BERMUDA MARITIME MUSEUM

National importance

*The value of (Bermuda) is known to
both France and America. Therefore
it is desirable that no time should be
lost in giving adequate security to it,
while it is still ours. To secure this
great naval station is an object of
much national importance.*

—*Letter from the First Lord of the
Admiralty, Thomas Grenvill, to the
British Prime Minister, recommending
Bermuda as a western Atlantic base
for the Royal Navy, 1806*

Great strength

*This island, is, by an act of the
British Parliament, about to
become a place of great strength
and resort as a naval depot and
arsenal for the British forces, which
may, at any time, be employed on
the American or West India station.
Upwards of 1,800 men were at the
last accounts employed upon its
fortifications, which it is said, when
completed will be mounted with
500 pieces of cannon.*
—The Niles Register, *August 22, 1829*

*British warships at anchor
off the new Dockyard*

since prisoners of war had to be fed, as well as the regular population.
According to one estimate, only about a tenth of the needed provisions
were arriving in port because of the conflict.

Still, islanders were not ready to cast off their ties to the Crown. While
many families had close connections to America, Bermuda as a whole
maintained a strong loyalty to Britain. That was perhaps less a show of
stout patriotism than a testimony to the islanders' opportunism. Just as
they had adapted so deftly to shifting loyalties in the past, Bermudians
would again play both sides to protect themselves while taking advantage
of profit-making opportunities wherever they could find them.

Before the end of the War of Independence, many of Bermuda's loyalist
privateers did just that, attacking American ships by the dozen and throwing
their prisoners into a seedy St. George's jail. By 1779, the Continental Congress
had allied with France and made plans to invade the island, even sending
four warships to the area. But timing was on Britain's side this time, for the
Royal Garrison Battalion had just arrived at Bermuda and their presence
kept the would-be invaders at bay. When peace between Britain and America
was finally signed in 1783, making official the independence of the United
States of America, Bermuda had weathered yet another threat to its survival.

Having lost its precious American colonies, Britain now found itself
in a difficult position—her colonies in Canada and the West Indies
were separated by an independent America that was keen to flex
its newly-won political muscle. Bermuda, as a halfway post between
Britain's Atlantic colonies, took on a new strategic importance that would
figure throughout the next two centuries.

The following years would see Britain get serious about making the island
a prominent naval and military outpost, particularly in the wake of the Gunpowder Theft, which had underscored Bermuda's weak military protection.
In 1792, Royal Navy hydrographer Lieutenant Thomas Hurd surveyed

BERMUDA ARCHIVES

Commissioner's House

Bermuda's westernmost landmark, Commissioner's House, was constructed between 1822 and 1831, dominating Royal Navy fortifications at Dockyard.

The three-storey, 30,000-square-foot structure was designed by Britain's Navy Board chief architect Edward Holl. Using a cast-iron frame pre-fabricated in England and hard Bermuda limestone quarried at the Dockyard, it was built as a home for the commissioners who oversaw all activity at the West-End base. After the office of commissioner was abolished in 1837, the building served as army barracks and later became HMS *Malabar* until the Royal Navy left Dockyard in 1951. The house fell into ruin in the 20th Century, but with the establishment of the Bermuda Maritime Museum in 1974, a massive renovation campaign was launched and it was re-opened as a heritage museum in 2000.

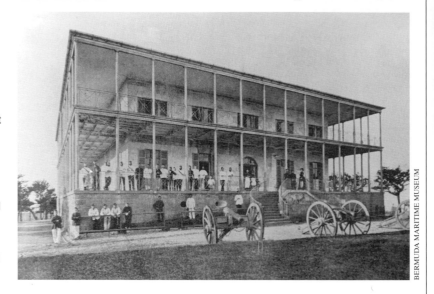

BERMUDA MARITIME MUSEUM

HMS Malabar V, *a Royal Navy warship used at Dockyard to house visiting sailors. The name was later transferred to Commissioner's House*

BERMUDA MARITIME MUSEUM

Royal Navy ships at Dockyard

Bermuda's reefs and identified two large anchorages suitable for battleships. He also proposed a dockyard for Grassy Bay, Sandys. Army engineer Captain Andrew Durnford was sent out to survey and upgrade Bermuda's fortifications; he repaired existing defences and built four new forts in the East End.

The military need grew more urgent when war broke out with Revolutionary France in 1793. The Royal Navy's North America Squadron comprised just a handful of ships, while French warships held virtual control of American waters. Vice-Admiral Sir George Murray was committed to making Bermuda the North Atlantic's major naval station—later dubbed "Gibraltar of the West"—and advised Britain to purchase 141 acres at Ireland Island as the site of a naval yard. The Bermuda legislature passed a bill later that year to make it official, though work on the Imperial Dockyard would not start until 1809.

The Napoleonic wars at the turn of the century devoured much of Britain's military budget and attention. Bermuda was not exempt from the conflict, for French privateers were running rampant through the Atlantic and many island ships were captured. Bermudian captains retaliated, however, preying on French vessels in the Caribbean around Haiti and elsewhere. Britain re-established its supremacy at sea with the defeat of Napoleon in the 1805 Battle of Trafalgar.

Construction began on the West-End Dockyard, employing both slaves and freemen who worked under the guidance of English engineers. The first buildings around Grassy Bay were built of cedar and soft stone; later construction made use of hard Bermuda limestone, excavated in blocks. And as Fortress Bermuda developed, the island became an employment hub for shipbuilders, craftsmen and sailors.

Britain's troubles with America were far from over. As British battles against the French continued, Royal Navy squadrons took to capturing armed American merchant ships and seizing their crew in an effort to prevent neutral countries trading with France. The practice annoyed the United

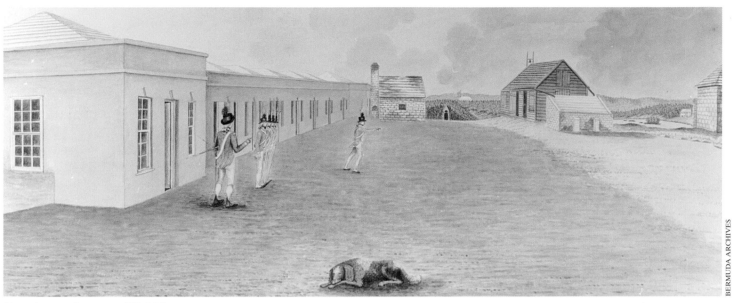

BERMUDA ARCHIVES

Rotating regiments of British
soldiers manned the island's
many forts

COURTESY OF LUCIANO AICARDI

Soldiers signalling during
manoeuvres in the 1890s

States, which had ties to France thanks to the 1803 Louisiana Purchase, which doubled its territory. Emboldened, America also set its sights on British possessions in Canada. Finally, the US declared war on Britain.

The so-called War of 1812 was largely a three-year naval conflict with maritime trade as its prime target. With one of three prize courts located in Bermuda (the other two were in Jamaica and Halifax), the war ignited a frenzy of activity in and around the island—especially after the British erected a retaliatory blockade of American ports and used the island as the staging post from which to launch a strike on Washington. St. George's was the focus of much maritime congestion; scores of ships would remain for months in the town's harbour while their captains and ship owners waged lengthy legal battles in the Admiralty Court. The island, itself, was spared attack and by the war's end, 43 vessels captured as prizes had bolstered its merchant marine of about 70 ships. Privateering was heavy during this period, with Bermudian ships making the most of the war to attack American and French prizes. Unscrupulous American privateers, like their Bermudian counterparts, knew the mercenary value of opportunism and some defied their own government to supply the British forces at Bermuda. Other American vessels proved irksome to Bermuda's trading ambitions for they caught many local sloops operating between the West Indies and Newfoundland and claimed thousands of pounds of cargo.

Work on Bermuda's defences, meantime, intensified. After an 1826 review of the island by British hero and general, the Duke of Wellington, who had defeated Napoleon's forces at the Battle of Waterloo, a slew of new fortifications began. The work centred on the Royal Naval Dockyard, which the British Admiralty intended to make a mid-Atlantic bastion for its busy fleet. This time, though, slaves were not the main source of labour for the project. Starting in 1823, English and Irish convicts were shipped across the Atlantic for use as cheap workers for the British government. Housed in prison hulks moored off the Dockyard, these convict gangs would build bridges, storehouses, barracks and ramparts, making the Dockyard an impregnable jewel among British naval fortifications. The island's western tip would remain a penal station for the next 40 years.

Thomas Moore

BERMUDA MEDIA

In January 1804, an Irish *bon vivant* arrived in Bermuda from Virginia aboard the HMS *Driver*. Thomas Moore stayed only a few months, but he made a lasting impression on the island, immortalising people and places in a series of romantic poems and ballads.

Moore, 25, took up the post of Registrar of the Court of Vice-Admiralty, keeping track of captured enemy ships brought to Bermuda to be certified as prizes. He made many friends, especially among the island's women. But it was not long before he began to find both the job and island lacking in excitement. In a series of letters to his mother, he bemoaned Bermuda's size and social scope, along with the parochial nature of its citizens.

"Certainly, the human face divine has degenerated wonderfully in these countries," he commented, "and if I were a painter, and wished to preserve my ideas of beauty immaculate, I would not suffer the brightest belle of Bermuda to be my housemaid."

Still, Moore, who lived on what is now Old Maids Lane in St. George's, spent his free time composing a series of 13 love poems to a woman he named "Nea," believed to be his teenaged neighbour, Hester Louisa Tucker, married to William Tucker. He wrote many of these at the Bailey's Bay Walsingham estate, where he found creative inspiration under a calabash tree for verse such as this:

Oh! Trust me, 'twas a place, an hour,
The worst that e'er temptation's power,
Could tangle me or you in!
Sweet Nea! Let us roam no more
Along that wild and lonely shore,
Such walks will be our ruin!

Despite his literary dalliances in Bermuda, Moore had had enough of the island by April that year, and left for New York.

In their own words
■ Tom Moore, *1804*

These little Bermuda islands form certainly one of the prettiest and most romantic spots that I could ever have imagined, and the descriptions which represent it as a place of fairy enchantment are very little beyond the truth. From my window, now as I write, I can see five or six different islands, the most distant not a mile from the others. They are covered with cedar groves, through the vistas of which you catch a few pretty white houses, which my practical shortsightedness always transforms into temples; and I often expect to see nymphs and graces come tripping from them, when to my great disappointment I find that a few miserable negroes are all the 'bloomy flush of life' it has to boast of. Indeed, you must not be surprised, dear mother, if I fall in love with the first pretty face I see on my return home; for certainly the human face divine has degenerated wonderfully in these countries, and if I were a painter and wished to preserve my ideas of beauty immaculate, I would not suffer the brightest belle of Bermuda to be my housemaid…

It is impossible to be ill in such a climate. Roses are in full bloom here now, and my favourite green peas smoke every day upon the table… I have been very fortunate here (as indeed Providence seems to please I should be everywhere) in conciliating friendship and interesting those around me in my welfare. The admiral, Sir Andrew Mitchell, has insisted upon my making his table my own during my stay here, and has promised to take me in his ship to America for the purpose of getting a direct passage to England—there being no direct conveyance from this corner thither…They threaten me here with impeachment, as being in a fair way to make bankrupts of the whole island. There has been nothing but gayety since I came, and there was never such a furor of dissipation known in the town of St. George's before. The music parties did not keep long up, because they found they were obliged to trust to me for their whole orchestra; but the dances have been innumerable, and still continue with great spirit indeed. The women dance in general extremely well, though, like Dogberry's 'writing and reading,' it comes by nature to them, for they never have any instruction except when some flying dancing-master, by the kindness of fortune, happens to be wrecked and driven ashore on the island. Poor things! I have real pity for them.

—*Tom Moore, in letters to his mother, 1804*

Life in 'Fortress Bermuda'

Lonely heart *To The Ladies, A Gentleman who is but very little acquainted with the fair sex of these Islands, and who wishes to settle here, would be happy to meet with an agreeable partner for life, between twenty and thirty years of age, and of an agreeable and lively disposition, with a fortune of about two hundred pounds per annum, which is not above half of his income. The gentleman is about middle stature, of genteel connections, and does not exceed twenty-five.*

Although he is aware of the censure of a number of persons, yet he hopes to find one who may be in nearly the same situation, and who will excuse this method of application, which is strictly honourable. A line directed for L.P. under cover to the Printer of this Paper will come safe to hand.

N.B. The strictest secrecy will be observed, and an answer sent immediately; or he will meet the party at any place and time appointed.

—*Personal ad in* The Bermuda Gazette, *August 1784*

Off-duty officers enjoy a game of 'American bowls' in 1888

Chaste and fair *The Bermudians are not inferior in any particular way to the people of the mother country; the women are as chaste and as fair, and the men as clever, as friendly, and as hospitable too in proportion to their means. It is true, that owing to the relaxation consequent to a warm climate, the ladies do not find it convenient to be at home at all times to receive idle visitors, but at the Governor's parties, public balls and amateur plays, they are neatly dressed, and each lady may claim the merit of being her own dress-maker.*

—*Richard Cotter,* Sketches of Bermuda, *1828*

The application of cockroaches *These troublesome, destructive and offensive vermin, have happily been found to form an article of incalculable value in the* **Materia Medica** *of the modern date; having been recently used with singular success in the cure of Lock-jaw, when every other supposed remedy had been perseveringly tried. The application of Cockroaches, as a medicated plaster, have proved of the greatest efficacy in removing external inflammation; in promoting suppuration in the most obstinate tumours; after the utmost skill of the surgeon has been unceasingly exerted in vain... The Cockroach, having the head, wings and legs removed, must be prepared with fresh cold hog's lard, or other sweet soft grease; and in that form applied in all cases to the parts affected... The above is offered in order that so valuable a discovery may become as extensively known as possible.*

—The Royal Gazette, *August 9, 1831*

Palmetto couture

Bermuda's lowly palmetto rose to the heights of urban style during the 18th Century, when woven hats became the accessory of choice among London fashionistas.

Ladies' palmetto hats, made of leaves that had been stripped, dried and bleached, were so popular, a thriving cottage industry developed on the island. Bermuda's palmetto was particularly in demand, and slaves were employed as weavers to plait and sew hats, along with fans, baskets and tablemats, for export. Up to £10,000 a year in palmetto products was exported to Britain at the height of the trend in the early 1700s.

By the century's end, the hats were no longer fashionable, and the overseas business died. A century later, however, the British Navy brought the palmetto briefly back into vogue, when garrison officers commonly wore hats made of woven fronds as protection against the sun.

...

Jingles all the way

All the way to Mangrove Bay,
There the old maids go to stay.

All the way to Crow Lane side,
Nothing there but foolish pride.

All the way roun' Harrington
*   Sound,*
One-wheel carriage rolling round.

All the way to Bailey's Bay,
Fish and taters every day.

All the way to Brackish Pon'
Cow's heel soup and damaged corn.

All the way to Spanish Point
There the times are out of joint.

—*Parish jingles of the 19th Century*

CHAPTER EIGHT

Freedom and Reform

EMANCIPATION AND ITS AFTERMATH

January 1834, and ended the 9th day of September following,

Vizt. :—

1.—An Act for the Abolition of Slavery in these Islands, in consideration of Compensation.

2.—An Act to repeal the Laws exclusively applicable to free black and free coloured persons and extend to them the Laws applicable to white persons ; and to fix the qualification for Jurors, Voters, and the Electors and Candidates for certain Offices and Places of Trust.

3.—An Act in addition to the Act to simplify and amend the mode of proceeding in the Court of General Assize.

4.—An Act for attaching the Money, Goods, Chattels and Debts of absent Debtors.

5.—An Act in addition to the "Act as well for the relief of the Poor, as for the putting out Apprentices, and setting idle persons to work."

6.—An Act for the protection of Landlords.

7.—An Act to amend the Acts relating to Conveyances of Real Estate by Women under Coverture.

8.—An Act to restrain and punish Vagrancy.

9.—An Act for raising a Public Revenue for

Banners, parades and church services throughout the island marked August 1, 1834 as a "new day" for Bermuda's black population. It was Emancipation Day, bringing the long-awaited abolition of slavery. Bermuda's population of almost 10,000 people included 3,600 slaves, as well as 1,200 free blacks, and both groups joined to celebrate the start of a new era. Joyful festivities, mostly religious gatherings of family and friends, began at midnight on July 31—the official end of more than 200 years of human bondage and indignity.

After much bitter debate, the British Parliament had finally moved to abolish the slave trade in 1807, followed by slavery itself in Britain on August 29, 1833. The next year, a bill was passed to eradicate slavery in all British colonies. In Bermuda, two abolition acts were passed: the first, the Act to Abolish Slavery, made all slaves free; the other repealed 200 years of discriminatory laws against blacks. America's Emancipation Proclamation was still 30 years away—Abraham Lincoln would not issue that decree until January 1, 1863, during the Civil War. An amendment to the Constitution two years later would finally end slavery in America. Elsewhere, Britain's Caribbean colonies followed the mother country's lead over the next few years, though Bermuda and Antigua were the only two territories which did away with slavery immediately. Others required black citizens to endure a six-year probationary period of 'apprenticeship' before winning full freedom, though this system ultimately collapsed.

Mercenary motives led Bermudian slaveholders to support the immediate end

ANNO TERTIO & QUARTO

GULIELMI IV. REGIS

C A P. LXXIII.

An Act for the Abolition of Slavery throughout the *British* Colonies ; for promoting the Industry of the manumitted Slaves ; and for compensating the Persons hitherto entitled to the Services of such Slaves.   [28th *August* 1833.]

WHEREAS divers Persons are holden in Slavery within divers of His Majesty's Colonies, and it is just and expedient that all such Persons should be manumitted and set free, and that a reasonable Compensation should be made to the Persons hitherto entitled to the Services of such Slaves for the Loss which they will incur by being deprived of their Right to such Services : And whereas it is also expedient that Provision should be made for promoting the Industry and securing the good Conduct of the Persons so to be manumitted, for a limited Period after such their Manumission : And whereas it is necessary that the Laws now in force in the said several Colonies should forthwith be adapted to the new State and Relations of Society therein which will follow upon such general Manumission as aforesaid of the said Slaves ; and that, in order to afford the necessary Time for such Adaptation of the said Laws, a short Interval should elapse before such Manumission should take effect : Be it therefore enacted by the King's most Excellent Majesty, by and with the Advice and Consent of the Lords Spiritual and Temporal, and Commons, in this present Parliament assembled, and by the Authority of the same, That from and after the First Day of *August* One thousand eight hundred and thirty-four

10 Y

Unfeigned thanks *But in a particular manner our unfeigned thanks and fervent prayers are due to our late Owners for their liberality, in giving up the four and six years apprenticeship which was theirs by right and we trust that through the assistance of that Divine Being who has and still continues to put into the heart of all men, that most excellent Gift, Charity—to Conduct ourselves in our new capacity as Freemen, in such a manner as to continue in the good graces of our superiors and further to gain the Confidence and good will of every Class of Society in these Islands.*
—*The Coloured Friendly Union Society of the Parish of Paget,* The Royal Gazette, *August 5, 1834*

Perfect order *The rubicon is passed; the step from Slavery to Freedom has been taken, and we sincerely trust that the movement has been effected with the same ease and security in other British Colonies…Four days of universal freedom have now passed; and four days of more perfect order, regularity and quiet have these famed peaceful Isles never witnessed.*
—The Royal Gazette, *August 5, 1834*

Free union *Upwards of 50 Marriages of Coloured people have been celebrated within the last fortnight.*
—The Royal Gazette, *August 5, 1834*

BERMUDA ARCHIVES

Blacks were free but remained second-class citizens for generations to come

to slavery. Under the new law, owners would be reimbursed for lost slave labour; from £20 million in compensation funds arranged by Britain, Bermuda's share was £50,584. That amount was based on average slave values around 1830, and worked out to roughly £20 per slave. Since many property owners owned 10 slaves each, and a few as many as 20 or 30, their compensation was a financial perk they did not wish to delay.

Emancipation, when it came, was the result of a massive humanitarian campaign waged for many years by abolitionist groups, slaves and free blacks. The Anti-Slavery Society in Britain hoped slaves would be treated to better living conditions after the 1807 law, because once the supply of slaves was drastically curtailed, owners would have to ensure the slaves already in their possession would lead long lives. But life on colonial plantations continued as it had in the past. Even in Bermuda, when questioned by the British Parliament about slavery, officials deemed living conditions "favourable" and claimed slaves enjoyed their share of "personal comfort."

Under pressure from Britain, local legislators allowed a few concessions in 1827. Slave marriages were legalised—but could not take place without the owner's permission. Blacks were permitted to give evidence in slave trials, but they could not testify against their owner or the owner's relatives, a restriction that allowed brutal acts to go unpunished. Such lingering restrictions were considered grossly unfair by Bermuda's free blacks, who,

In their own words
■ J. Holt, 1834

Messrs. Editors, Many friends in America will like to know how the British Colonists spent the 1st of August 1834. I can tell you how it was passed in this little town. The rejoicings of the day began, as our warm-hearted Irish friends would say, in the middle of the night. At 12 o'clock, the fife and triangle sounded merrily through the streets, and after a few "Hurrahs" for King William IV, all again was quiet as the "smooth surface of a summer's day." At sunrise I attended the usual prayer meeting of the people of colour in the Wesleyan Chapel.

As I entered, an elderly slave was imploring a blessing on the ministers of the Gospel…When the prayer was over, we went to the Parish Church to witness the marriage of two emancipated slaves whose owners had the day before refused consent to the marriage, though they were dressed in their bridals, and with several other couples stood at the altar. The rector told them, tho' he could not marry them that day without the owner's consent, to come the 1st of August, and he would unite them.

At 11 a.m. public thanksgiving was offered up in the Parish Church. The greater part of the Church was filled with coloured people, men, women and children dressed in their best, and presenting such a host of joyous faces as this little rock never before saw. Many of the late owners gave up their pews to their former slaves. Notwithstanding the heavy rain, many of the white inhabitants attended…Although the crowd of coloured people was great, perfect order and quietness prevailed, and every attention was paid by the officers of the vestry to accommodate. During the service the countenances of many manifested deep feeling of joy and thankfulness. The discourse of the rector was excellent, though in one sentiment advanced I differ from him; he asserted that they had no right to liberty; it was a free gift from government and their late owners. Similar services were held in all the parish churches throughout the island.

The day passed, and the day closed in happiness and peace. It was quite a holiday—the people of colour aptly termed it Good Friday. The next morning all was stir and bustle—masters hiring their late slaves, or the emancipated running around to look for work. I should have stated that at daylight of the 2nd, the fife and triangle, drum, flute, etc. (with all the little Negro boys who had heard of the plan, and had scrambled out of their lodgings to partake of the fun) went to the house of the commandant of the garrison and a few others, played "God save the King," gave three cheers for King William and then dispersed quietly.

After work was over at sunset the coloured people assembled in the market square with drum, fife and everything that would make a merry noise, played, sung "God Save the King" and "Rule Britannia," gave many a loud and ringing "Hurrah!", danced, capered, shook hands and the little fellows tumbled each other over head and ears in the mud, the old fellows rolled their trousers up to their knees to keep them from being spattered, and hand and foot, and tongue and head had full enjoyment till nine o'clock, when the gun-firing sent them all home in peace.

The mayor had been indefatigable to promote the public peace and give full enjoyment to the coloured people. He walked the streets on the night of July 31, but found no disturbance. He attended the merrymaking and paradings and found no cause for reproof.

It is my decided opinion that we owe the peace and happiness of the 1st of August to the influence of Sunday Schools, and the preaching of the gospel: The preaching of the Gospel and the schools that proceed from it are the only efficient means of preparing a people for the blessing of freedom.

—*J. Holt, a letter on Emancipation Day to the* The New York Observer, *1834*

Samuel Gilbert Pearman, of Flatts, was born to slaves in 1834

COURTESY OF GLORIA McPHEE

George Samuel Lambert was age seven at Emancipation

BERMUDA ARCHIVES

Mama Do (Julia Dill), brought to Bermuda as a child slave from Peru

COURTESY OF VIOLET BRANGMAN

Mary Warfield was freed at age nine from the slave ship Enterprise

COURTESY OF PATRICIA FERGUSON

Office of Asst. Commissioners of Compensation
FEBRUARY 14, 1835.

NOTICE IS HEREBY GIVEN that the following CLAIMS have been duly lodged in this Office, since those published under date of February 11.

Name and Description of Claimant or Person in possession of the Slaves.	Domicile of Slaves.	No. of Slaves.
John Fowle,	Sandy's.	3
Susannah B. Gilbert,	"	4
Mary H. Gilbert,	"	5
John A. M. Gilbert,	"	7
John W. Gilbert, by Richard G. Tatem, his Attorney,	"	2
Burrows Gilbert,	"	10
Susannah Gilbert, Executrix of Thos. Gilbert, deceased,	"	4
Benjamin H. Gilbert,	"	9
Benjamin H. Gilbert, Susan G. Morris, and John Durrant,	"	1
John A. M. Gilbert, Executor of Benj. H. Gilbert, Senior,	"	6
Elizabeth Gibbs,	"	7
Thomas Gray, by Attorney, John Seymour Burrows,	"	5
Jehonddan Green,	"	6
Robert Hunt, Senior,	"	10
William Hunt,	"	10
Mary Hunt,	"	3
Elizabeth Hunt,	"	1
Elizabeth Hunt,	"	2
Mary T. G. Hunt,	"	2
Eliza P. Hunt,	"	5
Joseph Henry Harvey, by Benjamin H. Gilbert, Attorney,	"	1
Susannah Harvey,	"	1
Susannah Harvey, and Mary Ann Morris,	"	5
George Hayes,	"	7
Thomas B. Hutchings,	"	2
Frances B. Jones,	"	6
Robert Jones, by Jesse Jones, Guardian,	"	1
Jesse Jones, Junr., by Jesse Jones, Senr., Guardian,	"	1
Jesse Jones,	"	11
Cyrus King,	"	4
Honora B. Ker,	"	4
Jane Kirkpatrick,	"	2
George Longhurst,	"	1
Marry Ann Morris,	"	7
Susan G. Morris,	"	1
William Morris,	"	4
Watlington Bethel, B. Young, Martha Saltus, and Alice Bethel,	"	1
Susan G. Morris, and John Durrant,	"	6
Augustus E. D. Morris, by William Morris, Guardian,	"	1
Eliza G. H. Morris, by William Morris, Guardian,	"	2
John Morgan,	"	11
James G. Murray,	"	1
Miles S. Morgan,	"	12
Benjamin H. Gilbert and others, Executors, of Elizabeth Gilbert, deceased,	"	14
Henry Morgan, by Attorney, Miles S. Morgan,	"	8
Sophia Nash,	"	3
Paul S. Outerbridge, by Cornelius B. Place, Admr.	"	7
Jonathan Outerbridge,	"	2
William R. Outerbridge,	"	3
Ephraim Paynter, by John Joseph Mathew Williams, Attorney,	"	2
Cornelius B. Place,	"	6
Richard Jennings Tucker, Executor of Mary King,	"	5
Thomas Place,	"	1
John Paynter, by Sarah J. Paynter, Executrix,	"	4
Sarah Paynter,	"	2
Paul Pitman, by J. J. M. Williams, Administrator,	"	2
Paul Paynter,	"	8
Martha G. Paynter,	"	1
Trimingham Tucker,	"	3
Jane Hayward Tucker,	"	2
Sophia B. Tucker,	"	1

Mercenary place *In this little mercenary place, nothing is esteemed but money: the people are chiefly all of one religion that of money, pleasure, vanity, while the Trinity they believe in and worship, is the world, the flesh and the devil.*
—*Methodist missionary Joshua Marsden, November 26, 1808*

A black family outside their modest cottage home; a list of slave-owners, left

in a January 1834 petition to the Council, argued they were still being treated as slaves despite their liberty. In response, the Legislature passed a bill repealing all laws that applied exclusively to free blacks and making applicable to them the same laws that governed white Bermudians. Yet, the act attempted to ensure white control, excluding free blacks from positions of authority and restricting voting rights based on land ownership.

Whites claimed Emancipation Day would encourage vindictive riots, drunkenness and general trouble-making, but the milestone was a thoroughly solemn and peaceful affair celebrated, as the government had requested, as a day of public worship. Churches throughout the island were full to over-

Conditions remained much the same for many after Emancipation

Friendly Societies and Odd-Fellows

Bermuda's black community formed "Friendly Societies" to provide a welfare net for newly-freed slaves and to lobby for rights. At least two such associations existed before abolition, and possibly more black social and informal action groups. Historians believe there might even have been a Bermudian version of America's famous "Underground Railroad," providing safe houses and protection for runaway slaves.

In 1832, the Young Men's Friendly Institution was formed in Pembroke to "promote Industry, Honesty and Frugality and for raising a Fund, by Contributions, for the relief of sick or distressed Members." Early in 1834, the Friendly Union followed in St. George's. By 1859, more than 15 formal organisations, with official charters and members, had been set up throughout the parishes. Among other achievements, they organised money-lending schemes, raised funds to build black schools, encouraged education and the performing arts, celebrated Emancipation anniversaries with church parades and services, and provided money and support to black widows, orphans and families.

Friendly Society women on parade

Odd-Fellowship, a more secret society which traced its origins back to mediaeval England, came to Bermuda in 1848. Like the Friendly Societies, its 19th-Century mandate was geared towards providing social support to the black community. The Somers Pride of India Lodge, Number 899 was established in St. George's, its name referring to the elegant tree under which its founding members held their first talks. Within a few years, Odd-Fellowship had taken root in Sandys and the city of Hamilton. Bermudian Odd-Fellows even travelled to group conventions in America.

A Friendly Society couple

flowing as the black community turned out in their Sunday best to give thanks. Pews normally reserved for white churchgoers were opened to all to accommodate the crowds. Folklore describes how Silk Alley and Petticoat Lane in St. George's were so named after two female slaves who wore silk petticoats to attend the Thanksgiving Service at St. Peter's Church, their rustling skirts evoking the new sound of freedom. Cobb's Hill Wesleyan Church in Warwick was also a focus for heart-felt celebrations, built as it had been by slaves for their community.

As a society, Bermuda made the transition from slave culture to free relatively easily, but individually, newly freed blacks had a long way to go to attain true equality. While many kept busy in the same occupations for which they had trained before Emancipation and some even continued working for the same families—albeit with wages—others found themselves struggling to survive financially once they had to find jobs suddenly, pay for housing and feed their families. Whites held the lion's share of land and wealth on the island, and also kept a firm grip on the reins of government and business, largely shutting blacks out of equal opportunity for another century.

The Brig *Enterprise*

The crowd assembled to welcome the landing of these people was immense, they were received with cheers. The court room was filled almost to suffocation. The feeling of commiseration exhibited throughout the proceeding by the Bermudian people of colour was really gratifying. Those persons who had but a short time since been owners of slaves spoke with disgust and utter detestation of the slavery system, and decried it, quite as much as any Anti-Slavery Society in the mother country could have wished, so thorough a change has taken place of late years in the minds of the people of this colony. The Court did not adjourn until near midnight, when a shelter was afforded to the now liberated people, by the Worshipful William M. Cox, Esq., in an unoccupied storeroom in the town of Hamilton. They have all been since, as we understand, provided for, either as domestic servants, or taken under the protection of the members of the Friendly Society.

— The Royal Gazette, *on the* Enterprise *affair, February 24, 1835*

The American Brigantine *Enterprise*, Smith, master, from Alexandria, bound to Charleston, out 21 days, short of provisions, put into Hamilton on Wednesday last, having been blown off the Coast.—She has 79 slaves on board.

Danger: Gombeys

We fully agree with our correspondent that the savage and nonsensical exhibition of the Gomba [Gombeys], practised here by the idle, should be done away with, as a thing not suited to a civilised Community, and highly dangerous to Passengers on horses or in carriages.

—The Royal Gazette, *1837*

Black families faced a difficult challenge trying to buy property, since they lacked ready funds; even those who had money found most land owned by whites was unavailable to them. A few, such as St. George's resident James Athill, overcame such hurdles; Athill had amassed enough assets to allow him to serve as parish constable in 1834. But most blacks faced a cycle of unemployment, overcrowding and poverty—a social quagmire that prevented them achieving any meaningful political power that could aid their struggle for self-improvement.

Notably, blacks were virtually denied the right to vote or run for office, as legislative changes made after August 1, 1834 demanded voters own property worth at least £100 (up from £40), or £400 (up from £200) to run as a member for the General Assembly—stipulations which excluded most of the black population.

Friendly Societies, or "lodges," run by the black community, stepped in to bridge the social gap in many ways. Lodges fought for and provided better education and healthcare and lent a needed hand to widows and children of black members. One such lodge, the Young Men's Friendly Institution, played a large part in securing the freedom of a shipload of American slaves which stopped at Bermuda in 1835 after being blown off course by a storm en route from Alexandria, Virginia to Charleston, South Carolina. On board the ship, an American brig named *Enterprise*, were 78 slaves and a master.

When news spread about the human cargo—a violation of island laws after Emancipation—lodge members pressed for the captives to be allowed to appear before the Chief Justice to declare whether they wished to continue the voyage and be sold, or stay on in Bermuda as free residents. All but one woman and her five children chose to remain on the island, and their descendants remain to this day.

One of the milestones of the late 18th Century was the debut of the island's first newspaper. In 1782 the General Assembly voted to spend £450 on a printing press to have laws printed and government proceedings published. In 1784, a 29-year-old Londoner named Joseph Stockdale arrived to take up the post of King's printer, bringing with him the first printing press.

The result was a weekly paper called the *Bermuda Gazette & Weekly Advertiser*, whose inaugural edition appeared on January 17, 1784. Proceedings from the General Assembly sessions were published for the first time, along with advertisements and island news, from ship arrivals and departures to crime reports and social events. In 1828, the newspaper was renamed *The Royal Gazette*.

Bermuda chose a new capital during this period. St. George's had served the growing colony well, but now shipping and nearly all commercial trade was centred in the Great Sound, and a port catering to the central and western parts of the island was needed. Foundations were laid for a town in Pembroke parish, then still called Spanish Point. Hamilton was named for the governor of the time, Henry Hamilton, and officially incorporated in 1793. While the new House of Assembly was being built, the General Assembly held its first meeting in Hamilton's Town Hall on January 23, 1815, symbolically moving the seat of government from the East End after 200 years.

Black Bermuda after Emancipation

Dr. CLARENCE V. H. MAXWELL

In January 1834, a group of 38 'free blacks' and 'free persons of colour' submitted a petition to the House of Assembly, the governor and council, and ultimately, the British government. Its context was the passage of the Emancipation Act of 1833 by the British Parliament, which had been sent to all colonial legislatures for amendment. Governor Stephen Chapman introduced the act to Bermuda's legislature on January 9, 1834, sparking debates on how Bermuda's post-abolition society was to be constituted. Of particular concern was the way the island would deal with a proposed apprenticeship scheme; as it turned out, Bermuda (and Antigua) would choose not to participate in this. As different parties got involved in the debate, so did this group of 38 men.

But their interests were particular. These men sought the removal of all legal restrictions which had governed their lives and fortunes: "Your Petitioners," they wrote, "most humbly pray that they may soon be relieved from the various disabilities and invidious distinctions to which they have hitherto been subjected, and may be admitted to the enjoyment of the rights and privileges which ought to be possessed in a state of Freedom." Fourteen of those who signed the petition were freeholders, their names topping the list. Some had been free since 1828.

A month later, in February 1834, two abolition acts were passed: An Act for the Abolition of Slavery in these Islands, in Consideration of Compensation, and An Act to repeal the Laws Exclusively Applicable to free Black and free Coloured Persons, and to Extend to them the Laws Applicable to White Persons, and to Fix the Qualifications for Jurors, Voters, and the Electors and Candidates for Certain Offices and Places of Trust. Both would take effect August 1, 1834. With the passage of these twin acts, much of the legal expression of Bermuda's so-called "customs of the country" came to an end. The obvious casualty was the institution of slavery—a behemoth which, though it had taken 211 years to build, needed just a single month to mortally wound. But this was on paper. How did blacks fare in the reality of post-Emancipation? What challenges faced them as they tried to navigate a new, free socio-political landscape which they had helped, in some part, to forge?

The first challenge was economic, and it faced white as well as black Bermudians. Bermuda's maritime economy was sinking, hit by North American competition to the carrying trade and the steamship's death blow to the island's shipbuilding industry. Agriculture, encouraged by political leaders and governors such as William Reid and Charles Elliot, would gradually fill the void, providing the main source of employment for both races, but it would take decades to become as viable a way of life as the seaborne trades.

Along with such economic changes of the time, there were demographic ones. For much of Bermuda's history, until the 1800s, white women dominated the local population. Indeed, Bermuda's females enjoyed a numerical superiority that effected many cultural and landowning traditions. But from the 1800s, a new trend emerged: the black population out-numbered whites in the colony for the first time

Shifting demographics: in the 1800s, blacks outnumbered whites for the first time

BERMUDA ARCHIVES

in Bermuda's social history. According to the census of 1851, of a total population of 11,092, there were 3,591 black women, 2,704 white women, 2,832 black men and 1,965 white men. Black women were the majority by the middle of the 19th Century, with white men the numerical minority. For some commentators, the emigration of white men from the island was in part responsible for their low numbers. Governor Charles Elliot noted, in a report to Whitehall on the census, this emigration of "young white men" was the result of "the peculiarly-depressed [economic] conditions of the poorer classes of that portion of [whites]."

But the most important question facing Bermuda's blacks lay in politics. On paper at least, the bulk of demands in the 1834 petition were satisfied, particularly the explicitly stated ones. The first bill paved the way for abolition, though as elsewhere, it assured that slaveowners be compensated for their "loss of property." Bermuda's share came out of the £20 million granted to all slaveowners in the British colonies. One group of proprietors believed slave-owners in Bermuda were due £171,855, or £45 per head. The Assembly also decided to bypass the apprenticeship scheme adopted by other colonies and, instead, to grant universal manumission immediately upon August 1.

Despite these changes, however, nothing was suggested about providing the newly freed with anything in the way of resources, much less financial compensation; nor was there any protection for blacks against eviction from the land once August 1 arrived. Not a few blacks began devising means to secure land ownership, and often these schemes were successful. Some worked for whites, occupying land, and later having it secured by them on the death of the landowner. It seems likely this type of labour relations scheme held for blacks the hope of eventually owning their own land. Others simply bought land outright, usually from the proceeds of successful businesses. Many black landowners appeared in St. George's in this way.

The second act was more complicated, and on the surface, appeared to satisfy the petitioners' "racial customs" concerns. No less in keeping with the petition tabled by the free 'Coloured' and 'Negro' group in January 1834, the Assembly repealed the Amelioration Act of 1827 and other pieces of legislation "imposing upon black or coloured persons…any penalty, duty, disability, or liabilities to which white persons are not subject by law, or taking away…any right, privilege or franchise from which white persons are not excluded." It thus gave freed coloureds and negroes what the

Black fishermen at Spanish Point

petitioners in January wanted: legal equality with whites.

But it did not guarantee social equality, as the petitioners had hoped. Race would remain a feature forging socio-political separation for a long time after 1834, and segregation became an entrenched way of Bermudian life. The most notable expression of this was in education, which was rigidly divided. Attempts mid-century to establish multi-racial education—the Reverend William Dowding's revitalisation of the Berkeley Plan, for example—would collapse in the face of local hostility.

The second part of the act held a far more blatant attempt to restrict the political power of Bermuda's blacks: it hiked the property value qualification needed to run for Assembly, parochial offices and municipal offices; raised criteria for voting eligibility; and banned all women from running for office. Ironically, as a result of this effort by the island's white elite to curb black political expression, a number of white Bermudians found themselves suddenly disenfranchised.

WANTED,

A Good WASHER and IRONER by the Year, with mutual liberty to end the contract on a month's notice ; or, if a Slave, until her qualified Emancipation on the 1st August next, with like liberty, but on condition of their having the refusal of their Parliamentary Apprenticeship from that date.

J. H. TUCKER

Somerville, March 15, 1834.

As the implications of the Abolition Act were being realised, questioned and criticised, Governor Chapman quickly sought to explain. "The effect," he wrote, "was designed to be that of securing to the Whites, as the wealthier class, the ascendancy which they lose as the European class…Wealth and poverty will divide Society much in the same way as European and African Descent have been wont to divide it."

Despite these challenges, the key feature of life within the black community after abolition was cooperation. The fulcrum behind the establishment of black Friendly Societies, educational facilities and even medical care, such cooperative spirit allowed blacks to overcome the enormous social, economic and political difficulties of the 19th Century. Moreover, it further fuelled their ambitions to live in the type of society the petitioners of 1834 had envisioned at the dawn of the post-Emancipation period.

■ *Dr. Clarence Maxwell is Director of Historical Research at the Bermuda Maritime Museum and Editor of the* Bermuda Journal of Archaeology and Maritime History

'Black women were the majority…white men the numerical minority'

Sacrifices *Through seven generations have they not been our obedient and attached slaves? For us and our ancestors they have risen early and late taken rest; they toiled through the live-long summer's day and in the sweat of their faces they have eaten the bread which we have provided for them. Their food was cheap, their clothes inexpensive, we have been enriched by the fruits of their labour; we have brought up our sons and our daughters and lived, many of us, in the enjoyment of luxuries…At our bidding they have undergone fatigue and labour; at our command they have perilled themselves on the ocean and hundreds and thousands have perished in the deep. And, in return for all these sacrifices, what do their children of the present generation demand of us?*
—*Chief Justice John Christie Esten,*
who in 1837 proposed a long-range
education plan to train the
children of former slaves

Untold wrongs *Bermuda, as if in contrition for the rigour which stamped her ancient slave laws, has been foremost to extirpate, without delay, every trace of slavery; and prompted by a sense of the justice which she owed the negro, for the untold wrongs that for upwards of two centuries had been legally sanctioned against him, determined altogether to discard the system of apprenticeship, and at once to give entire and unconditional freedom to the whole body of slaves.*
—*Humanitarian Susette H. Lloyd,*
Sketches of Bermuda, *1835*

Education, if it existed at all in these years, was rudimentary. During the days of the Bermuda Company, progressive steps had included the construction of three schoolhouses in 1662—one of which remains as Warwick Academy—and strides were made by individuals such as surveyor Richard Norwood, who returned to Bermuda and became a respected educator. But during the 18th Century and the first half of the 19th Century, education was sorely neglected.

It fell to the clergy to teach basic reading, writing and arithmetic, but instruction was mostly mediocre, and Bermudian children were generally allowed to spend their days outdoors, swimming, diving and fishing until they were old enough to work. Wealthier families sent their sons abroad—Yale and Harvard Colleges and the College of William & Mary were already established East Coast institutions, and English and Scottish universities were also highly-sought destinations, as much for the social status they conferred as for their curricula. As was the norm elsewhere, Bermudian daughters did not receive the same encouragement; girls were generally taught household arts and needlework, though a few also learned languages, art and music.

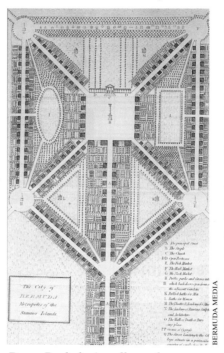

Dean Berkeley's college plan

In 1725, a zealous British missionary called Dr. George Berkeley set forth an ambitious educational plan that involved Bermuda. "A Proposal for the Supplying of Churches in our Foreign Plantations" laid out a vision for a Bermuda-based school to provide Christian education for English youth living on New World plantations along with Native Americans. The project won favour among London's elite, and Berkeley was swamped with donations and offers by scholars to participate. Dean Berkeley even managed a meeting with King George I and secured a charter for the college, to be called St. Paul's, on June 1 that year. Berkeley set sail for Rhode Island, where for three years he socialised with the East Coast pedagogy and tried to raise more funding. But by the time he was ready to pursue the project in Bermuda, the tide of popular opinion in England had turned against any scheme to educate the colonies.

Berkeley was forced to go home; after seven years, his dream had died. However, his good intentions and respect for learning left a legacy—if only in name. In Bermuda, Berkeley Institute was named for him a century later, and seen as the continuation of his plan. In the United States, several Ivy League schools were inspired by his beliefs: the University of California, Berkeley (and its home city) in California bear his name in tribute; Yale named a college for him, and both Columbia University in New York and the University of Pennsylvania were established using his advice.

Education and religion were closely linked in these years, and sermons often took the form of inspirational lectures on topics outside the church.

Birth of the new capital

COLIN BENBOW

Bermudians tended to be a lawless crowd and the avoidance of duty was endemic among the seafaring classes. While St. George's was well-defended and had the only Customs House, ships returning from the Caribbean or US seaboard normally approached Bermuda from the west.

Many captains developed the habit of offloading most of their cargo in coves and inlets (like Mangrove Bay) before reporting to St. George's to pay duty on what was left—that is, if they saw the authorities at all before watering and departing on another voyage. As Governor Henry Hamilton (1788–94) complained to the Under Secretary in London: "To a person who wishes to acquit himself to the approbation of his superiors, it is mortifying to see vessels hovering all day upon the coast, when it is known they only await a convenient opportunity to be piloted to a safe harbour under cover of night or for the coming of sail-boats to lighten them of part of their cargo, unknown to the Revenue Officers."

For much of the second half of the 18th Century, the big debate was between the townsmen of St. George's, clinging to their traditional monopoly, and a growing number of other Bermudians who wished to remove the capital to a more convenient place where smuggling could be countered and trade regularised. Indeed, the matter split the Legislature. All the governor's councillors lived in or near the town and preferred things to remain as they were. The majority of members of the 36-seat Assembly who found travel on non-existent roads, plus a ferry ride to St. George's, uncomfortable, if not downright dangerous, were of a different persuasion.

Crow Lane Harbour seemed a logical alternative. Situated on the south side of Pembroke Parish, it was already being used by local shipping. It was centrally located; it offered some protection against hurricanes and its approaches were being improved by Lt. Hurd's channel surveys. Some people, taking the gamble, had already bought land there.

In 1787, with the Treasury empty and government debts being met by notes payable, the Legislature agreed to petition King George III on behalf of "Pembroke Town," despite a counter petition from the St. Georgians. While the issue dragged on due to the king's ill health, the Assembly set up a committee to examine the terrain, map out the size of the proposed town, advise on land values and ratify the deeds of existing owners.

By May 1790, progress had been made. Naming the new town after Governor Hamilton, who had quietly backed the plan, the committee decided it should be one square mile in size and laid out the unusual colonial grid plan, with streets intersecting at right angles.

The needed land was to be acquired by voluntary conveyance and it was thought that £40 per acre would be suitable remuneration. Negotiations with landowners took place in Mrs. Wright's Coffee Shop at Crow Lane, the nearest building to the site. The property was then divided up into lots (each with 50-foot frontage and 150 feet in depth) and offered at auctions on the basis of one-eighth down and the rest to be repaid over seven years. The committee decided streets were to be 50 feet wide and that structures on the front street should be built more or less in line to give a

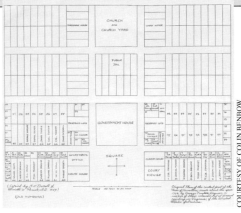

Proposed plan of central Hamilton, 1796

decent visual impression. Certain lots were withheld for government use and land between the front street and harbour was kept for wharves, cranes and cargo sheds.

In 1793, with royal permission granted, the Legislature agreed both towns could incorporate and run their own affairs. Hamilton did so immediately. Already its first major building was under construction; the spacious upper floor of the Customs Warehouse was completed in June 1794. The same year, Daniel Tucker had been elected the town's first mayor.

The new town was up and running with aldermen and common councillors, but little in the way of fanfare. Hamilton, with its new coat-of-arms and motto—*Sparsa Collegit* ("Gather Up the Pieces")—was starting out on the long road to 20th-Century prosperity. In 1793, public utilities and other urban conveniences were still a century away.

■ *Colin Benbow is a Bermudian educator, author and columnist*

Hamilton's waterfront was divided into lots and soon became a busy commercial area

BERMUDA ARCHIVES

BERMUDA ARCHIVES

After Emancipation, most blacks remained in their old employment, albeit paid. These women were nannies to white children

Oxford alumnus George Whitefield, an orator known for his magnetic voice, came to Bermuda in 1748 as a respite from his work in Georgia, where he ran several orphanages. The Evangelist preacher was so popular, he was invited to speak all over the island during his stay, in homes, churches and outdoors, to blacks and whites. Methodist preachers such as Reverend John Stephenson and Joshua Marsden continued the push to educate both races, and by 1832, there were nine Sunday schools, teaching white and black children. The Church of England followed suit, setting up schools of its own.

Chief Justice John Christie Esten was particularly concerned about the need to educate Bermuda's black population after Emancipation. As he saw it, training the children of former slaves was a moral obligation, and in 1837 he proposed a plan to school whites and blacks. While he failed to get the project off the ground, it appears he did sway public thinking, for two years later the government provided the first general grant for white and black education. It was the start of local government commitment towards education. The Elliot School in Devonshire was built by a group of artisans and opened in 1848 with a class of 34 boys and girls, supported by government and the Society for the Promotion of Christian Knowledge.

In 1853, educator William C. Dowding tried to resurrect Dean Berkeley's plan and again won support from English society, including the Archbishop of Canterbury. Dowding came to Bermuda and opened St. Paul's, mainly for black students. But he was criticised by many whites and when Dowding returned to England in 1856 to muster more financing, the school was closed.

A plan to create an elite school for white boys was briefly successful in 1829, when Devonshire College opened with a curriculum based on the classics. It closed a few years later, though some of its buildings were incorporated into St. Brendan's Hospital. Money raised for the college was split into two later projects. A school for white boys, Saltus Grammar School, opened in 1887 at Pembroke Sunday School. And after much debate, the Berkeley Educational Society was founded, with an aim to establish an integrated school. On September 1, 1897, the school opened at Samaritan's Hall, Hamilton. Of the 27 students, only one was white.

Such were the first faltering steps towards creating an education system that would keep Bermuda competitive with the rest of the world. By the century's end, a slate of new schools was founded with long-lasting ambitions for both sexes, among them Bermuda High School for Girls, Mount St. Agnes, Whitney Institute and St. George's Grammar School. While enrolment was restricted to white students, at some institutions through to the 1960s, they would forge a strong foundation for the island's future school system.

TIMELINE *1684–1834*

BERMUDA

1690 The island's population numbers 5,889, of whom 4,152 are white and 1,737 black

1700 The Bermuda 'fleet' counts 60 sloops, six brigantines and at least 400 two-masted boats

1712 Bermudians use more limestone to build houses after heavy hurricanes strike island

1755 Bermuda sells 130,000 bushels of salt a year to North America at height of salt trade

1761 The island is struck by serious slave revolt and smallpox epidemic

1775 Thieves steal gunpowder from St. George's for George Washington's armies

WORLD

1692 Witch trials captivate the community of Salem, Massachusetts

1695 The Ashanti kingdom expands and prospers on West Africa's Gold Coast

1700 Bach, Händel and Vivaldi bring Baroque music to its height in Europe

1759 Britain defeats French forces in Quebec, Canada

1770 Captain James Cook gets to Australia after exploring the South Pacific

1783 Britain and America sign peace accord, making official the United States of America

There were hard times ahead as the economy faltered once again

The Elliot School, Devonshire, opened in 1848, supported by government and a Christian organisation

When the American Revolutionary War came to a close in 1783, trade resumed between Bermuda, the West Indies and America and the island which had almost seen its people starve to death began to thrive. Bermudian entrepreneurial spirit was renewed, and over the next several decades, industrious locals made themselves busy—and rich—once again in their favourite occupations: privateering, shipbuilding and the salt trade.

But time was running out for all three pillars of the island's economy. The various wars of the period brought both advantages and hurdles for island commerce, but larger obstacles were looming that would soon signal an end to this heady period of maritime industry. After the War of 1812, Bermuda ports reopened to US and foreign vessels, which were banned from British ports in the Caribbean. As a result, Bermuda received a much-needed economic boost, not to mention a cash injection from the Admiralty Court established on the island to sort out the many prizes and prisoners involved in booming privateering ventures.

But when West Indian ports were finally opened to North American traders in 1822, Bermuda saw its carrying monopoly fold. Worse, the island had also lost control of the salt industry when the Turks Islands officially became Bahamian territory just after the turn of the century. Bermudian families had already made substantial profits from maritime pursuits, but now even shipbuilding was in decline.

Gradually, less costly American and Canadian vessels operated around the Caribbean, and the advent of steampower would in time put the swift Bermuda sloop out of business. Emancipation was the final nail in the coffin of the shipping and shipbuilding trades, because cheap slave labour could no longer be counted on.

It was the end of an era that had vastly shaped the island's fortunes and forged a Bermudian identity characterised by pluck, innovation and a wily ability to recognise and create profitable ventures. Bermudians would now have to draw on those same qualities to adapt and survive another period of shifting obstacles and opportunities.

BERMUDA					
1784 The premier issue of *The Bermuda Gazette*, the island's first newspaper, is published	**1809** Navy begins work to construct 'Fortress Bermuda' at the Royal Naval Dockyard	**1815** General Assembly meets in new capital, Hamilton, for the first time	**1823** English and Irish convicts are shipped as cheap labour to Dockyard	**1825** Church of England establishes school system for black Bermudians	**1834** Two abolition acts take effect on August 1, ending 200 years of slavery

WORLD					
1796 Smallpox vaccine is introduced to England	**1805** Britain regains supremacy at sea, defeating Napoleon in the Battle of Trafalgar	**1807** British abolish the slave trade, but slavery stays legal for nearly 30 years	**1825** England's first passenger railroad opens; steam-driven locomotives become common	**1832** American Samuel Morse invents the electric telegraph, used to send Morse code	**1837** Queen Victoria's reign begins, launching an era of progress and innovation

BERMUDA MARITIME MUSEUM

BERMUDA ARCHIVES

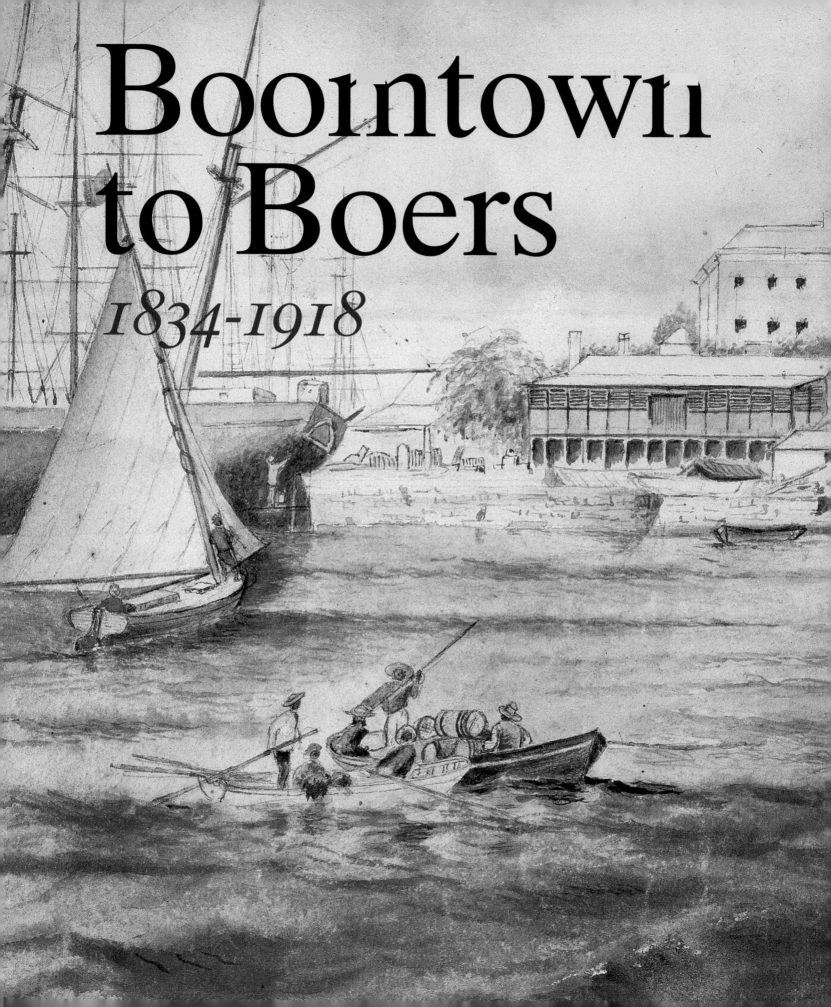

Boomtown to Boers

1834-1918

CHAPTER NINE

From Sea to Soil

CONVICT LABOUR AND THE SHIFT TO AGRICULTURE

As he craned his neck to get a better glimpse of Bermuda from his crowded ship quarters, Irishman John Mitchel was feeling decidedly homesick. It was June 20, 1848, and the 33-year-old native of County Derry, with the rest of the vessel's passengers, had spent the past several weeks journeying across the Atlantic. Even though he was immensely relieved to have finally reached land, Mitchel's first impressions of the island, recorded in a detailed diary, were not exactly glowing.

"Their houses are uniformly white, both walls and roof, but uncomfortable-looking for the want of chimneys; the cooking-house being usually a small detached building," he remarked, painting a drab image of what appeared to him "an unkindly and foreign" land.

"The rocks, wherever laid bare (except those long washed by the sea), are white or cream-coloured. The whole surface of all the islands is made up of hundreds of low hillocks, many of them covered with a pitiful scraggy brush of cedars; and cedars are their only tree," he wrote. "The land not under wood is of a brownish green colour, and of a most naked and arid, hungry and thirsty visage. No wonder: for not one single stream, not one spring, rill or well, gushes, trickles or bubbles in all the 300 isles, with their 3,000 hills. The hills are too low, and the land too narrow, and all the rock is a porous calcerous concretion, which drinks up all the rain that falls on it, and would drink ten times as much, and be thirsty afterwards. Heavens! What a burned and blasted country."

But Mitchel and the other new arrivals were no ordinary visitors. Exiled to Bermuda from Britain, they were among the 9,000 convicts—from petty thieves to brutal murderers and political prisoners like Mitchel—sentenced

Two convict hulks surrounded by British warships at Dockyard

BERMUDA MARITIME MUSEUM

Convicts were housed in old roofed-over warships called hulks, from 1824 to the end of penal exile in 1863

Road to sin *A penal settlement existed until recently in Bermuda, and the convicts were employed to hew out of the rock 120 miles of carriage roads. The question is, 'If these men had not sinned, would the islands be without these roads?'*

—S. G. W. Benjamin, The Atlantic Islands as Resorts of Health and Pleasure, *1878*

to hard labour at Bermuda's Dockyard for four consecutive decades in the 19th Century. Mitchel, an erudite lawyer and journalist, was somewhat of an anomaly among such a motley gang; he had been convicted and sentenced to 14 years' 'transportation' for political reasons after a career of criticising the British government for its failures in dealing with the Irish famine and other social problems. Mitchel's *Jail Journal*, which recorded his lengthy prison custody, including the 10 months he spent in Bermuda, was published in 1854 in *The New York Citizen*, a weekly newspaper he launched after finally escaping with his family from Sydney to America.

Mitchel's diary serves as an inside view of life aboard the dreary prison hulks—old warships stripped of their masts and roofed over as floating prisons. It reflects the monotony of daily life as well as graphic descriptions of the cruel punishments and cramped, dirty living quarters. In one entry, for November 22, 1848, Mitchel recounts the flogging of three would-be escapees. "They are caught, and brought back in heavy irons," he wrote. "One of them was found dressed in women's clothes. The Governor [Charles Elliot] came this morning in person to Ireland Island, though it is Sunday, to give special orders about the mangling of these culprits tomorrow. It is to be a most solemn and terrific butchery."

As a deterrent to others, the trio were ordered "flayed" in all three hulks, receiving 20 lashes each time for a total of 60. "I heard the horrid screams of one man plainly," Mitchel wrote the next day. "After being lashed in the *Medway*, they had all been carried to this ship, with blankets thrown over their bloody backs: and the first of them, after receiving a dozen blows with miserable shrieks, grew weak and swooned: the scourging stopped for about ten minutes while the surgeon used means to revive

How they lived The convicts of Bermuda

Despite mostly fair treatment at the hands of the British Navy, convicts sentenced to years of penal exile at Bermuda suffered hard labour, boredom, disease—and the occasional brutal beating.

A typical eight-hour day saw convicts get up, wash, have breakfast and go to prayers. Morning work hours ran from 7:30 a.m. to noon. Prisoners would be ferried from their hammock-strung sleeping quarters on the hulks to various worksites around Dockyard or St. George's.

After a midday meal break, they went back to work from 1:30 to 5 p.m. Supper, cleaning, washing clothes and prayers filled their evenings. In their spare time, the prisoners made intricate stone carvings and other artifacts, which they sold to supplement their prison wages of three-pence per day. Of that amount, one penny was put toward groceries, another was deducted for wear and tear of clothes, and the remaining sum was held by the commissariat until a convict's sentence expired and he left the island.

"They seldom, if ever, work in the rain or the heat of the sun, while those whose constitutions are delicate, spend much of their time in hospital," wrote Lieutenant E. Mitchell in *The Leisure Hour*, in 1863.

Convicts' daily rations were ample, consisting of: $1\frac{1}{4}$ pounds of uncooked meat such as salt pork, $1\frac{1}{2}$ pounds of bread, potatoes and other vegetables, a few ounces of chocolate and half a gill of rum. Care was taken to feed them adequately to ensure as many fit men as

BERMUDA MARITIME MUSEUM

possible were available to work—a policy that came under fire from some observers. Victorian novelist Anthony Trollope mocked the convicts' lifestyle after a visit to Bermuda in 1859. " 'Look at the prisoners' rations!' the soldiers say in Bermuda when they complain of their own," he later wrote, "and who can answer them?"

Convicts' jobs spanned the entire Dockyard and included both labouring on fortifications as well as general shipping duties. They blasted stone from limestone quarries, coaled ships, refitted vessels, caulked and coppered, built drawbridges

and repaired roads. Some prisoners worked as mat-makers, washermen, shoemakers, barbers and tailors as well as heavy labourers. Some were skilled sawyers, carpenters and smiths. They were outfitted in canvas trousers, smock frocks, straw hats and boots, each labelled with their name and prison. Education was provided to help convicts learn to read and write. Each received a half day a week of schooling in everything from geography to dictation. Convicts who fell ill received medical treatment at an onshore hospital.

Despite such provisions, life as a prisoner was harsh, with floggings for insubordination or escape. "Corporal punishment was rarely inflicted," claimed Lieutenant Mitchell, "but when it was, it was no joke, the convicts being flogged with a heavy naval cat-o-nine-tails, by men, not as soldiers are with a light cat, and by drummer boys. I witnessed one day, a flogging of 14 of these desperados; it was a painful sight, but, under the circumstances, quite necessary."

The convicts' cramped, hot quarters aided the spread of diseases like dysentery and yellow fever. Conditions became so overcrowded and dirty, the government bought Boaz Island in 1854 and built a prison there to house convicts ashore. The dead were buried in a nearby graveyard, their headstones often containing a simple reference to their status as felons:

48 lashes *Convict Henry Johnson (201) will receive 48 lashes according to the Customs and usages of the Service for refusing to perform the work allotted to him on the 4th Instant for inciting others to the like insubordination and for threatening language to the Overseer in presence of the assembled prisoners. His name will be struck off the list of prisoners to be sent to Australia by the Grace of the Crown and he will work in irons till he has expressed contrition for his conduct, without spirit ration. This order will be read to the Prisoners of the respective Hulks.* —*Governor Charles Elliot, March 5, 1848*

In affectionate remembrance of Don Willis, who departed this life November 18th, 1853, aged 27. Deeply regretted by his Fellow Prisoners.

Farewell my friends, we meet no more;
No aid on earth my life could save;
For, banished from my native shore,
In foreign clime I found a grave.

BERMUDA MARITIME MUSEUM

'Only half awake' *The sleepiness of the people appeared to me the most prevailing characteristic of the place. There seemed to be no energy among the natives, no idea of going ahead, none of that principle of constant motion which is found so strongly developed among their great neighbours in the United States. To say that they live for eating and drinking would be to wrong them. They want the energy for gratification of such vicious tastes. To live and die would seem to be enough for them…to live and die as their fathers and mothers did before them, in the same houses, using the same furniture, nurtured on the same food, and enjoying the same immunity from the dangers of excitement.*

~~~

I did not once encounter a piece of meat fit to be eaten, excepting when I dined on rations supplied by the convict establishment. English people whom I met declared that they were unable to get anything to eat. The people, both black and white, seemed to be only half awake. The land is only half cultivated, and hardly half is tilled of that which might be tilled.
—*Anthony Trollope,* The West Indies and the Spanish Main, *1860*

Convicts spent free time carving ornaments from soft stone

him—and then he had the remainder of his allowance. He was then carried groaning out of this ship into the *Coromandel,* instantly stripped again, and cross scarified with another twenty lashes."

Construction of the Royal Naval Dockyard had begun in 1809 with most of the heavy work being done by slaves hired out by their Bermudian owners to the British Navy. After Emancipation in 1834, labour was not so readily available, but Britain had already turned to the cheapest white labour instead, sending thousands of English and Irish convicts from crowded prisons to penal colonies in Gibraltar, Australia, Bermuda and Spike Island in Ireland. Sentenced to hard labour under the Royal Navy and Royal Engineers, the first batch of 300 prisoners arrived at Bermuda in 1824 aboard HMS *Antelope.* Convicts would be sent here until 1863 when penal exile was abolished.

As many as 2,500 convicts were stationed in Bermuda at any one time and for most of the period were housed on the hulks. Over the years, seven such hulks arrived at the island and became ominous landmarks: the *Antelope* in 1824, *Dromedary* in 1826, *Coromandel* in 1827, *Weymouth* in 1829, *Tenedos* in 1843, *Thames* in 1844, and *Medway* in 1848. The first five were moored at Ireland Island, within a stone breakwater that formed a camber or harbour; the *Thames* and *Medway* stayed at St. George's. Paid threepence a day, convicts would be kept busy in gangs quarrying stone, building bridges and storehouses and carrying out regular dockyard work like repairing ships, diving and handling cargoes.

Reports on convict conditions vary, but despite the brutality of beatings like the one Mitchel describes, history would seem to indicate that most prisoners were adequately cared for, with decent food, schooling and medical attention. Some imprisoned Irish, accustomed to famine at home, were astonished to receive so much food. However, their cramped quarters in the airless hulks did become a breeding ground for tropical diseases like yellow fever. The convicts were prone to epidemics which frequently ravaged Bermuda, killing close to a quarter of their population.

After the drama of the American wars and the sweeping social change of Emancipation, Bermuda fell back into life as a sleepy backwater, largely isolated from the outside world. Like Mitchel, foreign visitors of the mid-19th Century—mostly military officers posted to the island— were less than enchanted by the tiny colony which many claimed was rife with heat, disease, lethargic locals and strange flora and fauna.

Typical was the letter Featherstone Osler wrote to his father on October 12, 1828 from HMS *Tribune.* In it, the naval officer condescendingly described the island as a "miserable hole which is chiefly populated by convicts," an outpost swarming with "musquetoes…almost as thick as bees" and where dinner in the capital comprised nothing more appetising than "starved fowl and a little ham and eggs."

The leisurely pace of life was doing Bermudians no favours, either. Rather than enjoying a prosperous new era, peacetime saw the island slipping into the economic doldrums. The salt-trade monopoly was over and ship-building had been dealt a lethal blow by a bold newcomer—steam power. Early industrial steam engines designed by Thomas Newcomen and James Watt had long been used in European and American mines and factories. But as the Industrial Revolution gained pace, they were also being adapted

A place of 'dread pestilence'

Nineteenth-Century life embraced a mixed share of gradual progress and debilitating pitfalls. The island's increased contact with other nations via trade and travel brought economic and social advantages, along with fresh ideas and new citizens. But it also opened the door to virulent infectious diseases which the primitive medical knowledge of the time was poorly equipped to deal with.

Bermuda was considered far healthier a destination than West Indian islands, but the age was one of widespread insanitary conditions and poor personal hygiene, which allowed scourges to linger for months and sometimes wipe out entire families or regiments, indiscriminately killing all ages, the rich and poor, black and white. In the worst epidemics, hundreds might die in a single year. Typhoid, measles, smallpox, yellow fever, cholera and influenza ravaged the island for more than 200 years.

Smallpox epidemics hit the island in 1701, 1761, 1782 and '83, disfiguring victims and filling local graveyards. But it was yellow fever, a tropical blood disease carried by mosquitoes, which proved a perennial menace to the island, breaking out in 1699, 1779 and 1796, and sweeping the parishes throughout the 1800s. A particularly severe outbreak occurred in 1819 in St. George's, as well as in 1837, 1843, 1856 and 1864. Known as "yellow jack" after the flag which ships hoisted when carrying contagious sufferers, yellow fever came to Bermuda via the West Indies or America and flared during summer. Superstition blamed its spread on everything from comet sightings to low tides.

In the 1700s, yellow fever was known as "Gaol Fever" and blamed on the crowded and dirty jail conditions of the time. Medical authorities suspected infected bedding of French sailors—thrown overboard, washed ashore and re-used—as the cause. The 1819 attack saw a quarter of the garrison fall prey, including 170 soldiers, 34 women and children, 43 civilians and 42 seamen.

One of the hardest-hit groups was the convict community. The prison hulks moored off Dockyard were rife with disease, due to crowded, dirty conditions that allowed infection to spread rapidly among the inhabitants. Around 1843, 119 prisoners died. A decade later, another particularly bad outbreak occurred, affecting mostly convicts and garrison troops. In St. George's, a third of the 339 soldiers were casualties, reducing the number of available guards. Troops were moved to Prospect, which brought an end to the fever, perhaps thanks to the distance from infected ships.

Later in the century, when the US Civil War made St. George's a hotbed of activity, yellow fever again hit hard. Medical records pointed an accusing finger at the town's poor living conditions, as St. George's was in a "filthy state, having no drains or sewers, cess-pits abounding and the streets filled with abominable odours, rendered worse by the mass of shipping in the harbour and the large numbers of dissipated, dirty sailors, who were generally to be seen on shore, more or less intoxicated and always in a perpetual state of debauch." The second battalion of the 2nd Regiment lost 120 of 148 soldiers, and across the island a total of 513 people died. From 1860–67, soldiers stationed at Bermuda were said to suffer the highest death rate of any posting in the world, with the exception of China.

Stories of such "dread pestilence" cast Bermuda as a disease-ridden backwater in the eyes of many foreigners observers. It was no consolation when Henry Tapp, author of the island's first tourist guide, published in 1852, contracted yellow fever. He died the following year.

In their own words
■ Anonymous, *1843*

Bermuda, 20th October, 1843: A dreadful and treacherous fever has made its appearance in these lovely isles—and now amidst our cedar forests and lemon groves, is truly heard the voice of lamentation. In tracing the origin of the disease at this time, the prevailing opinion ascribes its importation to the royal West Indian mail steamers. It broke out in St. George's about the beginning of August—extending to the barracks, convict hulk and magnificent fortifications which nearly cover that island. Soon after, it appeared at Ireland Island, in the hulks, and also in the naval yard. Finally it found its way to the town and barracks of Hamilton.

I would not recall the harrowing scenes, which presented themselves while the grave was closing over all ranks without distinction, nor the individual suffering and grief while the fever raged for two months with uncontrolled fury. One scene I cannot omit, as it affected all spectators: The chaplain in St. George's, whose duty it was to perform the burial service, day and night, without intermission, having on one occasion 16 coffins placed before him, was quite unmanned and wept aloud.

The barracks are now deserted, and the splendid band of the 20th Regiment, which used to perform on the Hamilton Parade every Tuesday, is heard only in subdued and mournful tones, accompanying the remains of some gallant soldier to the tomb. These military funerals, especially in the calm and bright moonlight, and amidst the volleys of musketry, are exceedingly solemn and impressive…I fear upwards of 300 have already perished.

—*A letter from Bermuda published in* The Inverness Courier

In their own words

■ John Harvey Darrell, *1819*

About Sunset on the evening of the 9th of September, 1819, I landed at St. George's, Bermuda. We had been becalmed for eight or 10 days within 70 miles of the land. I, having spoken to a vessel lately come out, was somewhat prepared for the dismal scene which awaited us on our landing, though the reality seemed even to exceed our terrified apprehensions. The Yellow Fever, which had appeared here the last year, returned again this Summer, and was now raging with a malignancy almost beyond what even it assumes in climates more frequently visited but it. It seemed, too, to have confined itself to the Town. And though to embark from a crowded little vessel, after a Voyage of almost ten weeks upon the Sea, to reach the Shore, and that, too, my native shore, is a luxury of the highest order—yet never can I forget the horror that thrilled thro' me on beholding the situation of the Town;—its streets deserted, its houses vacant, silence and solemnity prevailing even amongst the shipping that lay at their moorings. The fever, the dead, and the dying, were the topics, the only topics of enquiry or communication.

Dying almost with impatience to learn the fate of my friends, I flew on to a Gentleman's House, where I was intimately acquainted. But it was closed and forsaken. Returning, I met one of the servants, who told me that her Master, Mistress and Family had fled into the country to avoid the Fever, as it was thought to be less prevalent there. But some were dead—who, she knew not. I hurried on to another friend's, which was also deserted, to a

third, and that was the same—and indeed, three parts of the Town seemed stripped of its Inhabitants.

At length I found a house which seemed still inhabited. I entered the Porch. Nobody answered my knocking: I passed on, and after crossing three or four rooms in which the disorder of the furniture left it doubtful whether its possessors were alive or not, was recognised, with a burst of joy, by a Lady who darted from an adjoining Apartment. In her surprise, she drew

Officers of the 39th Regiment of Foot stationed in Bermuda in 1859. Hundreds of British soldiers died in epidemics on the island

me in to see her Son of whose recovery there was some hope. But recollecting the danger to me she sent me suddenly from the Chamber, expressing her anguish that I should have arrived at Bermuda in such a fatal conjunction, for almost all the English and those lately from England had fallen victims to the Fever. She told me, too, who had died and who recovered. That six or eight persons had been buried every day for several weeks; but, which to me was of the first importance, my friends were all well in the country a few days

past. Another Lady whom I saw told me how fortunate she had been to lose only one of her darling children. And not an individual that I met but had had a loss in his family—though it was wonderful to observe with what levity they bore it, as if it were more astonishing that some were left alive than that many had died.

I shall not enlarge upon the difficulty I found in procuring a Horse to carry me an Hour from this scene of confusion. Suffice it to say, that after all my pains, on arriving at the Ferry, it was so late and the weather so dark and rainy that I was unable to cross the Ferry and was compelled to turn back and lodge for the night at Cedar Hill. No fewer than seven persons were then confined at that House with the Fever. One favourite Servant Girl, brought from England to attend upon Miss T(ill), had died a few days before, and this very night a Mr. Gibbons, to whom it was supposed Miss T(ill) was attached, breathed his last at his Lodgings in Town. Miss T. went the same path, deceasing three weeks afterwards. I need not say that this night, spent by me watching the tedious hours, seemed the longest that I had ever known— though at break of day, I continued my journey, crossed the Ferry and actually set foot in our breakfast parlour when the family were just assembled, before one of them suspected that I was come, or even on my way to them.

The happiness of such a return is one of those occurrences which does not happen twice in one's lifetime. After such an absence, to meet my Parents, my Sisters and Brothers in perfect health, amid such dreadful visitations of the stroke of Destiny, was indeed a joy!

—John Harvey Darrell, returning to Bermuda after several years in England

First steamboat *The Steam Boat* **Marco Bozzaris** *quitted our port for St. George, with her paddles in full operation. Her owner condescendingly plied her up and down the harbour of Hamilton several times for the gratification and amusement of its inhabitants. The* **Marco Bozzaris** *is the first steamer that ever came to these Islands; she naturally excited much curiosity.*

—The Royal Gazette,
January 7, 1834

Almost nil *Today agriculture is almost nil in Bermuda; formerly it flourished. The actual inhabitants employ the few negroes they have to cultivate vegetables and maize and to raise poultry. They have very few animals and I have only seen a dozen cows on the island. Provisions of all kinds are so rare and so expensive that the warships which come continually to Bermuda are only able to procure some potatoes and onions. On the streets one meets very few people and the inhabitants appear extremely indolent. In the town there are only five or six merchants who sell at great cost groceries, hardware and drapery. Americans bring to the country planks, maize, flour, butter and some other provisions for which one pays cash.*

—*French botanist François Michaux,
writing in the* Annals of the
Museum of Natural History, *Paris,
after a 1806 visit to the island*

All quiet *Bermuda is a quiet land where I have heard people ask: Did you hear the dog barking yesterday? Two carriages in St. George's on the same day would be an exceptional event.*

—*English adventurer
J. W. Boddam-Whetham, 1879*

BERMUDA ARCHIVES

Bermuda's shipbuilders began to suffer as European steamships took over

for use at sea. The Royal Navy was cautious and took many years to fully embrace the new technology. But before long, British and American businessmen saw the commercial potential of steam. The days of sail were far from over, and sailing ships would continue to ply the oceans in decreasing numbers for at least another century. But their days were numbered.

For Bermuda, it spelled economic disaster. Bermuda sloops had long been the envy of the maritime world, but gradually island shipyards began to close as steamships from Europe and North America took over their trade routes. Many Bermudians continued to go to sea, offering their skills in home waters and around the globe. But the once-proud shipbuilding industry had begun its slide into obscurity.

Bermudians also faced a growing crisis ashore—though many failed to recognise it. While the embargoes of the American Revolutionary War had starkly illustrated the dire consequences of the island's lack of food production, Bermudians still had not addressed the problem. Instead, they faced a perennial shortage of food assuaged only by costly, and politically precarious, imports from the United States. Economically, Bermuda was also dependent —on English taxpayers, for money was pouring in to finance construction of the British Naval Dockyard, up to £200,000 a year. But as for self-sustaining industry, the island had none.

Strong leadership was needed to shift the island's narrow economic focus to suit the challenges ahead. Luckily, the right candidate for such a job arrived from Britain in 1839. Governor William Reid would be remembered as the "Good Governor" for his empathy, enthusiasm and innovative energy. His seven-year tenure would witness the arrival of new technology and immigrants, which together would guide islanders' fortunes for the next half-century from the sea to the soil.

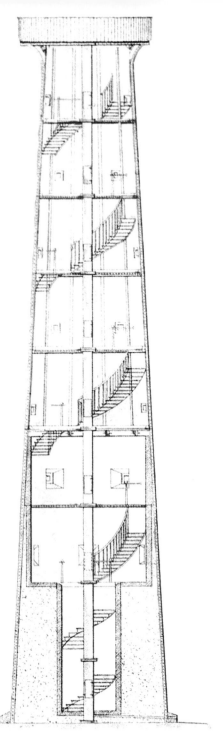

Lieutenant-Colonel William Reid was the first governor to be sent to Bermuda following the young Queen Victoria's 1837 ascension to the throne, and it was perhaps fitting that under a monarch who would come to define an Empire driven by the inventive capitalism of the Industrial Revolution, he embodied a keen understanding of science, machines and economics. In Britain, it was a time of rapid progress, a period that saw the country evolve rapidly into the world's first industrial power. Vast prosperity was built on a wave of scientific inventions such as the spinning jenny, the powered loom and various steam-powered machines, and these, in turn, gave birth to factory networks and a more sophisticated economy. Canals, railroads and steamships changed the scale of transportation, linking the nation's cities and bringing farflung communities closer, while advances in sanitation, medicine and agriculture saw Britain's population nearly triple between 1750 and 1850 to more than 20 million.

No doubt Reid came to Bermuda infused with the buzz of such exciting times, and his zeal proved contagious to the whole island. The multi-talented governor was instrumental in bringing numerous 'firsts' to Bermuda. He

Governor William Reid

Cast a light *The Ship with the Cast Iron Light House for Gibbs Hill arrived at Ireland Island on Wednesday last from London, and on Saturday proceeded through Stagg's Channel to Port Royal. The Light, which will be a revolving one, will stand at an elevation of 375 feet above the level of the Sea, and will be a most brilliant one. This will be the second Iron Light House in the world.*

—The Royal Gazette, *November 26, 1844*

After Reid's wake-up call, Bermuda onions became a profitable export

The cast-iron Gibbs Hill Lighthouse was shipped in pieces from Britain
BERMUDA ARCHIVES

BERMUDA MEDIA

Ready for inspection in a garrison bunkhouse

pushed for the creation of a public library, which opened in the Secretariat building with 276 volumes dedicated to science, shipbuilding and history. He had the channels to local harbours cut deeper, opening the island to larger ships in a bid to boost exports. And he undertook the construction of a revolutionary lighthouse, whose 30-mile lamp would help prevent shipwrecks on the island's infamous reefs. Gibbs Hill Lighthouse, erected from pre-fabricated panels shipped from England, was first lit on May 1, 1846. Under his administration, also, the British Army moved ahead on plans to locate its garrison at Prospect, buying up strategic Devonshire land to house a large camp for the mobile reserve. Reid, for whom Reid Street (formerly "Second Street") was named, was also a world authority on hurricanes. The author of *Law of Storms*, he had long studied weather prediction and had helped Barbados rebuild after a devastating seven-hour hurricane in 1831. But he had never experienced a hurricane first-hand until one hit Bermuda on September 12, 1839. It was not a deadly storm, but was later dubbed "Reid's Hurricane" out of respect for his passion for such tempests.

Reid's main challenge was coaxing Bermudians to switch their attentions from maritime pursuits to feeding themselves. He was dismayed when he arrived to find a population of 11,000 whose agricultural system was in a shambles. Few Bermudians had any personal interest in farming—a fact underscored by the existence of just two ploughs on the entire island. The US was Bermuda's main food source—and Reid recognised that could quickly lead to starvation in the face of frequent wars and blockades. He wasted no time in introducing new farming methods along with the latest tools and equipment, and he also imported many species of plants and trees. Indeed, the gardens of his official residence at Mount Langton boasted exotica such as gru gru palms, India rubber trees, bamboos and wampee and litchi trees, which Reid planted around 1841. More importantly, he helped rekindle Bermudians' interest in agriculture by holding events like ploughing contests and launching an annual Agricultural Exhibition, which continues as a public fair. Before long, crops like arrowroot, potatoes, squash, tomatoes and the Bermuda onion were being harvested.

But the island's most urgent need was for skilled agricultural workers to kick-start the industry and teach Bermudians how to earn a living from their land. Reid convinced the island legislature to fund immigrants from Europe, at first identifying Britons and Germans as good candidates. Under Reid's successor, Charles Elliot, the new policy would focus on the Portuguese farmers of Madeira and the Azores whose emigration would bring lasting benefits. Over time, the

As agriculture blossomed, lilies became an important export product and thousands were grown each year

> ## *Playing on 'vurds'*
>
> Bermudians of the 19th Century were said to speak with a pronounced drawl and their writing displayed a plethora of parochial spelling, which captured much of the dialect that still identifies a native-born islander: *bad* for bed, *chears* for chairs, *fathers* for feathers, *fur* for far, *sarvis* for service, *gaile* for girl, *Bir*-muda, *pint* for point, *owld* for old, *wedo* for widow, *hondred* for hundred and *hur* for her.

changes fuelled enough agricultural production to satisfy both home consumption and exports: Bermudian arrowroot, potatoes, onions and tomatoes would become highly sought in overseas markets, generating precious income for the island through to the start of the 1900s.

By the time his governorship ended in 1846, Reid could be proud his efforts had turned around the island's economic prospects, invigorated Bermudian farming, and, as a direct result, had encouraged a rise in Bermuda's population after a 65-year decline.

The old horse ferry to Coney Island

CHAPTER TEN

The Portuguese

IMMIGRANTS FORGE A THRIVING NEW COMMUNITY

Naomi and Manuel DeCouto in 1924 with their children, a Portuguese-Bermudian family which emigrated to Fall River, Massachusetts. At right, Naomi's parents, Bermuda immigrants Frank Medeiros Simon and his wife Antoinette

COURTESY OF ROBERT PIRES

COURTESY OF ROBERT PIRES

COURTESY OF ROBERT PIRES

I n the 1880s, a 30-year-old farmer named Frank Medeiros Simon traded life on one remote Atlantic island for another. Both islands were important whaling hubs, military outposts and ports of call for mariners. Yet in every other way, they were worlds apart. In São Miguel, the Azores, Simon bid farewell to his wife Antoinette and their five children and sailed west to Bermuda a thousand miles away. In a foreign culture where he neither spoke the language nor understood British customs, he got busy building a new life, one rooted in the harvests of Bermuda onions, potatoes and arrowroot.

In 1890, a few years after his arrival, Simon sent for his family to join him and over the next two decades, they prospered and grew. Frank and Antoinette would have seven more sons and daughters, whose lives and those of their children and grandchildren were infused with common threads of community activism, intellectual thought and indefatigable industry. Today, the names of their descendants—Marshall, Mello, Pires, Souza, DeCouto, Barboza, Johnson, Correia, Martin—touch family roots throughout Bermuda's Portuguese community.

The names and circumstances may change, but Simon's story is that of many ancestors of Portuguese-Bermudians. His journey followed the 1849 path of Bermuda's first Portuguese immigrants and would be repeated thousands of times in the following century and a half as the story of Portuguese emigration unfolded. Like communities in the United States, Canada and elsewhere, Bermuda offered a better future for migrants fleeing poverty and persecution, but the island also desperately needed their agricultural and work skills and reaped the rewards.

"The benefit I look forward to from your introducing a few European

Portuguese families patronised the studio of photographer Nicholas Lusher in the early 1900s. Centre left, Samuel (son of Frank) and Carrie Simon c. 1920

agricultural labourers," Governor William Reid told the House of Assembly in September 1845, "is not so much from the amount of additional labour which may be thereby obtained, as from these persons bringing with them habits of active industry, improved methods of applying manual labour and combining with it the labour of cattle and mechanical contrivances."

It was Reid's closing speech to the House after a seven-year governorship that had injected energy to the colony after a lethargic few decades following the American wars. Most notably, he had laid firm foundations for a shift of the island's withering economy—one that for the next half-century would see Bermudians put less emphasis on maritime pursuits and instead make their living from the land. They would not only become more self-reliant by growing their own produce for local consumption, but before the end of the century, Bermudian exports of island-grown crops would generate a major new source of income. Reid had reinvented the art of agriculture in Bermudian eyes, bringing new farming tools and machinery to the island and convincing people they had a stake in making it work. Lastly, he recommended the House provide for what he felt was the most important ingredient in his plan—skilled labour

Governor Charles Elliot

*A proud Portuguese couple
in their wedding attire*

BERMUDA ARCHIVES

Tomato coup

*A distinguished farmer of one
of the lower Parishes [east of
Devonshire], sent to New York
lately a small soapbox, not quite
full, of Bermuda tomatoes, and the
same was sold in that city for Eight
shillings and four pence. This
vegetable can be grown throughout
the year in Bermuda, by the tun,
and sold by the tun in New York
during the half-year when the far
and wide outstretching region,
of which that rising city is the
emporium, is ice-bound and
cheerless.*

—The Royal Gazette, *June 13, 1848*

from overseas—and he urged his successor, Charles Elliot, to support the policy.

"The chief object," Reid reasoned, "in bringing in new agricultural settlers should be, in my opinion, to re-implant here those arts in agriculture which have been gradually lost from the time the people of these islands betook themselves exclusively to seafaring habits."

Reid's suggestion that Bermuda entice European workers opened the door for the Portuguese, known for their work ethic and agricultural talents. The House took little convincing; strong measures were needed to revitalise Bermuda, and Reid and his progressive ideas were popular. Within two years, the legislature voted to offer £400 in bounties to vessels bringing Portuguese settlers to be indentured farm labourers. Willing captains obliged. On August 14, 1849, an advertisement in *The Royal Gazette* asked Bermudians to sign up to employ farm labourers and house servants who would be shipped from Madeira aboard Captain Benjamin Watlington's brigantine *Golden Rule*. On November 4 that year, the first boatload of 58 Portuguese arrived.

Reid had guessed accurately that such a recommendation would pay off handsomely for the island in the short-term. But he could not have predicted how far-reaching his efforts would prove for Bermuda's future. And not only for its economy. Reid's policies would re-shape the island's social, ethnic and cultural heritage—bringing into its community a new people to build families, learn new vocations and establish vibrant traditions under the inclusive umbrella of 'Bermudian' culture. The handful of peasant labourers in 1849 would form the vanguard of a 150-year influx of Portuguese citizens, from Madeira, Cape Verde and the Azores, which then were known as the "Western Islands." In time, Portuguese-Bermudians would become doctors, lawyers, architects and educators, making up close to a quarter of the island's population and forming an enduring link with the wide diaspora of Portuguese people throughout the world.

Bermuda's connection with the Portuguese began more than 300 years earlier. During the 15th and 16th Centuries—the Age of Discovery which marked the zenith of Portugal's imperialism—the island served as a navigational landmark for seafarers on their homeward journeys from New World forays. Many Portuguese, like their Spanish, French and British counterparts, were shipwrecked on Bermuda during that period, and some survived thanks to the cache of natural provisions they found on the "Isle of Devils." Later, in the 1700s and 1800s, Portuguese whalers and seamen were frequent visitors to Bermuda aboard passing vessels.

The Portuguese laid claim to a seafaring legacy, yet it was their understanding of the earth that brought them to Bermuda and North America in later years. By the 18th Century, many Portuguese were emigrating across the Atlantic from the impoverished islands of Madeira and the Azores. Many of the first migrants headed for Brazil or the Caribbean; others followed to America and Canada, forming close-knit communities in Rhode Island, New England (New Bedford and Fall River, Massachusetts, for example) and Newfoundland, where their whaling and farming skills were appreciated.

Bermuda was an attractive alternative for Madeirans and Azoreans, skilled island farmers who were familiar with the Atlantic environment. Their islands presented neat parallels with Bermuda: all were whaling hubs and Atlantic ports of call for maritime trade and travel. All were deserted islands before being discovered and settled between the 1400s and 1600s.

And just as Bermuda was to Britain, so Madeira and the Azores became outposts of Portugal's maritime empire, providing strategic ports and much-needed provisions for westward expansion. In subsequent years, the Azores, like Bermuda, would become a military base and weather station.

Mountainous and forested, Madeira is named for the Portuguese word for 'wood.' Located 360 miles west of Morocco, the archipelago was discovered in 1419 after Portugal's maritime exploration of the African coast. Infante Dom Henrique, "Prince Henry the Navigator," ordered Madeira colonised as part of his programme of financed maritime expeditions. Eight-hundred miles west of Portugal, the Azores were known to Arab navigators of the 12th Century, but settlement did not occur until 1432 when Portuguese captain Gonçalo Velho named them for the hawks, or birds of prey, which flocked around his vessel. The nine islands of the Azores—Santa Maria, São Miguel, Faial, Pico, São Jorge, Terceira, Graciosa, Flores and Corvo—are scattered over 500 miles of ocean and their people comprise a melting pot of ethnicities and religions, including an early Flemish heritage.

By the 19th Century, though, Madeira, Cape Verde and the Azores were suffering from failing economies. In the Azores, emigration was particularly fuelled by a blight that wiped out the islands' vineyard and orange groves, propelling farmers across the Atlantic to carve out better lives for their families. Bermuda, with its virgin farming tracts, advertised labour shortage, and relatively rich work contracts, fed their dreams. The colony must have seemed like a land of plenty to eager Portuguese farmers and their families, who wasted no time in signing up to emigrate.

Captain "B. W. Watlington Esq. contemplates sending his vessel—the *Golden Rule*—to Madeira for Immigrants, and has, we understand, a List containing applications for 50 persons," read the August 28, 1849 advertisement in *The Gazette*. "The Report of Lord Harris, Governor of Trinidad, speaks in favourable terms of the Portuguese Immigrants in that Colony. At Bermuda, inhabitants of Madeira would find very nearly their own climate, and probably more profitable employment than they could in their own country."

TO
Farmers, Householders, &c.

FOR MADEIRA,
TO RETURN DIRECT,
With a Number of Farming Labor-
ers and House Servants.

The Brigantine
GOLDEN RULE,
Will be Despatched on or about the 20th Inst., for the ABOVE PORT, for the purpose of procuring GOOD LABOURERS for Farming purposes, &c.

Persons desirous of Subscribing for them will please make *Immediate* application to Mr. CHAS. H. GILBERT, or to the SUBSCRIBER who will furnish them with every information ; a part of the Number have been already Subscribed for.—A Sum for passage money is allowed from the Immigration Fund.

B. W. WATLINGTON.
Hamilton, August 14th, 1849.

EMIGRANTS FROM MADEIRA.— The Brigt. Golden Rule, Captain Watlington, arrived on Sunday evening last, in 21 days from Madeira, with fifty-eight emigrants —7 children, 16 women and the remainder male adults. They are all engaged to persons residing in various parts of the Island. We understand they are an orderly and well-behaved people and were obtained chiefly from the country. We sincerely trust this importation of laborers will answer the end contemplated ; and we hope they will be the means of inducing the cultivation of the vine more extensively than at present.

The *Golden Rule*
The Watlington ship Golden Rule *brought the first Madeiran immigrants to Bermuda in 1849, the beginning of the island's Portuguese community*

How they lived

Portuguese immigrants brought a wealth of new customs and culture when they came to live in Bermuda. Their language, religions, cuisine, sport, horticulture and family traditions gradually permeated island life beginning in 1849, and over the next century and a half would help shape Bermuda's modern identity. While generations of Portuguese bridged the cultural gap, the community also kept alive its distinctive heritage.

A strong work ethic and tight family bonds were the hallmarks of the migrant community, as new arrivals laboured long hours to provide a better life for their families. The dream of a prosperous future became reality for many who, in time, came to run their own businesses, buy homes and land, win Bermudian status and carve out a stake

COURTESY OF SANDRA ROUJA

Portuguese waitresses c. 1925

NIGEL RICHARDSON

A colourful festa decoration

in the island's political and economic future.

Traditionally a patriarchal society, the Portuguese respected men as the family heads, and unmarried sons were expected to help support their parents and siblings. Women cooked and cleaned and raised large families, aided by daughters and female relatives. As was typical in European farming communities of the time, children were

expected to contribute to family earnings, and youngsters, like their adult relatives, worked long days on Bermudian farms.

The Portuguese heritage introduced dishes such as chourico (spicy sausage), São Jorge cheese, cozido (stew), polvo (octopus), and baked goods such as malacádas (sugar doughnuts) and massa cevada (egg bread) to the island's culinary lexicon. Its colourful religious festivals (or

festas) honouring saints and the Holy Trinity have also become popular spectacles. While Bermuda's Portuguese are mostly Roman Catholic, Evangelical and Seventh Day Adventist denominations also have a strong following.

Unfortunately, years of prejudices sidelined Portuguese immigrants from island society, casting a stigma over generations of men, women and children who often felt pressured to abandon their native language and ideas in favour of assimilation. In later years, however, Bermudians of Portuguese descent have reclaimed their heritage and the island is proud of a community now estimated as close to 20 percent of the population. By the end of the 20th Century, Portuguese was used in newspaper advertisements, exhibits, banks and other public facilities.

Early onions *I was delighted to see Bermuda fresh Vegetables in the Washington Market, and immediately shook hands with the large Onions mentioned in last week's Albion. Bermuda sends her stuff sooner to us in the season than Charleston; so get your Steamer going as soon as possible. Tell the Bermuda Ladies of every degree that early Onions, peas and potatoes will, in New York, buy them Silk Dresses and satin Bonnets…*
—*Letter from a New York resident to a friend in Bermuda, reprinted in* The Royal Gazette, *August 3, 1847*

The government's immigration fund underwrote the voyage. Its main targets, based on Governor Reid's recommendation, were farm labourers, but Bermudian subscribers also sought domestic workers to carry out household duties. Two weeks later, the *Golden Rule*, captained by Watlington's nephew John Thomas Watlington, set sail for Madeira. And less than two months later, on Sunday, November 6, the ship returned to Hamilton carrying the first Portuguese arrivals.

"The Brigt. *Golden Rule*, Capt. Watlington, arrived on Sunday last, in 21 days from Madeira, with 58 emigrants—seven children, 16 women and the reminder male adults," reported *The Gazette*. "They are all engaged to persons residing in various parts of the Island. We understand they are an orderly and well-behaved people and were obtained chiefly from the country. We sincerely trust this importation will answer the end contemplated and we hope they will induce the cultivation of the vine more extensively than at present."

Salaries offered to the new immigrants were meagre, but compared to their previous livelihoods, the Bermuda contracts offered hope for a fresh start. Adult workers would be paid £12 a year, women £8, and children £2— meagre sums, yet more than they could earn in their homeland. For their part, the Watlingtons were paid £274.10s for making the journey.

BERMUDA MARITIME MUSEUM: PAINTING BY JOSEPH MONK

*Portuguese whaler António
Marshall and his crew rowed to
the rescue of 33 people when the
vessel* Pollokshields *ran aground
off the South Shore in 1915*

Very industrious *I have
had frequent conversations with
Gentlemen now here that have been
residing in Demerara a number of
years; they speak very highly of the
Portuguese. A Portuguese will live
entirely on Onions and Potatoes
(articles that we have in abundance)
and are a very industrious race.
They can be imported here in
10 weeks.*

—*Letter to the editor,* The Royal
Gazette, *August 23, 1847*

The Madeira immigrants quickly established themselves as willing
and skilled workers, and their hard labour was instrumental in the
push to revitalise Bermuda's agriculture. By the 1860s, even more
Portuguese followed, from the Cape Verde islands and the Azores. By 1851,
just two years after the first immigrants' arrival, productivity was on the
upswing—and the largest-ever cargo of produce sailed to New York: 1,075
barrels of potatoes, 491 barrels of onions, 17,900 pounds of onions in baskets
and loose, 550 boxes of tomatoes and 2,681 pounds of arrowroot.

As agriculture began to thrive, the legislature looked to other sources
to import labour. In 1850, it voted to allow an additional £200 to bring more
immigrants—this time from the United Kingdom. Two years later, the
British government offered Bermuda workers from the Hebridean island of
Skye, off Scotland's northwest coast. But the immigrants did not stay. Similar
attempts to import agricultural labour from Germany and Sweden were
mostly unsuccessful. Small groups of Swedes were brought to the island in
1872 and '78, but remained only a short period.

The later part of the century saw a steady drift of Portuguese immigrants
to Bermuda. From 1849–80, most immigrants came from Madeira; later
decades saw a shift to the Azores. Their names are found on passenger lists
from visiting vessels such as the *San Francisco*, the *Canima* and *Beta*, as well
as ships travelling from New York. Some arrived directly from Massachusetts,
where towns like New Bedford and Fall River had strong Portuguese
communities. Throughout the 1880s and '90s, records show a total of 69
immigration applications for Portuguese workers to the government; of
those, 59 were submitted by Portuguese residents themselves—indicating

COURTESY OF ABEL CABRAL

COURTESY OF SANDRA ROUJA

DEPARTMENT OF COMMUNICATION

COURTESY OF ABEL CABRAL

Portuguese immigrants quickly brought new vigour to agriculture

Thrifty, intelligent

We have a great many Portuguese in these islands and they are, on the whole, a thrifty, intelligent and progressive element. Scarcely more than a generation ago the first of them began to settle down in this Colony; thenceforth a steady influx continued. We are lucky in having attracted to Bermuda so desirable a class of people and it is noted with satisfaction that they are prospering in a money way and earning that reward which their industry and knowledge of farming entitles them to.

—*Editorial,* The Royal Gazette, *1917*

many sponsored friends and relatives to follow them to Bermuda. On arrival, they joined a tight community network which served to aid newcomers as they settled in. Slowly, through work, marriage and community interaction, the Portuguese began to adapt and enter the fabric of Bermudian life.

Some of the new immigrants owned property, but most Portuguese planters leased acres of land from Bermudian landlords, and farmed these tracts for a wide array of produce—primarily lilies, onions, potatoes and arrowroot. Some spent the winters farming in Bermuda, and worked during the summers in New Bedford, but over the years more began to put down permanent roots on the island. Many Portuguese came to Bermuda under contract; some brought their wives and families to also work—including children as young as five. Portuguese workers became so popular, the government passed a law in 1856 banning the "enticement of a contract immigrant" from one employer to another.

By the 1870s, the island's export trade had developed to a level that was generating a handsome income for government, with an average 70,000 barrels and 350,000 crates of onions, among other products, shipped annually to the US. Portuguese emigrants continued to pour in; in 1878, a total of 350 arrived. The number of Portuguese employed in agriculture grew steadily: from

DEPARTMENT OF COMMUNICATION

*Arrowroot awaits shipment
on St. David's Island*

1,290 in 1871, to 2,477 in 1881 and 3,054 in 1891. Bermuda's economy, thanks to its new Portuguese residents, had been revitalised once again.

By the turn of the century, many Portuguese had become naturalised Bermudians, bringing relatives to the island, purchasing homes and land, and hiring immigrant workers of their own from the Azores. Agriculture continued to be the focus of Portuguese workers until the height of Bermuda's export production the 1920s, when most of the island's farms were owned by Portuguese residents. The island's liberal immigration policies during this period allowed for an open-door system between Bermuda and the Azores—a scenario that would change later in the 20th Century when restrictive measures on immigrants, particularly the Portuguese, began to be enforced.

Most Portuguese workers were recruited as planters and farm labourers, especially during the manpower shortages of the First World War. After the 1920s, the island would continue to need workers for farming, but also for large construction projects such as renovations to the Dockyard, the building of the Causeway and Kindley Field airbase, and the development of Tucker's Town.

The Evangelists

Three Azorean brothers helped spur the spread of evangelism among Bermuda's largely Roman Catholic Portuguese community.

José, Augusto and João Paulo emigrated to the US from the Azorean island of São Miguel in 1881. When Augusto moved to Bermuda two years later, he had converted from Catholicism, bringing Gospel teachings he had learned from the Salvation Army in America. As a layman missionary, he was known among agricultural workers for preaching evangelism, the Protestant school that believes in the doctrine of salvation by faith. Augusto was joined by his brothers and the trio led lively religious debates at the Paget farm, Tankfield, attended by a growing Portuguese following.

More Azorean missionaries came to Bermuda and evangelical services were held around the island, from living-room Sunday schools to open-air baptisms at Devonshire Bay, which drew both converts and critics. In December 1890, the Church of God was established with a congregation of 11 members. It would become the Evangelical Church of Bermuda, now at Mission Road, Paget.

BERMUDA ARCHIVES

Portuguese farmers helped make the Bermuda onion a famous commodity

In their own words
■ Sandra Rouja

Documents tell us more than what is written. The very appearance of a signature on a document can have surprising revelations. Having always heard "Vovo," my maternal Portuguese grandfather, could neither read nor write, I was surprised to find his signature on his Certificate of (Bermuda) Naturalisation dated August 1924.

When I showed it to my mother, she said, "Well, of course, I remember us teaching him to write his name so he could sign that certificate. We would sit around the dining room table every night until he got it right." I have a mental image of him in my mind; strong, quiet, handsome, at age 52 the head of a household of 11 children.

Manuel DeCosta Silva, c. 1924

COURTESY OF SANDRA ROUJA

He has just finished his dinner after a long day on the farm and is tired, but he is not relaxing. He is trying to master his hand around a pen instead of a hoe so that when he takes the oath to become 'a Bermudian' he can proudly sign his name instead of making an 'X.'

—Sandra Rouja, grand-daughter of Southampton farmer Manuel DeCosta Silva, born November 1, 1873, in São Miguel, the Azores. He was granted Bermudian status in 1924

In the early 1900s, the pattern of Azorean immigration to Bermuda mirrored the influx to the US and Canada, and entrenched networks of migrant workers helped ease new immigrants into North American society. Portuguese communities grew strong in Toronto, Montreal and Boston—and each developed lasting familial and community links with Bermuda's own Portuguese. In Bermuda, the Azorean community continued to expand and schools like Mount St. Agnes opened to cater to the growing Roman Catholic population. Portuguese radio kept the community informed and Portuguese social clubs were established. As generations grew up on the island, fewer Portuguese children followed the farming footsteps of their fathers and grandfathers. By the 1920s, second- and third-generation Portuguese worked in a wide array of careers, as hospital attendants, police officers, construction labourers, grocers, sailors, plumbers. Gradually, children travelled overseas for education and returned as trained professionals—doctors, lawyers, educators—who became an integral and influential part of Bermuda society.

The Portuguese celebrated their distinctive heritage and held firm to their language, their cuisine, their social events and religious festivals, and like other immigrant segments of island life—the West Indians, and later the Filipinos—they would become important parts of Bermuda's overall culture. Bermudians found the Azoreans to be an industrious and conservative people whose driving ambition was simply a better life for themselves and their families. Many sent money earned in Bermuda back to the Azores to support relatives left behind; others returned with enough saved wages to buy farms of their own. But in time, thousands of Portuguese people would come to call Bermuda home.

Portuguese were industrious and conservative

COURTESY OF ABEL CABRAL

Going to church by horse and buggy, c. 1927

COURTESY OF ROBERT PIRES

The Portuguese had become an intrinsic part of Bermudian life, and their input and influence would grow as the island developed through the 20th Century. When agricultural exports, the island's economic mainstay for more than 50 years, began to decline and finally disappeared, Portuguese-Bermudians, like their fellow islanders, would have to find another way forward to survive and prosper.

The fight for rights

If I'm good enough to work, I'm good enough to stay here," remarked dairyman Anthony Barboza in a poignant plea to remain on the island in 1966. Barboza, who had come to Bermuda from the Azores as a contract farm labourer and had lived and worked on the island for eight years, was being refused naturalisation papers by the government. The reason? Because he could not read.

Sadly, his case was not uncommon. Azorean immigrants struggled against blatant discrimination by Bermudians, not only in the form of social barriers, but also bureaucratic ones. Bermuda's government imposed strict regulations from the 1920s onwards aimed at banning the immigration of whole families and restricting those workers who were permitted to enter the country to farming and menial labour.

Although most Portuguese were far removed from their peasant roots by this era, social prejudices also persisted against them. Banned from many of the island's white social clubs, the Portuguese community formed the Vasco da Gama Club, which became a refuge for its members. The club organised festive and sporting events, helped newcomers network into island life, provided healthcare support and led lobbying efforts to

secure Portuguese residents the same rights afforded immigrants of other nationalities.

After the Second World War, Portuguese families were banned from joining relatives already working in Bermuda—the so-called "no-wives rule." The policy meant long separations for Azorean men from their wives and children; most sent home their earnings to loved ones left behind and hoped one day they could join them. In April 1957, Bermuda and Lisbon signed an agreement allowing wives and dependent children to move to the island, but only

Done more *The Portuguese have done more for this Colony in the last 50 years than any other people, including the British.* —*J.E.P. Vesey, MCP House of Assembly, 1959*

House Votes Down Immigration of Portuguese Wives

There is to be no change in the "no wives" rule for Portuguese labourers in Bermuda.

The House of Assembly decided this on Friday when by a vote of 16-13 they threw out the report of a committee headed by Mr. Morris Gibbons.

It was Mr. Gibbons' second try — and second defeat — within a year on the question of Portuguese wives.

Why can't the law be the same so that we are like others who immigrate?
—*Wife of Portuguese resident worker in Bermuda on the severe regulations imposed on Azorean emigrant families,*
The Royal Gazette, *January 26, 1966*

after workers had spent seven years in Bermuda. Officials cited housing and population pressures, but Portuguese families felt unjustly discriminated against, since other European immigrants, notably British workers, faced

no such restrictions.

Monsignor Felipe Macedo, a Catholic priest and the Portuguese Vice-Consul in Bermuda, became an heroic ally of the community during these years. He gave a voice to the unheard community—most of whom were afraid of the repercussions of complaining—and was outspoken in his criticism of the lack of rights for Portuguese workers and their families. For example, Portuguese workers were interrogated by the Currency Exchange Control Board, he said. They were asked why they were sending money home, rather than placing it in island

banks. "One man with no family in the Azores was told that since he had no dependents, he had no business sending money and should keep it here," reported *The Royal Gazette*. Such ethnic discrimination saw years of hardship and legal confrontations. The community eventually formed the Portuguese-Bermudian Association to carry on the lobby effort, particularly the fight for the rights of long-term residents.

Employment freedom for Portuguese workers was restricted for decades, keeping many immigrants confined to jobs as farmers, cleaners or gardeners until later in the 20th Century. It was not until 1982 that the job-category restriction was lifted. A year later, the government ordered an end to all labour discrimination against the Portuguese.

Club together *Portuguese may now enter the Colony only under strict Government surveillance and control, and then may only stay for a limited period. Supposing Joe, Manuel and Pete come here for farm work, they are apt to club together and live as frugally as possible, doing their own cooking, acting as house-wives when not out in the fields, often living in done-over out-houses or barns, where a negligible rent is charged by the land-owner or farm-owner. Their pay? Well, probably one-half or two-thirds goes back to the little wife in the Azores, as none may bring in either wife or children under recent legislation.* —The Bermudian, *1938*

CHAPTER ELEVEN

American Civil War

BLOCKADE-RUNNERS BRING FLEETING FORTUNE

Georgiana Gholson Walker, who braved the Union blockade to be with her husband in Bermuda

BERMUDA NATIONAL TRUST

In March 1863, a 29-year-old Southern belle set out on a brief journey that could have been considered either an act of commendable audacity or an incredibly foolish stunt. Six months pregnant and with her three young children in tow, Georgiana Gholson Walker boarded the blockade-runner *Cornubia* in Wilmington, North Carolina and set off in a bid to successfully dodge a fleet of enemy vessels and reach Bermuda. It was the middle of the American Civil War, and Walker's husband, Major Norman Stewart Walker, had spent the past four months on the island in his new post as political agent for the besieged Confederacy. Desperate to see him again, she ignored the advice of friends and convinced the ship's captain to take her on the daring escapade. "No one gave me one word of encouragement or hope," she later wrote, "except that brave and blessed friend—my Father, who said, 'My child, you are in the path of duty, I doubt not all will be well.'"

No woman had ever run the Union blockade, but the plucky Petersburg, Virginia native, daughter of lawyer and politician George Saunders Gholson, was determined to try. The dangers were substantial. The captain "laid plainly before me the perils of the trip, saying that the last vessel which had gone out had just been captured, that the Northern Fleet was large and stationed for many miles out. I said nevertheless I should go," she recalled in her journal. As the ship prepared to sail, the Confederate general in command in Wilmington came on board to urge her to reconsider, as did her good friend, the wife of Confederate president Jefferson Davis. She "besought me to consider my children, if not myself, and to return to Richmond." But Walker was resolute, though privately she admitted "occasional misgivings as I looked upon my innocents and thought of the dangers to which I was going to expose them. But I had weighed the matter well and I believed it to be my duty."

Walker and her children—eight-year-old Carey, nicknamed "Lillie," Norman Stewart, Jr., seven, and Georgie Gholson, two—boarded the ship on March 18 and with the captain and crew, waited for the safety of nightfall.

St. George's became a bustling boomtown as Bermudians rushed to meet the needs of blockade-runners

Most important *Bermuda is the most important of our naval stations in the Atlantic. Its central position in that ocean, within three days steaming distance of the shores of North America, its dockyard, its capacious deep-water harbours, together with its natural capabilities for defence, contribute to render it the citadel of our naval power in the western world. There is reason to believe that the desire of the Americans for its possession is in proportion to its value to this country.*
—*Colonel William F. Drummond Jervois, Royal Engineers*

"I did not altogether relish these 'deeds of darkness,'" she remarked. "There is a feeling of wounded pride, that we must seek the protection of the night, and slip by our foes as noiselessly as we can. We feel that this should not be the necessity of a nation, a noble and proud nation, as is the Confederate States! Oh for a few staunch 'Iron clads' that we could dash in among these Yankee hirelings and scatter them to the winds and then steam out in the broad light of day."

The crew prepared a cloak of secrecy; portholes were closed and blanketed, the skylight was covered and lights extinguished. Letters and important Confederate dispatches were collected together in a weighted bag so that, should the ship be captured, they could be quickly disposed of. As preparations were underway, Walker sat in the saloon with Lillie on one side of her, "Normy" on the other and Georgie on her lap, trying to distract them with

Major Norman Stewart Walker

stories. Finally, the *Cornubia* crept stealthily out of port to test her luck in the waters of war. The captain kept his passenger informed of their progress. "We have passed one blockader, Madame," he called to Walker from the saloon door. The ship passed another, then another, and the captain kept up a running commentary. After a couple of hours, the anxious mother, along with the rest of the ship, could breathe in relief. The *Cornubia* had evaded the entire Northern fleet; the rest of the journey would be relatively safe.

Four days later, on Sunday, March 22, land was spotted and Walker and the ship entered St. George's Harbour. "What a perfect vision of beauty it seemed to my wearied heart!" she exclaimed. "Wearied by the cares and sufferings of my troubled country and sickened by the separation from my Husband. I thought I had never seen so lovely a spot: the little white cottages dotting the green hills in the distance; the beautiful white village on the side of the water, with the

BERMUDA NATIONAL TRUST

THE BERMUDIAN

The Union gunboats Tioga *and* Sonoma *blockaded Bermuda in 1863, prompting fears Britain would enter the war. Inset, the* Tioga *crew*

Great spoils *The inhabitants are well satisfied with their government, and the large amounts of money circulated among them by the Sailors and Soldiers, tends to sustain and increase that spirit. They anticipate great spoils in case of another war with the United States. The opinion is prevalent, that the Americans are very desirous of obtaining possession of these islands, and they are particularly jealous and distrustful of American visitors, and also of Frenchmen, whom they consider as our probable allies. They boast, however, that their isles have remained in obscurity, until their defences have become strong enough to defy the world.*
—*US secret agent Albert Fitz, in his report,* The Naval and Military Strength of the British West India Islands, *1842*

magnificent hill rising at the back." As they approached the town, she asked a sailor to hoist her youngest high above his shoulders—a greeting to alert her husband his family had arrived.

Georgiana came to the island as Bermuda was warming to its role as a key trans-shipment hub for the Confederate States, and the high activity, intrigue, prosperity and gaiety of those years would be chronicled in her journal. It was a time of overnight fortune, booming industry and reckless derring-do, a dramatic wakeup call for the erstwhile sleepy island, which suddenly found itself playing a strategic role on the international stage. Georgiana's journey, an impudent dash across the treacherous 674-mile stretch of Atlantic, would be repeated hundreds of times by others in both directions over the next two years as Southern vessels defied the Yankee siege—and sought Bermuda's help to win their cause.

Peace had been shattered on April 12, 1861 when the United States plunged into civil war. Over the next four years, until April 1865, the nation would tear itself apart in a chilling spectacle of blood-letting that would represent a grim foreshadow of modern mechanised warfare. The so-called "American War of Secession" pitted southern Confederate States against northern Unionists in a bitter conflict which was rooted in the socio-economic split between the North and South, but ignited directly by the federal push to abolish slavery as southern states took steps towards independence.

It was the first modern war, with more than 2,400 battles and over 600,000 dead—the greatest combat casualties until the First World War a half-century later. At stake for the South was its agrarian economy, supported by the labour-heavy plantation system of agriculture that relied on slavery to survive. The North, in its push for abolition, was also fighting for the concept

Royal thanks *Gentlemen,*

In thanking you for the kind welcome which you have given me, and for your loyal address, I do so with the same sentiments of gratitude which I have always experienced upon similar occasions. It is true that Bermuda is but a small colony, but I am well aware of the spirit of loyalty with which its inhabitants are actuated; and the reception which they have afforded me, is a pleasing indication of the affection which they bear towards the Queen, and one which I shall not fail to communicate to Her Majesty. From their geographical position and configuration, the importance of these Islands to the Mother country cannot be overrated, and I shall always regard them with a peculiar interest, from the benefits which our navy and commerce derive from their harbours and resources. I thank you sincerely for your prayers for my prosperity in my profession.

—Reply to Members of Council by Prince Alfred, Duke of Edinburgh, May 1861

of country itself—the clash between federal power and state rights to self-determination. Bermuda was on the sidelines, a non-combatant which nevertheless would play a major role in the struggle, thanks to its location.

Britain, and by extension, its colony Bermuda, officially declared itself neutral in the conflict. Queen Victoria's May 13, 1861 proclamation barred "all British subjects from taking part, or participating in any way whatsoever, either by land or sea, in existing hostilities between the United States and the Confederate States." Later royal proclamations banned the export of military supplies from Britain to the North or South. But such orders were ignored, for in reality, the British strongly favoured the rebel South, because of its cotton supply for England's mills. For Bermuda, the war was more personal. For generations, Bermudians kept close contact with America, particularly the South. Many locals had relatives there and trade had always been brisk between Southern ports and the island. Now Bermudians found themselves perfectly placed as a staging post for a daring group of seafarers —the blockade-runners.

Anxious to quickly choke the rebels, Union President Abraham Lincoln moved to cut off their lifeline to the world. The South was the world's major cotton exporter, and Lincoln urgently needed to prevent the Confederacy selling cotton as a means to fund shipments of weapons and supplies. Within days of the war's outbreak, he ordered a huge naval blockade of southern ports.

Southern strategists recognised the move as potentially crippling, and Confederate States reacted quickly to circumvent economic strangulation. Swift steamers began running the Yankee blockade of "men-of-war" gunboats. These blockade-runners carried food, munitions, even luxury consumer items, to the South from Europe, Canada and the US in return for bales of raw cotton. The precious cotton would be shipped via wharves in Bermuda —as well as Nassau and Havana—for England, where it was destined for Lancashire's textile mills. As the cotton supply became scarce, cotton prices skyrocketed and "white gold" became the coveted currency of war.

British-US tensions mounted throughout these years and several flare-ups could have plunged Britain into war— more than likely on the side of the Confederates. While there were several minor incidents with Union captains trying to blockade Bermuda, their clandestine antics never amounted to anything more serious, leaving Bermudians free to line their pockets while they could.

Rapidly, the war brought about the sudden transformation of the island of 11,000 people from a place of relative poverty and isolation to a thriving

Seal of the Confederacy

Bermuda played a part in the secret trans-Atlantic shipment of the Great Seal of the Confederacy during the US Civil War. The Congress of the Confederate States ordered the seal's manufacture in Britain in April 1863, for use as an independent stamp for all Southern documents. The seal was smuggled back to America via Halifax and Bermuda before a blockade-runner carried it on to Richmond, Virginia. After several failed attempts, the last leg of the journey was finally completed in August 1864. But the seal press and wax, which had been sent with it from England, were left behind in Bermuda, and copies of the historic item were made and remain in local collections today. The seal depicted George Washington on horseback encircled by a crop-decorated wreath of cotton, tobacco and sugarcane. It bore the date, February 22, 1862—marking the inaugural session of the Confederate Congress, and Washington's birthday. Made of silver, the seal also carried the Latin motto, *Deo Vindice*, or "God Will Judge."

In their own words

■ US Consul Charles Maxwell Allen, *1861*

Dec. 30, 1861

For some days I have been in a very unsettled state as regards to my remaining here. Everybody here thinks there is no escape from war between England and the United States and if it should prove so, of course I should be compelled to leave but I am more hopeful than most others and think the difficulties will in some way be settled without War. The present state of things makes it very unpleasant for me here just now as there is very bitter feeling against everything and everybody belonging to the United States and many here seem to go upon the supposition that I am responsible for the whole difficulty. I have learned to keep quiet and enter into no arguments. Every hole and corner is filled with Southerners.

The military men of whom there are a great many are very busy and I am informed that they have been at work all day today making "cartridges and mounting guns." They seem to be of the opinion that our people will be after this island first thing. I told them at the dinner table today that "they need have no fear, as our people would not have such a God-forsaken place as this if they could get it for nothing."

March 10, 1862

We had news from Charleston that the "South had whipped the Northern Army and killed and taken them all prisoners." There was great rejoicing here and everyone seemed to believe it. Next day a steamer came from New York with some days' later news and it appeared that the victory was on the other side but no one would believe it. It is wonderful to see how ready they are to believe anything that favours the South and disbelieve anything that favours the North. The fact is they are afraid of the growth of our country and want to see it divided. I don't know of a person here that expresses an idea that the States will ever be united again. I have no patience to talk with them so I have learned to keep quiet and enter into no arguments. Every hole and corner is filled up with Southerners, some have left today but there are plenty left. If they will only catch the steamers *Bermuda* and *Stettin* that have gone today, I shall be thankful.

July 15, 1862

I had my flagstaff cut down on 3rd July so could not hoist my flag on the 4th.

You complain of loneliness when you are surrounded by friends; what can you think of me in such a God-forsaken place as this with scarcely one friendly person to speak to? I have once been attacked in my office and once knocked down in the street within a few days; the general sentiment is: "It's good enough for him; he's a damn Yankee."

—*From Allen's letters to his wife in Alleghany County, New York*

Expert pilots *Taking an elevated position in the ship, up the shrouds, in the top, or on the forecastle, and by the appearance of the bottom, they direct the course of the vessel. It must be insisted on that only the practised eye of the Bermudian pilots can be depended on for conducting a ship safely. The pilots are the most expert I ever met.*
—*Alex G. Findlay, FRGS,*
Description of the Bermudas
or Somers Islands; with
Nautical Directions, *1864*

crucible of wealth, industry and cosmopolitan affairs. Foreigners poured into the island, from captains seeking well-paying work to merchants, political agents and spies. Meantime, Bermudians' innate commercial greed took full advantage of what, for the island, was a serendipitous event. By the winter of 1861–62, Bermuda's flagging economy was already eyeing the prospect of a turnaround. By 1863, the island had become an important entrepôt for the Confederates. Indeed, Union commander Charles Wilkes declared Bermuda the "principal depot of arms and munitions of war" for blockade-runners— some 1,800 of which would stop at Bermuda over the four-year period. The good fortune wouldn't last long, but while it did, Bermudians would ride a giddy wave of prosperity.

Supplies for the rebels were brought into Bermuda (or Nassau or Havana) from Europe on regular large vessels, then transferred to smaller ships that made the fast dash to Confederate ports like Wilmington, always hoping to elude the line of Union warships blocking their path. At first, regular coastal packets made uneventful runs to Wilmington and easily evaded enemy ships. But when the Union reinforced its blockade, throwing a tight defensive line across the approaches to southern ports, Confederate States had to devise an even craftier tactic.

The blockade-runners in Bermuda commissioned specially-built ships to take on the challenge. These were fast, sleek, mostly paddlewheel vessels between 100 and 900 tons with shallow drafts to help them slip across sandbars off the Confederate coast. Many were designed with collapsible smokestacks, which could also blow off steam underwater to make them less visible to the enemy. All were camouflaged a dull lead colour—and even roosters were forbidden in the ships' poultry cargoes, for fear their crowing might tip off the enemy. The blockade-runners made desperate dashes to port on moonless nights, preferably at high tide, their lights extinguished as they slipped under the noses of Union crews.

Once safely ashore, the runners exchanged their cargoes for cotton, and prepared for the dangerous run back to Bermuda. Some blockade-runners made their daring passages out of patriotism, but most were driven by the lure of riches. Blockade-running was the most profitable business of its day,

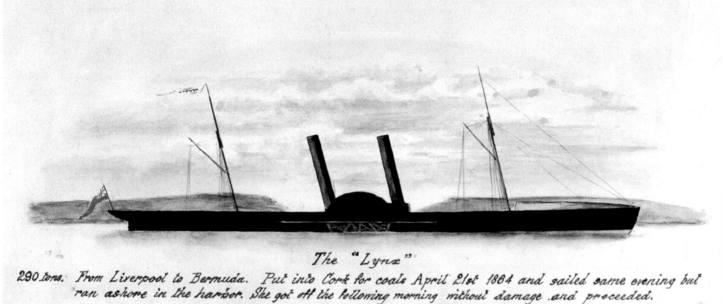

The "Lynx"

290 tons. From Liverpool to Bermuda. Put into Cork for coals April 21st 1864 and sailed same evening but ran ashore in the harbor. She got off the following morning without damage and proceeded.

ST. GEORGE'S HISTORICAL SOCIETY

The sleek, low-riding Lynx *was specially designed for blockade-running*

with a single bale of cotton likely to make $500 profit. Captains could make $5,000 a journey—a terrific sum that attracted many Royal Navy officers who took leave to earn a fortune. Two well-known Bermudian captains involved in blockade-running were Hezekiah Frith, who ferried a cargo of boots and shoes to Wilmington aboard his schooner the *Harkaway*, and Jeremiah Peniston, who served as a pilot on the *Cornubia*, the same vessel that transported Georgiana Walker to the island. Crews usually comprised of foreigners, including Bermudians, would make more money than they had ever dreamed possible. The runners stacked their ships high with cotton bales, making tens of thousands of dollars on each successful run, often many more times the worth of the ship itself.

On paper, cargoes from Bermuda were cleared for Nassau, but this bureaucratic sleight of hand saw goods delivered directly to the South, most frequently to the nearest major port, Wilmington. Only in the last months of 1864, did Halifax eclipse Bermuda as the key hub for blockade-runners after the island, along with Nassau, was stricken by another epidemic of yellow fever.

BERMUDA NATIONAL TRUST

Joseph Hayne Rainey

Born a slave in South Carolina, Joseph Hayne Rainey fled to Bermuda during the US Civil War aboard a blockade-runner. Many slaves escaped to the safety of British soil in this way, and most usually sailed back to the US to live as free men and women in the North. But Rainey and his wife Susan decided to stay on the island: he opened a barber shop (Barber's Alley in St. George's pays tribute to him today), while his wife, a talented dressmaker, started a business making fashionable clothes for the island's socialites.

The couple fled the 1865 yellow-fever epidemic to Hamilton, where Rainey continued to work as a barber, and bartender, at the Hamilton Hotel. He was also respected in the community as an officer of Alexandrina Lodge, No. 1026.

But Rainey became best known after the war, when he returned to the South and ran for public office. A South Carolina Republican, he was among the first black members of the US House of Representatives.

St. George's became the focus of blockade-running activity, and was soon transformed from a quiet village into a hurly-burly boomtown. Its proximity to the open sea made it a more popular port than Hamilton, which nevertheless saw its share of vessels connected to the war. Only decades earlier, Hamilton had become the new capital of Bermuda, taking over the role from St. George's. But now the old town reclaimed its energy and status as the island's commercial centre. Steamers packed the harbour at anchor and their crews swarmed the streets, laden with cash payments and ready to spend. Hundreds of Bermudians from other parishes also moved east to snare jobs and higher wages. The town's warehouses were used to store cotton awaiting trans-shipment, as well as large quantities of Welsh coal—180 tons of which was required by blockade-runners for every voyage.

Local businesses made small fortunes supplying everything the newcomers needed, from food and lodging to supplies and ferrymen. Bermudian pilots were in great demand to guide the blockade-runners through the reefs. Local craftsmen such as carpenters offered their skills and Bermuda sailors often signed on as crew, anxious to line their pockets with the huge profits possible from a successful blockade run, even it meant ending up as prisoners of war in Union prisons, as often happened. As well as manpower, the runners needed many other things, all of which Bermudians eagerly provided. Local rents doubled and prices for all manner of goods went through the roof.

BERMUDA NATIONAL TRUST

John Tory Bourne made a fortune from the war as a shipping agent

The first Bermudian to realise fortunes were to be made was shipping agent John Tory Bourne, who became middleman for a large English shipping company that sent supplies to Confederate merchants. At first, Bourne stockpiled hundreds of tons of coal; then he leased Penno's Wharf and began warehousing cargoes destined for Wilmington. After a while, the merchants relied on Bourne heavily, even asking him for advice on what goods the Confederates would want each trip. Bourne and his family made so much money that within two years he bought a large mansion, Rose Hill.

A huge assortment of mail and goods passed through St. George's on the way to the rebels: gunpowder, ammunition, rifles, swords, uniforms, boots, saddles, blankets, medicine and tons of food were shipped. The Great Seal of the Confederacy was brought from England via Bermuda, although the press it was made on never made it past the island, where it remains. Bourne and other agents even found room in their cargoes for luxury goods that could be sold for exorbitant prices in Confederate cities.

The demand was so great, local merchants could barely keep up, and eventually the Confederate government decided to send its own agent to

In their own words

■ Blockade-runner T. L. Outerbridge, *1864*

I was in the steamer *Robert E. Lee*. We left Wilmington, North Carolina, one night about 9 o'clock, just as the moon was rising, so as to have high water to get over the bar, because she could only cross at that time. She was about the largest boat running the blockade and drew most water. With the moon rising, we found ourselves among the Blockade Squadron just in time for them to make us out.

In a few minutes we saw two men-of-war, one on our right and one on our left. They began to fire big cannon shot at us, twenty-four in all. One struck our deck, hitting the bulwark forward of the sponson and the winch, splitting it into a thousand pieces. The foreigners on board were all sitting around the winch and several were severely wounded. The men-of-war soon came near enough to fire small arms at us, but strange to say, no one was hit.

The captain, Wilkinson by name, all this time was walking up and down the bridge, to all appearances paying no attention to them whatever. While the firing was going on, the mate, myself and the rest of the crew were on the fo'c'sle looking for other craft. One of the round shot came so close to me that I was made unconscious for a time. The others ran away. Next day I was praised by the officers for not running off; I didn't tell them I couldn't run. Not a man was hit although we could pick the bullets out of the wood all round where we had been.

I'll tell you about my experiences in the steamer *Siren*. She was a small boat which the British government had used for running about Bermuda but they had condemned her and she was then sold to Mr. Fininsey, Confederate Consul, who was in Bermuda. He bought her to send to Wilmington and her crew were to bring back the steamer *Cape of Good Hope*, which was being used as a passenger ship between Smithfield and Wilmington.

The *Cape of Good Hope* was a large boat and their idea was to load her with cotton for Bermuda and use the *Siren* for running between Wilmington and Smithfield.

Capt. Jeremiah Peniston went as Master of the *Siren*; my brother, Eldon Outerbridge, was First Officer, I was Second Officer, and Mr. Tabb, a gentleman from Virginia, was Purser. After a passage of seven days, we reached Bowford, North Carolina. We proceeded down the coast under sail towards Cape Fear, thinking this would deceive the blockaders. After going along about an hour, the man-of-war *Key Stone State* came up and spoke to us,

The Robert E. Lee, *which was eventually captured by Union warships in 1863*

ordering us to heave to, which we did. They sent a boat, took us in tow, carried us into Bowford Harbour and anchored us close to a receiving ship. The officers of the *Key Stone State* laughed at us for trying to run the blockade in such a vessel.

We were sent to Camp Hamilton where we came under military authority. The treatment there was very severe. After being there four days, we were called out into the yard and those who were masons were picked out and sent to New York. The rest of us went to Point Lookout Prison where about fifteen-thousand Confederate soldiers were imprisoned. We were stripped and all our possessions taken with the promise that all would be returned when we came out.

Point Lookout was a hard-looking place. It was a mile square, boarded up with planks to a height of fifteen feet. Four

feet from the top was a platform where soldiers were stationed every thirty feet. These were coloured men which the North had taken from the South and made soldiers. They delighted in shooting Southerners. Every morning we saw fifteen or twenty who had been shot during the night.

We were given half a loaf of bread a day and three times a week a quarter pound of fresh beef. All the time we were there, about two months, we had to sleep in the open. Fortunately for us, my brother Eldon, while being searched, managed to conceal a sovereign under his tongue. This money enabled us with economy to buy from settlers outside the camp. They were stationed where we could buy through a little hole in the fence. We wrote several letters to Lord Lyons, the British Ambassador in Washington, asking him to get us released but he never received them; they were all torn up or burnt.

At last, Mr. Tabb, our Purser, with the help of the Chaplain, managed to get a letter through to Lord Lyons. He interceded for us at once and we were soon let loose to come to Bermuda. We were given enough money to take us to New York and there we went to Mr. Middleton, the Bermuda agent. Mr. Middleton told us Capt. William Peniston was at New York in his Barque *Lapflerene*. He was going to Bermuda and wanted a crew.

Accordingly, we went to the wharf and saw Capt. Peniston who welcomed us, saying "Boys, come along with me. I'm going to Bermuda and you're welcome."

—Bermudian blockade-runner Captain T. L. Outerbridge on his capture by the Union

James captured a spectacular cotton-bale fire at Penno's Wharf, as well as more leisurely scenes

COURTESY OF JOHN COX

ST. GEORGE'S HISTORICAL SOCIETY

Painting the news ■ Artist Edward James, *1861–67*

Edward James was a prolific English watercolourist who chronicled on canvas much of Civil War-era life in Bermuda. The arrival of blockade-runners, sinking ships, the fiery sabotage of a cotton cargo, town festivals, the opening of the East-End Causeway—all were subjects of James's paintings during his 16 years on the island, from 1861–77,

when he died at 57 of a stroke.

James worked as a Crown surveyor during his first few years in Bermuda, but after losing that job in 1865, he turned to painting full-time. Based in St. George's, the hub of social and commercial activity during the Civil War years, he sold his sketches and paintings to tourists and locals, and also gave art lessons to Bermudian students.

His paintings, many of which remain in local collections, are noteworthy for the way they captured daily life and historic events of the period. Many of the characters he painted into his scenes were facsimiles of real islanders; indeed, a man in a wide-brimmed hat and yellow jacket portrayed in one well-known work (pictured above, left) is believed to be the painter himself.

Mr. Edward James,

BEGS to announce that he has now accumula-
ted a complete Collection of **DRAW-
INGS** of the Various STEAMERS and other
VESSELS, now, and recently visiting the Port
of St. Georges. The prices of these Sketches vary
from 10s. 6d. up to £3 3s.
Specimens are to be seen at the Store of Mr.
JOSEPH F. PICKERING, Water Street, St. Georges.
List of Drawings so far made :—

C. S. S. Florida	Gibraltar
Robert E. Lee	Beauregard
A. D. Vauce	Lady Davis
Eugenie	Banshee
Phantom	Venus
Gladiator	Mirian
Hansa	Ella & Annie
Harriet Pinkuey	Phœbe
Nashville	Merrimac
Adela	Londona
Quachita	Minho
Herald	Emma

September 14, 1863.

James's newspaper advertisement offering for sale his drawings of vessels visiting St. George's

Bermuda to take charge. Major Norman S. Walker, Georgiana's husband, had joined the Confederate Army as a soldier at the start of the war in 1861, and had quickly risen through the ranks. Arriving in November 1862, he set up Confederate operations at the Globe Hotel and began his duties. While Bourne continued to handle the commercial details of supplying the Confederates, Walker acted as political agent for the transfer of cargoes consigned for the South. He also handled cotton shipments to England via the old town, helped procure coal for the Confederate navy and blockade-runners, and took care of stranded Confederates on the island.

By the time Georgiana joined him, the Walkers were the lifeblood of the boisterous Confederate community in Bermuda, and their lavish parties made them favourites among Bermuda society. The Walker family lived first in the Globe Hotel, and then in a nearby cottage, where on June 15, 1863, their fourth child was born. His name paid tribute to their temporary home: Randolph St. George.

Walker was the political nemesis of US Consul Charles Maxwell Allen, the Union's man in Bermuda during these years. Surrounded by rebel

The Globe Hotel, where Confederate Agent Norman Walker made his home and office

BERMUDA NATIONAL TRUST

Bermudian soldier

One of the negroes is a remarkably sprightly fellow from Bermuda where he was educated as a soldier. His position is that of an Orderly Sergeant, but he has lost an arm, and probably one leg will go. A third of the "glory" for which he says he came to fight, being thus amputated, he will in the future be a wiser man.

—Dispatch from the army correspondent, Weekly Columbus Enquirer, *Columbus, Georgia, July 28, 1863*

sympathisers, Allen had an impossible task as he tried to remind Bermudians of their supposed neutrality. However, he stuck to it through the duration of the war, despite numerous pranks, death threats, and even physical assault. He constantly petitioned the Governor, Colonel Harry St. George Ord, when he saw flagrant breaches of the rules, helped escaped Union prisoners who made their way to Bermuda, and also took care of runaway Southern slaves who stowed away on returning blockade-runners' ships. Yet despite the harsh treatment, Allen loved Bermuda and after the war, he retired to live in Flatts Village for the rest of his life.

Confederate crews and stranded Union sailors prowled the countless drinking dens of St. George's town and violence often flared. The Army garrison was frequently called out to quell trouble, sometimes between black Bermudian workers and pro-slavery Confederate crews. But the biggest threat to Bermudian residents and visitors during the war's later years was yellow fever. A deadly outbreak of the epidemic between mid-1864–65 saw nearly 3,000 people contract the disease, with over 500 fatalities, more than a third in St. George's. For ships arriving from Europe and the US, the scourge was dreaded.

"We landed 1,140 bales of cotton at Bermuda, and it was after we started back for Wilmington that the horrid yellow fever broke out among us," recounted Captain Augustus Roberts, of the 400-ton steamer *Don*. "I believe that every precaution was taken by the government of the island to prevent the disease from spreading, but, increased by the drunkenness, dissipation and dirty habits of the crews of the blockade-runners, and the wretchedly bad drainage of the town of St. George, it had lately broken out with great violence and had spread like wildfire both on shore and among

BERMUDA ARCHIVES

A Confederate star flutters over King's Square in pro-South St. George's

St. George's was a sleepy colonial town until the outbreak of war. In five years, boosted by war trade, its revenue soared by 250 percent						
REVENUE IN £ STERLING						
	1860	*1861*	*1862*	*1863*	*1864*	*1865*
Hamilton	11,210	10,245	13,135	16,251	19,642	24,079
St. George's	56.050	51,225	65,675	81,255	98,210	120,395

In their own words
■ Georgiana Walker, *1863*

December 26, 1863. Last night was one of the happiest of my Bermuda life; because I felt that I was giving happiness to others. My Xmas party included most of the Confederate citizens in the Island (& they number now about one hundred). Of course there were many among them who scarcely expected to be invited, but I felt that all had a right, at least on this night, to come, & I wanted to feel that no respectable countryman of mine could say that there was no one to wish him a "Merry Xmas," & at whose home he could break bread. The Confederate Flag gaily decorated my little cottage; we had Confederate songs, dancing & games. At supper, I myself, proposed the health of "Our President" & hearty cheers resounded to every corner of the house in honour of his name. I do not know whether my guests availed themselves of my permission to "cheer their own Flag, and abuse all other governments to their hearts content." We parted almost at "rosy dawn" & all declared that they had been happier than they believed they could be, out of "Dixie."

January 4. The *Presto* leaves at 3 o'clock today & she is to be taken in by Capt. Wilkinson. That augurs well for her safe arrival. I send a package by Col. Ball for my Mother & a box of Brandy to my Father. A note from our landlady today with the very pleasing intelligence that she wished £20 more a year for her house! Truly the spirit of extortion is stalking through this land, as well as through some others. Poor Confederate countrymen! We are fleeced on every side.

February 11. Yesterday the *Vance* arrived from Wilmington, & we have the happiness of hearing from home. The news from our "own dear land" is better than I feared it would be. I had heard that our soldiers were becoming dispirited & dissatisfied, while the enemy were replenishing their ranks daily with new men. On the contrary, we hear that our men are re-enlisting to a man, and all seem to have stout hearts. God bless them! They are noble fellows, & I trust that their labours & their trials & their sorrows may soon all end in victory. The news which gives us most concern is the rumour that the new Congress has been postponed, the people fearing the disloyalty of some of the newly elected members from North Carolina & Georgia. This is truly disturbing, if so. What will become of us, if, added to the toil & strife & welfare with our enemy, we are rent by internal discords!

April 10. We came down from Hamilton yesterday morning where we had gone to dine with the Governor. We received an invitation about a week before, & went up on Friday morning to the Hamilton Hotel. A little before seven o'clock, after making an elaborate (& altho I say it) a very beautiful toilette, we drove to Mount Langton. My dress swept a quarter of a mile (more or less) behind me & the company had the good taste not to step on it, for which I felt much obliged. My seat was by the Governor's side at dinner & Mrs. Ord was in front of us. His Excellency is one of the most charming and social men. I felt particularly bright & in good spirits, so we had not only a pleasant but shocking to say, really a jolly time! The Governor was kind enough to declare to Mrs. Ord that I had fully converted him to the Southern cause, which of course was a pleasantry only, for I made no efforts to do so, moreover, I am glad to say, His Excellency needed no conversion. As I bid him good night, after having been detained several times by him, he remarked, "Well, Mrs. Walker, after the War is over, I am coming to the South to pay you a visit & I shall expect you to take me into the mountains. Moreover not to show me the beauties of Richmond in a Yankee-made carriage!" I replied, "I shall hold Your Excellency to this promise, when the War is over, & you may depend upon my valuing your life too much to trust you to anything so treacherous as a Yankee manufacture."

—*From the private journal of Georgiana Gholson Walker, 1862–65*

Menu

~ Turtle Soup ~

~ Boiled Fish ~ Boiled Potatoes ~
~ Cucumbers ~

~ Fillet Boeuf au Champignons ~
~ Oyster Pates ~

~ Mutton Chops ~ Tomato Sauce ~
~ Croquettes on Rice ~

~ Roast Saddle Mutton ~
~ Boiled Chickens ~ Egg Sauce ~

~ Asparagus ~ Green Peas ~
~ Tomatoes ~ Baked Potatoes ~

~ Duck with Truffles ~

~ Plum Pudding ~
~ Cocoanut Pudding Tartlets ~

~ Salad ~ Macaroni Omlette ~
~ Cheese ~ Bread & Butter ~

~ Ice Cream ~ Fresh Peaches ~
~ Ambrosia ~ Jelly ~

~ Blanc Mange ~ Bananas ~ Oranges ~
~ Citron ~ Strawberries ~

~ Table set "a la Russe" Coffee ~

~ Champaign ~ Sherry Madeira ~
~ Claret ~ Cherry Cordial ~
~ Noyau ~ Curacoa ~

—Menu for a dinner party hosted by Georgiana Gholson Walker in honour of the Archbishop of Halifax, May 12, 1864

Ordnance Island, St. George's after the Civil War

An Edward James painting of the Camber at Dockyard

All quiet: Bermuda returns to tranquillity at war's end

the shipping. It must have been brought on board our ship by some of the men who had been spending much time on shore: we had not been twenty-four hours at sea before the fever got a deadly hold on our crew."

Roberts, who survived, earned a reputation as a daring blockade-runner, and it was only after the war that he was discovered to be using an alias. A Royal Navy captain, he was actually an English nobleman, Augustus Charles Hobart-Hampden, son of the Sixth Earl of Buckingham, and a close friend of Governor Ord.

As yellow fever ravaged Bermuda, a shady character named Dr. Luke P. Blackburn caused a stir on the island. Billed as a specialist in the treatment of the disease, he attended numerous patients free of charge and was considered a boon to the local medical community. In fact, Blackburn had been collecting infected bed linen with the intent of shipping it off to Union ports to infect the Northern troops. US Consul Allen uncovered the plot in April 1865 through a spy, and ordered the sheets, pillowcases and blankets to be taken to a quarantine station at Nonsuch Island, where they were sterilised and buried. Blackburn was later arrested in Canada, but the case was dismissed for lack of evidence.

By the war's end stages, yellow-fever outbreaks in Bermuda and Nassau had forced the bulk of blockade-runners to do their business via Halifax. But by then, the galloping good times which had indulged Bermuda were almost over.

In April 1865, the South finally surrendered, its economy shattered. Lincoln's Emancipation Proclamation of 1863, followed by the 13th Amendment in 1865, brought an end to slavery in the US. Now the States began to try to rebuild their shaken Union.

The war was over even earlier for Bermuda, and with it, the prosperity of St. George's. The fall of two key North Carolina ports—Fort Fisher and Wilmington—over the winter of 1864–65 left runners stranded in Bermuda. When the victorious Union forces finally lifted their blockade of the South the following spring, the defeated Confederates melted away from Bermuda almost overnight. The four-year frenzy of excitement and profiteering had created an inflated prosperity that blinded Bermudians to the possibility of a Confederate defeat. So it came as a shock when just as quickly as good fortune had arrived, their financial well-being collapsed. Noted US Consul Allen: "Had they known that the islands were to sink in 20 minutes, there could hardly have been greater consternation."

Georgiana and Norman Walker, who had returned to Bermuda in January, 1865 from Halifax, finally left the island at the war's end. She headed to England with their children; the Major went to Nassau briefly, before joining his family in Liverpool.

Notably, news of Lincoln's assassination on April 15, 1865 received little sympathy in pro-South Bermuda. The only flags lowered were those of the US and French consuls, though the island's black community did mourn the death of the anti-slavery president whom members of Alexandrina Lodge described in a condolence message as "an invaluable friend."

With the Confederates gone, Bermuda's use as a shipping hub vanished. Hundreds of destitute sailors were left without work on the island. Merchants suffered debts that took years to liquidate. Prices sank back to pre-war levels. And once again, Bermuda was left to its own devices.

CHAPTER TWELVE

Tourism Takes Off

NATURE'S FAIRYLAND COURTS THE RICH AND FAMOUS

The enticing cover of the first
official guidebook, 1914

Bermuda is not the place for consumptives," declared American visitor Julia Dorr. "But for the overworked and weary, for those who need rest and recreation and quiet amusement, for those who love the beauty of sea and sky better than noisy crowds and fashionable display, and can dispense with some accustomed conveniences for the sake of what they may gain in other ways, it is truly a paradise."

Dorr spent two months in the spring of 1883 on the island she would later describe as "Eden" in her book *Bermuda: An Idyl of the Summer Islands*, published the following year. In the memoir, Dorr described how she and her companion, "H.," fled the late snows of New England for Bermuda aboard the New York steamer *Orinoco* after ignoring the advice of friends to tour Europe instead.

"What a contrast to icy mountains and valleys of drifted snow!" she exclaimed on her first morning in Bermuda. "Before me were large pride-of-India trees, laden with their long, pendulous racemes of pale lavender, each separate blossom having a drop of maroon at its heart…Beneath me were glowing beds of geraniums, callas, roses, Easter lilies, and the many-hued coleus…As far as the eye could reach was one stretch of unbroken bloom and verdure."

Dorr spent her bucolic holiday exploring the island on foot or by boat, admiring quaint gardens and pondering traditions such as limestone-quarrying. She attended events such as the Pembroke boys' school sports day, and rhapsodised over the colours and climate of a place where people enjoyed a state of "perpetual summer." She rode the ferry (a rowboat) across Hamilton Harbour, climbed Gibbs Hill Lighthouse, took a horse and carriage to St. George's and visited Pembroke Church (St. John's), home of the gravesite of Governor R. M. Laffan, who had died the previous year.

"I found myself continually wondering how life looked, what the wide world was like, to eyes that had seen nothing but blue seas, blue skies…and the narrow spaces of this island group," Dorr marvelled. "It would be

Blooming marvellous

They will bloom when New York is seventy degrees below zero and London is black with fog or slopped with mud and rain. And on this island there is not a motor or a train, or a smoking, rattling thing.

—Author Frances Hodgson Burnett
on the rose garden she planted
in Bailey's Bay, 1911

Prefer Bermuda *Over 50,000 American travellers seek the soft air of Florida every winter. I have never met one who had seen both places that did not prefer Bermuda. Is it not worthwhile to attract some of them to St. George's?*

—Governor Sir John Henry
Lefroy, 1875

Amusements *Life is not nearly as dull in Bermuda as might be supposed. There are plenty of outdoor amusements: driving, rowing, yachting, cricket, croquet. Dinner parties and balls enliven the time, especially in the winter.*

—Stark's Illustrated Bermuda
Guide, 1902

Too modest *The people of Bermuda are too modest. If they pushed their claims further, and made people in the United Sates understand what a delightful country they have, they would have far more visitors.*

—The New York Times, 1883

Princess Louise's visit in 1883, above and left, sparked tremendous overseas interest in Bermuda and led directly to the modern tourism industry

strange if a certain insular narrowness were not sometimes felt, as when a lady said to her friend, 'I wonder what the world would do without Bermuda! Just think how many potatoes and onions we export!'"

Yet, Bermuda's isolation was ironically also its biggest selling point to foreigners.

"Perhaps in this isolation, this fact of being absolutely cut off from one's old life, lies one of the chief causes of the recuperative power, the restfulness, of a few weeks in Bermuda," she said, quoting a colleague: "'I positively draw a breath of relief every time the steamer sails,' said one whose life had been spent in the eager stress and strain of business, and whose nerves had suffered therefrom. 'It is such a comfort to know that I cannot get a letter, or a New York paper, for a fortnight.'"

Dorr's impressions are noteworthy because she belonged to the vanguard of a new phenomenon in Bermuda—the first true 'tourists' to the island. Her stay actually coincided with that of Louise Carolina Albertha, the fourth daughter of Queen Victoria and Prince Albert. The princess, whose husband the Marquis of Lorne was serving as Canada's governor-general, left Ottawa's harsh winter for Bermuda and arrived on January 29, 1883 aboard the British warship HMS *Dido*. Some 3,000 spectators turned out to greet her, along with Mayor Nathaniel Butterfield, but for most of her stay,

Fatal error *This is one of the last refuges now left in the world to which one can come to escape such persons [motorists]. It would, in our opinion, be a fatal error to attract to Bermuda the extravagant and sporting set who have made so many other places entirely intolerable to persons of taste and cultivation.*

—Extract from a 1908 petition signed by Woodrow Wilson (later US president, 1913–21) and Samuel L. Clemens (Mark Twain), decrying the advent of cars in Bermuda

American humourist Mark Twain spent many idyllic holidays in Bermuda

BERMUDA ARCHIVES

Come on in! Early bathing fashions

BERMUDA ARCHIVES

the princess enjoyed relative privacy as she travelled around the island. An accomplished artist, she stayed at "Inglewood," the Paget home of James Trimingham, and filled her days painting watercolours of the island.

The royal sojourn, the first of its kind, proved a landmark event in promoting Bermuda. Foreign reporters covering the princess's visit were impressed by the island, which until then had been virtually unknown among world travellers. Media stories, sent back to North America by ship, helped stoke interest in Bermuda overseas. "Bermuda needs only to be known to be appreciated," wrote a *New York Times* reporter on the island. "It is not a little paradise, but it is as near it as any place I know." Almost immediately, visitors began arriving, swamping the small number of hotels and guest houses. A new era had dawned for Bermuda, a new avenue of opportunity which for the next century would successfully parlay the island's physical attributes into a much-needed economic lifeline.

Bermuda's re-invention in the late 19th Century came at a time when the world's philosophy towards travel was changing. The concept of visiting places such as Bermuda for a holiday was previously unknown. In Europe, sea-bathing for pleasure was not yet in practice, and long-distance ventures to broaden the mind were still the exclusive preserve of the very wealthy. Until the 1880s, arrivals in Bermuda had been health-seekers, traders or military personnel posted to the island, and since the latter often resented being forced to live in what they considered a backwater, their reports were frequently unflattering.

Gradually, attitudes about the erstwhile "sleepy outpost" began to change, largely thanks to influential writers and artists passing through Bermuda. Luminaries such as painter Winslow Homer began visiting the island and were captivated by its light and blue-tinged shadows. They showed their work in galleries across America, unintentionally promoting a previously unseen image of the tranquil islands. American humourist Samuel L. Clemens (Mark Twain) also stopped in Bermuda on his way home from a grand tour of Europe, and was so entranced by the island, he visited numerous times more. Early visitors also included geologists and natural scientists in the wake of Charles Darwin's evolutionary theories, which had sparked a scientific boom by the turn of the century.

Others ventured to the island in the hope its climate would help cure ailments such as tuberculosis, but while the beauty of Bermuda might have raised their spirits, the intense humidity usually worsened the health of consumptive invalids, many of whom died while struggling to recuperate. Due to improved medical understanding and living conditions, however, Bermuda's onetime reputation—shared by islands of the Caribbean—as a haven for disease and pestilence was cleared, and by the time Princess Louise and Dorr arrived, the island stage was set for tourism to develop on a large scale.

The new surge in visitors was primarily Americans—some attracted by the island's racial segregation. It prompted a boom in investment by Bermuda's usually conservative businessmen in the island's tourism infrastructure. A few small, tavern-like hotels had existed sporadically in Hamilton throughout

Terrace of Hamilton Hotel, Bermuda.

Busy hostelries (from bottom left, clockwise): St. George's Hotel, American House and the Hamilton Hotel. Below, an advertisement for the Hamilton

What it cost

The Hamilton Hotel on the hillside above the city. Board and lodging, $7 per day and upwards. The Princess Hotel at the west end of the city, so called after HRH Princess Louise, who visited Bermuda in 1883, $7 per day and upwards. The American House and the Imperial Hotel below the Hamilton, $6 per day and up. The Point Pleasant Hotel, situated along the city's waterfront, $6 per day and up. Paget. Hotel Inverurie, $6 per day and up. Warwick. Belmont Hotel, $6 per day and up. Flatts. Frascati Hotel, $6 per day and up. St. George's. The St. George Hotel, on the Rose Hill property, once owned by Governor Tucker, $6 per day and up. Somerset. Summerside, $4 per day. The above quotations are for accommodation during the winter months. In summer the Hamilton and Princess Hotels are both closed; the other hotels accept guests at slightly reduced rates.

—The Pocket Guide to the
West Indies, *1923*

the 19th Century, but most had gone out of business. In 1885, following the princess's visit, the island saw the opening of a grand new hotel named in her honour: the Princess Hotel at Pitts Bay on Hamilton Harbour. Known simply as "The Princess," it was the island's first waterfront hotel, and as a self-styled 'resort,' offered guests hot and cold running seawater, luxurious furnishings and, by the 1900s, the island's first hotel swimming pool and golf-course.

Dorr noted in her memoir that board and lodging costs of the time amounted to about $10 a week at the island's nicer hotels (Bermuda then had four other operating hotels: the Hamilton Hotel and American House in the capital, and the Globe Hotel and Bermuda House in St. George's). Standards at island establishments were raised to accommodate travellers used to international luxury hotels; telephones, electricity and elevators soon became *de rigueur* as competing hotels vied for visitors. Small businesses also sprang up to cater to new tourists, with excursions to popular sights like Walsingham Cave and Devil's Hole.

Improved transport was urgently needed to get people to the island. Steamships had been contracted since the 1860s to provide regular runs between Bermuda and New York, but service had always been problematic. In 1874, the Quebec and Gulf Ports Steamship Company took up the contract, providing weekly service during the spring aboard its sturdy boats like *Canima*, *Georgia* and *Orinoco* (on which Dorr travelled), and aggressively promoting Bermuda in New York City through leaflet campaigns. Travellers also arrived via Cunard's monthly Halifax-Bermuda-Jamaica run. By 1904, *Bermudian*—the first liner built specifically for the Quebec Steamship line's Bermuda run—was in service. The liner would be a regular visitor to the island for the next 13 years, until the First World War put Bermuda's tourism aspirations on hold.

On the island, visitors travelled around by bicycle, horse and carriage and

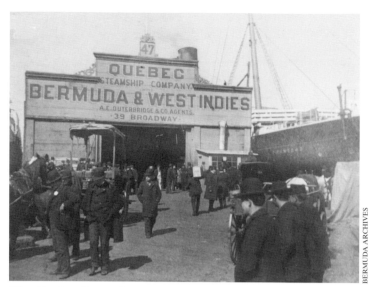

BERMUDA ARCHIVES

The Quebec Steamship Company berth in New York City, 1899

BERMUDA ARCHIVES

Carriage trips to Devil's Hole, Harrington Sound were popular

QUO·FATA·FERUNT

Coat of arms

On October 4, 1910, Bermuda won royal approval to use its own coat of arms, a redesign of the original seal adopted by the Bermuda Company in 1615. The coat of arms bears a silver shield, depicting a red lion holding a blue antique shield on which is pictured the shipwrecked *Sea Venture*. The arms carries the Latin motto *Quo Fata Ferunt*, meaning "Whither the Fates Carry Us"—a line from Virgil's *Aeneid:* "And so we set sail, not knowing whither the fates may carry us." The coat of arms is used as an emblem on everything from the Bermudian flag to official documents.

boat. In January 1908, entrepreneur Albert Spurling opened an automobile service offering sightseeing via a single touring car he had imported, dubbed "The Scarlet Runner." But the phenomenon created such a stir, particularly among horse-and-carriage owners whose animals were startled by the car, that a petition was sent to the government urging lawmakers to ban the use of all motor vehicles. Woodrow Wilson, who would later become America's 28th president, serving through the First World War, and Mark Twain, both ardent Bermudaphiles, signed the lobby effort, and within weeks the Scarlet Runner was banished, along with a handful of private automobiles during the early part of the century. Bermuda became known as one of three places in the world where cars were forbidden by law—along with the islands of Brioni in the Adriatic and the Republic of San Marino. While a few lorries, an ambulance and a fire engine were allowed in Bermuda, cars would not return for another 30 years.

BERMUDA ARCHIVES

Visitors take a ride in a St. David's whaleboat

Golfing was a major attraction, even in 1898

BERMUDA ARCHIVES

Sleepy South Road near Warwick Camp in the 1870s

BERMUDA MARITIME MUSEUM

Rigging the gangplank to a visiting passenger ship in 1880

THE BERMUDIAN

Ring your bell *On overtaking another vehicle or traveller, keep to the right until past and then go over to the left again. Much confusion and accidents are caused by American cyclists through ignorance of this rule of the road. Cyclists must not overtake foot-passengers without ringing their bell when at a reasonable distance.*

—Stark's Illustrated Bermuda
Guide, *James H. Stark, 1902*

In their own words
■ Helen Fessenden

The kindling was a ceremony at which we children were allowed to assist. Slender sticks wound with strips of bright paper were made ready for us; these, as I can now see, were strangely like the Hermes wand of old, the caduceus, though evoked by what remote echo is hard to imagine. Down the slope to the gaping mouth of that huge oven we would go to thrust our small faggots into the first, mild, crackling flames. Gnarled cedar roots filled the oven to its dome; gradually as the firing proceeded, intense heat was worked up and this was maintained throughout the entire period.

Meantime at the house, the kitchen was the scene of Herculean labours, a neck-and-neck race between supply and demand; the brick oven usually fired only once a week was in daily requisition, turning out its twenty or twenty-four loaves a day. As the bread finished baking, boilers with salt beef or pork or smoked shoulder took its place in what was in reality a fireless cooker of large capacity and exceptional efficiency, for it heated water almost to boiling point twenty-four hours after the fire had been drawn and two or three stages of cooking accomplished. Pea soup and dumplings, pumpkin and sweet potatoes, coffee by the gallon added to the menu and pails of water sweetened with molasses and a dash of pepper vinegar was considered safer than immoderate water drinking after a spell of stoking. Last but not least, an occasional judicious tot of Jamaica rum.

As the days passed, our burning kiln became a Mecca; every evening visitors from our own [and] adjoining parishes came to watch the progress and the men threw themselves into the job with immense zest.

It was indeed a scene that Dante might have pictured—that gaping oven mouth at the foot of the slope and the seething cauldron of flames within. Half-naked figures, black bodies gleaming with sweat, clustered in the runway for the short but terrific job of raking and stoking, one after another endured to the limit the inferno of heat as fierce blasts poured out. Raucous shouts reached the ears of the onlookers as man after man took his place "God-a-mighty, Water—Forebreast me—Water" and with the shouting, steam rose from the drenched figures as dipper after dipper of water was doused over them. Then a respite until the next period.

Slowly the great mass of lime-stone heated; first quivering heat waves vibrated over the top, then a dim red glow growing always more intense, till at last heat and time had done their appointed job and the kiln 'was burnt.'

Quiet descended upon the scene and the cooling process went on till it was safe to begin to reap the harvest. This carried with it the penalty of working for hours in an alkali-laden atmosphere, filling bag after bag with lime. My father did much of this himself, emerging from the pit with skin, eyes, nose, lungs saturated with harsh powder but with the comforting thought that every bushel sold added one shilling and sixpence to the farm budget.

—*Helen Fessenden on her memories of lime manufacture using a kiln in the 1870s. She was married to Reginald Fessenden, the father of modern radio transmission*

Tennis, anyone?

Two Bermudian women, both named Mary, were responsible for the popularity of tennis in Bermuda and its introduction to America in the late 1800s.

While versions of the game had been played by English royalty as far back as the early 1600s and later became a spectacle sport in France, tennis failed to win widespread popularity in Europe until the late 19th Century. In 1873, Thomas Middleton brought the first tennis set to Bermuda and gave the equipment to Attorney General Sir Samuel Brownlow Gray, who had a private court laid at his Paget home, Clermont.

It was Gray's daughter, Mary, who became fascinated by the game, which soon began to draw a following of keen players on private courts throughout the island. Tennis scoring rules of the time were different to today, with 15 points to a game. Members of the British military introduced the current scoring method with its game-set-match structure, when the sport finally became known in England as 'tennis.' By the late 1870s, Mary Gray had staked her claim as a keen sportswoman, winning numerous tournaments and promoting the game among her Bermudian friends. She even played tennis with the future King George V when he was a naval

officer stationed in Bermuda.

It was another Mary—Mary Outerbridge —who introduced tennis to the United States. In 1874, she travelled from Bermuda to New York City taking with her tennis racquets, a net, balls and rule book —paraphernalia that garnered puzzled looks from US customs officers. Through business connections of her brother, Joseph Outerbridge, she was given permission to design a tennis court on the grounds of the Staten Island Cricket Club—the first such court in the nation. The venerable US Lawn Tennis Association was established seven years later.

Tennis at Clermont, Paget, in 1893, where Bermuda's first court was installed by Sir Samuel Brownlow Gray. The sport soon caught on, below

Future calling *I remember [Thomas Alva] Edison coming to Bermuda. He came up to Mount Langton and fixed up some primitive telephone arrangement by which he, sitting in a room at one end of the house, talked to my Father who was at the other end. My Mother told me that my Father said afterwards: "That is an invention which may revolutionise trade."*
—*Laura Gertrude Berners (nee Laffan), the youngest daughter of Bermuda's governor, 1877–82*

Bermuda's reinvention proved fortuitous. The island's once-prosperous tomato and onion industries were being undercut by cheaper products from California, Florida, Texas and elsewhere. The Bermuda onion crop had once enjoyed a monopoly in the US, but this was soon destroyed by American competitors. Higher US import tariffs were also being levied to protect domestic producers, hurting Bermudian growers. While the bulk of island produce was sold at New York markets, prices fluctuated drastically, making the quest for profits a guessing game. Potato and arrowroot exports were lucrative for many years, but these, too, eventually collapsed in the early 1900s. Easter-lily exports continued, but on a small scale. Agriculture's potential as an integral support of the colony had once again been lost.

"Here we have the most remarkable and probably the most valuable climate in the world, within two days' sail of the very best market, utterly wasted for want of expert agriculturalists and sufficient capital," lamented a

Front Street: newly prosperous

Language of flags

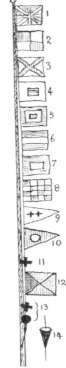

Flags talk in Bermuda after a most bewildering fashion. They give you all kinds of information if you are only quick-witted enough to take it in: when it is church time, and when it is noon; when an unknown ship is in sight; when the mails will close; when they go out, and when they come in; when a boat is wanted at Mount Langton; when there is a vessel on the rocks; when the **Pioneer** *will call at the Ducking Stool—whatever that may be—and when it will not call. There is no end to the signals; but it would take a lifetime and the patience of Job to master their language.*

—*Julia Dorr,* Bermuda: An Idyl of the Summer Islands, *1884*

Board of Agriculture report in 1906. "What Bermuda might have been if the proper attention had been paid to agriculture it is not very difficult to conceive; one only has to imagine each cultivated valley surrounded by the choicest varieties of all kinds of fruit trees to gain some idea of the terrific waste of valuable forces that has been going on all these years."

While British military and naval establishments continued to pour a relatively healthy sum into the island's coffers, Bermuda soon looked to tourism to fill the widening economic void. With the US undergoing an economic boom, the island realised it was time to jump wholeheartedly into promoting the island among newly prosperous Americans.

In 1913, the Bermuda government created the Trade Development Board with the mandate of building up tourist facilities and promoting the island overseas. The board quickly decided it wanted the so-called 'better class' of visitor, who was looking for a retreat not just from North America's cold winters, but also the hectic pace of industrial life. A decision was made: Bermuda would be promoted as the "Isles of Rest," an island paradise devoid of stressful factories, railroads, trolley cars and automobiles. Within a year, the board had produced its first booklet, Bermuda's first official guide-book. *Nature's Fairyland* created a persuasive image of a restful Bermuda far from the madding crowd of American cities.

To make sure the reality matched the promise, laws were passed to keep Bermuda beautiful—no billboards or garish advertisements were allowed. Motorcars, just beginning to appear on Bermuda's streets, were

BERMUDA ARCHIVES

*Bermudians take to the water
to watch a dinghy regatta*

banned. The strategy worked perfectly. Like Woodrow Wilson, celebrities and the super-rich soon found themselves charmed by the island and began making it their private playground. The list was a virtual *Who's Who* of America's elite: William H. Vanderbilt, Vincent Astor, William Howard Taft, Helen Hayes and Endicott Peabody were all regular island guests and their visits helped stoke Bermuda's image as the place to go. Tourists began arriving in droves, and the prosperous Bermuda tourism industry was born.

Modern-day travellers would be amused to learn that during the years which witnessed the birth of island tourism, Bermuda's forts—now marketed as cultural heritage sights—were then working structures manned by British soldiers…and strictly off-limits to visitors. Dorr describes watching British "redcoats" at target practice outside "Camp Warwick" and on another occasion, looking at a fort across Castle Harbour and trying to count the cannonball stacks at the ready.

*West Indian "Bully Rooster"
troops guard Government House
on Langton Hill, Pembroke, in 1899*

BERMUDA MARITIME MUSEUM

America might have torn itself apart with civil war, but Britain still feared its old foe during the late 19th Century. The lessons of four years of hard fighting had turned the reunited States into a hardened and experienced war machine, which Britain worried might turn against isolated strategic outposts like Bermuda.

As a result, Britain set about strengthening Bermuda's defences yet again. The military began improvements to allow island fortifications to withstand the very latest in military technology. Existing forts had been built to repel wooden warships, but now stood little chance of challenging modern, ironclad steamships armed with powerful rifled guns. To do so, new breech-loading guns had to be installed, requiring new or improved mounts. Forts like St. Catherine's and

The write stuff

Bermuda became a magnet for world-renowned writers beginning in the late 19th Century. Like their art and music counterparts, novelists, poets, playwrights and critics, most from the US East Coast, found creative inspiration in a place so close to home, yet so far-removed from the modern world. Literary stars such as humourist Samuel Clemens (Mark Twain), dramatist Eugene O'Neill and Rudyard Kipling were intrigued by the island's balmy climate, quaint beauty and privacy and made Bermuda a favourite retreat. Several became repeat visitors and their influence helped fuel Bermuda tourism through the 20th Century.

After his first visit in 1867, Twain admitted being charmed by "the lovely vistas of blue water that went curving in and out, disappearing and anon again appearing through jungle walls of brilliant foliage." He enjoyed playing croquet, miniature golf and watching ships arrive at Hamilton Harbour. Plagued by angina in his later years, Twain surmised that Bermuda was the right country "for a jaded man to loaf in. There are no harassments," he added. "The deep peace and quiet sink into one's body and bones and give his conscience a rest."

When he steamed to the island from New York in 1924, O'Neill brought a family entourage with him, including his wife, children and Irish wolfhound. They rented Spithead Lodge on Harbour Road and spent more than a year on the island, which O'Neill thought might help him conquer alcoholism and depression. It didn't, but he was prolific nonetheless, writing *Strange Interlude*, among other works, during his sojourn.

English children's author Frances Hodgson Burnett stayed at Bailey's Bay with her son Vivian in 1911—the same year she published *The Secret Garden*. The Nobel Prize-winner Kipling, visited twice, in 1898 and 1930, and was moved to write an article in the London *Spectator* linking places in Bermuda with settings in Shakespeare's *The Tempest*. Other literati in Bermuda over these years included E.B. White, Stephen Leacock, Charles Hanson Towne, Langston Hughes, C.L.R. James and Arthur Samuels.

BERMUDA MEDIA

*Dramatist Eugene O'Neill
spent more than a year writing
in Bermuda*

Fort Cunningham were greatly renovated, as was Buildings Bay Battery near St. George's, later known as Alexandra Battery. Some of the new guns were installed with heavy iron shields for protection.

During the 1870s and '80s, other fortifications were improved or built from scratch. The Dockyard Keep was remodelled and a brand new fort erected at Scaur Hill, Sandys to protect the Dockyard from any invasion army approaching by land. The Bermuda garrison was also strengthened, with Prospect Camp as its headquarters and other large facilities at St. George's, Boaz Island and the training camp at Warwick, today the headquarters of the Bermuda Regiment.

With the convict labour system gone after the Crimean War, Bermuda again faced a labour shortage to carry out these construction works. This time, the island turned to the Caribbean for help at the end of the 1800s. Hundreds of workers, facing an economic downturn at home, came to the island through St. Kitts from Nevis, Anguilla, St. Eustatius and Saba. Others were recruited in Jamaica. The six-year Dockyard Extension Works, begun in 1900, included the repair of bridges, construction of the South Wharf as well as the huge floating dock, a massive undertaking responsible for a major wave of West Indian immigration in the form of skilled carpenters, masons and labourers. By 1904, there were more than 3,000 West Indians working in Bermuda.

Other newcomers included members of the British West India Regiment, the "Bully Roosters," so-called due to their colourful, Moorish-style uniforms. Posted to Bermuda in 1899 to replace the Boer War-bound Worcester Regiment, the BWIR included members from Jamaica, Barbados, and other islands. Most would eventually return home after a two-year tour of duty in which they served as the resident battalion at Prospect's garrison. Some BWIR soldiers remained in Bermuda, and their descendants live on the island today.

In their own words
■ August Carl Schulenburg, 1901

On the 8th of May 1901, 32 of us from Area 2 were surrounded by the British and taken prisoner. I had little with me, except my rifle and the clothes I was wearing. Our pockets were emptied by the enemy. I had a cop notebook, with entries in Dutch shorthand. For three successive days I had to appear before the general for interrogation, especially about the notes in my diary. I persistently refused to say anything and, as they could not make out what I had written in the pocketbook, they refused to give it back.

In Durban, we were marched to the Point and then taken out on a small boat to a large ship The Armenian that lay outside the harbour. They used a large basket and crane to get us up on deck, four at a time. On the ship we learnt that we were to be taken to Cape Town, where a further 600 prisoners of war would be embarked, and then on to Bermuda.

The trip from the Cape to Bermuda lasted 30 days and was most boring, especially in the tropics. There were a number of Hollanders aboard, as well as other volunteers from foreign countries who had fought for the Boers. These decided to hijack the ship, but I knew nothing of this plan. I later learnt that the idea was to take over the vessel near the Azores and then carry on to Portugal. But because of squealers, the plan did not succeed, and the ringleaders were locked up until arrival in Bermuda.

In the early morning of the 28th we saw land again, and this time, it was Bermuda. The Bermudas were thickly wooded with cedar trees. The Boer POWs were accommodated in tents on the

Boer prisoners of war held in Bermuda. Below, some of the cedar items they created

BERMUDA ARCHIVES

following islands: Darrell's, Burt's, Morgan's, Tucker's and Hawkins. Later, another island housed the children prisoners of war. A prison hospital under canvas was situated on Ports Island and some of our men lie buried on an island close by.

On the 1st of July we were taken to Burt's Island. It was pleasant to be on land again, even though so far from home. The island was very small, about 500 square yards in size, and it was divided in two by a high double barbed-wire fence with a gate in the middle. We were on one side and the English guards on the other. Two warships also guarded us, illuminating the island at night with their strong searchlights. At first, we numbered 450 men. The English guards were under the command of Major G.D. Armstrong. The tents were erected in rows and these were known as "lines." There were nine lines at first, but this was soon reduced to seven when some men were transferred to Morgan's Island. Seven men shared a

tent. Each line chose its line captain and each tent had a corporal responsible for the cleanliness of the tent and its surroundings. Roll call was held twice a day on the parade ground: mornings and evenings at six o'clock. Each line captain was responsible for his men, but officers were not counted. Rations had to be drawn each day and every tent inhabitant had to see to his own preparation and cooking. Daily rations for each man on Burt's Island were:

*Bread 1^{1}/$_{4}$ lbs or Biscuits 1 lb
Fresh meat 1 lb
Preserved meat ^{3}/$_{4}$ lb
Coffee ^{2}/$_{3}$ oz
Salt ^{1}/$_{2}$ oz
Fresh vegetables ^{1}/$_{2}$ lb
Preserved vegetables 1 oz*

Lime juice with sugar was issued if fresh vegetables were not available, or on the recommendation of the medical officer. There were five marquees in our camp; three were used as school tents, one as a library and one as a mess for officers. A large wood and canvas building was erected for use as a church.

The boring soul-killing life on the island was made bearable, and enjoyable to a certain extent, by the friendly help of American and Bermudian residents who sympathised with us...

I was also secretary of the POW Industrial Association. This was started by the makers of curios and toys. Hundreds of these items were made out of cedar wood at the request of Americans and other visitors. We had to concoct a plan to get these items away to Hamilton. Through the English commander, I was able to contact Miss Katherine Elwes at Government House, and she undertook to receive the curios, sell them and let me have the money to divide among the makers. A large wooden box with a padlock was given to me; I had

BERMUDA MARITIME MUSEUM

one key and Miss Elwes had the other. I received the objects, supplied each with a label and price and packed them in the box. A fair amount of money came into the camp by this means.

In July 1901, I became seriously ill with dysentry and had to go to the hospital on Ports Island. Something which was hard and which I shall never forget was the fact that I had to row the boat myself, while the guard with his rifle and equipment sat opposite me. The trip was some distance and the fever, headache and stomach pains were unbearable. On arrival, I was taken to the hospital marquee. I had to strip naked and then the guard, with bayonet fixed, escorted me to the sea where I took a sea bath. Then back to the hospital and into bed at last. What a relief!

The doctors came every day, but I became worse. After eight days, they gave me enemas of potassium permanganate and from then on, I recovered slowly.

Life in camp went on routinely. Classes were organised to provide lessons for all who were anxious to make use of the offer. Each day I taught English and History—general as well as South African. A Frenchman, Fleumer, started a French class and since I had learnt the language in school, I joined. We were able to construct a tennis court, but swimming was our greatest sport and exercise. We had a debating society with the name "Nil Desperandum"; I was secretary of this. *The Burt's Trompet*, with teacher Willie Bachofner as editor, was our camp newspaper. It was written by hand, contained news received from secret sources and was sold once a week. We were forbidden actual newspapers and all outgoing and incoming letters were censored. We received our mail once a week and this was an occasion for much excitement.

—*From the diaries of August Carl Schulenburg, a Boer War prisoner of war in Bermuda from June 1901 to July 1902*

Tourists were not the only foreign visitors to Bermuda during these years. In 1901–2, more than 4,000 South African men and boys were brought to the island and held as prisoners of war on the islands of the Great Sound. Begun in 1899, the Boer War, or South African War, was waged between the British and the Boers—whose agile army was well-equipped by the Germans. At the heart of the conflict was the Boer resistance to British territorial expansion in the bid for a united South Africa.

The POWs, as young as six years and as old as 80, were kept in tents under heavy guard by British troops on Tucker's, Morgan's, Ports, Darrell's, Burt's and Hawkins Islands. Unlike internment camps in South Africa, which were rife with disease, the Bermudian camps appear to have been well organised and peaceful. Each island ran its own self-contained community, with church, school, library and dining and wash tents. Interned children were educated, while the older men spent hours carving ornaments and mementoes from cedar wood, which were sold for them by relief associations.

At the war's end, most of the Boers were shipped home after swearing allegiance to Britain, or went on to North America to begin new lives there. A few remained in Bermuda, and ran small souvenir or craft shops.

Members of the BVRC First Contingent in the First World War

THE BERMUDIAN

The First Contingent embarking for Europe from Front Street in 1915

BERMUDA ARCHIVES

BERMUDA MARITIME MUSEUM

*Men of the Bermuda Contingent,
Royal Garrison Artillery in
Europe during the Great War*

A far more explosive war was about to engulf the world. In 1914, Britain and Germany, along with their respective allies, began a four-year conflict that would involve many nations. The First World War—the "Great War"—pitted Germany, Austria and Hungary against France, Britain, Russia, and the United States in the deadliest, most intense conflict in human history to that point—a war which despite its political scope, devolved into a dismal stalemate waged largely in the trenches of western Europe.

Bermuda's two militia groups, divided by race, were soon taking part in the fighting. Some 250 members of the black Bermuda Militia Artillery were attached to the Royal Garrison Artillery and set to work in munitions dumps near the front lines in France. A further 122 men of the white Bermuda Volunteer Rifle Corps joined the Lincolnshire Regiment and saw action in trench warfare, where gas, gangrene and raids destroyed a generation of men. Eighty Bermudians, from both the BVRC and BMA, were among the war's dead.

POW issue *Four pairs of strong boots, seven pairs of linen trousers, eight shirts, eight pairs of socks, two pairs of underdrawers and two handkerchiefs. Suspenders, caps and straw hats were furnished on request.*

—British government issue to German prisoner of war, sailor Ernest Allrecht, held on Ports Island 1916–17

Bermuda experienced disrupted shipping, food shortages and a downturn in its nascent tourism due to the war, but also strengthened local defences. Locally, troops from both the BMA and BVRC served as military police, coastal patrols and also carried out signalling duties. Members of the BVRC ran a camp on Ports Island for prisoners of war—this time Germans—along with a few German citizens interned during the war.

On November 11, 1918, the war ended with the signing of the Armistice between Germany and the Allies, and a shell-shocked world began picking up the pieces. Bermudians would face an even more terrifying world war in two decades. In the meantime, they had plenty to adjust to. The modern age was now in full swing and with it came a whole new set of social, technological and economic challenges.

TIMELINE *1834–1918*

BERMUDA

1849 Fifty-eight men, women and children from Madeira are first Portuguese immigrants

1851 Record crop shipment to New York includes onions, tomatoes and arrowroot

1871 Causeway links St. George's to the main island, replacing ferry

1879 First police force is created: nine full-time officers and 21 part-time parish constables

1883 The visit of Princess Louise marks celebrity launch of Bermuda tourism

1887 Telephone service is installed between Hamilton and St. George's

WORLD

1840 Britain issues first postage stamp, the Penny Black, a prelude to postal service

1860 David Livingstone explores Africa's Zambezi River

1861 Breakaway of southern states launches four-year American Civil War

1865 North wins US Civil War; slavery is abolished; Abraham Lincoln assassinated

1877 European powers race to colonise inner Africa, seeking new markets and resources

1878 British scientist Joseph Swan invents the lightbulb

In their own words

■ Cassie B. White, *1918*

We drove all night and it seemed as if we were going right in the front-line trenches, for the roll of the guns and the flashes from them really made us feel a little frightened, but just the same we kept on going. Several airplanes were going up from the different airdromes that we passed and it was on that night about 12 that we saw our first air fight. The Captain that was in charge of us had to keep getting out of the ambulance asking the way to our famous Emergency Hospital Unit (EHU). At last, after many stops, we finally reached our destination…

Miss Morse was appointed acting chief nurse and she put us all to work on making dressings, the frightful guns keeping us on the alert all the time. After dinner, patients began to pour in and, oh, how they came—the worst cases that I have ever seen, ambulance drivers putting them all over everywhere, the surgeon not being able to operate fast enough. I was put in the Operating Room for the afternoon and all next day, everything being upside down for we were not prepared for patients. That afternoon several more nurses arriving on the scene to help us and we were

COURTESY OF KATHLEEN SHARPE KEANE

Bermudian nurse Cassie White witnessed horrors of the battlefield

very glad to have them. Such wounds, and oh, the poor boys dying so fast, it was murder and just made your blood run cold to see the boys, but not a word from any of them, they were so patient and oh so good.

I was put on night duty the following night in eight wards, one being the officers' ward. Working without lights is no joke, for we had to treat the wounds and try to relieve the patient. Oh, how we did dread to see the moon shine, and it happens that the moon shone brighter than ever at that time.

It did help us in one way, for it gave a little light for us to see how to work, but on the other, it aided the [enemy] to find us. They were flying over us all the time and oh, one night when [a German plane] came down so close to me to leave his card, I, for one, almost died, being the first time that I have ever heard him so close. Happily, he flew over my tent before dropping his bomb and after he left us I went to my other tents to see if my [patients] were okay.

He came the very next night and used his machine gun. Patients with splints on both legs got up and ran for the wheat field and all the day nurses and officers and men slept in the wheat field, too. Quite a sight to watch the different people getting up out of the wheat field bringing their blankets with them in the morning.

—*Cassie B. White, a Bermudian nurse who served at a US Army Base Hospital in France during the First World War, writing in her diary August 7 to September 13, 1918*

'Such wounds, and oh, the poor boys dying so fast. It was murder and just made your blood run cold. Not a word from any of them'

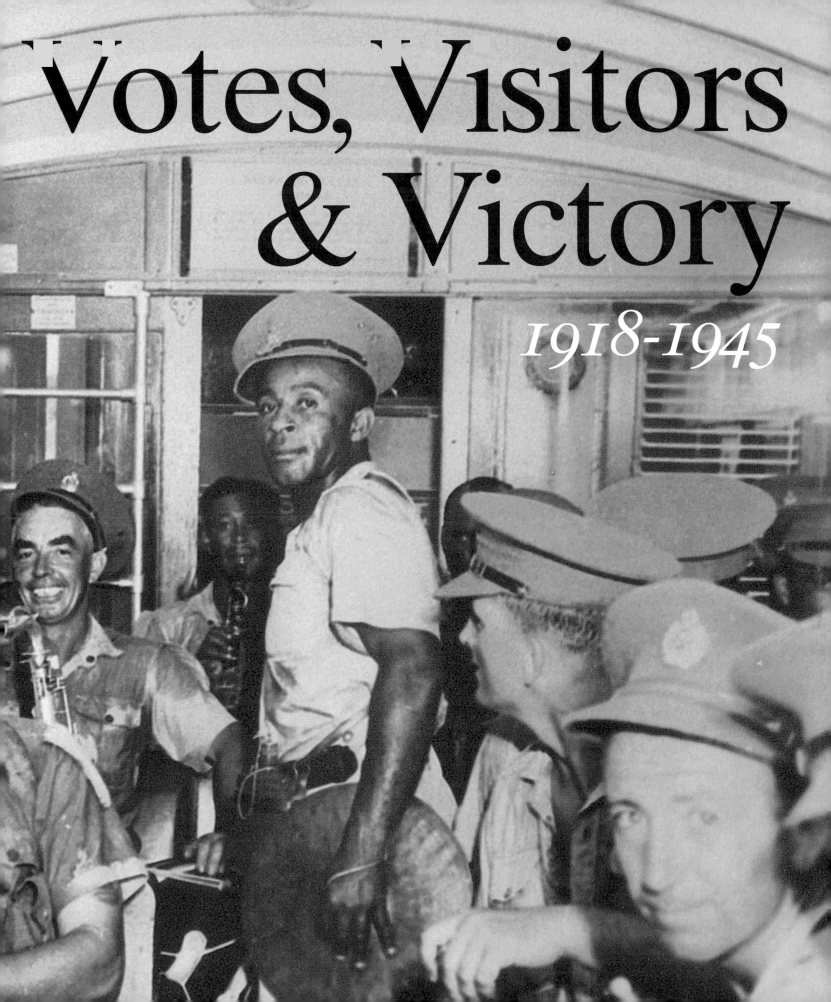

Votes, Visitors & Victory

1918-1945

CHAPTER THIRTEEN

The Fight for Rights

WOMEN, BLACKS AND WORKERS DEMAND FAIR PLAY

T he large crowd which gathered outside Mangrove Bay police station on December 18, 1930 was abuzz with excitement. A week before Christmas, the usually quiet streets of Somerset rippled with high anticipation, as journalists, photographers and Bermudian men, women and children made their way to the West End, eager to see the outcome of a bizarre showdown—an 'auction' pitting a group of the island's society women against Parliament itself.

They would, indeed, witness an historic spectacle that Thursday morning, but one whose larger impact would not be felt for a further 14 years. While the day marked the climax of a single courageous act of civil disobedience, it would best be remembered in newspaper photos as symbolising the quarter-century-long crusade for women's rights.

At 10 o'clock, the streets erupted into equal parts cheers and boos as a horse-drawn bus arrived from Hamilton carrying a group of well-dressed

Suffragettes protest outside Somerset police station as they auction an antique cedar table

THE BERMUDIAN

women who, with their dignified hats, cardigans and pearls, looked as if they were en route to a tea party rather than a protest rally. Draped in red, green and white, the hallmark colours of the Women's Suffrage Movement, the bus wound its way slowly through Sandys parish until it pulled up in front of the police station. On board were Sue Masters, Henrietta Tucker, May Hutchings, Kate Seon and Nellie Rees, among others, all proud 'suffragettes' who had come to lend moral support, not to mention bidding power, to the day's heroine—Gladys Morrell.

At issue was the paltry sum of £6/14 shillings—the amount Morrell had withheld in parochial taxes (plus costs) to protest the lack of voting rights for women in Bermuda. That sum would now be raised through the parish vestry's auction of Morrell's furniture, confiscated by order of Magistrates Court. At 11 o'clock, police sergeant A. T. Burrows appeared atop the station's steps to act as auctioneer. The hushed crowd bristled with curiosity as an antique cedar table was displayed, the first item on the block (and the only property auctioned, as it turned out). The bidding began, and to the dismay of Morrell and her colleagues, some of their opponents entered the fray. But the suffragettes banded together to control the auction's outcome; bidding up the table to cover its tax assessment, they outbid the others, ensuring it was returned to one of their own. When the hammer came down, at £20, the table went to the wife of the Sandys rector, who promptly paid for her prize in cash and returned it to Morrell.

The suffragettes turned the day into a festive milestone, joining Morrell for lunch at her house, and later celebrating their solidarity with a dinner and parish rally. They had reason to be jubilant, having scored the latest and most militant—if only totemic—victory in their campaign to extend voting privileges to Bermuda's women. Later that day, Morrell received a cable from a veteran leader of the suffrage movement in Quebec. It read: "Good for you. Quebec women wish you all success and speedy victory."

But the fight for equality by Morrell and her phalanx of suffragettes still had a long way to go; it would last nearly to the end of the Second World War, when the contributions of women to both the workforce and warfront could no longer be ignored. And when change came, it not only offered the vote to white women (and black female property owners), but also opened the first door of hope to all Bermudian blacks for universal adult suffrage which would follow later in the century, overturning the island's archaic voting restrictions.

The suffragettes' struggle was launched in 1919 amid the worldwide outpouring of relief and thanksgiving following the Great War of 1914–18. For five years during the bloody conflict, everything but war and the dream of victory had been put aside. Once the war was over, though, ordinary people began looking to a prosperous future accompanied by, they hoped, a new world fit for heroes.

Women, among others, were demanding the right to vote. In Britain, they got their wish in 1919, but in Bermuda, the very notion of women voting for members of the Colonial Parliament—or worse, actually standing for Parliament—filled most of the island's male population with dread. The idea was privately ridiculed and publically dismissed. Bermuda still followed restrictive voting laws enacted at the time of Emancipation in 1834 with the aim of barring newly-freed blacks from achieving true equality. As a result,

BERMUDA ARCHIVES

Gladys Morrell spearheaded Bermuda's votes-for-women campaign

On the attack *Our society has embarked on a policy of attacking on two fronts. We have attacked on the Downing Street and Westminster front; and at present we are attacking on the home front.*
—Bermudian suffragette Gladys Morrell

Valuable women *Women are a valuable asset in the life of the Colony, and, if their share in public affairs should be undertaken in the same energetic way in which their private duties are carried out, it is difficult to see where any adverse opinion to their being admitted to the franchise could possibly be sustained.*
—The Royal Gazette, *1919*

Suffragette Rose Gosling with pupils at Bermuda High School

Long overdue *We hope that the whole question of the franchise will be thoroughly investigated by the Colonial Office and many changes that have been long overdue, made, so that all races and classes in this community may have proper representation.*
—The Bermuda Recorder *on the Bermuda Women's Suffrage Society petition sent to the secretary of state for the colonies, March 15, 1930*

only men who owned property worth £60 could vote, and if they wanted to run for local councils or the House of Assembly, that figure was hiked to £240. Particularly galling to property-owning women was a clause which denied them the vote, but gladly gave it to their husbands—even though the property belonged to the wives.

Born in Somerset on June 2, 1888, Gladys Carlyon De Courcy Misick (later Morrell) was, perhaps, the perfect champion of the suffragettes' cause. The daughter of Thalia J.D. Misick and Terence Misick, a Member of the Colonial Parliament (MCP), she attended Bermuda High School for Girls before leaving the island to study history at London University—against her father's wishes. It was a time of infectious social change, both in Britain and the United States, and women were at the forefront as they marched and demonstrated for social freedoms beyond their traditional roles at home or in 'helpful' occupations such as nursing and teaching. As they challenged long-held assumptions about women's place in society, the right to vote as equal citizens was paramount among their demands, and the suffragette movement was born. Inspired by the suffragette movement's enigmatic British leaders like Emmeline Pankhurst and Millicent Fawcett, Misick joined the campaign and was soon helping to form suffragette groups in southwest England. On one occasion she led a 100-mile march from Land's End to Taunton.

Misick returned to Bermuda after the First World War, fired with the resolve to bring the same progressive changes to the colony. As a property owner in Bermuda, she was annoyed at being denied a stake in the political process, and with the help of like-minded friends such as Rose Gosling, Doris Trott Butterfield and Isobel Lockward, was determined to make changes. At first it seemed she might achieve her goal quickly; she won the support of the local media and enlisted the backing of politician Salisbury Stanley Spurling, who raised the matter of women's suffrage in the House of Assembly during the summer of 1919. He proposed "a committee be appointed with leave to bring in a bill providing that women shall have the right of voting at all Parliamentary, Parochial and Municipal elections on the same conditions and with the same restrictions that apply to men." Surprisingly, the motion passed with just three objections, although an amendment to also give qualified women the right of election was immediately quashed.

Legislators seemed to be receptive to debating the issue of female suffrage—but Misick would soon learn not to be overly optimistic. Three years passed with no committee report, no mention of the issue in the Assembly, and all attempts at pursuing the issue stonewalled. Misick was not the first woman to try to change the status quo in Bermuda. Elizabeth Smith had attempted to do the same with a petition in 1785, and Anna Maria Outerbridge also fought for female equality with bills that were accepted by the Assembly in 1895 and 1896, before being defeated by the president of the Legislative Council.

In November 1922, the women wrote a letter probing the status of the report promised in Spurling's motion. In January the following year, all they received was a non-committal reply from the clerk of the legislature. Misick and her largely white, well-off supporters decided it was time for a new

THE BERMUDIAN

*Hamilton and the House of
Assembly in 1920. Just 1,400 men
elected the island's representatives*

Antiquated *As democracies go,
Bermuda is unique and antiquated;
its form of government is one that
is almost extinct. Strictly speaking,
it is not a democracy at all. For
Bermuda is governed, not by the
people, but by the people who own
real estate. You must be an adult
male, owning £60 worth of land
(about $288) to vote. Or your wife
must own that amount. But your
wife may not vote.*

—Residence in Bermuda, *published
by the Bermuda Trade Development
Board, 1936*

No representation

*There are 86 women freeholders in
Paget who are being denied the
vote. The whole of the foreshore,
from east to west, is owned by
women. They pay taxes on property
worth well over £100,000, but have
no representation whatsoever.*

—*Bermudian suffragette Henrietta
Frith Tucker, explaining in court why
she refused to pay parish taxes*

initiative, and in April 1923, they officially formed the Bermuda Women's
Suffrage Society (BWSS).

They were taking up a long-standing cause, but they had no idea how
long their fight was going to take. Defeat followed defeat as the years of
campaigning wore on. The suffragists tried to get official support from the
British Parliament, but failed. They brought in heavy-hitting supporters
such as Viscountess Nancy Astor and Emmeline Pankhurst—who told
Bermudians she was surprised one of Britain's oldest colonies was so slow
to extend equal rights to women. Still, the Bermuda Assembly would not
give in. By this time, Misick had married naval officer John S. Morrell and
the couple had a daughter, Rachel. Misick's mother also remained a faithful
supporter—as did Sir Stanley Spurling. In 1925, Spurling presented the
House with the draft of the Women's Suffrage Act 1925, a document drafted
by the BWSS. Among other provisions, it proposed that "all rights, privileges
and franchises which are now enjoyed by men with regard to Qualification
for election as members of Parish vestries and Parish officers and for voting
at such elections shall henceforth equally be enjoyed by women." In less
than a half-hour, the bill was defeated 25 votes to nine.

The suffragists knew it was time to take a tougher line. Yet, the Bermuda
activists were not like the earlier militant suffragettes of Emmeline
Pankhurst's movement. There would be no chaining themselves to railings
or throwing themselves under racehorses like their English counterparts.
Instead, taking a page from Mahatma Gandhi's belief in "passive resistance,"
Morrell and her suffragettes withheld parish taxes (provoking auctions
such as the cedar-table episode), held rallies, tea parties and letter-writing
campaigns, and affiliated with similar groups overseas. One year, the
suffragists played up to the press by holding a mock funeral before an
auction, mourning "the passing of justice."

A BWSS survey found that of a population of 30,000, Bermuda had 36
government representatives elected by just 1,400 men, a fact that riled
island progressives—particularly in the 1930s when the concept of freedom
was so embattled by overseas dictatorships. In 1931, the Assembly reconsidered

152

THE
FIGHT FOR
RIGHTS

Call for review *It has been brought to my notice that the proportion of registered electors to the total population of Bermuda is less than six percent, which must be regarded as an abnormally low figure. I also wish to point out that the franchise has been very generally granted to women in the British Empire, at ages varying from 21 to 30 years, and that in this respect also the position in Bermuda would appear to call for review.*

> —Lord Passfield, Secretary of State
> for the Colonies, to the Bermuda
> government, 1930

Outstanding job *Women have done an outstanding job in their willingness to serve the causes of the local and free world community. They are entitled to the same allowance that the men get.*

> —Nathaniel Henry Vesey during the
> Assembly's debate on voting franchise
> for women, April 21, 1944

Legitimate rights *When one speaks about keeping the vote from women on the basis of sex, one must also think about keeping certain people from getting jobs because of the colour of their skin. Some say there is no race issue here. I say there is. I shall vote for this measure today because I hate to see any group enslaved by the power of others and refused their legitimate rights.*

> —Dr. Eustace Cann, MCP, in the
> Assembly's April 21, 1944 vote on
> giving women the franchise

the women's suffrage issue, but legislators remained intransigent after an hour's debate. Six years later, the vote was held again, and this time it was closer: 15 to 13.

But it was not until 1943, when an ambitious young politician named Henry "Jack" Tucker (later government leader) piloted their bill through the Assembly, that victory actually felt imminent—with a heartening 18-to-16 outcome. The following year, the 21-year-old BWSS finally saw its dream come true. On April 21, 1944, Tucker again led the charge, invoking female participation in the Second World War to stir both guilt and patriotism among his male audience. This time, the vote was 20 to 13—in favour— thanks to swing votes. The Upper House later approved the bill five to three. Bermuda's suffragettes had won their war. On March 5, 1945, the Society planted a cedar tree on the House of Assembly grounds to mark the milestone, though it later died, a victim of the cedar-blight infestation.

While suffragists included women and men who supported the extension of voting rights to women on democratic principle, most of the island's white, male establishment had openly opposed female suffrage, claiming it would undermine 'the family.' If women were helping to run the country, who would be raising their children and keeping order in their homes? they argued. Opponents also felt a 'yes' vote would endorse the greater question of universal adult suffrage (which it eventually did). But many blacks, including the handful of black 'permitted' MCPs, opposed female voting rights. Some were afraid of social and economic repercussions if they took a public stand on the controversial issue—not an unreasonable fear, given the balance of power in Bermuda's deeply segregated society. Many also believed that far from expediting the cause of black rights, allowing white women to vote would pose yet another hurdle to black equality by doubling white voting power and thus further blocking the blacks from gaining a meaningful place in Parliament.

"Though the coloured people, in the main, seemed perturbed over the granting of women's suffrage, they had little to be thankful for under the old system," wrote black MCP David Tucker in the May, 1944 edition of *The Recorder*. "We are told that in the future not only will matters be no worse for us, but a decided improvement is to be expected. If such proves to be the case, the day of universal franchise will be postponed, but nothing must deter us from working to that end; after all, we cannot have real democracy until that day arrives."

The suffragettes expressed disappointment that so few blacks had supported their campaign, for they saw their victory as a positive stride forward for women of both races. In the meantime, the first women—including Morrell—were elected to parish councils in 1945. The BWSS, its work done, was disbanded, and the Bermuda Women's Civic & Political Association was formed to lobby for the feminist cause. During the general election of 1948, the group helped elect the first two women to Parliament: Hilda Aitken and Edna Watson. Both women finished third on the ballots of Smith's and Paget parishes, respectively, and each served one term.

Morell died at age 81 on January 6, 1969. Her life's work had set the stage for the next political battle: the 20-year campaign for universal adult suffrage—along with the abolition of the exclusive property restriction— by black Bermudians.

In their own words
■ Charles Monk, 1900

THE POOR BLIND SAMPSON

There is a poor blind Sampson in this land. Shorn of his strength and bound in bonds of steel. Some of the Jamaicans have honoured Hamilton gaol some months ago by an unjust imprisonment for simply demanding justice from Walker & Company sub-contractors, but justice will not be done until some of the other contracting parties shall disgrace the gaol by an imprisonment for an open, brazen, barefaced violation of nearly every tenet of the contract and some having control shall be brought to account for a perversion of it...

There is being perpetrated in Bermuda today one of the most brazen-faced pieces of diabolical rascality in the violation of contracts, thereby starving wives and children in Jamaica and keeping honest workmen with hardly anything to cover their nakedness. Although their contract guaranteed continuous work from the landing to the termination of the two years, there are nearly 100 of them without work. One Jamaican with a contract in his pocket was told by Robinson (the foreman) to go about his business or he would give him a kick and pay 10 shillings for it. Some of the men working have not received a farthing for over a fortnight. For humanity's sake, we feel glad that His Excellency the Governor has done what he could do to get these men justice and to alleviate their condition, but they have a hard road to travel.

—Charles Monk's front-page story in the November 28, 1900 edition of The New Era, *resulting in libel charges and a four-month jail term*

BERMUDA MARITIME MUSEUM

Jamaican workers build the major Dockyard extension in 1902

It was to be many years, however, before everyone in Bermuda was allowed to vote. There had been a few black representatives in the Assembly for many years, but most of the black population was still excluded from voting or standing for office under the island's restrictive laws, which favoured property-owners. As early as the turn of the 20th Century, individuals began canvassing for black rights.

In 1902, trouble erupted when foreign workers were hired for massive extension works at the Royal Naval Dockyard. The four-year contract for the job, worth £610,000, had been awarded to C.H. Walker & Company of London. The firm set about seeking labourers from Barbados and Italy, and built barracks to accommodate the workers on a plot of Somerset land called King's Point (now the location of the Cambridge Beaches resort). The first workers to arrive were 25 Italian masons and their families who were boarded on a ship at Dockyard. Paid a shilling and sixpence per day, the workers eventually began to complain about living conditions and were subsequently replaced by Jamaicans.

Hundreds of Jamaican men, women and children were recruited, arriving on ships in cramped, uncomfortable conditions. With no food or water provided, they were housed in a building with 17 rooms, though some were forced to live in tents outside. The Jamaicans complained about substandard lodging and claimed they often were underpaid, or were not employed at all. Industrial accidents on the Dockyard worksite also led to several deaths. Within a month, there was rioting.

The workers' cause was taken up by an American named Charles Vinton Monk. The Wilmington, Delaware-born Monk had been posted to Bermuda in 1898 at the age of 31 to serve as pastor of the Allen Temple African Methodist Episcopal Church in Somerset and the Mount Zion AME Church in Southampton. He married Bermudian Fannie Parker, daughter of editor and publisher John J. Parker, and the couple had six children.

Monk, who was also a printer and journalist, resurrected *The New Era*, a crusading black newspaper in which he lashed out against the Dockyard

The West Indians

Immigrants change face of island life

Hundreds of West Indian immigrants began arriving in Bermuda in the 1890s and by the start of the 20th Century the community made up close to 20 percent of the island's population. Emigrants came from across the Caribbean, including Jamaica, Antigua, St. Kitts, Nevis, Barbados and Trinidad.

Fleeing economic depression in their home islands, particularly due to the collapse of the sugar industry, they sought employment in a wide variety of jobs, from farming and construction to the maritime trades. Like the Portuguese, however, the newcomers faced a backlash of social prejudice from Bermudians black and white, despite centuries of seaborne connections and family ties between Bermuda and the islands to the south. Lawmakers, fearful of the West Indian influx, imposed a tax of four shillings on every West Indian arrival in 1898, a levy raised to 10 shillings four years later. Once here, immigrants suffered discrimination in the form of poor housing and unemployment.

The floodgates of West Indian immigration opened in the 20th Century. The massive five-year extension of the Royal Naval Dockyard beginning in 1900 brought many skilled West Indian masons, carpenters and tradesmen; most returned home, but some remained in Bermuda, settling in tightly-knit communities in Pembroke, Devonshire and North Hamilton. Berkeley Institute, which opened on Court Street in 1897, employed West Indian teachers and provided academic schooling for Bermudian blacks, including an increasing number of children of Caribbean parentage.

More workers from the Caribbean were recruited in the 1920s to help build the Bermuda Railway. By then, a strong West Indian network had developed throughout Bermuda. Many immigrants owned property and businesses, and Caribbean cultural influences, from architecture to calypso, gombey troupes to cricket, had permeated island life.

INSTITUTE OF JAMAICA

The junkanoo—a West Indian relative of Bermuda's gombey

BERMUDA MARITIME MUSEUM

Women in Tortola: immigrants came to Bermuda from across the Caribbean

Right: West Indian fruit-seller in Bermuda

BERMUDA ARCHIVES

LIBRARY OF CONGRESS

Marcus Garvey

Garveyism in Bermuda

Jamaican-born black-rights activist Marcus Mosiah Garvey founded the United Negro Improvement Association in 1914, promoting the "Back-to-Africa" movement that spread through the US and Caribbean.

A secret UNIA chapter was formed in Bermuda to help lobby for Garvey's dream of unifying black people through trade and government.

In November 1928, Garvey passed through Bermuda en route to Jamaica aboard the SS *Canadian Forester*. Restricted by a Canadian deportation order, however, he was barred from landing on the island—though his wife did so, and met local supporters during her visit.

The first newspapers

By 1900, Bermuda had five newspapers catering to both black and white readers. *The Royal Gazette* was the island's oldest publication. Launched in St. George's as the *Bermuda Gazette & Weekly Advertiser* by Joseph Stockdale in 1784, it moved to Hamilton in 1816 as *The Bermuda Gazette & Hamilton and St. George's Weekly Advertiser*. In 1828, the first issue of *The Royal Gazette* appeared; the paper later incorporated the *Bermuda Colonist & Daily News*, which had opened in 1866.

The island's first black newspaper, *The Bermuda Times*, was launched in 1871 by Nova Scotia-born Samuel J. Parker, Sr. who formed a family enterprise with his sons John and Samuel, Jr. called Parker and Company. *The Times* changed its name to the *Times and Advocate* in 1875, and declared it would stand:

> *For the Cause that Lacks Assistance*
> *For the Wrong that needs Resistance*
> *For the Future in the Distance*
> *And the Good that we can do.*

Parker and his sons worked together until 1882, when John Parker launched the *Home and People's Journal*. The following year, John and his father consolidated to form the *Bermuda Times and People's Journal*, which became known simply as *The People's Journal*.

American minister and black-rights activist Charles Vinton Monk joined the Parker publishing empire when he married John Parker's daughter Fannie. After his father-in-law died in 1899, Monk—who was also a printer and journalist—served as

co-editor with William H. Lacey of *The People's Journal* for a year. He and his wife then resurrected *The New Era*, a weekly that had been established in 1881 by A. L. Spedon, a white Scottish publisher from Canada, who died three years later. The Monks, who had bought title to the paper, continued publishing *The New Era* until 1904.

Bermuda then remained without a black-owned newspaper until July 18, 1925, when Alfred Brownlow Place—a

musician and keen supporter of activist Marcus Garvey—raised enough money to open *The Recorder*. There had earlier been a short-lived publication called *The Bermuda Recorder*, launched in 1899 by a white Paget resident, John J. Bushell. The new *Recorder*, run by Place himself for 47 years, continued as the island's only black newspaper for a half-century, becoming

The Bermuda Recorder, *run by Alfred Brownlow Place, was the island's only black newspaper for 49 years, before closing in 1975*

BRIMSTONE MEDIA

The Bermuda Recorder. It dedicated itself to serving the black community under the motto *Pro Bono Publico* ("For the Good of the Public"). The paper, which evolved from a weekly tabloid to a broadsheet published every Wednesday and Saturday, celebrated the achievements of Bermuda's black community, cataloguing its struggles and exposing injustices.

The Recorder closed its doors on Friday, July 11, 1975, one week before its 50th anniversary.

Favoured few *In 1936 less than 10 percent of the population could vote. Of 30,000 men, women and children, there were just 2,456 voters. Of the 2,456 voters, 1,404 were white. To qualify for election, a candidate must possess freehold property worth £240 ($1,152) and he must deposit £50 ($240) in the Colonial Treasury (forfeited if not elected).*
—Residence in Bermuda, *published by the Bermuda Trade Development Board, 1936*

contractors who employed the Jamaicans, and also criticised Bermuda's "tyrannical oligarchy."

But Monk, 35, paid the price for speaking up. He was charged by Bermuda's attorney general with four counts of criminal libel for his fiery articles, and went to trial in Supreme Court on March 20, 1903. Monk defended himself in the long and sensational trial, after his Jamaican lawyer, the highly-respected Matthew Henry Spencer-Joseph, died suddenly in his hotel room at age 42 (rumours of the day speculated that he was poisoned).

The trial's outcome on December 16, 1903 saw Monk convicted and jailed for four months and fined heavily. Eventually, he moved back to the United States. But a beginning had been made for black people standing up for their rights in an increasingly modernising island. Notably, the episode gave impetus to the first labour union lobbyists. In 1919, the Bermuda Union of Teachers was formed by black teachers; years later, they would be followed by their white counterparts, and the two groups would finally amalgamate after desegregation.

CHAPTER FOURTEEN

A Perfect Paradise

PROTECTING OUR UNIQUE BUT FRAGILE ENVIRONMENT

Dr. William Beebe, left, and Otis Barton with the bathysphere

The morning of June 6, 1930 dawned perfectly calm, the late spring gales of the previous days giving way to a silky stillness along Bermuda's South Shore. Brooklyn-born biologist, explorer and author Dr. Charles William Beebe decided to take advantage of the good weather and, with his colleagues, struck out to sea early in an entourage that included the tugboat *Gladisfen* and a converted Royal Navy gunboat, the *Ready*. Leaving their East-End headquarters at Nonsuch Island, they chugged through the island-sprinkled Castle Roads channel, where the clifftop ruins of Richard Moore's forts looked down on the flotilla. The timewarp wasn't lost on Beebe, 52, who wondered what Moore might have said 300 years earlier, "if he could have watched our strange procession steaming past. In all likelihood, the steaming part would have mystified and interested him far more than our chief object."

The "chief object" of the day was to be a test run of the bathysphere, an odd-looking contraption that would make history in Bermuda's waters by carrying Beebe and its inventor Otis Barton to record-breaking ocean depths which until then, had been strictly the realm of science fiction. Brought to Bermuda that year, the bathysphere was a steel pod attached to 3,500 feet of $7/8$-inch steel cable that would be lowered and raised by a seven-ton steam winch that had been installed, along with boilers, on the barge. With three window ports made of three-inch-thick fused quartz, a circular bolted door, and a diameter of four feet, nine inches, the bathysphere was designed to carry to record depths a maximum of two people—even a couple of six-footers, as Beebe and Barton happened to be.

An hour later, 10 miles offshore amid mildly heaving swells, Beebe stopped the group. Here, where Bermuda's sea floor fell away to more than a mile and a half, they would attempt their first manned descent. The half-

> **Bermuda:** *a perfect paradise in which an earnest Naturalist may luxuriate.*
> —The Canadian Naturalist and Geologist *on Bermuda, 1857*

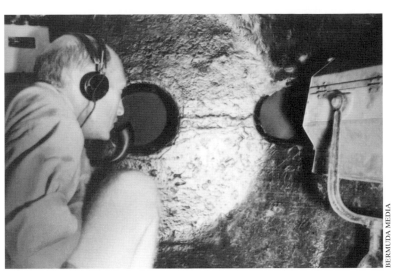

Dr. William Beebe in the cramped confines of the bathysphere

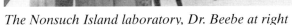

The Nonsuch Island laboratory, Dr. Beebe at right

'We are still alive'

- *We have just splashed below the surface.*
- *We are at our deepest helmet dive.*
  ...60 feet
- *The Lusitania is resting at this level.*
  ...285 feet
- *This is the greatest depth reached in a regulation suit by Navy divers.*
  ...306 feet
- *We are passing the deepest submarine record.*
  ...383 feet
- *The Egypt was found at this level by divers in rigid shells.*
  ...400 feet
- *A diver in an armoured suit descended this far into a Bavarian lake—the deepest point which a live human has ever reached.*
  ...525 feet
- *Only dead men have sunk below this.*
  ...600 feet
- *We are still alive and one quarter of a mile down.*
  ...1,426 feet

  —*Messages sent by William Beebe and Otis Barton from the bathysphere up a telephone line to their colleagues at the surface off Bermuda, June 1930*

mile of rubber hose containing telephone and electric-light wires leading from the bathysphere to the surface was unravelled. The necessary oxygen tanks and chemicals were installed in the bathysphere—calcium chloride for absorbing moisture and soda lime for removing carbon dioxide from their self-contained atmosphere. Finally, it was time to launch. Beebe crawled into the cold metal capsule and Barton clambered in after him. At their signal, the 400-pound door was swung shut, and its huge bolts screwed tight.

Inside, Beebe and Barton adjusted the phone, tested their searchlight and opened the oxygen valve that would keep them alive for the next hour. "I remembered what I had read of Houdini's method of remaining in a closed coffin for a long time," said Beebe, "and we both began conscientiously regulating our breathing and conversing in low tones."

The pair felt the bathysphere tremble and lift off the *Ready*'s deck as the crew manoeuvred the winch and swung the metal globe over the side of the barge. Beebe and Barton, peering through their magnifying ports, saw a "froth of foam and bubbles" as the bathysphere plunged through the surface. The *Ready*'s quickly vanishing keel was their last visible link with the "upper world." Their unprecedented journey had begun.

Down, down they went, to 50 feet, then 100, as the bathysphere sank lower and lower into what Beebe would describe as the "ever-deepening twilight." Beyond, the sea's brilliant bluish-green haze seemed to swallow them up as they descended farther than any human, all the while talking to their colleagues at the surface, who noted every observation. "The sound of the human voice had, all unconsciously to us, seemed a much surer bond than the steel cable or the sturdiness of the sphere," Beebe would later write.

At 300 feet, Barton called out in surprise. Beebe turned his flashlight on the door and to his shock, saw "a slow trickle of water beneath it. About a pint had already collected in the bottom of the sphere. I wiped away the meandering stream," he said, "and still it came." Beebe and Barton watched the trickle, trying to stay confident in the knowledge a solid-steel door protected them. Knowing the inward pressure was increasing with every foot of depth, Beebe gave the command to descend even further. The tactic worked; the trickle stopped.

In their own words

■ William Beebe, 1934

At 10:44 we were sitting in absolute silence, our faces reflecting a faint bluish sheen. I became conscious of the pulse throb in my temples and remember that I kept time to it with my fingers on the cold damp steel of the window ledge. I shifted the handkerchief on my face and carefully wiped the glass, and at this moment we felt the sphere check in its course—we felt ourselves press slightly more heavily on the floor, and the telephone said, "Fourteen-hundred feet." I had the feeling of a few more meters' descent, and then we swung quietly at our lowest floor, over a quarter of a mile beneath the surface.

I pressed my face against the glass and looked upward, and in the slight segment which I could manage I saw a faint paling of the blue. I peered down, and again I felt the old longing to go further, although it looked like the black pit mouth of hell itself—yet still showed blue. I thought I saw a new fish flapping close to the sphere, but it proved to be the waving edge of The Explorers' Club flag—black as jet at this depth.

My window was clear as crystal, in fact clearer, for, as I have said before and want to emphasize, fused quartz is one of the most transparent of all substances and transmits all wave lengths of sunlight. The outside world I now saw through it was, however, a solid, blue-black world, one which seemed born of a single vibration—blue, blue, forever and forever blue…

When, at any time in our earthly life, we come to a moment or place of tremendous interest, it often happens that we realise the full significance only after it is all over. In the present instance the opposite was true, and this very fact makes any vivid record of feelings and emotions a very difficult thing. At the very deepest point we reached I deliberately took stock of the interior of the bathysphere: I was curled up in a ball on the cold damp steel, Barton's voice relayed my observations

Deep-sea fish chasing squid, as described by Beebe from the bathysphere and painted by his artist colleague Else Bostelmann

BERMUDA AQUARIUM, MUSEUM & ZOO

and assurances of our safety, a fan swished back and forth through the air, and the ticking of my wrist watch came as a strange sound of another world.

Soon after this there came a moment which stands out clearly, unpunctuated by any word of ours, with no fish or creature visible outside. I sat crouched with mouth and nose wrapped in a handkerchief and my forehead pressed close to the cold glass—that transparent bit of old earth which so sturdily held back nine tons of water from my face. There came to me at that instant a tremendous wave of emotion, a real appreciation of what was momentarily almost superhuman, cosmic, of the whole situation: our barge slowly rolling high overhead in the blazing sunlight, like the merest chip in the midst of ocean, the long cobweb of cable leading down through the spectrum to our lonely sphere, where, sealed tight, two conscious human beings sat and peered into the abyssal darkness as we dangled in mid-water, isolated as a lost planet in outermost space. Here, under a pressure which, if loosened, in a fraction of a second would make amorphous tissue of our bodies, breathing our own homemade atmosphere, sending a few comforting words chasing up and down a string of hose—here I was privileged to peer out and actually see the creatures which had evolved in the blackness of a blue midnight which, since the ocean was born, had known no following day; here I was privileged to sit and try to crystallise what I observed through inadequate eyes and to interpret with a mind wholly unequal to the task.

To the ever-recurring question, "How does it feel?" I can only quote the words of Herbert Spencer: I felt like "an infinitesimal atom floating in illimitable space." No wonder my sole written contribution to science and literature at the time was: "Am writing at a depth of a quarter of a mile. A luminous fish is outside the window."

—*William Beebe, on a descent in the bathysphere off Bermuda, in* Half Mile Down, *1934*

Greatest interest *About 8.7 per cent of the total native flora is endemic, there being 61 species in Bermuda or its waters not known to grow naturally anywhere else in the world. These plants are of the greatest interest to naturalists, as they presumably developed in Bermuda from related plants formerly existing but now mostly extinct here.*

—Nathaniel Lord Britton, director of the New York Botanical Gardens and a professor at Columbia University, New York, in Flora of Bermuda, *1918*

Excellent position *That the Bermudas afford an excellent position from whence to observe the annual migration of many species of the feathered tribes of America, cannot be doubted.*

—John Matthew Jones, The Naturalist in Bermuda, *1859*

Fairy world *What a revelation of beauty! Different forms of plant and animal life. Plants and corals, shells and fishes, in all shades of colour. To look into the sea gardens of Bermuda is like a glimpse into a fairy world.*

•••

Bermuda is a little world, and will bear study; there is much to be seen, there is much to be learned, and very much to enjoy.

—Frank R. Bell, in Beautiful Bermuda: The Standard Guide to Bermuda, *9th edition, 1946*

The bathysphere dropped to 400 feet, then to 600 before pausing at 700. Thousands of human beings had reached this depth and even gone to lower levels, Beebe noted, "but all of these were dead, drowned victims of war, tempest, or other Acts of God. We were the first living men to look out at the strange illumination—and it was of an indefinable translucent blue quite unlike anything I have ever seen in the upper world."

Finally, at 803 feet, Beebe felt they had achieved enough on this particular adventure and they returned to the surface to celebrate their history-making dive with "the memory of living scenes in a world as strange as that of Mars."

The two scientists would return to the bathysphere in the following days, months and years, marvelling at the spectacle of themselves dangling "in a hollow pea on a swaying cobweb a quarter of a mile below the deck of a ship rolling in mid-ocean." On August 15, 1934, Beebe and Barton reached a new record depth of 3,028 feet (half a nautical mile), winning themselves, and Bermuda, headlines around the world.

As well as the actual physical achievement, their dives garnered eye-popping images and important information for the world of science. Some 300 paintings and drawings, published in *National Geographic* magazine, *The New York Times* and other media, were the result of their deep-ocean observations, as Beebe's detailed comments were relayed by phone to an artist, Else Bostelmann, who also observed first-hand specimens brought back to the Bermuda laboratory. Beebe's findings were populated by what looked like imaginary creatures—iridescent fish, silvery eels, flying snails, mists of crustaceans, even a "golden-tailed serpent dragon"—though most of the exotic fauna seen from the bathysphere was captured and preserved for empirical study.

Beebe, the erstwhile assistant curator of birds at the New York Zoological Society (today the Wildlife Conservation Society) had later shifted his focus to fish. He was the first director of the Society's Institute for Tropical Research when he came to Bermuda in the 1920s, interested in studying life in the depths of the Atlantic. Beebe was offered the use of Nonsuch Island as a marine research station, and there he established the Bermuda Oceanographic Expedition from 1928–31. Beebe's research would continue periodically through to the Second World War, using Bermuda as a base for his pioneering expeditions.

Over the years, many renowned scientists like Beebe carried out their work either in Bermuda or its surrounding waters. The island's mid-Atlantic location was an ideal laboratory from which to study the environment, thanks to its unique marine habitat, mild climate and depths of more than 12,000 feet that could be quickly reached from the shore year-round. As the world's northernmost coral atoll, Bermuda posed an enigma which also attracted numerous visiting geologists. The trend was heightened by the fact that scientific inquiry was booming during the first half of the 20th Century —especially during the peaceful years between the World Wars when expeditions such as Beebe's were carried out by explorers around the globe.

The wave of scientific curiosity had been triggered by groundbreaking discoveries in evolutionary science, engineering and physics in the mid-1800s which revolutionised Western society during the Victorian Age and set the stage for the continuing global progress of the 1900s. The world of flora and fauna was particularly under the microscope. Darwinism, based on

A pioneering environmentalist

Born in 1877, Louis Leon Arthur Mowbray was a pioneering Bermudian environmentalist who became a world-renowned aquarium designer.

As a child, he was fascinated with birds and animals and collected specimens to learn more about them. Later he became interested in photography; after apprenticing in New York, he opened a small studio in which an exhibit of his zoological oddities attracted walk-in customers.

Ironically, it was Mowbray who actually discovered a live Bermuda petrel, or cahow, at Castle Island as early as 1910—more than 40 years before his son, Louis Septaime, who followed him as curator of the Bermuda Aquarium, made the official rediscovery of the nearly extinct bird in 1951 with Robert Cushman Murphy and David Wingate. As was custom among scientists of the time, Mowbray, Sr. killed the bird to send its specimen to the American Museum, along with fossilised seabird bones he had turned up while exploring the newly-found Crystal Cave. It was not until 1916, when the world was embroiled in the First World War, that the bones were proven to be exactly the same as those in Mowbray's specimen, and a definitive identification of the petrel was possible. Even then, efforts to clearly establish the bird's existence in Bermuda would wait several decades.

But it was Mowbray's love for the sea—and everything in it—which was to guide his professional success. After crewing on vessels in Europe and the Black Sea, he returned home, and in 1907 was hired to help create and operate the island's first aquarium and marine research centre, on Agar's Island, Hamilton Harbour. Mowbray ran the facility for three years, collaborating with American institutions to which he shipped Bermuda fish for exhibit.

In 1911, Mowbray moved to Boston with his wife and two sons to design and direct a new aquarium. Three years later, he was chosen by the New York Zoological Society to serve as superintendent of the New York Aquarium. In the 1920s, he took time out from this post to build and run the Miami Beach Aquarium, Florida.

Mowbray returned to Bermuda in 1926, invited by the government to design and curate the new Bermuda Aquarium at Flatts. It opened two years later and has been a prime attraction for tourists and locals ever since. Mowbray took part in overseas expeditions to bring back many interesting specimens. Several trips were organised by his friend and colleague Dr. Charles Townsend of the New York Zoological Society and sponsored by US philanthropist (and Bermuda resident) Vincent Astor. After a voyage to the Galapagos Islands, he returned with 30 tortoises, paving the Aquarium's expansion into a zoo. He also added penguins to the menagerie. Their breeding in 1936 put the Bermuda Aquarium & Zoo on the conservation map. Mowbray died in 1952.

COURTESY OF LOUIS K. MOWBRAY

Louis L. A. Mowbray with an Allison tuna, the species he named

English naturalist Charles Darwin's theory of evolution by natural selection, had triggered a new interest in animal life and its relevance to humankind, and even by the 1930s, the fantastical, sometimes grotesque, nature of Beebe's sea life would have enthralled scientists and laymen, alike.

Perhaps as a result, Bermudian society witnessed a renewed sense of responsibility for the environment, with the government acting to prevent over-fishing and damage to the island's fragile coral reef system. MPs were following a long tradition of concern for Bermuda's nature. Turtles had been protected by law since 1615, and as early as 1627, a bill had been enacted to preserve the cedar tree, whose numbers were being destroyed by shipbuilding, house construction and the crating of exports. Further conservation measures were enforced in 1657, when the export of cedar was banned, and again in 1704 when the harvest of young trees was forbidden. The arrival of the first settlers, along with their cats, dogs, domestic animals and pests such as rats, had also wreaked havoc on the island's wildlife. Animals such as green turtles and docile cahows were killed in huge numbers, severely endangering their future and leading to their status as protected species centuries later.

The Victorian interest in natural history came to Bermuda largely through the British military garrison. Officers stationed on the island during this period hailed mostly from England's highly-educated upper classes, their interests ranging from geology and meteorology to biology, ornithology and anthropology. Their individual studies of the island's flora and fauna

In their own words
■ John Matthew Jones, *1859*

At seven o'clock on Monday evening, September 29, 1851, the heavens became beautifully illuminated by the Aurora Borealis, which extended over the crest of the intervening hills of the North Shore, far to the east and west. The lower portion visible from my residence, exhibited the usual white light of the Aurora, more or less vividly at intervals, and was bounded by a wide and luminous arc of the most beautiful roseate or carmine, extending almost to the altitude of the Polar star, and ultimately much above it. Through this reddened portion of the sky, evanescent rays of white light were continually shooting upwards. At nine o'clock the brilliancy of the phenomenon had passed away.

This is the second time that I have observed the Aurora Borealis in the Bermudas, during a residence of nearly eleven years. Familiar as I have been with this phenomenon in the latitude of 46 degrees of the North American colonies, I never before observed the heavens radiant with the beautiful deep rose colour which prevailed on both occasions.
—*John Matthew Jones,*
"Meteorological Observations"
in The Naturalist in Bermuda, *1859*

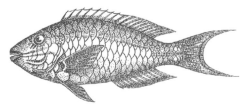

Parrotfish drawing, from Yale University professor of zoology Addison E. Verrill's book, The Bermuda Islands, *1902*

would generate international interest in Bermuda's natural history over the next century. Two of Bermuda's 19th-Century governors, Sir William Reid and Sir J. H. Lefroy, both held scientific qualifications and were deeply interested in natural Bermuda. Lefroy published the first purely scientific treatise on the island, compiling early colonial records that helped lead naturalists to Bermuda's biggest environmental success story: the rediscovery of the long-forgotten cahow.

Sir J. H. Lefroy

The endemic cahow, or Bermuda petrel, was thought to be extinct for 300 years until January 1951, when seven breeding pairs were rediscovered on the small, isolated islands of Castle Harbour. Gadfly petrels are specific to a single oceanic island, and Bermuda's cahow had taken refuge from human and animal predators on the East-End islets. After much celebration, both in Bermuda and overseas, the islands were formally declared wildlife sanctuaries. Just 10 years later, biologist David Wingate set up the nearby Nonsuch Island Nature Reserve to restore and protect not only the cahow, but all of Bermuda's wildlife, a "living laboratory" of the island's indigenous flora and fauna. Nonsuch has remained an essential oasis for nature against the problems of the modern world.

Unfortunately no scientist was able to predict the catastrophic infestation that began destroying Bermuda's endemic cedar tree in the mid-1940s, leaving a swathe of silver skeletons from one end of the island to the other. Two species of scale insect, the oystershell and the cedar scale, arrived accidentally on an ornamental species of juniper, carrying and spreading cedar blight. Before long, the infestation multiplied, the voracious, sap-sucking insects killing thousands of cedars in a short time and irrevocably changing the Bermuda landscape. Until the 1940s, cedars made up more than 90 per cent of the island's trees, with an estimated average of 13 cedars for every acre; now their numbers were depleted en masse. Scale-eating beetles, mites, wasps, ladybirds and other predators brought in to control the attack proved useless and within a decade, close to a million cedars were gone. Only 10 percent remained alive—a tragic end to the trees that had provided Bermudians with speedy ships, house frames and furniture, and shaped so much of the island's look and character. The Department of Agriculture removed the dead cedars and replanted with fast-growing casuarina pines from Australia. Despite intensive replanting efforts, the cedar forests which had blanketed the island for centuries would never return due to the trappings of modern progress: buildings, cars and roads. Still, the cedar is today making a partial comeback as biologists carry out the careful planting of scale-resistant trees.

Like the casuarinas, many foreign species were introduced to the island in the 20th Century. More often than not, these efforts at biological control brought with them a domino effect of unforeseen repercussions. Newcomers included the Jamaican anole, a lizard which was brought to Bermuda in 1905 to control the Mediterranean fruit fly, but ended up a pest by eating insects like the ladybird, which were vital to the island's ecosystem. The yellow tropical flycatcher (better known as the great kiskadee) was introduced in 1957 to control the burgeoning lizard population. But like the anole, the kiskadee also failed to perform as expected, multiplying in large numbers and devouring the eggs of bluebirds and other native birds instead.

In their own words

■ David Wingate, 2003

The 1948 hurricane had really turned me on to birds. The eye of the storm came right over Bermuda and the winds dumped hundreds of thousands of birds into the leaf-stripped forests. Instead of leaves and flowers, there were colourful birds everywhere, dead, or struggling. I didn't know what any of them were, so I was frantically painting them and drawing them and taking my pictures to [Bermuda Aquarium curator] Louis S. Mowbray. That's when he realised how serious I was.

In 1951, Mowbray invited Robert Cushman Murphy [curator of birds at the American Museum of Natural History]—the world authority on seabirds at that point —to come to Bermuda to search for the cahow, or Bermuda petrel, on Castle Islands, St. George's, where they were believed to be nesting. When Murphy arrived, Louis mentioned me to him, and Murphy said, "Bring the boy along."

I was 15, a student at Saltus Grammar School. To my good fortune, the weather was too bad for them to search the Castle Harbour islands until a Sunday, January 28, when the gale broke, I was invited to join them. That's how I came to be there when it happened: when they dug a cahow out of an incredibly deep—14-foot—crevice and noosed it. It was a life-defining moment for me, because I knew exactly what I wanted to do for a career from then on.

I was fully aware of the cahow by the time the invitation came to join the Murphy-Mowbray expedition. The previous year, 1950, I had attempted my own search. Like so many boys of my era, we used to go exploring—this was before television—and one of the great places to explore in Bermuda was "Tom Moore's Jungle" [Walsingham Nature Reserve, Hamilton Parish]. To us, it was like the undiscovered Amazon. There were lots of caves. You could go underground and

Louis S. Mowbray (left) and Robert Cushman Murphy with the rediscovered Bermuda petrel, or cahow

come out in a sinkhole. On one occasion when I was doing that, I stumbled on my first connection with the cahow. On prehistoric Bermuda, the birds would go into cave openings to find nests, then fall down and get trapped. I was climbing up a cone of soil and my hand felt something hard. In the light of day, I recognised it as a cahow bone.

I looked up. Across the water I could see the Castle Harbour islands in the distance. I realised that was the place where the cahows might have survived. The islands seemed to beckon. So, along with a couple of friends, I made a canvas-covered kayak and we paddled it all the way out there. But the water was so rough, we never plucked up the courage to land.

Finally, on that day in January, I saw my first live cahow. Murphy, Mowbray and I travelled out to Castle Harbour on the old Aquarium boat *Iridio* and landed on one of the islands. My job was to help search the crevices. Being young and agile, I could climb about and look into holes with a flashlight. The crevices were on cliff ledges, little sandy cavelets with a small hole at the back dug by the birds. One hole went off so far into the rock, we couldn't see the end of it, as there was a mound of soil in front. Murphy knew what to look for. He knew petrels were incredibly cryptic, nesting deep, remaining totally silent and staying in the dark in the daytime. But he also knew they leave a telltale type of excrement —and the first thing we found in front of that hole was the white and green excrement. There are no other seabirds known to nest in Bermuda in winter, so

Well relished Fowle *A kind of webbe-footed Fowle there is, of the bignesse of an English green Plouer, or Sea-Meawe, which all the Summer wee saw not, and in the darkest nights of Nouember and December (for in the night they only feed) they would come forth, but not flye farre from home, and houering in the ayre, and oure the Sea, made a strange hollow and harsh howling. Our men found a prettie way to take them, which was by standing on the Rockes or Sands by the Sea side, and hollowing, laughing, and making the strangest outcry that possibly they could; with the noyse wherof the Birds would come flocking to that place, and settle vpon the very armes and head of him that so cryed, and still creepe neerer and neerer, answering the noyse themselues by which our men would weigh them with their hand, and which weighed heauiest they tooke for the best, and let the others alone, and so our men would take twentie dozen in two houres of the chiefest of them: and they were a good and well relished Fowle, fat and full as a partridge.*

—William Strachey, on Bermuda's cahows, July 15, 1610

this was telling. There were also webbed footprints in the sand.

Murphy and Mowbray spent most of the day digging out sand so they could see the end of the burrow. Sure enough, there was a bird inside! Mowbray went back to the boat and got a long pole. He made a noose and pulled out the bird so they could get photographs. It resulted in the breaking of the egg the bird was sitting on—but considering it also resulted in the rediscovery of the cahow and the establishment of a conservation programme, it was probably worth it. Murphy had chosen January because it was the peak of the cahow's nesting season. Turned out he was absolutely right. Seven pairs were found on three islands.

The next day, we went back with the press and the famous photograph was taken with Murphy and Mowbray holding the cahow with its wings spread. That picture made headlines around the world. The cahow story has always captured the imagination of the press. It's kind of like rediscovering the dodo, and you can imagine what kind of sensation it caused.

Afterwards, I always thought how close I had come to actually being the rediscoverer of the cahow—that, had I explored the islands during my own expedition, it might have been me instead of Murphy. I was just the tag-along on this trip. But the experience inspired me to devote the rest of my life to bringing back that species from the edge of extinction. When I graduated from Cornell University and returned to Bermuda, Louis Mowbray put me in charge of the cahow programme and I found an additional island with eight new pairs in 1959. In 1963, I led my own expedition to Haiti, where I rediscovered the closely-related black-capped petrel, lost to science since the 1870s.

—Naturalist David Wingate on the January 28, 1951 rediscovery of the cahow on islands in Castle Harbour

As early as 1901, the Bermuda Natural History Society was promoting research into the island's plant and animal life and lobbying for both a public aquarium and a place for visiting scientists to conduct their studies. Two sister institutes were eventually born: the Bermuda Aquarium, Museum & Zoo and the Bermuda Biological Station for Research.

Society members teamed with American scientists from Harvard and New York Universities in 1903, and with the help of the Bermuda government established a biology and zoology research station in Flatts Village at the Frascati Hotel. The facility remained there until 1906.

In 1907, the British War Department leased Agar's Island in Hamilton Harbour—formerly a munitions storage site—to the Society. The group converted the former gunpowder magazine into the island's first public aquarium, and made the residences and storehouses a research station. The Agar's Island Aquarium opened on New Year's Day, 1908, and the research station also operated there until 1916. A boat ferried visitors to the facility from the foot of Queen Street, as well as from the Princess Hotel's dock. When Agar's was repossessed by the military during the First World War, neither the station nor the aquarium had a permanent home for the next decade, though the station did operate from nearby Dyer's Island between 1917–18, and then moved back to Agar's from 1919–31.

Work on a new site for the aquarium, on the other side of Flatts Inlet, began in 1926, and on February 1, 1928, the Bermuda Aquarium opened, attracting 12,000 of the island's 19,000 tourists that year. In 1926, the Bermuda Biological Station for Research, Inc. was also incorporated, as a non-profit, independent organisation serving scientists, professors and students who came to the island from around the world. The station found a permanent site in 1932 at Ferry Reach, St. George's, thanks to an endowment and facilities provided through a joint effort between the government and the Rockefeller Foundation. It remained largely a summer operation during these early years.

In 1898, the Botanical Gardens in Paget opened as a 10-acre park called the Public Gardens. In 1921, another 10 acres was added to the property and seven years later, a horticulturist was hired to develop the facility. It was not until 1958 that the park was officially named Bermuda Botanical Gardens. The neighbouring Camden Estate was added in 1966, and the whole property planted with exotic seeds and plants imported from around the globe. Other early groups promoting environmental awareness were the Bermuda Garden Club, set up in 1921 to tout the merits of horticulture and the beautification of the island through gardening, and the Historical Monuments Trust, which preserved Paget Marsh and Spittal Pond.

Bermudians' growing interest in the protection of their surroundings would only intensify as the threat of human progress and development increased. As a space-crunched microcosm, the island would need strong efforts to protect its extremely fragile natural environment. But the explorative steps made by the scientific community in the first half of the century would lay the foundations for widespread grassroots initiatives later and the creation of modern organisations such as the Bermuda National Trust and the Bermuda Audubon Society. By the time the fierce global environmentalism of the 1960s erupted, branding concepts like 'conservation' as mainstream buzzwords on the public imagination, islanders would share with the world at large a strong sensitivity to protecting their planet.

CHAPTER FIFTEEN

The New Tourism

ADVENT OF AIR TRAVEL AND LUXURY CRUISES

BERMUDA MARITIME MUSEUM

A Furness Bermuda Line cruise brochure promises fun in the sun for shivering North Americans

As the First World War neared its end, Bermuda's tourism industry hit a major snag. Visitor numbers had been declining drastically, and in 1917, Canadian Steamship Lines decided not to renew the island's regular service, citing high costs and the not insignificant dangers of sailing in war-troubled waters. Moreover, *Bermudian*, which had been kept on the New York-to-Bermuda route, was requisitioned in March that year as a British troop carrier. Suddenly, Bermuda had no way to export its agricultural goods or to bring in visitors. The island needed to attract another large shipping company.

In the summer of 1919, the New York arm of British steamship company Furness Withy came to the rescue, promising to refit *Bermudian* in return for a five-year, $15,000 annual subsidy from the island government. The deal, signed in June, marked the beginning of a long and mutually fruitful relationship between the island and Furness that would continue until 1966. During that time, the shipping company acted as a partner in the business of Bermuda tourism, providing not only luxury liners such as *Bermuda*, *Monarch of Bermuda* and *Queen of Bermuda* to bring in thousands of visitors, but also investing in capital projects such as new hotels to modernise the island's infrastructure. Above all, Furness helped generally to hone Bermuda's image as an upscale resort—a "Mid-Ocean Playground"—that would attract the type of American visitor who would fuel the island's economy throughout the 20th Century.

By 1920, it was decided by government and subsidiary Furness Bermuda Line officials that the answer to Bermuda's tourism question lay in giving America's ruling classes what they wanted—an exclusive enclave where the mega-rich could rub shoulders while they wintered in Bermuda. All eyes eventually fell on Tucker's Town, the quiet peninsula community overlooking Castle Harbour which had been named for Governor Daniel Tucker (whose early 17th-Century aim to relocate Bermuda's capital there never went ahead). The plan envisioned a self-contained neighbourhood of more than 500 acres for America's aristocracy, complete with golf-courses, tennis

The Yanks are Coming   Landing in Bermuda
The Yanks are Coming

*A hand-coloured postcard shows
Furness passengers arriving in
Bermuda*

*Other shipping lines saw profit
in calling at the island*

courts, a country club, and hotels and cottages for both winter and summer
visitors. Furness, led by local merchants, petitioned the government to
buy the land and after lengthy negotiations, got the green light.

The area had long been abandoned by most white families, but there
remained a community of black farmers, boat-builders and fishermen with
two churches, a cricket pitch, a school and a post office. A group of 24 angry
residents petitioned the government to stay on their land, though many
Bermudians, excited by the prospect of a post-war tourism revival, were in
favour of the project. The black landowners ultimately lost their fight to
keep their Tucker's Town properties. Under a special act, the hold-outs had
their land forcibly taken; in return, they were paid market value or offered
homes in other parishes. The last objector to leave was a woman named
Dinna Smith, who was physically evicted in 1923 and moved to Smith's Parish.

Before long, the elegant homes of millionaires crowded Tucker's Town,
surrounding the 18-hole golf-course of the exclusive Mid Ocean Club.
Baseball legend Babe Ruth was photographed playing the links, one of
many stars who helped boost Bermuda's monied image, including scientist
Albert Einstein, actor Harpo Marx, composer Irving Berlin and child movie
star Shirley Temple. Tourist arrivals flourished in the next few years as other
Americans followed the lead of their super-rich countrymen. Suddenly
Bermuda was the place to be, and not just in the winter time.

Furness, meantime, began investing in the island's hotels. The company

The Bermuda experience

Government and cruise line chiefs were anxious to sell Bermuda as a romantic, relaxing getaway far removed from the bustle of American cities. Thousands arrived to sample the island's charms.

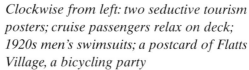

Clockwise from left: two seductive tourism posters; cruise passengers relax on deck; 1920s men's swimsuits; a postcard of Flatts Village, a bicycling party

THE BERMUDIAN

BERMUDA MARITIME MUSEUM

BERMUDA MEDIA

THE BERMUDIAN

BERMUDA ARCHIVES

*Clockwise from top:
American students frolic on
the beach; a romantic lane
near Elba (Elbow) Beach;
on a bicycle made for two;
the Kenwood Hotel on Reid
Street; an East Coast 'society'
visitor; a tourism brochure
depicts a languid day on the
water*

THE BERMUDIAN

FAMOUS FACES *Some of the world figures who were drawn to Bermuda's charms*

The Prince of Wales, who abdicated as King Edward VIII, arrives in 1931

New York Yankees slugger Babe Ruth tries his luck on the links

Frequent visitor Woodrow Wilson, who later became US president. He even signed a petition against allowing cars on Bermuda's crushed-coral roads

Colony of contentment

Your voyage to the Bermuda Islands will bring you more than a change of scene and climate. It may even work a miracle in your mental viewpoint, because of the cheerfulness of the Bermuda environment. The depression has happily missed these little islands, and instead you find an almost unbelievable era of contentment and good cheer. The proverbial restfulness and scenic charm of Bermuda were never so helpful as now; here one finds peace of mind and new strength and energy…Come during the fall or winter, for relaxation and recreation in Bermuda's equable climate. You need no passport to enter this mid-ocean haven.

—*Bermuda Trade Development Board advertisement, October 1931*

bought the St. George's Hotel in 1921, and the Bermudiana in Hamilton three years later. But its flagship property would be the Castle Harbour, which, with a golf-course, docks and beaches, demanded a massive labour force that resulted in the recruitment of 600 Azorean contractors. The project took two years, and on November 30, 1931, Governor Lieutenant-General Sir Thomas Astley Cubitt opened the 400-room hotel, the latest star in Bermuda's expanding tourism firmament.

'Tourism' was truly coming of age. With the horrors of the Great War behind them, western societies embraced the new freedom and affluence, which, with the advent of modernised transport, led to a whole new breed of traveller. Throughout the 1920s and '30s, the whole concept of travel would evolve—from a solitary pursuit to a collective mentality shaped by careful marketing that created and sold Bermuda to the world at large.

Along with its relaxed lifestyle and pretty aesthetic, Bermuda lured American visitors with yet another advantage: alcohol. Prohibition—a US policy banning liquor sale or consumption—stretched from 1919–33, and like their predecessors throughout the centuries, Bermudian entrepreneurs were not about to miss a lucrative opportunity. Rum-runners used the island as a trans-shipment headquarters to smuggle liquor into the States. But tourists were not complaining; in the face of a 'dry' America, they turned to Bermuda, where during the 1920s, bars, restaurants and hotels had become, according to a British associate of the Trade Development Board, "one continual carousal."

On April Fool's Day, 1930, a seaplane carrying three Americans left New York City on what would later be hailed as an "epochal flight." The Stinson cabin monoplane, powered by a 300-horsepower Wright engine, would become the first airplane to cross the 666 miles of water between North America and Bermuda.

Its three crew, navigator Captain Lewis A. Yancey, pilot William Alexander and radio engineer Zeh Bouck, made history at 10 o'clock the following morning, a Wednesday, when they swooped down for a landing on Hamilton Harbour aboard the *Pilot Radio*. It had not been the smoothest flight. The trio had departed New York at 9:39 a.m. the previous day, expecting to reach the island in eight hours. But strong winds delayed them and they decided to land and spend the night at sea rather than risk missing Bermuda completely in the darkness. At one minute to six that evening, they had set the plane down 60 miles north of the island, notifying *The New York Times* of their decision. The Canadian National Steamship Line's *Lady Somers*, en route to Halifax, turned back to offer the plane assistance, but when it found the trio in no difficulty, the liner continued its trans-Atlantic journey as scheduled.

Early the next morning, pilot Alexander took off again, braving the heavy swells in what *The Bermudian* magazine would later describe as "a great feat of airmanship." At 6:30 a.m., ebbing fuel forced the plane down once again, this time just four miles off the island. The three Americans swapped gasoline between the plane's various tanks and managed to make another takeoff. Finally, after five more minutes of flying, the pioneering *Pilot Radio* came down in Murray's Anchorage, off St. George's. After refuelling, the plane, carrying a handful of local VIPs including Trade Development Board chairman John "J. P." Hand, flew down the South Shore and finally came to a triumphant stop on the Hamilton waterfront. Their maverick journey won the trio $1,000 each and headlines around the globe.

The race now began to bring the first visitors by air. There had been a short-lived aviation company in Bermuda in 1919, offering charters to fly over the island, but the first air arrival did not occur until 1926, when an American dirigible, an airship named *Los Angeles*, made a long, slow journey to the island, buffeted by high winds. It was Charles Lindbergh's trail-blazing solo flight across the Atlantic the following year that ignited a new fervour for aviation; the glamour and novelty of airplanes attracted rapt media coverage and public interest. It would be years before commercial airliners braved the distance from the American mainland, but the Bermuda government realised the potential and in July 1927, the Trade Development Board offered £2,000 to the first non-stop flight from America in the next four months. No one claimed the prize.

Nine months after *Pilot Radio*'s expedition, another floatplane successfully completed the journey without a hitch. On Wednesday, January 7, 1931, the Bellanca seaplane *Tradewind*, piloted by Beryl Hart and navigated by Lieutenant William S. MacLaren, flew from Norfolk, Virginia to Bermuda in about seven hours. It marked the first leg of "a journey calculated to demonstrate the commercial possibilities of trans-Atlantic flight between America and Europe, with Bermuda and the Azores as intermediate refuelling points," according to *The Bermudian*. Unfortunately, Hart and

Pilot Radio and crew at Murray's Anchorage, St. George's, after the historic flight from New York

Beryl Hart and William MacLaren celebrate in Bermuda before vanishing over the Atlantic in their plane, Tradewind, *below*

Cruising on the *Queen of Bermuda*

In their own words

■ Captain Bill Motts, c. *1935*

On a Christmas Cruise, the ship is fully booked with a total of 800 First Class passengers, who will be seen off by 3,000 visitors. Outside the pier, a steady stream of taxis disgorge passengers and visitors, as porters whisk away their baggage. Florist vans deliver dozens of magnificent Bon Voyage Vases and arrangements of flowers; while others have huge baskets of fruit or cases of champagne for going-away parties. Most of the women are fur-coated, and adorned with orchid corsages and, with their husbands, sweethearts and friends, stream aboard, where they are taken to their various decks in elevators operated by pill-boxed, silver-buttoned and white-gloved bellboys.

I shall never forget our smallest boy bellboy, 'Jimmy,' who is undoubtedly a millionaire by now. He was 16 years old and four-feet, six inches tall,

> *The* Queen of Bermuda *became symbolic of the age of luxury liners*

with a freckled face and an infectious grin, and was an all-round good youngster liked by everyone. Passengers would pat him on the head and say: "Oh, isn't he cute." Jimmy would beam, and they would make some remark like: "Are you always so happy?" He would beam more and say: "Well, madam, today is my birthday," which invariably brought forth a dollar tip. That boy always had two birthdays a trip—one outwards and one homewards, when there was a different crowd of passengers on board. We did upwards of 50 cruises a year, and, so far as I know, he was never caught out.

Soon the whole ship is controlled bedlam. Cocktail parties in dozens of state-rooms, and the stewards making a fortune in tips, with buckets of ice and trays of hors d'oeuvres. Millions of questions are asked. A lady once asked me: "Officer, which way do we go out?" and pointing towards the bow of the ship, continued, "That way?" "Well, madam, if we go out that way, we go right up 55th Street and land in Roosevelt Hospital." That was rewarded with a somewhat blank look and: "Oh, I see, thank you." Then you smile and put her right.

Sunset in New York on December 22nd comes at 4:31 p.m., and this is the time that

BERMUDA MEDIA

all flags are lowered. At 4:20 p.m., the crews are stood by the various halyards and winches. The Officer of the Watch is on the bridge with the Bugler. At exactly 4:31, the officer gives the signal and, as the first plaintive note of the bugle rings out, every flag begins to descend slowly and with absolute precision, all reaching the deck as the final note from the bugle sounds. On the deck, even the most boisterous of the passengers and visitors are silenced by this magnificent piece of pageantry. Immediately, the masthead Christmas tree lights, together with the flood-lights on the three red- and black-banded funnels and superstructure are switched on, accompanied by oohs and aahs, and "How on earth did they get up there?"

At 5:55, the engines are put on 'Standby' and the Senior Bridge Officer reports to the captain that everything is in readiness for sailing. Somehow by 5:58 p.m., all visitors are ashore—a few a little the worse for wear—and a minute later the gangways are clear and the doors closed. Passengers line the decks shouting to their friends and vice versa. Thousands of coloured paper streamers fragilely join the ship to shore.

In five minutes from 'Letting Go,' the tugs are dismissed, and the six ships slide silently down the North River in line ahead, each a blaze of light topped off with

the masthead Christmas trees. New York City is a veritable fairyland with literally millions of lights and, as we approach the downtown skyline of sky-scrapers, one in particular stands out; every light in every room has been switched off, except those which form a gigantic White Cross 40 storeys high—spectacular!

The brilliantly floodlit Statue of Liberty from her great height gazes down benignly as we glide past, and hundreds of passengers line the decks of the large Staten Island ferries, and shouts of "Bon Voyage" and "Merry Christmas" can be heard as we pass. Tugs towing strings of barges (many with garbage), invisible except for their navigation lights are passed, and the myriad lights on shore decrease rapidly as we approach the flashing lights of the buoyed channel leading to the open sea. Promenade decks have emptied, as there is a chill wind blowing and most passengers are dressing for dinner.

Down below, the Cocktail Lounges are full of passengers in evening dress. The main Dining Saloon with its tables of snow-white napery and gleaming silverware is filled with the first dinner sitting. Quiet and efficient stewards anticipate every wish and help with the menu that seems to include just about every conceivable gourmet dish.

In an alcove on the deck above overlooking the Dining

A magazine advertisement glamourises cruising on the Queen

Saloon, an eight-piece orchestra softly play suitable music, and after dinner they will play for those who wish to dance in the beautiful ballroom, 70 feet long and 60 feet wide, with its twinkling starlit ceiling and Verandah Cafes on each side. Others will spend their time in the Smoking Room—a quieter atmosphere with its rich rugs, exquisite French tapestries, and the sofas and lounge chairs upholstered in soft deep red leather, with a huge fire-place and mantel.

Chuckles emanate from the Bar, as the affable bar-tender regales his customers with jokes and stories. Still others will go to the Lounge to watch latest movies, or to the well-stocked Library and Writing Room. Everywhere is the essence of comfort.

—Captain A. W. "Bill" Motts, *navigation officer of the* Queen of Bermuda, *on the ship's annual Christmas cruise from New York to the island, a popular tradition at the peak of the pre-Second World War season*

'The menu seems to include just about every conceivable gourmet dish'

NEW YORK—in 5 Hours!

R. M. A. CAVALIER
IMPERIAL AIRWAYS
To Bermuda
TUESDAYS
AND
SATURDAYS
Return
MONDAYS
AND
FRIDAYS

U. S. A. BERMUDA CLIPPER
PAN AMERICAN AIRWAYS
To Bermuda
WEDNESDAYS
AND
FRIDAYS
Return
THURSDAYS
AND
SUNDAYS

BERMUDA ARCHIVES

The Cavalier *(right, at Darrell's Island) and the* Bermuda Clipper *began the revolution in air travel to the island*

BERMUDA ARCHIVES

BERMUDA MARITIME MUSEUM

From a Furness Bermuda Line tourist brochure

MacLaren never lived to see that dream become reality. After a celebration in Bermuda, they departed for the Azores—and were never seen again.

Such early pioneers paved the way for the coming travel revolution. Anticipating the new era on the horizon, Bermuda's Assembly voted in 1934 to subsidise a seaplane base at Darrell's Island—a prelude to a deal signed by Pan American Airways and Imperial Airways that year to establish a New York-Bermuda passenger and mail service. Finally, on June 12, 1937, the first Empire-class flying-boat, Imperial's *Cavalier* left the Great Sound (where it had been assembled) for Port Washington, Long Island. Almost simultaneously, Pan Am's *Bermuda Clipper* touched down at Darrell's Island after completing the same flight in the opposite direction. Bermuda found itself in the vanguard of trans-Atlantic air travel.

Tourist air arrivals began in earnest over the next few years as both airlines launched regular services to the island aboard luxurious passenger flying-boats. Not only was the new mode of transport quick and easy—five hours as opposed to 40 during a three-day steam from New York—but it also gave Bermudians a spectacular aerial view of the island few had seen before. "Around the reefs swirl whorls of blue water in all the shades from turquoise, jade and emerald to aquamarine, cobalt and Prussian blue," wrote *The Bermudian's* editor Ronald Williams on the *Cavalier's* inaugural flight. "So breathtaking is the sight that like every other man on board the flying boat I am desperately aware that adequate description is beyond me."

Tragically, the *Cavalier* went down in the Gulf Stream in 1939 during its 290th scheduled trip to Bermuda, killing three of its 13 passengers and crew.

THE BERMUDIAN

Old versus new: a Bermuda Railway train passes a horse and cart

Even more an Eden?

A few weeks more and another season will be here. And with it will come the new **Monarch of Bermuda,** *the new Castle Harbour Hotel, the new golf-course, the new wing to the* **Princess** *[Hotel], the new railroad— maybe the new water project, work going forward on the new play-ground, the new telephone building, new street pavements, the renovated "Bermuda." In the minds of some persons, all this newness will conjure up thoughts of a completely changing Bermuda. "Keep Bermuda quaint," has been their plea. It has never been our impression that Bermuda was made quaint by the bumps on Front Street, by the difficulties and lack of comfortable transportation, by flies or by mediaeval methods of shop-keeping. Bermuda's quaintness, as we conceive it, is embodied in its gardens, its little white coral-stone houses, its flower-bordered paths, its unequalled waters, its vegetation. Bermuda can be made still more of an Eden than it is—or ever was.*

—Editor Ronald John Williams,
The Bermudian, *November 1931*

But the clock could not be turned back. American travellers for the most part had faith in the safety of the seaplanes and visitor numbers began their predicted upswing: by 1937, the island welcomed more than 82,000 tourists a year aboard planes and cruise ships, compared to just 13,000 in 1920. Bermuda was well on its way into the age of aviation.

It was Halloween, 1931, when a ceremony outside Number One Shed in Hamilton set in motion a short-lived, but beloved addition to Bermuda's landscape that became dubbed "Old Rattle and Shake." Some 150 invited guests gathered on Front Street to take part in the inaugural run of the Bermuda Railway to Somerset. The dignitaries—including the governor and his wife, British Royal Navy officials, the American consul, the police chief and the bishop of Bermuda—climbed aboard four coaches and waited excitedly. Crowds of spectators lined the sidewalk and leaned over shop balconies as Lady Cubitt entered the train's motor compartment and pressed the engine's electric starter. The train, which would be described by one journalist as "an iron serpent in the Garden of Eden," rolled into action.

THE BERMUDIAN

One of 33 bridges linking Bermuda's islands for the Bermuda Railway

Central command

When the dial telephone supplants the present "central" system in the coming winter, one of the most agreeable features of the Islands' civilisation will go. Nowhere in the world is a telephone service so intimate and companionable. "Central" is a kindly self-appointed information bureau, seemingly possessed of second sight. One never has to ask for a number—merely the name of a house or person will do. "Mr. X is boarding with some people out in Devonshire," you say, "do you think you could find him for me?" "Central" will tell you the time at any hour of day or night, and most pleasantly, and where the fire is. She tells a woman whether her husband is in the Hamilton Bar or the New Windsor Bar. When you can't get the telephone of your friends to answer, she will say, "They are dining with their father and mother this evening, I think. Shall I ring them there for you?
—The Story of Bermuda,
by Hudson Strode, 1932

Holiday shopping

Once the man in your party has purchased a pair of Doeskin trousers, he should not object to your buying a few pairs of white doeskin gloves, which wash as easily and satisfactorily as a linen handkerchief.
—Bermuda in Three Colours,
by Carveth Wells, 1935

No equal *I've been all over the world, and have seen many of the famous places noted for their beauty, but I have never seen any other to equal Bermuda.*
—Canadian Prime Minister Mackenzie
King on a 1930 visit to the island

The fanfare had been a long time coming. As far back as 1899, the railway idea had been proposed, but it was not until the 1920s that plans began to take shape. The privately-financed Bermuda Railway built the line from Somerset to St. George's, through Hamilton, amid a slew of problems, controversies and delays. When the 22-mile line opened on October 31, it was already three years late, but Bermudians embraced it as a huge step forward on an island where motor cars were banned and transportation between the parishes had, until then, been restricted to boat, carriage or bicycle along primitive roads.

The train, by contrast, offered all-weather comfort, travelling the length of Bermuda via 33 bridges which linked the islands and crossed coastal inlets. Once aboard, passengers got a whole new view of Bermuda. Service was racially segregated. The train's first-class coaches offered wicker chairs, while benches were provided for cheaper seats. Locals could now easily commute to work in Hamilton, and tourists could load on their bicycles, ready to use once they reached their destination.

Unfortunately, the railway's glory days were soon to be over. Bermuda's climate corroded the train's iron parts and the cost of importing diesel fuel was exorbitant. Wartime use by the military also left the line and rolling stock in very poor shape. Engineers also discovered the railway needed extensive, and expensive, repairs totalling an estimated £1 million. Eventually, the Bermuda government stepped in and bought the railway, which had never made a profit, for a mere $115,000. They operated the line at a loss for a short while before finally selling the whole operation to British Guyana. The long-delayed advent of automobiles to Bermuda after the Second World War also helped put the nail in the railway's coffin, and after just 17 years in operation, Old Rattle and Shake was no more.

The impact of changes brought about by surging post-war tourism, modern modes of transport, new hotels and new-fangled technology during these years was keenly felt by everyday Bermudians. Many feared the quickening speed of modern life and resented the steady invasion of foreigners. Even those who realised change was inevitable worried the new pressures on the island could quickly erase the quaint character that had made Bermuda unique.

Horse carriages await customers on Front Street of the late 1920s

Competing at the Agricultural Show

HORSE HEAVEN

Until the advent of mechanical transport, horses were the only form of locomotion on land and a large equine population was employed in many ways, both commercial and recreational.

The Somerset Express makes a stop

Racing at the Shelly Bay track in 1930

The Somerset Express

It stops for deliveries at various gates—a bale of hay here, a pound of beef there, a baby's high chair, a half-yard of silk to piece out a dress, a broody hen lent for setting. When the bus driver blows his whistle, out comes the person for whom the commission has been performed. The 'Express-bus' is a primitive convenience whose popularity the railway has not diminished, because the railway is too up-to-date to stop at private gates and tell the latest gossip of Hamilton.

—*Hudson Strode on the "Somerset Express," a horse-drawn bus which carried freight and passengers between Hamilton and the West End, 1932*

A hand-coloured postcard

An entry in the annual Floral Parade

The Bermuda Hunt Club. Deprived of foxes, riders instead enjoyed paper chases

All aboard the Bermuda Railway

In their own words

■ Jane A. Dublon, *1931*

It's not every day in the week that one can hop down in a strange country and be a "first passenger." What luck for me! A mere visiting American tourist, I had an invitation to ride on the first train ever to run on the Bermuda Railroad with a load of passengers—the very first.

A carriage took me to the Elbow Beach crossing and there I sat on the morning of May 15th. The driver was resting, the horse was resting, but I was waiting impatiently for the locomotive to come along and pick me up. I pictured a black, round-bellied caboose like the steam-puffers we have in the States and waited to hear its hoarse screech.

"Tootle-de-oot!" There sounds a cross between a whistle and an automobile horn and up the track comes a strange conveyance, not at all like my advance ideas. It looks like an enormous truck whose owner has dressed it up for a picnic. It does not belch steam, for it is, I discover later, a well-behaved petrol [diesel]-eater. Its previous role has been that of ballast carrier, but "Sally," as I immediately name her, has now been scrubbed as clean as the deck of a ship. Three double rows of benches have been built and anchored firmly. They could seat two on each side, or twelve in all.

The new white wood glistens invitingly, but there are only five passengers in this first "coach" which has already made the fifteen-minute run from Hamilton to Elbow Beach Crossing. Two more fares, myself and a construction engineer, climb up the new steps in the back. Those who are already at home in Sally are Mr. Geoffrey P. Barker, the inspecting engineer, Mr. Dunn of Scotland, Mr. Jones, another Englishman, chief Bermuda engineer in charge of the road. That comprises the

official testing inspection party…The whistle-horn shrills again, and we are off at high speed, fifteen miles an hour, for this is solid road-bed here in Paget Parish and Warwick. Our locomotive engineer is invisible in the caboose, but a man stands up above in front to relay instructions from Chief Engineer Jones to the driver. "Slow down: it is at crossings, "crawl along" when we come to places where the road-bed is not completely finished. We wind through a green and cut across the smooth, velvety turf of the Belmont Manor golf-links. On the landward side lie the rolling cedar-covered hills at the centre of the island, while northwards, on our right is blue Hamilton Harbour. I have driven through Warwick in a carriage to Gibbs

A popular stop on the Bermuda Railway

Inside the first-class carriage

Hill, and I have followed the soft crunchy South Shore roads with Jimmy the Groom and Ginger the Hired Mount, but never before have I had so perfect a view of the island. The height of the car, added to the elevated road bed, makes a perfect vantage point. Railroads spoil Bermuda for the visitor in search of quaint spots and natural beauty? Never…

But no time to stop, we must hurry on to a rendezvous with a speed boat. For

when we took our ride, the bridge to Somerset Island was not completed and we had to leave Sally behind. At the Southampton end of the road-bed we climbed down to the waterfront, embarked and poked around Ely's Harbour…and then came back to the Bermuda Railroad. But what a change! No nice, new ballast car this time. No, nothing but narrow gauge construction tracks to ride upon and flat cars hitched together. Long logs tied on lengthwise were the seats this time, with the one luxury of new steamer blankets. I picked a seat and was advised to move, because it was just where two cars were tied together and they might decide to part company!

A little ride, then a walk over tracks as yet unsafe…Ten minutes' walk brought us to more solid track, and again we found a flat-bed car awaiting us for the last lap of the journey. This part of the road is the oldest and the sides of the fill are already overgrown with bright blue morning glories.

It wasn't long before we reached Somerset terminus and the end of our exciting, thrilling "first" ride. But by the time this appears in print, railroad rides in Bermuda should be no novelty. Real cars will probably be going at thirty miles an hour crossing the completed bridge to Somerset Island.

—*Janet A. Dublon,* The Bermudian, *1931*

Tourist brochures promised grace and luxury on a paradise island

BERMUDA MARITIME MUSEUM

BERMUDA MEDIA

The first, narrow, cut of Khyber Pass, Warwick

THE BERMUDIAN

Lily fields were an attractive subject for visiting artists and photographers

"If she continues her progressive pace the pleasant slogan stamped on outgoing mail—'Come to the Isles of Rest'—may soon become a quaint joke," commented Hudson Strode in his book, *The Story of Bermuda*, published in 1932. "The Bermudians themselves are more or less dazed by the rapid developments in their little country. Those few not in trade and those not owning houses to rent to Americans are justified in resenting tourists, for the Islands stand perilously in danger of becoming merely the rich American's playground and the 'tripper's delight.' American gold is tempting and progress is insidious."

And 'progress' continued. On December 21, 1931, the Bermuda Telephone Company opened its new automatic telephone exchange. A series of conversations took place between Washington DC and Bermuda to commemorate the milestone—with the governor sending greetings to the under secretary of state, and the American consul in Bermuda exchanging pleasantries with the British ambassador in Washington. The dial telephone would replace the central system between 1932–33.

Another project that garnered public interest and debate was the so-called "Watlington Waterworks" project in which Hamilton Mayor Sir Harry Watlington tapped into a natural lens in a Devonshire hillside in a bid to alleviate the island's perennial water shortage. Pipelines were laid in Hamilton and construction began on a purification plant with a reservoir capacity of 240,000 gallons, allowing residents and businesses to purchase water during times of drought when their own water tanks ran dry. It became the island's first public water system.

Bermuda's improving facilities and increasing attraction to tourists insulated the island from the Depression when most parts of America and Europe were suffering from the economic and social catastrophe. The island's allure as an unspoiled "Fairyland" stayed intact throughout the 1930s—a testament to the painstaking 'branding' of Bermuda as an elite escape. Yet just as all signs pointed to unstoppable success for the island's tourist trade, a dark cloud was just around the corner. The Second World War would wreak havoc on Bermuda's tourism aspirations and bring both personal triumph and tragedy to island families and their relatives. But it would also change Bermuda as never before, hurling the island from the idyllic isolation it had embraced for centuries, and into the modern world.

CHAPTER SIXTEEN

Second World War

CONFLICT MAKES HEROES AT HOME AND ABROAD

I t may sound ridiculous," Bermudian Anthony "Toby" Smith wrote to his wife Faith from war-ravaged England in the 1940s, "but my work and efforts are helping—if ever so little. Some critics might say that I was wrong to leave you and the babies. My answer is they wouldn't say it if they had heard the terrifying, anticipatory drone of enemy planes, the roar of anti-aircraft guns, the fluttering scream of bombs, the crash of bombs and the almost dead silence which follows.

"And I would tell them that this isn't that rather indefinite place, 'the battlefield.' These are the towns, villages, valleys, hills and roads of England, of people like you, women, children and old fellows. God be willing, I hope you and the children will never hear them like so many people of this country have."

Thanks to heroic islanders like Smith, and his counterparts from all over the world who joined the Allied forces of the Second World War, they never had to. Smith was among the first contingent of 21 Bermudians who volunteered for overseas service; the group of 17 Bermuda Volunteer Rifles Corps (BVRC) and four Bermuda Volunteer Engineers (BVE) boarded the troop ship *Mataroa* on June 24, 1940 and sailed out of St. George's Harbour for England. Like many to follow, these soldiers would join the Royal Lincolnshire Regiment which saw action throughout Europe. Driven by duty and patriotism, Bermuda's soldiers, sailors, pilots, engineers, doctors and nurses shared both the horror and exhilaration of a dark global conflict that split the world in a showdown viewed in the most basic of terms, between 'good' and 'evil.' It was a war waged for the first time with modern mechanised weaponry against ordinary citizens. And ordinary citizens like Smith realised the unprecedented bloodshed and barbarity could be stopped only by their own determination.

"Do you suppose that German planes will stop murdering our people by our wishing it?" wrote Smith to his family. "No. I know you realise as well

Major "Toby" Smith (standing, second right) and others from the first contingent of Bermudians, sail to war aboard the troop ship Mataroa *in 1940*

BERMUDA MARITIME MUSEUM

Those who served

Hundreds of Bermudians served in the Second World War in a variety of roles around the globe. Clockwise from left: Bermudians with the First Battalion Caribbean Regiment in Egypt; members of the Bermuda Volunteer Rifle Corps in training before fighting in Europe; Randolph Richardson, an air gunner in RAF raids over Germany

BERMUDA MARITIME MUSEUM

COURTESY OF HELENE PAYNTER

BERMUDA MARITIME MUSEUM

as I do that the only thing that will stop them is to defeat them, smash them and destroy evil itself—Germany. And whose job is it to stop them? Well, it is everyone's job, everyone with a sense of decency."

Yet the decision that saw so many abandon their families in order to save the world was not an easy one to make, and soldiers like Smith found themselves bitterly torn, wrestling between their personal duty to wives and children, and the larger moral one. Driven by the commitment to country, most felt the mission which called them to arms could not be ignored.

"I often think I am a fool, an idiotic fool, but you are my love and the children our very own, and I realise that I had to come and do my bit," Smith reasoned. "And if you have ever read what the Germans have done, and are doing, in Europe— all of it, but particularly Poland and Greece—tens of thousands of people, people like us, dear, starving to death, being shot, murdered for nothing more than that they loved their homes just like us. We will be together again, and separation is better than life under Germans I believe…"

For six long years of war—from September 1, 1939 when Hitler's troops invaded Poland, to the victory celebrations of '45—Bermuda and Bermudians played a role on the world stage. Almost 500 local men left the island, joining British, Canadian and American forces to fight in theatres of war around

THE BERMUDIAN

The Nazi swastika on a German seaplane during a pre-war visit to Bermuda in 1936

In their own words
■ Major Anthony 'Toby' Smith, *1944*

COURTESY OF JONATHAN SMITH

Do you remember how I first saw you and searched and searched until I found you; my visit to you in Philadelphia; your return to Bermuda and what I shall never, never forget, the day we were crossing the little white bridge near Miamba—and our first kiss? Do you remember? I was so excited that I didn't know what to do. Then our getting engaged, your return to America and my seeing you again there, your return to Bermuda, our wedding. Then our happy times, our worries, the wonders of our babies. The joys and problems, tears and happiness and all the time, we loved one another and we managed to get along somehow. How, I am not sure, but I feel certain that a great many of our problems were due to the fact that we steadfastly loved and believed in one another.

Then my feeling that I should go to join up in England. I often think that it was wrong, very wrong, and then I am certain that I would have hated myself for not doing something to help dear old England. And in the final analysis, I am certain that little though it has been, I have done best by coming here, and I can say with some pride, "I have served my King and Country"—and woe betide the man who laughs at me.

May God grant us both health and strength to see the end of the war and may the day when we can be together come soon. Please hear our prayer, O Christ, and please take care of and keep happy and well my darling and brave wife and our dear children.

—Major Anthony F. "Toby" Smith, April, 1944, to his wife Faith, in Bermuda with their five children. A member of the BVRC, Smith left the island on June 24, 1940, serving as Commander of B Company, Royal Lincolnshire Regiment, and as an army instructor. Smith died on the battlefield in the German-occupied territory near Overloon, Holland, along with 200 Allied soldiers, including several BVRC members, on October 14, 1944

Profoundly loyal

Bermudians, easygoing, friendly and insularly self-complacent, are just as faithful in their adherence to many a British custom in their daily lives. And by some of their gardens, churches, narrow lanes and cobbled streets they have even contrived to create what impresses some romantic observers as a sort of semi-tropical Little England. Just now, of course, they are most concerned with what the effects of US military occupation will be on their placid life and landscape. But though they deeply resent and fear such innovations as hot dogs and the motor cars allowed to the US "base people," just as they resent English interference in their affairs (they were not even consulted about the base deal), they remain profoundly loyal to the Empire and are proud to be helping it survive.

—Life *magazine, August 18, 1941*

the world. More than 100 members of the predominantly black Bermuda Militia Infantry and Bermuda Militia Artillery joined the First Battalion Caribbean Regiment in North Africa and Italy. Their mission included guarding German POWs. Contingents from the exclusively white BVRC, some 182 men in total, and BVE, joined air, land and sea services. Bermudian men, and some 29 women, joined the Royal Navy, the Royal Artillery, the Royal Air Force, the Merchant Navy, the Royal Marines and Royal Engineers, the Lincolnshire Regiment, the Royal Canadian Air Force and Navy, the Tank Brigade, the Parachute Regiment, the Women's Auxilliary, the United States Army and Air Force, among other services. Several were decorated for bravery and, in all, 36 gave their lives.

Major Smith was among them. At age 36, he was killed on October 14, 1944 in a German attack near Overloon, Holland. Today a British military cemetery stands on the quiet spot, where many of the 200 graves belong to men of the "Lincolns." Among the tombstones, visitors strolling through the carefully-tended site will recognise those bearing familiar names: White, Patterson, DeSilva, Smith—all Bermudians who made the ultimate sacrifice.

Like its citizens, Bermuda itself would be called upon to play an important part in the Second World War—a role that would catapult the island into the modern age and expose it to the world at large. This identity shift would occur as a result of a landmark agreement which US President Franklin D. Roosevelt would describe as "the most important event in United States defence since Jefferson's Louisiana Purchase in 1803." The British press hailed it as "one of the most far-reaching commitments in world history."

BERMUDA ARCHIVES

American work-crews lay runways at the new US airfield in St. David's. The huge endeavour created 750 acres of new land

Deeply disturbed

The people of Bermuda are deeply disturbed lest some new conception of American hemisphere defence may affect the status of this ancient Colony as an integral part of the British Commonwealth. We re-affirm our unswerving loyalty to His Majesty the King. We earnestly pray that the ties of tradition and the bonds of affection which unite us to the Mother Country may never be severed. We pledge our support to any agreement reached, but pray that such an agreement may take heed of our deep-rooted and fervent attachment to the Crown.

—Memorial sent August 20, 1940 to the secretary of state for the colonies after the US land-lease deal

His Majesty's Government are deeply touched by the loyal sentiment which inspired the Memorial and the pledges of sturdy and continued support which it contains. These are but in keeping with the traditions of the ancient Colony. His Majesty's Government desire to assure the House that there is no question of Bermuda, or any part of it, being separated from the British Empire or of the people of Bermuda ceasing to be British subjects.

—Reply from the British secretary of state, read to the House of Commons

They were referring to the 99-year 'destroyers-for-bases' deal, struck in 1940, one year into the war, between Roosevelt and British leader Winston Churchill. Under the agreement, British lands were leased to the US, some in exchange for military hardware, to provide America with air and sea facilities. In the case of Newfoundland and Bermuda, however, Britain agreed to lease land as outright gifts to the US for its naval and air bases— a diplomatic decision which, given the circumstances of the war, made political and strategic sense.

The war against Nazi Germany was going badly, and Britain urgently needed support from the US, at that time still neutral. The Americans, in turn, feared a Nazi takeover of Bermuda would have terrible consequences to their own security. Although the US was a longtime friend, Bermudians feared—even expected—the island would either be given to, or annexed by, the Americans. In fact, secret negotiations for baselands in Bermuda had been going on since before the outbreak of war.

US gunners practise at a newly-installed battery in Bermuda

BERMUDA MARITIME MUSEUM

Winston Churchill (wearing hat) at Government House in 1942

Pillars of the bridge

In this great world struggle, in this convulsion, you in Bermuda happen to be called upon to play a part of special importance and distinction ...I wish to express to you my conviction that these [US] bases are important pillars of the bridge connecting the two great English-speaking democracies. You have cause to be proud it has fallen to your lot to make this important contribution to a better world ...and for your contribution to these supreme and even, if I may say, sublime ends, I am very happy to have found myself here today to express on behalf of the Motherland and of the British House of Commons my profound gratitude.

—Winston Churchill's 7 p.m. address to a hurriedly assembled joint session of the House of Assembly and Senate at the Sessions House during his January 15, 1942 visit to Bermuda. He left for London aboard a flying-boat the following morning

The Americans expected to install 4,500 troops and, at first, planned to build a huge new air base covering most of Warwick and some of Southampton parishes, effectively cutting Bermuda in two. Bermudians were appalled, but also felt duty-bound to oblige. Their fears were eased when British authorities proposed a different site for the US Army airfield: on the islands of Castle Harbour. A second base, a US Navy station for seaplanes, would be built by connecting islands in the Great Sound, off Southampton. Under the deal, Britain and the US signed a 99-year lease, allowing America rent-free use of the Bermuda lands.

Work began in the Great Sound to connect Morgan's and Tucker's islands and King's Point, creating the first ever American naval operating base on British soil. On March 1, 1941, the Stars and Stripes was raised here. The huge project was followed by construction of the East-End airfield, an even more colossal endeavour. Squadrons of heavy machinery began bulldozing the islands of Castle Harbour, and dredging 35-million square yards of rock and coral to make landfill. The formerly peaceful backwater became a screeching, thundering mass of dust and industry. American engineers had obliterated Cooper's Island, Long Bird Island and a large portion of St. David's, which had been connected to the mainland only since 1934. Once complete by the close of 1941, the project created more than 750 acres of new land and a glistening new airstrip called Kindley Field stretched across the East End. Before long, thousands of Americans arrived.

Churchill came to Bermuda to thank the island on a closely-guarded, one-day visit on January 15, 1942 on his way back to England after signing the 26 United Nations pact in Washington DC. Arriving aboard a Boeing 314 flying-boat, Churchill landed at Darrell's Island, and was ferried to Albuoy's Point accompanied by Lord Beaverbrook, Admiral of the Fleet Sir Dudley Pound, Air Chief Marshal Sir Charles Portal and Sir Charles Wilson, his personal medical adviser. Bermuda Governor the Viscount Knollys and Lady Knollys also accompanied him, since they had been visiting the US. At 7 p.m., Churchill made his address to a joint session of the House of Assembly and the Senate, congratulating Bermuda for making such an "important contribution to a better world." Churchill called the two US bases on the island "pillars of the bridge" connecting the democracies of Britain and America. The following morning, he boarded another flying-boat for the return journey to England.

Once the dust settled, Bermudians began to feel more positive about the arrangement. Thousands of Americans meant thousands of dollars waiting to be spent, and there was a large void to be filled with the wartime departure of the tourist trade. Islanders and Americans soon got along famously, especially once the US entered the war following the December 7, 1941 attack on Pearl Harbour. That year, the Immigration Department recorded some 9,500 American base workers entering Bermuda.

American military cars and their servicewomen drivers

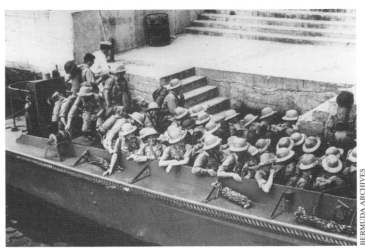

The first American troops arrive in Bermuda

Give up your homes

For centuries, St. David's Island
occupied a unique position in this
little Colony…Seafarers they were,
born with the taste of salt sea spray
in their mouths and a barometer in
their brains. They were proud of
their homes…built by their forefathers
…Suspicious of anything new,
they…clung stubbornly to a tiny
island in a changing world. These
were the people who yesterday were
asked to give up their homes. They
might just as well have been told
that they would have to give up
their lives. The request, judged by
their standards, amounted to the
same thing.

The Mid-Ocean News,
November 1940

In Bermuda where land is so precious,
it is an easier thing to offer our lives
for our country than to give up the
homes which embody traditions of
the past and hope of the future. With
the disappearance of St. David's as
we have known it goes our last link
with the simple way of life of our
forefathers and it is in this sense that
all Bermuda shares in this great
renunciation.

—*Letter to* The Royal Gazette,
November 1940

Vacation tourism might have dried up, but Bermuda rapidly became a hive of wartime activity. The island evolved into a vital naval and air hub serving warships, merchant and Allied defences. The Castle Harbour and St. George's hotels were taken over as military dormitories for US Army servicemen, and the Elbow Beach Hotel was used for storage. Ships' crews, airmen and military personnel of many types passed through the island during these years, filling the fiscal and physical void left by holidaymakers.

At the West End, the Royal Navy's West Atlantic Squadron operated out of Dockyard, playing a deadly game of pursuit with Nazi pocket battleships. The Royal Air Force took over facilities on Darrell's Island, where Imperial Airways' and Pan Am's seaplanes had flown in and out with tourists immediately before the war. At Boaz Island, Sandys, the British Fleet Air Arm ran anti-German spotter planes and anti-submarine patrols.

The Americans, who in 1942 had installed anti-aircraft artillery to cover both their bases, successfully flew missions from the island to search and destroy German U-boats. There was a small Allied submarine depot at Ordnance Island in St. George's. Bermuda also provided safe harbours for merchant ships to gather while they waited to cross the Atlantic under the protection of huge convoys escorted by navy warships. Such convoys were the only protection against German U-boats and battleships, which represented a constant threat in their campaign to cut the chain of food and materials to Allied nations.

Bermuda was also chosen as an ideal intelligence-gathering headquarters for screening trans-Atlantic communications. Radio towers were erected and deciphering equipment installed at island forts, allowing the military to monitor electronic signals sent from enemy submarines in the Atlantic, and thereby providing Allied forces with key information on Axis military operations.

In August 1940, the British Imperial Censor brought in the first of 1,200 "censorettes" or "trappers"—young English women trained to speedily sift through transit mail and telecommunications, checking for secrets being passed to Germany. Installed in temporary offices set up in the Princess Hotel's basement and boarded at the Bermudiana and Inverurie hotels, they examined letters for coded messages, invisible ink and black-listed addressees, and could often open and re-seal mail without a trace.

Shot down over France

In their own words

■ John Hartley Watlington, *1943*

In the summer of 1943, England was subjected a good deal to what were called "tip-and-run" raids by German fighter-bombers. One of our defensive tactics was known as "intruder operations." It consisted of sending single-seater fighters over to particular aerodromes in France and Belgium to intercept raiders on their return. As soon as the approach of raiders was picked up by radar, pilots were detailed to take off on one of these missions.

Thus it was on the evening of June 21, 1943, several of us pilots were ordered to the RAF Station at Ford [Aerodrome] on the South Coast for night operations. We spent a couple of hours after briefing in making up individual flight plans to prospective aerodromes in France which we might be called on to visit. About midnight, I ate a very hearty meal of bacon and eggs, etc. (strictly aircrew rations) and then, sure enough, I was alerted shortly after 2 a.m. (June 22) to patrol an aerodrome near Amiens.

I was at this time attached to 400 Squadron Royal Canadian Air Force. It came under the RAF Army Cooperation Command and later became known as the Tactical Air Force. With our photographic reconnaissance aircraft and medium bombers, we were the eyes and aerial striking power for the Army. But up to this time we had done little, apart from the epic attack on Dieppe in August 1942. Having become proficient as the Canadian Army's "seeing-eye," we had been allowed to carry out such active operations as train-busting over the French countryside (we were limited to freight trains). We then advanced to

Watlington in the cockpit of his fighter plane

some earnest night-flying training preparatory to "Ranger" operations which again involved a bit of train-busting, beating up road convoys and generally making a nuisance of ourselves, all by the light of the moon.

These operations put us in good stead for being used to counteract the tip-and-run attacks, as carried out by the Focke-Wolf 190 fighter-bombers. We were equipped with the Allison-powered North American Mustang, a single-seat fighter aircraft suitable for low-altitude reconnaissance work. It was armed with eight machine guns firing forward and could be coaxed to 350 miles per hour.

It took me but a couple of minutes to get into the air, fly to Beachy Head where I set course for the estuary of the Somme River. It was a clear moonlight night and I easily picked up the French coast and the estuary. Here I climbed to a thousand feet, then opened throttle and made a long dive, parallel with the coast, picking up speed of 350 to 400 miles an hour before turning, crossing the coast at some 50 feet. At this altitude and speed, my aircraft presented a poor target to any ground defences. Everything was very clear with a full moon in front of me, and the field, hedgerows and farmsteads stood out from the landscape through which the silvery river twisted and turned. There was not a light to be seen anywhere… [He opens fire on an enemy-run locomotive, then heads back down the line to Amiens.]

As I neared the town, there was a locomotive coming out, travelling slowly in an easterly direction. Thinking that the shooting was pretty good tonight and that the aerodrome patrolling could wait a couple more minutes, I decided to have a 'go' at this second opportunity. I

COURTESY OF THE WATLINGTON FAMILY

flew out to the side of my new target going up to 800 feet preparatory to making a slow gliding approach down to it; the slower the glide, the longer the attack. When, at 500 feet and concentrating on the locomotive, all hell seemed to break loose and I was rudely awakened to the fact that I was directly over a very heavily defended area. An intense barrage of light ack-ack fire had opened up from below…

The flak was tracer, making a very bright streak of light, resembling water from a fire hose. At the same moment, on came the Jerry searchlights, which caught and held me in their beam. I immediately took violent evasive action. The light was blinding and the overall effect of this treatment was considerably demoralising to say the least. While thus engaged, the plane was hit by a solitary bullet, which pierced the radiator situated just behind and under my seat. I heard the bullet as it struck and it sounded like someone using a can opener on the old 'kite.' Anyway, it prompted a little more violent evasive tactics, and I was ready at this point to try anything to quit all this attention.

The intense light of the tracers and searchlights had blinded me temporarily. I must have been at 500 feet when I was struck. The throttle had been bent well open at the first signs of tracer, but because of my rough handling of the controls in trying to shake off the searchlights, it was impossible to pick up much speed and despite my efforts, the searchlights still held me…

In a moment or two, the cockpit filled with fumes and a fine spray of engine coolant liquid from my damaged radiator; this irritated my eyes, making it difficult to see, and if it hadn't been for my oxygen mask, I would certainly have suffocated. Having flown well away to the eastward, I turned on to a southerly course putting the moon over my left shoulder and started a normal climb. With the emergency lever, I next jettisoned the cockpit cover, which leaves just the windscreen in front of the pilot. This had little effect, as I hoped it would, of dispersing the fumes and spray coming up from the radiator. The windscreen and instrument panel was covered with this coolant liquid spray, so I had to wipe off each instrument to see its reading… [Watlington radios to England, outlining his predicament and his plan to abandon the aircraft.]

I was climbing to make it as safe as possible when I had to leave the aircraft. I probably overdid it as I reached approximately 9,000 feet, or about two miles, before making my exit, which is plenty of height to allow a parachute to open. My engine gave an excellent performance although its cooling system was rapidly being drained.

At 5,000 feet, the temperature was indicating its highest reading, but nothing abnormal happened until another 4,000 feet had been gained when the engine commenced running roughly. At this sign I throttled back, released my cockpit safety straps and holding the nose in a climbing position thus reducing speed, I waited a few seconds before the stalling speed was reached and then shoved the stick forward, making the nose drop, and jumped upwards and out to one side. I was very much concerned over clearing the rail surface, as we had had reports of pilots injuring themselves in jumping from Mustangs. However, I must have hit on the right procedure as I floated slowly past the tail at some 10 feet to spare.

The aircraft fell out of sight before I remembered all about the rip-cord, which I gripped and gave a ruddy good yank. This was immediately followed by a violent jerk and on looking up there was the parachute all spread out as it should be. After blessing Scotty, the Squadron's parachute man, I was stunned to find myself in the midst of so complete and vast a silence after listening for an hour or so to a 1,200-horsepower engine perform. The moonlight was brilliant and below me lay a great countryside, which I began to observe with growing interest. Faintly, in the distance, I could hear my plane falling; and soon afterwards saw the fire on the ground where it crashed.

—*Bermudian John Hartley Watlington,*
a pilot with the Royal Canadian Air
Force, who stayed undercover in France
for nearly a year between 1943–44
before he returned to Bermuda

1939 Bermuda troops prepare to join Allies in war against Germany	**1940** Britain announces deal to lease Bermuda land to America for military bases	**1941** Bermuda Workers Association, later Bermuda Industrial Union, is founded	**1942** US pilots and Royal Navy fleets make Bermuda HQ for attacking German U-boats	**1944** Bermuda's land-owning women win 20-year campaign for right to vote	**1945** Islanders celebrate Victory in Europe (VE) Day on May 8 with public holiday	**BERMUDA**
1939 Hitler's troops invade Poland on September 1, triggering Second World War	**1940** Penicillin is discovered and the Xerox photocopier invented	**1941** Japan captures Singapore, Malaya, the Philippines, Hong Kong, Burma and Indonesia	**1941** US enters war after Japanese attack on fleet at Pearl Harbour, Hawaii	**1945** US drops atomic bomb on Hiroshima, killing 80,000; war ends	**1945** United Nations founded to avoid future wars through mediation	**WORLD**

Censorship, powdered milk and rations

How they lived

The war transformed Bermuda's easy-going way of life and changed it forever. Sporadic mail, few tourists, censorship and rations were the hallmarks of wartime Bermuda as the island hunkered down to weather the hardships and uncertainty of these years.

The German U-boat offensive of 1942 restricted food supplies, as cargo ships made the dangerous journey to the island far less frequently. As a result, Bermudians had to limit their consumption of basic foodstuffs, available only with ration coupons distributed by the local War Supply Board. Sugar, powdered milk, bread and butter were all rationed. A sailing ship service was launched from the Caribbean, but supplies remained very scarce. In a move that perhaps made sense in theory, but only worsened the shortage, island authorities decided to sell bread that was aged a day, in the assumption Bermudians would eat less of it. But due to the lack of preservatives in this era, the tactic wasted precious loaves because by the time they were officially put on sale, they were often mould-ridden.

A shortage of rubber forced a rationing of other materials like tyres and shoes. The government encouraged people to grow their own fruit and vegetables, and a canning factory was opened to preserve Bermuda produce. Some people

Civilians and servicemen get together at a dance

BERMUDA MARITIME MUSEUM

Servicemen at the island's Victory 'V' Club

COURTESY OF MAISIE FARGE

tried to make soap, which was another rare commodity.

Bermuda householders covered up their windows with blackout curtains and shut off their lights at night to deter a

feared strike by German bombers (which never came). Car headlights were also painted black and the Air Raid Patrol (ARP) held a constant vigil for enemy planes and

submarine raiders. On the home front, post-office staff censored all mail coming to and from Bermuda to prevent details of Allied operations reaching enemy hands.

Bermudians were hardest hit by unemployment during these years, thanks to the instant drop-off of tourism and its trickle-down effect on jobs such as those in retail stores. Public-works projects were therefore increased during the war years to provide low-paying work for people who needed it. Under the Bermuda Labour Corps initiatives, workers built several public parks, including Bernard Park.

The condition of the soft, coral roads deteriorated into potholes as US and British trucks and tanks thundered through the parishes. The railway was kept busy, carrying troops and supplies around the island, since Bermudians would not be allowed private cars until 1946.

Socially, wartime Bermuda was active as civilians met British and American sailors and soldiers at the island's hotels, bars and restaurants. Local women's groups served tea to Allied servicemen at the United Services Club at the former Hamilton Hotel on Queen Street, where frequent dances were also held.

The staff of the censorship office were unable to talk about their classified work, but were kept busy through badminton, table-tennis and bridge events, and also put on amateur theatre productions.

Censors stationed in Bermuda check the trans-Atlantic mail

The BVRC operated gunboat patrols around the island's shallow waters

Suspicious letters were detained in Bermuda. Indeed, by 1944 when mail examination finally ended, a Prize Court was established on the island to decide the fate of more than a million seized parcels and letters. Sometimes, the censorettes intercepted contraband or valuables such as diamonds on their way to swell Nazi coffers. Censorettes checked ship passengers' luggage, and, since many were proficient in several languages, they frequently acted as translators. Their work infuriated Nazi Germany, and Berlin Radio publicly decried them.

Notably, the censors uncovered German spies in the United States and on October 3, 1940, intercepted a shipment of 500 French Impressionist paintings aboard the American Export Line ship, SS *Excalibur*, in Hamilton. Hidden behind steel bars in the liner's vaults, the artwork, known as the Vollard Collection, had been en route to New York, where British authorities believed its sale would have generated several hundred thousand pounds for Hitler's campaign. Instead, the paintings were stored temporarily at the Bank of Bermuda before being shipped for safe-keeping to the Canadian National Gallery.

At home, the Bermuda Militia Artillery and the Bermuda Volunteer Engineers manned the six-inch guns and searchlights of St. David's Battery, while the Volunteer Rifles and Militia Infantry guarded strategic landing sites from possible enemy attack. More huge guns were brought to the island by both Americans and British and installed in a flurry of work. Bermudian riflemen and militiamen were called on to guard installations like the Atlantic cable hut in Tucker's Town, the docks and telephone and electricity stations.

Interned enemies also came under their guard. At first, a handful of German and Austrian nationals were interned at Huntley Towers, Paget. Over the course of the war, a number of prisoners of war were taken, usually from captured shipping and these Germans, Italians, Poles and Finns were held at Fort Cunningham, on Paget Island.

But just as it had during the previous centuries, Bermuda avoided invasion. Hitler's forces disintegrated and Germany finally went down in defeat in 1945. "Yesterday morning at 2:41 a.m. at General [Dwight D.] Eisenhower's headquarters, General [Alfred] Jodl, the representative of the German High Command, signed an act of unconditional surrender," Britain's Prime Minister Churchill announced on the morning of May 8 at 10 o'clock Bermuda time.

Like the rest of the Allied world, the island exploded with "VE" (Victory in Europe) Day celebrations. "Sirens were blown and church bells rung and all shops and businesses were closed," reported the *Bermuda Historical Quarterly*. "An hour later a large proportion of the population attended services of thanksgiving in churches throughout the island."

The following week, after a Cathedral service packed with legislative and military officials, Bermudians crowded the decorated streets of Hamilton to celebrate. Hundreds of troops took part in a huge victory parade down Front Street, among them members of the Royal Navy, Royal Canadian Navy and US Navy, the US Army, the Merchant Navy, the Marine Corps, the Royal Artillery, the Pictou Highlanders, and the Royal Airforce and Royal Canadian Air Force. In a proud procession, Bermuda's First World War veterans also took part, marching alongside local troops and firefighters. Even children joined the march wearing their Girl Guides and Boy Scouts uniforms.

Standing guard over military seaplanes at Darrell's Island

Three months later, on the night of August 14, 1945, Japan surrendered. Bermudians lit bonfires and set off fireworks as boats and ferries sounded their whistles. The next two days, declared public holidays, marked the end of an era—yet islanders shared "a general feeling of thankfulness rather than jubilation," according to one contemporary account, "the desire to celebrate being curtailed to a great extent by anxiety concerning the atomic bomb, which had played such an important part in the defeat of Japan."

A US gun crew runs a drill

The war against tyranny was over. Bermuda had played its part in gaining victory, but the peaceful, sleepy island of yesteryear was never to be seen again. Bermuda neither looked nor thought the way it had done just six years earlier. The Americans would stay on, their airbase becoming a civilian airport that would bring hundreds of thousands of tourists to the island. War had thrust Bermuda into the mechanised, industrial age—now it was time for the island and its people to join the world at large.

The secret of U-505

German submarines, or U-boats, were a constant threat during the war, and both American and British troops used Bermuda as a base from which to launch searches and attacks on marauding vessels throughout the Atlantic.

One particular sub, U-505, involved Bermuda in a clandestine wartime cover-up operation. On June 4, 1944, U-505 was attacked by the USS *Guadalcanal* and then boarded and captured by sailors from the destroyer escort USS *Pillsbury*. It was a milestone event, marking the first time an enemy ship of war had been seized by the US Navy since the War of 1812. A US Navy tug towed the German submarine to Bermuda, where U-505 was kept hidden until war's end, when it was taken to the US.

Today an American National Historic Landmark, U-505 is on permanent exhibit at Chicago's Museum of Science and Industry, a memorial to Americans who gave their lives at sea in both World Wars.

Japan surrenders

On August 14th, at 8 p.m. Bermuda time, the news that Japan had accepted the surrender terms of the Allies was announced from London by the Prime Minister, Mr. Clement Attlee, and from Washington by President [Harry S.] Truman. Almost immediately the sirens sounded all over the Colony, to be followed shortly afterwards by the whistles of the ferry steamers and of the small Furness liner Fort Townshend *which had arrived from New York the day before, inaugurating the first scheduled passenger service since the early days of the war. Bonfires were lighted and fireworks were set off in several parts of the Island. Within an hour, a service of thanksgiving was held in the Cathedral. His Excellency the Governor, Lord Burghley, proclaimed the two following days to be public holidays. The holidays were marked by a general feeling of thankfulness, rather than jubilation, the desire to celebrate being curtailed, to a great extent, by anxiety concerning the atomic bomb, which had played such an important part in the defeat of Japan.*

—Bermuda Historical Quarterly,
Vol. 2, Autumn, 1945

A great deliverance

At this momentous hour, when the arms of our country and allies have, under Divine providence, been crowned with victory in Europe, the feeling uppermost in the mind of each one of us must surely be of gratitude to Almighty God for a great deliverance.

—*Acting Governor W. L. Murphy's message to Bermuda on Victory in Europe (V.E.) Day celebrations, May 8, 1945*

BERMUDA MARITIME MUSEUM

Bermudian women volunteers at the Hamilton Princess canteen

Women at war

The war would forever change the role of women throughout western societies, including Bermuda. Restricted in career and education choices, political rights and public expectation before the war, women emerged from the conflict in 1945 empowered by their hard experiences and important contributions.

The sea-change in sentiment had everything to do with the equalising power of the war itself. Bermudian women, like their male and female counterparts through North America and Europe, were sorely needed at home and abroad to help win the war. A total of 29 local women volunteered and joined overseas services including the Royal Air Force and the Royal Canadian Air Force, Women's Division, as well as special auxiliary services such as the Women's Royal Naval Services (WRNS) and the British Auxiliary Territorial Services. Armed combat roles were off-limits in this era, but women fulfilled a gamut of non-combat duties ranging from medical and clerical jobs to Morse code instruction and convoy-plotting for which they took intensive courses or received on-the-job training. One woman, Daisy Vallis, died in a car accident while enlisted.

Many women joined humanitarian efforts such as the British Red Cross, the United Nations Relief and Rehabilitation, and the Imperial Order Daughters of the Empire (IODE), which had set up a Bermuda chapter in 1911. Throughout the war, women helped raise money and provide services for soldiers, their widows and children, and refugees through the Bermuda Women's Auxiliary Force. The BWAF ran a canteen for Allied forces and helped war veterans once the conflict ended.

At home, women worked as teachers and nurses, joined local services such as the BVRC and BMA, and raised families alone when men were called to duty overseas. Many were left widows by the war.

Such participation changed society and could not be ignored. On April 21, 1944, the Women's Suffrage Bill was finally passed by the island's Parliament, vindicating the 25-year struggle by Gladys Morrell and her army of suffragists. Propertied women in Bermuda at last had the right to vote. As the war wound down in the spring of 1945, they celebrated their own victory with a symbolic tree-planting outside the House of Assembly.

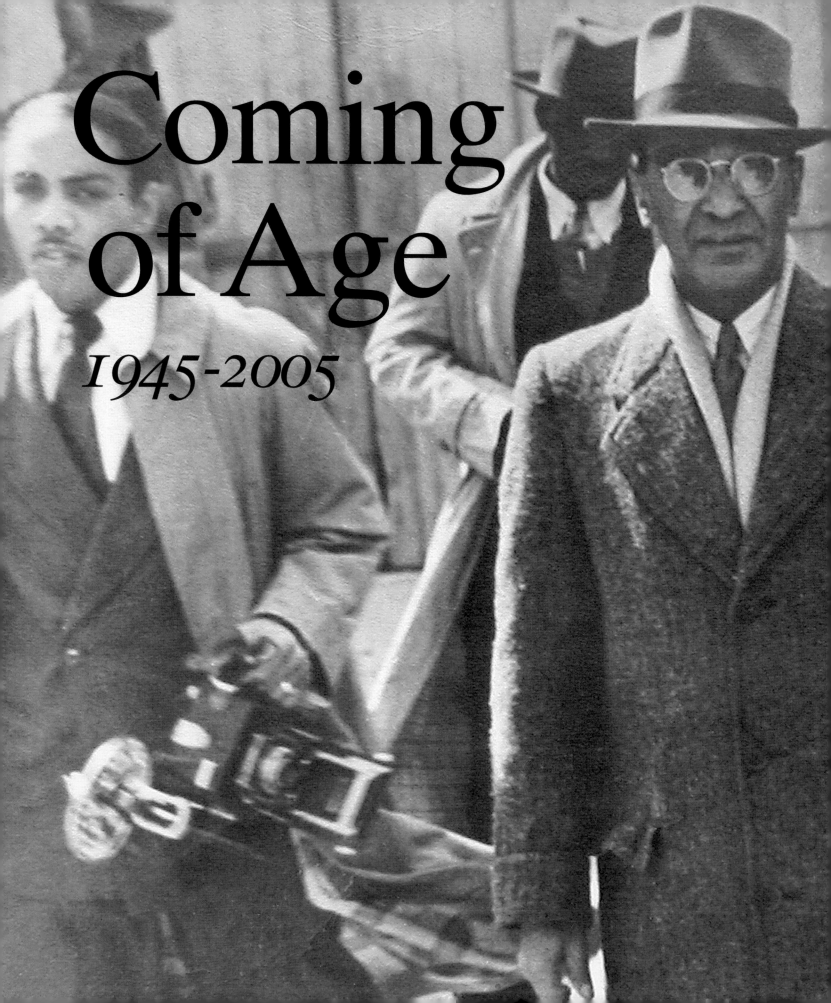

Coming of Age

1945-2005

CHAPTER SEVENTEEN

Progress in Peace

THE COMING OF CARS AND COLD WARRIORS

Company manager John Plowman was 34 years old when a revolution of sorts rolled through Bermuda in 1946. Automobiles, long forbidden on the island, were finally legal and available —and Bermudians raced to get their driving permits and buy one of the shiny first models to make their way out of Hamilton's showrooms and on to the parishes' newly-paved roads, attracting rubber-neckers everywhere they went. Plowman, himself, was in a perfect position to witness the phenomenon; not only did he run Holmes Williams & Purvey, the island's first car importer, but he was one of the first Bermudians to actually get behind the wheel of a car.

"I bought a Hillman convertible in January 1947," he later told *The Bermudian*. "Licence plate 5281. The numbers were supposed to finish at 5,501, because people thought there would be only 300 or so cars on the road."

Legislators assumed the cost of buying and licensing a car would restrict ownership, but such conservative predictions soon proved short-sighted. Bermudians fast developed an appetite for American-style consumerism that began to permeate island life in the post-war years. The Motor Car Act, passed by the Legislature in early 1946, allowed private cars and taxis, while limiting vehicle size and cars per household, and curbing their speed to 20 miles per hour.

More than merely a status symbol, the car was a greater visible token of the victory of capitalism and democracy generally, as well as a catalyst for sweeping social, economic and political changes as the island emerged from its quiet, isolated past. Bermuda no longer could be considered an insignificant outpost or a colonial backwater. The war had changed the island and its people, and the world's perception of them. Now Bermuda could enjoy the shared victory by Allied countries, its soldiers home from years of fighting, its national sentiment one of hope, energy and far-reaching ambition.

The world at large was never to be the same again, and nor was Bermuda. Aside from the positive mood of its people, the island had transformed dramatically in physical ways, thanks to the advent of cars, commercial aviation

Ambulances stand ready in post-war Bermuda

BERMUDA ARCHIVES

THE BERMUDIAN

*Private cars were finally allowed
in 1946. This colourful taxi was
taking visitors to the beach in 1959*

Prosperity *We are now in an
unprecedented era of prosperity.*
— *Sir John Cox, Speaker of the
House of Assembly, 1958*

and the American military presence. The huge influx of American troops
and machinery during the war had altered the face and feel of Bermuda
immeasurably. The US bases had swallowed up more than eight per cent of
the island's land mass, though during construction, the Americans had actually
created 800 acres of land which did not exist in 1941. The East-End airfield
built by the Army at Kindley Field now became a civilian airport—opening
Bermuda to the world of mass tourism for the first time.

Bermuda's human face had changed, too. The island had welcomed
5,000 American troops, and later their families, increasing its population by
20 percent. The post-war decades would see the population expand even
further, as Bermuda's birth-rate soared and immigration increased, mirroring
Europe and America. In 1939, Bermudians numbered 32,000; by 1970, the
island's population stood at 53,000. Homebuilding was carried out with a
vengeance and population growth also brought employment, environmental
and social challenges.

Keep left: horse carriages swiftly gave way to cars on busy Front Street, Hamilton

Birth control *The report of the Commission of Inquiry, set up last year to survey the growth of population and the problem of illegitimacy, was submitted to the House of Assembly on May 30. Among the Commission's recommendations are restriction of population, expansion of birth-control and planned-parenthood measures by the Department of Health; sex education in the schools, sterilization, under certain conditions, of men (or women) with large families of illegitimate children; better housing for low-income groups, and more facilities for recreation in the parishes.*

—Bermuda Historical
Quarterly, *1951*

Bermudians of this era were embarking on their own journey of change that would shape the society we know today. More than anything, transport was to herald the transformation. For centuries, the island had been a place of horses and carts and long walks or bicycle trips to the schoolroom and workplace. But by the second half of 1945, the soft, crushed coral roads were being paved over with asphalt and after the 1946 law was passed, quiet country lanes throbbed to the sound of motor engines as Bermudians explored their new freedom to quickly move around the island.

They found the East End vibrant with operations at Kindley Air Force Base, the sprawling American compound at St. David's. At the West End, life at the US naval base in Southampton continued, and would become increasingly active as the base developed into a strategic mid-Atlantic hub for NATO nuclear submarines during the long years of the Cold War. The Royal Naval Dockyard was busier than ever, a community in itself known to locals as "Little England." Up to 1,000 Bermudians worked at the Dockyard, helping the British Navy look after its warships. With its own shops and cinema, a school and medical facilities, the Dockyard also provided an enviable apprenticeship scheme which, over the years, taught the trades to hundreds of Bermudians. They became shipwrights, fitters, mechanics, masons, carpenters, plumbers, and many went on to use those skills in their own companies around the island.

Motor cars would open the floodgates to a whole spectrum of post-war

THE BERMUDIAN

*After years of war, Bermudians
gladly bought into the modern
world of convenience*

innovations—trends and technologies that reflected a society newly optimistic about its fortunes and future. The wonder of television had reached the island; at first, locals tuned in to fuzzy black-and-white broadcasts from the American base station, but by 1958 Bermuda got its own station, ZBM TV-10, and seven years later, a second station, ZFB, began broadcasting on channel eight. Household appliances and newfangled consumer goods such as refrigerators, record-players, lawn-mowers and washing machines soon became must-haves in Bermudian homes, as islanders watched their closest neighbour pursue the "American Dream"—and embraced it as their own. It was an age promising peace and prosperity and Bermudians were determined to take advantage of the benign climate to forge a solid long-term future.

The late 1940s and '50s marked a time of rebuilding—particularly in Bermuda's tourism industry, which had been growing so well before 1939. When the war ended, the Bermuda tourist trade had to be relaunched, the island again promising a unique slice of British serenity just a short hop from America. Wartime military service had claimed many of Bermuda's regular cruise ships. The door was now open for a boom in arrivals by air. Yet tourism's recovery was slow; indeed, it took until 1951, with 99,162 visitors, to break the pre-war annual tourist peak of 82,000. Over the 1960s and '70s, that number would more than quadruple, establishing the industry as the island's core economic pillar, its so-called "bread-and-butter" trade.

Catering to the upswing was a surge in hotel construction. The historic Hamilton Hotel went up in flames two days before Christmas in 1955 and the Bermudiana suffered a similar fate three years later. In April 1960, the new Bermudiana opened on the same site, triggering a spree of hotel-building that would revitalise tourism's infrastructure. In 1947, Furness Withy had sold its stake in Bermuda property—including the Bermudiana, Castle Harbour and St. George's hotels—but it continued to operate its grand

BERMUDA MARITIME MUSEUM

Barbadian workers at the sprawling Dockyard, Sandys

The Talbot Brothers were
a popular calypso group

BERMUDA MEDIA

The 92-year-old Hamilton Hotel,
Bermuda's first, is destroyed
by fire in 1955

THE BERMUDIAN

Another World

Bermuda is another world
Seven-hundred miles at sea,
And the way the people greet you
Is like a friendly melody.

—*Verse from the unofficial Bermuda*
anthem, by Hubert Smith, c. 1969

cruise ships. Crowds thronged Front Street in 1949 when *Queen of Bermuda* returned to the island after wartime service amid much fanfare; the beloved vessel would continue to sail the New York-Bermuda run for a further 17 years.

Still, the old-time elegance of cruising, along with the essence of tourism which it promoted, was fast disappearing, soon to be eclipsed by the coming Jet Age. Soon after the war, Pan Am brought in Boeing 314 flying-boats, whose route now continued from Bermuda across the Atlantic to the Azores and Europe. BOAC launched a seaplane service from Baltimore to Darrell's Island in 1945. Then, on January 3, 1946, a Pan Am DC-4 Skymaster became the first commercial airliner to land on Kindley Field, forging a new era for the island. Before long, land planes would replace the Darrell's Island flying-boats; the last passenger seaplane flew out in 1948.

The post-war years saw a network of airfields and routes spring up around the world and Kindley Air Force Base began to get daily airliner landings. Eventually, the US Navy took over the base from the Air Force, and military and civilian operations were separated. The St. George's base was renamed the US Naval Air Station (USNAS), while the Southampton base became the USNAS Annex. Travellers were processed at Kindley's revamped Civil Air Terminal, later renamed Bermuda International Airport. In 1959, the first commercial jet touched down at the island, a Pan Am Boeing 707 on a non-stop journey from Seattle. Bermuda was now a destination easily accessible from some of the world's major gateway cities. Tourism was in full swing, pumping money into the local economy and creating many jobs. Most visitors were from the eastern seaboard of the United States, but tourists from further afield began taking advantage of new rapid air services to Bermuda and arrival numbers soared.

Times had changed. Prestige ship travel, bringing the super-rich to the island for a leisurely winter sojourn, was fast evolving into mass tourism—regular Americans and Europeans flying in for shorter beach and golfing getaways, increasingly during the spring and summer. The trend spelled far greater benefits for Bermuda, but as travel grew more competitive, it also required the island to spend more time, effort and resources promoting itself overseas. Honeymooners were courted. The Newport-Bermuda Ocean Race restarted, bringing yachtsmen and their vessels from New England. Spirited annual College Weeks, beginning in 1950, saw thousands of teenagers and 20-somethings fly in from East Coast schools for subtropical frivolity on Bermuda's beaches, not to mention fun—and fractures—aboard rented mopeds. For many, it was their first experience of Bermuda, and they liked the holiday island so much, they returned for honeymoons and regular family vacations. Easter floral pageants were promoted, along with a quaint array of local highlights such as dog shows, duty-free shopping, military tattoos and bridge tournaments.

Eventually, cruise-ship fleets were again built up and began a boom period of their own. After the mid-1960s, when tourist arrivals had already passed 200,000 a year, large new hotels like the Southampton Princess sprang up to meet the demand.

Bermuda continued to be sold to travellers as an otherworldly destination, an upmarket paradise. The 'exclusive' factor was a key attraction; visitors—of whom nearly 90 percent were American—found the esoteric nature of Bermuda appealing. And like destinations round the world, the island's tourism industry began to reap steady growth.

TV troubles *The TV set is nothing more or less than an advertising machine, for which payment should be made to the owners. There is as much beer advertising on ZBM-TV as is advertised in any liquor store or pool room. Instead of the children lisping "Gentle Jesus Meek and Mild" on their way to bed, we hear them singing, "Better have one now, now, now." It comes on at 7 p.m., the children's bedtime. What a prospect for Bermuda, the Isles of Rest…When I bought my TV set we had some good and interesting entertainment from Kindley Field and it was well worth the money I paid for it. I have heard there are some good stories on at 10 p.m. but my working day begins at 6 a.m. and it's too late for me.*

—*Letter to* The Royal Gazette,
June 6, 1959

A new era of travel: commercial land-based planes in 1952

The Dockyard's use was limited in a world no longer at war, and on March 31, 1951, the Royal Navy shut down its operations there. The decision brought a traumatic change to the West End. The Navy sent remaining apprentices to England to finish their training, but hundreds of other Bermudians lost their jobs and gradually moved their families closer to Hamilton in search of work. As the Dockyard fell silent, Sandys reverted to the quiet country parish it once was. The Bermuda government bought out Imperial interests in the former military property to develop the area for retail and tourism use, a scheme that would not properly take shape until the West End Development Corporation was established 30 years later.

The military again reshaped local life when the British Army garrison was finally withdrawn in 1957, ending a 256-year connection. For generations, British soldiers had mingled and often intermarried with locals, contributing to the sporting and social scene. But suddenly they were gone, leaving empty the huge Prospect camp in Devonshire, which would become the headquarters for Bermuda's police force.

In their bases in Southampton and St. David's, by contrast, the Americans picked up the pace of their military activities. By the 1950s, world war had been replaced by a sinister Cold War between the West and the Soviet bloc. Once again, Bermuda became an important part of the free world's defences, this time as a refuelling station for American nuclear bombers. A Strategic Air Command (SAC) squadron was sent to Bermuda and clandestine aircraft flew missions from the island to support US Polaris nuclear submarines, which also were supplied at bases on the island. A by-product of the SAC unit was the establishment of the Roger B. Chaffee School for American children on the US bases.

In 1954, the Americans set up a secretive electronic listening post at Tudor Hill in Southampton, as did the Canadian military in Somerset, to eavesdrop on Soviet submarines operating in the Atlantic. The US Navy constructed a "Texas Tower" in 1960 on Argus Bank; along the lines of an

A quiet day on Front Street in 1949

The pall of prejudice

Bermuda gave a warm welcome to tourists in the 1930s, '40s and '50s—unless they happened to be Jewish or black. Racial segregation, which permeated much of island life until the 1960s, barred black visitors from staying in white-owned hotels and guesthouses until these finally dropped the colour bar starting in 1959. Instead, African-Americans and other black guests checked into a growing number of black-owned establishments, which benefitted from their patronage during the 1940s and '50s. Though some visiting black celebrities—boxers Joe Louis and Cassius Clay (later Muhammed Ali)

and musician Louis Armstrong—were embraced by Bermuda, most black tourists found the island highly unwelcoming. Black travellers were even obliged to sleep on benches at the island's airport during unplanned layovers.

Anti-semitism was also an unspoken undercurrent of the island's hospitality industry, which stirred bitter controversy in the 1930s. Jewish-American visitors found themselves increasingly shut out of Bermuda's hotels and guesthouses, whose advertisements openly preferred a "restricted clientèle." Under island law, hoteliers were allowed to turn away guests if they chose; their bigoted criteria for doing so was

cloaked in the justification Bermuda sought a "better class of tourists." In 1937, outraged British Jews complained to the secretary of state for the colonies in London and cruise-line officials warned that excluding Jews could irreparably damage the island's tourism industry.

The post-war world was less tolerant of such bigotry, though social change came more slowly to Bermuda. For many years, Jews, blacks and Portuguese continued to face a social stigma, barred, for instance, from golf-courses and institutions such as the Royal Bermuda Yacht Club. The issue of exclusion in the tourism industry, however, dissolved gradually, though prejudices continued to ripple below the island's benevolent façade.

Black tourism *The time has come for us to seriously begin our own tourist trade. It is the island's biggest and best business. The building of a successful Negro tourist trade in Bermuda will be the means of strengthening our economy.*
—*Black tourism promoter Hilton G. Hill quoted in* Afro *magazine, 1950*

Contrast *Why is there such a contrast between the way Bermuda looks to the tourist and the way it looks to those of us who live here? Not because some Bermudians are black and others are white; not because of extravagance; not motor cars; and certainly not because Bermuda has to be the way it is. No, the answer is to be found in the actions of a small group of Bermudians who seem to have set as their aim in life the making of as much money as they possibly can.*
—An Analysis of Bermuda's Social Problems (The Limited Franchise, segregation and discrimination), *produced by the Association of Bermuda Affairs, a group of black Bermudians fighting segregation, 1953*

Boat Day: the arrival of the Ocean Monarch *was a regular treat for locals*

THE BERMUDIAN

Regiment soldiers fly the flag at the Senate Building

BERMUDA REGIMENT

The Bermuda Regiment

The formation of the Bermuda Regiment in September 1965 marked an end to racial segregation of local forces. It brought together the island's white Bermuda Volunteer Rifle Corps (BVRC), later called the Bermuda Rifles, and the black Bermuda Militia Artillery (BMA) to form a single army.

The Regiment, whose male recruits are conscripted, has supported local police and foreign troops during civil disturbances such as the 1977 riots and carried out disaster relief after hurricanes in both Bermuda and the Caribbean. The Regiment's Band & Corps performs ceremonial duties at events such as Beat Retreat.

The Regiment is affiliated with the Royal Anglian Regiment in England and the Lincoln and Welland Regiment in Canada.

Taboo

In Bermuda, it's taboo
Look out: don't let de cops catch you.
Keep your curlers out of sight
Don't let 'em show in broad daylight
Pretty girls are super fine
But no-one loves a porcupine.

—*Verse from a 1964 calypso song on Bermuda's conservative laws*

oil-drilling rig, it was used by the US Office of Naval Research, which took part in classified anti-submarine projects. Lockheed P-3 Orion surveillance aircraft routinely flew in and out of USNAS, St. George's during these years, shadowing missile-loaded Soviet subs during intelligence-gathering missions along the Eastern Seaboard and over the Atlantic. At the same time, squadrons of modified C-130 Hercules transports, called 'TACAMO' aircraft, for "Take Charge and Move Out," patrolled the North Atlantic on potentially catastrophic missions. Acting as liaisons between the US Defence Department and American nuclear submarines on patrol, these aircraft could deliver, in the event of war, crucial "go-codes" that would launch atomic missiles—Trident, Polaris, Poseidon—from US subs below. Bermuda was a communications hub for this programme, and also a site for placement of US nuclear bombs at times of "advanced readiness" against the Soviets.

While secret manoeuvrings continued at sea, the world's imagination was captured by the age of space travel. No longer was "outer space" the stuff of science fiction; now human beings could leave the earth's atmosphere in fire-breathing spaceships—and return. On a political level, the new frontier triggered an intense race between the Americans and Soviets to see whose scientists could conquer space first. The Russians achieved the

THE BERMUDIAN

US Navy dirigibles at St. David's

first milestone, sending its *Sputnik* satellite around the world in October 1957, followed immediately by *Sputnik II*, which carried the first passenger —a dog named Laika. Just a decade later, on July 20, 1969, American Neil Armstrong and his *Apollo XI* crewmates successfully landed on the moon.

Bermuda was to play no small part in the new push for non-military space exploration. Under US President Dwight Eisenhower, the National Aeronautics & Space Administration (NASA) set up a sophisticated station on Cooper's Island in 1961, the largest of 18 tracking, data and communications stations around the world. Its primary mission was to relay data, including voice communications, for all high-profile space missions, including the orbital flights of John Glenn and Walter Schirra in 1962 and the later lunar landings. The Bermuda station also provided tracking support for many test launches of missiles from US submarines and monitored the launches of NASA shuttles from the Kennedy Space Center on Merritt Island, Florida, as well as scientific, communications and military satellites from the adjacent US Air Force Station at Cape Canaveral.

From the first test flights of Project Mercury and Project Gemini through the Apollo programme—17 missions which resulted in the first photos of Earth from space in 1968 and lunar landings a year later—the Bermuda station played a key communications link between manned spacecraft and Mission Control. After Apollo missions concluded in 1972, the station continued to support NASA through its development of reusable space shuttles and unmanned probes to other planets.

When NASA eventually deployed a constellation of tracking satellites 23,300 miles above the Equator, its land-based stations were no longer needed. As a result, the Bermuda outpost began winding down operations in 1998 and finally closed in 2001.

'Magic years' of moonshots and heroes

In their own words
■ William Way

From 1960 to 2001, NASA operated a tracking station on Cooper's Island, St. David's, one of 18 radar and telemetry outposts around the world which provided crucial links for launches from the Kennedy Space Center and Cape Canaveral.

It was the beginning of the space era for America. They were magic years. At one time or another, all seven of the original astronauts came to Bermuda on flight-control teams, including Gus Grissom and Alan Shepard. They were revered. People would peek out of their offices at them as they walked in. They were even more famous at Cape Canaveral. They had reputations for driving fast in their sports cars all over the Cape. One got injured in a motorcycle accident in Bermuda and it made the news all over the world. We used to tell the astronauts when they got on their bikes, "You guys, stay on the left—and don't go 100 miles an hour!"

NASA began its Apollo programme in 1967 with President John F. Kennedy's objective of landing on the moon before the end of the decade. But the first Apollo mission ground test, Apollo I, resulted in a catastrophe on January 27 that year. The Bermuda station was involved in a full countdown called a 'plugs-out test,' which means a simulation of launch day. We were sending and receiving data back and forth from the Cape. All of a sudden, somebody came on the 'net' and said, "The test is terminated." Then the network director came on and said, "Leave all your equipment as it is. Turn off all tape recorders, and don't do or change anything on any of the equipment. There's been a problem." We called back and they told us something terribly bad had happened. There had been a fire in the command

William Way at the NASA station at St. David's

COURTESY OF WILLIAM WAY

module on the launch pad and Gus Grissom, Ed White and Roger B. Chaffee had all been killed. There was a deep sense of loss at the station, especially for Gus who had been a flight controller for many missions.

Along with subsequent successes, including Apollo 11's first lunar landing on July 20, 1969, this was one of several dramatic moments at the Bermuda Station. I will never forget the launch of Apollo 13, on April 13, 1970. It was supposed to be another standard moon landing. We were taping data and sending it on to Houston in "real" time. Data's going up, data's coming down. Voice is going up and down.

It was a normal day.

And then the whole mood was broken by: "Houston, we've had a problem." With the spacecraft halfway to the moon, an explosion had occurred when two oxygen tanks ruptured and most of the spacecraft's systems were destroyed. It broke hydraulic lines and electrical power and control lines, leaving the spacecraft completely inoperative. We were later to find out that previously damaged oxygen-tank wiring had shorted and started a fire, and shortly afterwards: "Boom!"

The objective of landing on the moon was immediately discarded and all efforts were refocussed on somehow, against enormous odds, bringing the crew back alive. That was the beginning of days of agony and consternation on everyone's part. We didn't know how bad the Apollo 13 problem was. The flight-controllers in Houston were reading the numbers and saying, "Hey, almost all your systems in the service module are down, your hydraulics are down, your battery power's gone, your oxygen tanks show no pressure"—they had a good assessment from the ground. We heard this going back and forth and as it went on, we gradually realised how bad it was.

Mission Control devised a plan for the astronauts: get out of the command module and transfer to the lunar module, a craft that had not actually been designed to bring them home. The computer people had to change the software, allowing the lunar module to sling around the moon and come back to land in the Pacific. The guys on the spacecraft were worried they would go careening off into space instead, but to a man, the astronauts maintained their professionalism, objectivity and optimism.

We were measuring oxygen, which was going down, and carbon dioxide, which was going up. Houston devised a reverse process using air-handling canisters on the spacecraft containing lithium hydroxide. Held together by duct tape, this improvised system slowly started generating oxygen—not much, but enough to reverse the steady decline.

The astronauts spent three miserable days coming back—three days with no heat, and almost no power or water. In Bermuda, we had to sleep at the station. We had military cots all over the place for about 45 people. The guys who lived in St. David's used to sneak home for a few hours' sleep. We were there around the clock for three or four days— but at least we were warm and had plenty of food, water and power.

Once the moon pulled them around, and they made the right entry point towards the Earth, we knew they were going to be okay. As the spacecraft approached Earth, the astronauts climbed back into the command module from the lunar module, cast off the service and lunar modules and landed safely in the Pacific. They came down in a perfect landing. The US was steaming every nearby ship in the Pacific towards the predicted landing point. It was like the proverbial child come home. I just remember everyone was so happy. It happened late at night for us, because it was daytime in the Pacific when they landed. But it was sheer euphoria— that we'd had an almost catastrophic problem and solved it, and in doing so, saved the lives of three astronauts, James Lovell, Fred Haise and Jack Swigert. It felt great.

—Philadelphia-born William Way,
a telemetry supervisor and later
manager for 20 years at Bermuda's
NASA tracking station

THE BERMUDIAN

The Queen and Prince Philip leave the House of Assembly in 1953

Bermuda may have been hosting thousands of North American tourists in these years, but the island remained fiercely patriotic. The pageantry of the colony's British ties filled the streets in November 1953 during the visit of the Queen, Elizabeth II, and her husband Prince Philip. The monarch, who had been crowned in June that year, heralded a fresh beginning, and her stopover, part of a Coronation world tour, marked the first by a reigning monarch to the island. Like Princess Louise before her, the Queen stoked Bermudian pride in both the island and its British heritage, and also gave Bermuda headlines overseas.

Indeed, the island had become a favourite for VIP visitors. Even during the war, Allied leaders met in Bermuda to decide the boundaries of the post-war world. Celebrities included Joseph Kennedy, who stopped over in 1939 as the newly appointed American ambassador to London. In August 1940, the Duke and Duchess of Windsor visited en route to the Bahamas. Commonwealth prime ministers were frequent visitors. And in 1943, Bermuda hosted an Allied conference on refugees. Even US President Harry Truman dropped in aboard the USS *Williamsburg* in August 1946.

After the war, Bermuda became a popular staging point for 'summit' talks between world powers, giving Bermudians an unprecedented front-row seat to some of the era's most dramatic global political discussions.

Cottage industry

Opened in February 1960, Hamilton's City Hall was the masterpiece of a Bermudian renowned for turning cottage aesthetics into architecture that symbolised the island.

The son of a Somerset merchant, Wilfred ("Wil") Richmond Onions was the imagination behind many of the island's hallmark homes, buildings which reinvigorated traditions and inspired generations of architects. Low-slung rooflines, cedar highlights, buttresses and welcoming-arms staircases—all were his signature style.

At the start of his career, he studied the construction and proportion of old buildings and adapted the sturdy Bermuda cottage into everything he built, including City Hall. The grand project was launched via a 1938 design contest won by Onions and his partner, Valmer Bouchard. Their design, essentially a

Wil Onions

mammoth cottage with slate roof and tower, was inspired by Stockholm's City Hall. But when the Second World War intervened, the plan was shelved for 20 years.

The post-war era brought a boom in residential architecture and Onions became the designer of choice for homes with classic lines emblematic of a reinvigorated vernacular. His firm, Onions & Bouchard (today OBM) constructed 50 such homes in six years for VIPs during the 1950s, as well as big projects like Waterloo House and the Elbow Beach Hotel.

Work on City Hall, based on his design, began in 1957. But Onions died before its completion; despondent over various construction problems and artistic differences, he took his own life on July 2, 1959.

In particular, the island was a showcase for the strong Anglo-American partnership between Second World War heroes Prime Minister Winston Churchill and President General Dwight Eisenhower. During the early 1950s, the pair corresponded frequently over issues ranging from the threat of another war—this time a nuclear one—to Communism, the Middle East, the Korean War and German re-armament, and in 1953 Bermuda was chosen as the mid-way meeting spot for their talks whose outcome would reverberate around the world. The so-called "Big Three" conference on December 4 that year brought Churchill and Eisenhower together with French Prime Minister Joseph Laniel at the Mid Ocean Club. Among other issues, they discussed the Soviet Union, the hydrogen bomb, uses of atomic energy, and increasing tensions over Egypt's interests in the Suez Canal.

Three years later, in March 1956, Churchill's successor, Harold Macmillan, travelled to the island to meet for "Big Two" talks with Eisenhower. Macmillan held similar talks in December 1961 with Eisenhower's successor, statesman John F. Kennedy. The American president would be assassinated two years later, on November 22, 1963.

The 1950s also witnessed a trickle to the island of multi-national companies fleeing taxes and cumbersome restrictions elsewhere. Paving the way was the landmark American International Company Limited (AICO) Act, passed in December 1947, which allowed foreign ownership of Bermuda-registered companies to exceed 40 percent if they did business outside the island only. The island's stable government and economy, English law and tax-free status proved an offshore magnet for British and American corporations and trusts, shipping companies, and particularly, insurance and reinsurance firms. They were described as 'exempted' companies, free as they were from corporate requirements faced by companies serving Bermudians. Instead, they chose Bermuda as a letter-head—and sometimes as a tangible headquarters—from which to conduct business outside the island, in countries around the world.

The first major insurance company to take advantage of Bermuda as an offshore base was AICO's parent, American International Group (AIG), a conglomerate of insurance agencies around the world whose visionary founder, C.V. Starr, saw the benefits of the island in the late 1940s. Bermuda reaped its own rewards, since AIG created 300 jobs, becoming one of the largest private employers within 10 years. The trend multiplied over the next four decades, and as more international companies put down stakes, they created a corporate torrent of foreign exchange so substantial, it formed a new economic pillar for Bermuda, surpassing even tourism before the century's end.

A wave of new companies rolled in during the 1960s. Formed by Fortune 500 companies and dubbed "captives," they acted as insurance subsidiaries for big corporate entities such as industrial, oil or shipping companies. Entrepreneur Fred Reiss, an Ohio-born fire-protection engineer, coined the captive title, and spearheaded the movement that allowed multi-nationals to bypass traditional insurance markets by financing their own risks and profit by doing so. The incorporation of captives burgeoned by the thousands through the 1970s, '80s and '90s, forming the foundation of Bermuda's new economic future. The captive insurance industry in Bermuda would become the world's largest and prove to be the genesis of what would grow into the island's multi-billion-dollar insurance industry.

Confronting the 'nuclear monster'

In their own words

■ Winston Churchill, 1954

March 9, 1954

Thank you for your letter. I am honoured by the kind personal things you say. There is no difference between us upon the major issues which overhang the world, namely resistance to Communism, the unity of the free nations, the concentration of the English-speaking world, United Europe and NATO. All these will and must increase if we are to come through the anxious years and perhaps decades which lie ahead of hopeful but puzzled mankind.

On the day the Soviets discovered and developed the Atomic Bomb the consequences of war became far more terrible. But that brief tremendous phase now lies in the past…

Of course I recur to my earlier proposal of a personal meeting between Three. Men have to settle with men, no matter how vast, and in part beyond their comprehension, the business in hand may be. I can even imagine that a few simple words, spoken in the awe which may at once oppress and inspire the speakers might lift this nuclear monster from our world.

It might be that the proposals which you made at Bermuda and which are accepted by the Soviets for parleys on this subject, could without raising the issue formally give a better chance of survival than any yet mentioned. The advantage of the process you have set in motion is that it might probe the chances of settlement to the heart without at the same time bringing nearer the explosion we seek to escape.

—Letter to US President General Dwight Eisenhower from British Prime Minister Winston Churchill three months after the Big Three conference in Bermuda

In their own words

■ Dwight Eisenhower, 1954

March 19, 1954

I have pondered over your letter. You are quite right in your estimate of my grave concern at the steady increase in methods of mass destruction. Whether or not the specific possibilities of devastation that you mention are indeed demonstrated capabilities, the prospects are truly appalling. Ways of lessening, or, if possible, of eliminating the danger must be found. That has been my principal preoccupation throughout the last year.

It was after many weeks of thinking and study with political and technical advisers that I finally reached the conclusion which we talked over at Bermuda and embodied in my address to the United Nations Assembly…That plan was designed primarily as a means of opening the door of worldwide discussion —with some confidence on both sides—rather than as a substantive foundation of an international plan for the control or elimination of nuclear weapons. But honest, open technical discussions on an internationally supported plan to promote peaceful uses of this new science might lead to something much more comprehensive.

Since last December, we have been following up this matter as actively as its technical character permits.

Eisenhower and Churchill meet in Bermuda

BERMUDA ARCHIVES

Foster [US Secretary of State John Foster Dulles] had two or more talks with [Soviet Foreign Minister Vyacheslav] Molotov when they were at Berlin. We have a draft plan which, after consultation with your people and those of two or three other countries, will, I expect, be transmitted to the Soviet Union through diplomatic channels, as agreed, probably next week.

While there have been some indications that the Soviets might want to confuse the issues with extraneous political matters, on the whole it is encouraging that they so far seem prepared to accept businesslike procedures. In its entirety the problem is one of immensity and difficulty, as you graphically stated. But I repeat I deem it important to make a beginning in an exchange of views, which, as you suggest, could open up new and more hopeful vistas for the future…

My impression is that matters are in a reasonably good way, but that they require constant concern and vigilance and, I hope, frequent and intimate personal exchanges of views between the two of us.

—Eisenhower's reply

CHAPTER EIGHTEEN

Growing Pains

HURDLES ON THE PATH TOWARDS EQUALITY

The Floral Pageant parade was an unlikely prelude to a riot

Unsustainable *In Bermuda —even though everyone is politically equal—it has too often been supposed that, to preserve an old-world atmosphere for American visitors, the coloured people must appear mainly as servants or hewers of wood. Socially and politically, this has proved unsustainable.*
—From a front-page story headlined "Riots in the Sun" in The Times *of London, April 1968*

O n April 25, 1968, thousands of Bermudians and tourists packed into Hamilton to watch what had become a highly popular rite of spring—the Floral Pageant parade. Vying for choice vantage spots, many arrived as early as noon, three hours before the event was to start, and took their seats on the Front Street stands or sidewalks, some bringing picnic lunches to eat as they waited for the colourful spectacle. As the parade, in its 18th year and boasting 52 flower-bedecked floats, prepared to wind its way around the city, youngsters clambered up the branches of harbourfront trees for a better view and spectators lined balconies and windows.

But what happened later that balmy Thursday was as far from the innocent gaiety of blossoms, pageant queens and community bonhomie as anyone could imagine. As darkness fell, gangs of rioters suddenly erupted within the crowded streets, hurling bottles and firebombs at helmeted police officers armed with truncheons and shields. Hundreds of youths charged through the city, overturning cars, shattering windows and setting storefronts ablaze. When it was all over, five officers had been beaten, 17 people arrested and a state of emergency, with dusk-to-dawn curfew, had been declared. Petals and glass intermingled on Hamilton's tear-gassed avenues, an incongruous testimony to the fact that beneath Bermuda's pretty façade, ugly truths could no longer be ignored.

In hindsight, the so-called "Floral Pageant Day Riot" was dramatically symbolic, a clash of the island's quaint past and rebellious present, of its economically and socially segregated black and white societies, of their respective fears and concerns—a flashpoint which would have far-reaching consequences for Bermudian culture. Its direct cause may have been linked to the barring of a black youth from a party held in a Front Street building that evening, but its true roots were far more widespread. The night represented a snapshot of racial tensions affecting not only the island, but the whole western world, particularly America. The 1960s and '70s, for the most part, would prove a jarring passage into the latter decades of the century, and

Warning signs

Lip service *There are no old-age pensions, no low-cost housing schemes, no unemployment insurance. The level of education is very low by British standards, and trade unions are only slowly being accepted. Negroes have many complaints about racial discrimination. The UBP pays lip service to integration but little has taken place in schools or social life.*
—Margaret Fishley, in a story on Bermuda in the Daily Telegraph, October 1966

Invisible people *Some white people seemed to regard coloured people as invisible people, non-existent. The only way he can feel he is there is to do something to attract attention.*
—Alma Hunt, cricketer, to an August 1968 commission investigating the Floral Pageant Day Riot

Much to do *Only the blind and the prejudiced will not agree that the progress has been great. And only the blind and the prejudiced will not agree that there is much to do.*
—Sir Henry Tucker, May 20, 1968

Oligarchy *We here are an oligarchy or government of the people, by the few, for the few, at the expense of the people.*
—Dr. Edgar Fitzgerald Gordon

Powderkeg *In my opinion, in this country we are sitting on what might be called a keg of gunpowder.*
—Wesley Leroy Tucker, MCP, in the House of Assembly, June 22, 1959

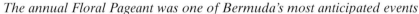

The annual Floral Pageant was one of Bermuda's most anticipated events

while Bermuda was spared the violent scale of civil unrest experienced by its larger neighbour, the island's path to maturity during these years would be pockmarked by many of the same kinds of social upheavals.

The Second World War had effected a physical transformation on Bermuda, but over the next three decades, the island would undergo a psychic metamorphosis. Among other milestones, the era saw the end of largely tolerated segregation, the introduction of universal suffrage, the creation of political parties, the first elections, and the establishment of labour standards and workers' rights. Such wholesale changes shaped a stronger future for Bermuda, but also provoked growing pains of a society in the throes of radical transformation.

In many ways, Bermuda's social unrest was a necessary process shared by other western democracies of the time. Against the backdrop of Vietnam's bloodshed, political assassinations and the tinderbox of civil-rights struggles and student uprisings across the US, Bermudians watched, listened and felt the fractious fallout even within their own tiny microcosm. Ripples of rebellion that surged beneath the tidy surface of the island during these years essentially sprang from the birth of new hopes and ambitions instilled by modernisation and spreading affluence. Bermuda had ridden the crest of the post-war boom and investments in tourism and international business were beginning to pay off. But the island's good life was far from inclusive. Bermuda's white establishment still held the bulk of wealth and power, a 300-year status quo that fed a building resentment in the black community.

The rhetoric of Malcolm X and Martin Luther King, Jr., together with black civic-lobby campaigns and labour protests in Britain and elsewhere, had seized the popular imagination of blacks and white libertarians, demonstrating the power of vocal solidarity. Deep within the social fabric of Bermuda, the words and events of the changing outside world held resonance. Indeed, Bermuda in the 1950s and '60s was a polarised community, an island split into two societies so distinct, they might as well have been different islands—one white, the other black.

"As separate entities, they can never be contained peaceably in so confined a space as ours, any more than they can co-exist peaceably in such large countries as America and Britain," noted an April 30, 1968 editorial in

THE BERMUDIAN

Supporters of the 1946 human-rights petition to Westminster

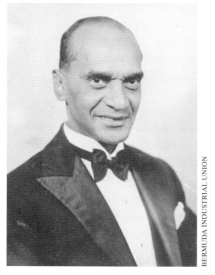

'Double-talk' *In Bermuda, they tell you that if there was universal franchise the island would blow up; that the tourist trade would vanish if they had to mingle freely with Negroes. But why is it that one could hardly get into the Clay House and Mount Area restaurants because of the number of tourists who go there to be with the coloured people? It is your duty to send me to Parliament to ask them to explain their double-talk."*

—Dr. E. F. Gordon, during the campaign that won him a St. George's seat in the House of Assembly in 1946

The Royal Gazette. "That, surely, is the prime lesson to be learned from recent events both here and abroad…all questions facing us in the political arena hinge upon a single one: the process of integration."

Before that could happen, Bermuda was to suffer through times of turbulence. Bermudian blacks, long shut out from both visible material rewards, equal rights and a genuine stake in their country, wanted changes—and the catalyst for their dream was a man named Dr. Edgar Fitzgerald Gordon.

As early as 1946, the Trinidad-born Gordon was well-known to most Bermudians, white and black. A firebrand physician who made as many enemies as he did friends, Gordon served as president of the Bermuda Workers Association (BWA), which became the Bermuda Industrial

Dr. E. F. Gordon (second right) during the 1946 petition campaign

Black Bermudian nurses and the
Cottage Hospital, below

'A useful bomb' *I had forgotten
that this is not a democracy, but an
oligarchy and even the horrors of total
and global warfare have not softened the
hearts of the slave drivers. An atomic
bomb would be very useful here. The new
generation might be chastened.*
— Dr. E. F. Gordon in a letter to
The Royal Gazette, *November 9, 1945*

Union (BIU) in 1947. He was also a Member of the Colonial Parliament (MCP) for St. George's. Outraged by social conditions such as substandard housing and poor sanitation in his adopted island, Gordon presented a petition in August 1946 demanding a review of Bermuda's human rights record to the British government. "Unless we can have human rights and fundamental freedoms, the Isles of Rest will become the Isles of Unrest," he predicted.

The colonial secretary was sympathetic, but no change came about. In March 1947, a white paper on Bermuda was published for the British House of Commons, but the issues described in Gordon's petition were simply referred back to the island for the local Assembly to deal with.

Undeterred, Gordon spent the next decade rallying blacks to challenge Bermuda's white power structure, becoming an indefatigable mouthpiece against racial injustice on behalf of the working class. Issues such as the island's dual school system, racial bias in the civil service and property-skewed voting rights dominated his many public speeches and letters to newspapers. Like Malcolm X, who was shot and killed in 1965, and Martin Luther King, who was murdered in 1968, Gordon was not afraid of being provocative or unpopular. He understood the uphill battle blacks were facing but also realised a steady crusade of protest could achieve positive results. In his own profession, he faced serious prejudices. As a black doctor, he was not allowed to practise inside King Edward VII Memorial Hospital; instead, he had to refer patients to a white counterpart who would attend to them.

Among his many crusades for equality, Gordon championed black nurses, who were shut out of lucrative jobs and, like him, barred from the hospital during the 1930s and '40s; underpaid local tradesmen during construction of the US Naval bases in 1940, a conflict that gave birth to the Bermuda Workers Association; and black cricket players who were overlooked for consideration for Bermuda's touring teams. But it was in 1953, during the Queen's first visit to the island, that Gordon won an international audience. In a small-minded political faux pas that would mushroom into a public relations disaster, the government failed to invite a single black guest to the state dinner held to welcome Elizabeth II, and selected just 60 black Bermudians—of a total of 1,200 guests—to attend a garden party in her honour.

In Parliament afterwards, Gordon lambasted the government's blatant racism, calling it a humiliating injustice to a community that made up 60 percent of the population. The British media, which had accompanied the royal entourage, agreed. Front-page headlines in the mass-circulation national dailies ridiculed the blunder, prompting 48 MPs in the British House of Commons to sign a motion protesting colour discrimination.

"To blazes with the first families of Bermuda and an end to blind snobbery!" demanded the London *Daily Mirror*, while the *Daily Herald* said: "Bermudians should know how Britain has reacted. It does not wipe out what happened. But it shows what Britons feel about colour discrimination, social snobbery and ham-handed Governors."

The same year, Gordon was asked to join the Inter-Racial Committee, a group formed by the government to look into equality issues. But he found himself powerless to sway its findings, which proved mostly disappointing to the black community: education would stay separate; a new tennis court

BERMUDA ARCHIVES

BERMUDA ARCHIVES

No more muddling

*Four years ago I arrived in a country
which had for three hundred years,
most successfully, in your own
words, 'muddled through.' Today,
there is a new Bermuda—a
Bermuda which can no longer
muddle through, a Bermuda which
has to plan, to organise, to become
a modern state. From now on, you
have got to plan; to organise your
political, your social and your
economic systems.*

—Outgoing Governor General Sir
Julian Gascoigne, the Speaker's
Dinner, January 8, 1964

Tension and violence

*Bermuda is nearing the end of a
long era in which political rule has
been the virtual prerogative of a
handful of wealthy families.
Discontent among Negroes that
was brought to light recently in the
tension and violence of strikes
indicate that this oldest of the
British crown-colonies will move
steadily to end some of the more
serious political grievances.*

—The New York Times, *1965*

'Don't give up'

*We wish to thank everyone for their
cooperation and to beg them to
continue to keep up the good work.
There are certain 'do nots' that we
would like to bring to the mind of
our supporters: 1. Don't use
violence; 2. Don't block traffic;
3. Don't get excited; 4. Don't give up.*

—Letter signed by the Progressive
Group published in The Recorder *on
the third day of the Theatre Boycott,
June 17, 1959*

would be built for blacks, but not at Hamilton's stadium; the hospital would accept black nurses, but they had to live off its property; no changes would be made in the racial makeup of Bermuda's armed forces; and hotels and restaurants would be allowed to continue to turn away certain clientèle—reinforcing a longtime prejudice against blacks and Jews that was legal under the 1930 Hotel and Innkeepers Act.

Gordon died on April 20, 1955, but his vehement campaigns against injustices had forever changed the way all Bermudians viewed their society. For the first time, blacks and all working-class people had been heard at a national level, and the campaign for their rights and freedoms was now set in motion. It would still take years for key civil-rights goals to become reality, but there would be no turning back. Gordon had paved the way for blacks to speak out, and also to make effective inroads in politics. Moreover, he had demonstrated to the island's leaders that Bermuda could benefit enormously from encouraging its people—both black and white—to be politically educated. Even his political opponent, Henry "Jack"—later Sir Henry—Tucker, paid him posthumous tribute. "I am satisfied the community has suffered a loss," said Tucker. "I myself regret his death and hope members of his group and mine will agree that his methods of association and compromise have set a very admirable pattern. I am expressing a personal sense of deep regret that he can no longer be with us."

One of Gordon's black successors in Parliament was Sir Edward T. Richards, a Guyanese teacher who became Bermuda's first premier. In the 1950s, Richards was named to the Executive Council, and 10 years later joined the fledgling United Bermuda Party. He went on to become party leader and head of government, after Henry Tucker. In 1973, under the island's new constitution, Richards became premier. He achieved another milestone in 1970, becoming the first black Bermudian to be knighted.

As Bermudians drove to work on June 15, 1959, they were met with posters and banners throughout the island proclaiming, "Down with Segregation in Theatres." Bermuda was celebrating its 350th birthday, but what happened at the island's cinemas that summer would far outweigh the pomp and pride of any colonial celebrations.

Racial segregation existed throughout Bermuda—in the civil service, in schools, churches, hotels, restaurants, and in the movie theatres. Divided into upper and lower floors, cinemas owned by the Bermuda General Theatres monopoly allowed white patrons to choose any seat in the house, including the preferred balconies upstairs, while relegating blacks to the downstairs only. Movies were a favourite recreation of Bermudians, especially blacks, who found many other forms of recreation very limited in a divided society. Indeed, of all Bermuda's segregated venues, cinemas represented those which black men, women and children patronised the most—and white owners had much to lose if black clientèle disappeared.

That economic leverage was not lost on a group of black Bermudians, many of them 20-something university graduates who found Bermuda's racial barriers shocking when they returned home to the island in the '50s from more liberal environments in North America and Britain. They decided to fight segregation by forming a secret society called the "Progressive Group" to study the island's social ills and find ways to improve life for black Bermudians. In 1959, the group's 18 members chose theatres as their

THIS IS WHAT THE TOURISTS WANT ? NO NEGROES ADMITTED

Protesting segregation years before the successful cinema boycott, Georgine Hill, right, and Eva Robinson picket the Bermudiana Theatre in March 1951

Boycott! *In this the 350th year of Bermuda's history, we the undermentioned group wish you to make an effort to bring about the end of second-class citizenship. There is no reason why any person should not be allowed to sit any place in any theatre. You are well-behaved, well-dressed and you know only too well that you have to pay your admission. You have a sense of personal dignity, courage and leadership. Therefore, assert yourself and BOYCOTT ALL THEATRES AS OF JUNE 15th; encourage your friends to do likewise.*
A Progressive Group.
　—Letter distributed to the black community by The Progressive Group in June 1959

'Three days' *I'll give them three days. People love the movies too much to stay away.*
　—A movie theatre employee on the first night of the boycott

symbolic battlefield for civil rights. They risked total failure and social ostracism. But history would record success beyond their wildest expectations.

The Theatre Boycott began that June day, when blacks rallied to support a provocative memorandum which the Progressive Group had distributed to thousands in the black community, having acquired the mailing lists of both the Somerset and St. George's cricket clubs. A copy of the memo had also found its way into *The Royal Gazette*, which ran a story on the lobby effort. The memo asked black Bermudians to stage a simple protest: to boycott the island's movie cinemas to help "bring about the end of second-class citizenship."

The Progressive Group was adamant about two things: that the boycott be non-violent, like the celebrated Montgomery, Alabama bus protest inspired by Rosa Parks nearly four years earlier, and that they themselves would remain anonymous—thus avoiding reprisals and personal attacks and keeping the focus on their goal: peaceful resistance and desegregation. The tactic worked and the group managed to conceal its identity for 30 years. When it finally went public in 1989, its members were by then some of Bermuda's best-known black educators, dentists, lawyers and politicians.

The campaign won strong support from the start. Hundreds of black Bermudians turned out on the first evening to rally on Church Street outside two Hamilton cinemas, the Island and Playhouse theatres. Following nights saw the area become a gathering spot for huge crowds of supporters, encouraged by nightly speakers such as street activist Kingsley Tweed whose participation helped turn the boycott into a mass demonstration. As instructed by the organisers, protesters stayed on the sidewalk so as not to block traffic and as they listened to speeches, waved placards reading, "No violence" and "Keep it up, we are winning." A few blacks who defied the boycott and attended movies were escorted to taxis by police after the shows.

The Progressive Group

The triumphant 1959 Theatre Boycott helped topple Bermuda's discriminatory racial barriers, but its organisers had farther-reaching plans to become an influential political force on the island.

"Progressive Group" members decided to stage the boycott as a small yet heartfelt protest. But it quickly gained such momentum, the boycott actually achieved their long-term hopes by triggering the reshaping of the island's entire political and social structure. Within a fortnight, desegregation

swept through public places including cinemas and hotels; just a few years later, all blacks had won the right to vote without property-ownership barriers, opening the door for the face of government—and its policies —to forever change.

The group, largely made up of new university graduates, pretended to be a social organisation, with dinner parties and croquet games held at each other's homes. But the frivolous façade was simply a cover for members to meet for political brainstorming and

serious debates on the island's race barrier without attracting unwanted attention. Members adopted individual 'portfolios,' based on government ministries, and produced a weighty discussion paper on the island's social and racial problems, an analysis which street activists such as Kingsley Tweed read aloud to crowds who turned out for the nightly boycott.

The group managed to keep its members' identities a secret for 30 years. In 1989, they were commended during

a ceremony at City Hall, an occasion that would be repeated a decade later when they won official kudos from the first Progressive Labour Party government. The 18 members of the group were: Dr. Stanley Ratteray, Esme and Lancelot Swan, Gerald and Izola Harvey, Eugene Woods, Rudy and Vera Commissiong, Marva Phillips, Rosalind and Edouard Williams, William Francis, Clifford Wade, Coleridge Williams, Dr. Erskine Simmons, William Walwyn and Dr. Clifford and Florenz Maxwell.

Shining example?

Your country can be a shining example to the world of two races living together and enjoying peace and prosperity. I would like to suggest in all seriousness that your country has a duty to show the rest of the world how two races can live as one. I say a duty because I believe that in Bermuda you have conditions which are more favourable than in any other part of the world, where races live side by side. You speak the same tongue. You have men, and women of both races of great ability and courage— and I believe foresight—to provide the leaders which every country needs. You have a prosperous economy from which you all benefit and which, at present at least, provides full employment; and you live in a beautiful country. If with these conditions, you in Bermuda cannot make a success of race relations, I don't know who can.
—Fred Lee, British Colonial Secretary,
speaking at Bermuda's Constitutional
Conference, November 1966

Even children joined the boycott, staying away from 'junior' shows held at the theatres. On June 21, *Merry Andrew*, starring Danny Kaye as a teacher who joins the circus, and Cecil B. de Mille's *The Buccaneer*, played to half-empty kids' audiences in Hamilton. White children paid their two shillings and sixpence admission to go upstairs (or one shilling and sixpence for a seat downstairs), but the few black youngsters who turned up that day simply peered through the window before walking away.

One night, a motorcade of boycott supporters took their rally to St. George's, honking their way in 150 cars and bikes to King's Square where some 1,500 paraded with banners sloganed with epithets like, "The only thing they love is money" and "Our skin is black but our money is the same colour."

While some liberal whites supported the aims of the standoff, Bermuda's white establishment was largely resistant to change, seeing the boycott as nothing more than an unnecessary irritation, a "storm in a teacup" staged by "hoodlums," according to Bermuda General Theatres chairman Jim Pearman. He was wrong on both counts. Curiously, the company blamed a seating shortage for segregation, and claimed the policy would be abolished later in the year anyway, once construction of a new 1,150-seat theatre finished—a rather twisted logic that did nothing to alleviate black frustrations. But to the Progressive Group's delight, the nightly rallies were taking an economic toll. Ten days after the boycott began, Bermuda General Theatres, which owned or leased five cinemas—the Island and Playhouse theatres and the Colonial Opera House in Hamilton, Somerset's Sandys Theatre, and the Somers Playhouse in St. George's—decided to pull the plug on all its movies, citing safety concerns for staff and patrons. Finally, on July 2, the theatres re-opened—without segregation.

Such a milestone, achieved in just two weeks, would have been victory alone, but the Theatre Boycott proved a watershed event that spawned a

Talking up a storm

Self-styled street activist Kingsley Tweed helped turn the 1959 Theatre Boycott from a simple protest into a mass rally that changed the social norms in Bermuda.

A one-man force of fiery oratory blended with sharp-witted humour, Tweed, 28, galvanised the black community into a show of solidarity that toppled racial segregation throughout the island. The erstwhile carpenter, well known in labour union circles for his outspoken views,

appeared on the third night of the boycott. Using an improvised loudspeaker, he urged the demonstrators not to give up, and stressed the

Tweed in 2003

impact the protest could have if black people acted together.

"A storm is a tornado, a hurricane, a typhoon and a forest fire, all wrapped up into one. Now that's a storm—and you can't fit that into a teacup!" he later told an interviewer, hitting back at cinema boss Jim Pearman's controversial downplaying of the boycott at the time. His verbal *tour de force*—accompanied by other speakers whom Tweed invited to his microphone—became a highlight of the nightly rallies.

After the boycott, Tweed became secretary-general of the Bermuda Industrial Union and also joined the lobby effort that led to universal adult suffrage. But after receiving death threats, he left the island in 1961 for Britain, where he became a minister in the African Methodist Episcopal Church. He would not return to the island for another 42 years.

domino effect on discriminatory racial policies throughout the island. Even before the cinemas made their historic policy change, Bermuda's major hotels and guest houses had announced they would begin to accept reservations from local residents "without discrimination." The Anglican Church followed suit, saying it "needed to take a fresh look" at the segregation of pews. The following year, a Parliamentary committee officially recommended racial discrimination be done away with in hotels or restaurants, and in 1961, segregation in restaurants became a crime under Bermuda law.

Encouraged by the boycott's success, members of the Progressive Group turned their sights on a larger goal: voting rights for all Bermudians. Blacks had been given the franchise when slavery was abolished in 1834—but only on paper. In reality, the island's voting laws excluded most blacks from the polls by demanding voters meet strict property ownership rules. Members of the Progressive Group were instrumental in overturning that discriminatory barrier. They helped to form the Committee for Universal Adult Suffrage (CUAS), which chose Roosevelt Brown to lead the lobby for "one man, one vote."

In Parliament, Wesley Leroy Tucker, the first black appointed to Bermuda's Executive Council, shepherded the campaign through endless meetings in the Assembly. At last, in 1963, the dream came true when the vote was given to every Bermudian adult over the age of 25, along with every British subject who had lived in Bermuda for three years.

A new era had dawned in Bermuda, one in which blacks felt they finally had some measure of power to achieve their goals, as well as a say in their future.

W. L. Tucker

Sir Henry Tucker

Sir Edward Richards

Newly-enfranchised Bermudians immediately put their power to work. It was election year in 1963, and with it came the formation of Bermuda's first official political party, the Progressive Labour Party, which picked up six seats in the new Parliament. One year later, the United Bermuda Party was formed. The UBP's leader was Henry "Jack" Tucker, a charismatic man of vision who realised change was inevitable and that ruling whites could survive only by sharing power.

These were exciting times for politicians. Representatives of both parties met in London to initiate a new constitution, which came into effect in 1967, abolishing the "plus vote"—a clause which gave property-holders an extra vote in elections. Instead, the Parliamentary Election Act guaranteed two votes for every British subject over the age of 21 who had lived in Bermuda for three years or more. Under the new constitution, Pembroke was split into four constituencies; the other eight parishes had two, with

In their own words

■ Andrew Bermingham

It was a cold bright day. We were sent down to BELCO in a police van at 8:45 in the morning. We were told things were getting out of control, and when we got there, it was obvious a lot of men were sitting on the wall encouraging the demonstrators. Within minutes, the picket line had doubled. I was told to stand in the middle of the road at the junction of Rosemont Avenue and Serpentine Road and ensure any cars which wanted access to BELCO could go in. Before long, a car carrying a white man, a BELCO employee being driven to work by his wife, approached and was surrounded by the crowd. I told the driver to wait while I spoke to the picketers. The mob jockeyed around the car and enveloped it. Slowly, the car inched forward through the BELCO gates.

Once it was gone, I was totally surrounded. I recall a man grabbed my jacket and the buttons popped off like peas out of a pod. Suddenly, my world closed in. Time seemed to stop. It was just me surrounded by this mass of angry people. I could see no way out of it. It was truly frightening. I'd taken out my baton, my truncheon, and someone shouted: "If you use that, we're going to get you!" Before I could say anything, someone struck me with a heavy blow on the back of the head and I went down.

In retrospect, it was obvious many of these men were armed and had, in fact, previously hidden the arms—golf clubs, sticks, stones—behind the low wall which surrounded BELCO. I clearly remember seeing weapons behind the wall and then seeing golf clubs in people's hands. In a dazed condition, I was taken back to the police minivan. Some time later, we heard there was another commotion at the east gate of BELCO, some 200 yards away. We were told the police needed assistance.

PC Andrew Bermingham (far left) runs to the aid of beaten colleague Ian Davies, with officers George Linnen (centre) and Tim Burch

Although I didn't have my total wits about me, I jumped out of the truck and ran to help. Things were totally out of control. There were men carrying various assorted weapons and missiles looking for trouble. It was a free-for-all.

It was then I could see Ian Davies on the ground. He had a massive head injury. He was unconscious, he was out. He was lying in a pool of blood and I thought some of his brains might even have been on the road. I assumed he was fatally injured, though he turned out not to be. I saw [officers George] Linnen and [Tim] Burch trying to protect him. I think it would be fair to say this incident may have tempered things a bit. People were shocked. The crowd which had followed me up Serpentine Road to the east gate was still in an angry fighting mood, but many of the onlookers had begun to

Union members at the BELCO picket

realise the gravity of the situation. There were comments like, "This is dreadful! This is awful!" People were trying to get back some semblance of reason. It was as if a large number of them had sensed this was totally out of order.

A BELCO employee, Emily Moss, was trying to help Ian Davies. She also tended to the other injured policemen. She came out of BELCO and entered into the fray for humanitarian reasons. She took some of the injured back inside the building to treat their wounds. I tell you, she was an angel of mercy.

An ambulance arrived 15 minutes later and Ian was loaded in and taken to hospital. Seventeen policemen ended up that night in King Edward, myself included. I had a severe concussion. There were many casualties from this day who never recovered physically or psychologically. Ian Davies was one of them. He was flown out of the island and spent months recovering in hospital in England. It was the end of his police career. In fact, he never worked again.

I was 23 at the time and to me, it was shocking because it was totally unexpected. In retrospect, the powers that be sent the police down there totally unprepared that day.

They completely underestimated the anger that existed. The magnitude of this incident actually happening in Bermuda made it a benchmark. On many days since, I have gone by that junction where I was attacked. What happened there is cemented in my mind forever.

—*British-born Andrew Bermingham*
on being a police constable injured in
the February 2, 1965 BELCO riot.
Bermingham retired in 1994 as a
superintendent after serving 30 years
in the Bermuda Police Force

BERMUDA POLICE SERVICE

Police don
riot gear in
the 1959
dock strike

each constituency returning two MPs and the number of seats in the House of Assembly increased from 36 to 40.

The following year, on May 22, 1968, Bermudians voted in the first general election contested by political parties. The UBP won a landslide victory, 30 seats to the PLP's 10, and established control of the House of Assembly. Under the new constitution, Sir Henry Tucker became Bermuda's first government leader. He would hold that post for three years before retiring, to be replaced by Sir Edward Richards.

The Sixties marked a stormy period for industrial relations, as the island's largely black workforce began flexing its growing political muscle to bring about wage and benefit improvements. Tensions had been running high for years and as the Bermuda Industrial Union's power grew, angry workers came close to flare-ups with the mainly white police force on several occasions.

The 1905 Riot Act was read for the first time during a strike by dock-workers, stevedores and longshoremen in September 1959. Though violence was avoided, Bermuda Rifles soldiers and squads of riot police brandishing truncheons and wicker shields were called out to confront crowds of angry, armed picketers on Front Street. Various demonstrations, near-clashes and work stoppages continued over the next few years. But the most violent eruption of social discontent occurred in 1965, during a bitter labour dispute about union representation at the Bermuda Electric Light Company. On February 2, a bloody morning clash between police and armed demonstrators picketing BELCO headquarters on Serpentine Road, Pembroke left 17 officers injured, one of them beaten unconscious before horrified onlookers.

It was the lowest point in Bermuda's labour relations history, but it was only a preview of further social upheaval and overt racial battles. Over the next several years, picketing and sympathy strikes were frequent occurrences, sometimes shutting down whole segments of the island as the BIU called on its members to show their collective political strength. Dock labourers, construction workers, bus drivers, aviation and bakery employees, teachers—all would walk off the job in 1968 as the tensions of an election year burst the island's polite façade, and the news of Martin Luther King's assassination on April 3 stunned the world and underscored issues of racial disparity.

"What strange gyrations our American friends across the ocean are going through. We fear for them because any major development there usually has an effect on us," said a *Royal Gazette* editorial of America's "racial crossroads" later that month. "We in Bermuda have one advantage over those in big countries," the *Gazette* added. "Perhaps the biggest thing we have going for us is the realisation by all thinking people that no one section of our community can live without the other."

That maxim would be put to the test again and again over the next decade as political, social and labour frustrations continued to build and boil over.

CHAPTER NINETEEN

Troubled Times

TURBULENCE ROCKS A FRAUGHT ISLAND

Governor and aide killed instantly

At approximately 15 minutes before midnight on Saturday, His Excellency the Governor and Commander- Richard Sharples, was assassinated, and his A.D.C., Capt. Hugh Sayers, murdered.

The Royal Gazette, *March 13, 1973*

Rule of the gun *In a small tight-knit community there is a natural tendency to avoid getting involved or implicating others. But I must ask anyone who knows anything about this crime to think most seriously about the implications for themselves and the community as a whole if the rule of the gun becomes the way of life on this island.*
—*Acting Governor Ian Kinnear,*
The New York Times, *March 11, 1973*

Bermudians awoke on the morning of Sunday, March 11, 1973 to shocking news. Governor Sir Richard Sharples and his aide-de-camp, Captain Hugh Sayers, had been assassinated the previous night in the grounds of Government House— shot dead while taking a late stroll through the gardens with the Governor's great dane dog, Horsa, which was also killed. For all Bermuda's simmering social and racial turmoil, such cold-blooded murders in their own community stunned islanders so unused to violent crime.

"If we were uncertain about our diagnosis before, we are not now. A virulent cancer is threatening the life of Bermuda, and, without further delay or procrastination, it has got to be located and cut right out," said an editorial in *The Royal Gazette*. "The assassination clearly indicates there is a direct move by power-seeking bandits to disrupt the life of this peaceful nation."

Less than six months into his Bermuda posting, the governor had been verbally attacked in budget debates only the previous day when PLP Parliamentarians labelled him "a symbol of Colonialism" and criticised government spending on his salary and staff. But generally, Sharples was an affable administrator who had been well-liked by Bermudians. On the night of his murder, when many police officers had been attending a police choir performance at the Southampton Princess Hotel, the governor hosted a small informal dinner party at Government House before taking his regular walk around the 15-acre property. He was gunned down shortly before midnight, within sight of the main door to the House; he and Sayers died within minutes of the attack.

The double-slayings prompted the government to invoke a state of emergency—only the second in the island's history, and just five years after the first, imposed after the 1968 Floral Pageant Day Riot. The crackdown also slapped an unprecedented 48-hour ban on people leaving Bermuda, as a full-scale hunt for the killers was launched by Scotland Yard, local police and the Bermuda Regiment. Headlines around the world—"Murder in Paradise," "Guns in the Sun"—recorded the event with the kind of crude

In their own words
■ Sir Richard Sharples

One of the things to be considered, I think, is the mood of the island. Do you feel it in your responsibilities relating to internal security? How do you assess the mood here, with a wide variance between the black population and the white population? Is there a state of harmony or is there an undercurrent of tension?

I don't think there is on the whole, but obviously there are in many communities. There are tensions that exist and which could come to the surface given the right climate to do so, but that climate doesn't exist at the moment. I think that Bermuda has done a very remarkable job, but I think that the question of racial discrimination and the whole barriers that existed between the races have been broken down, and broken down completely and effectively in a very short space of time, and have been broken down by a willing of co-operation between black and white people in this island, who realised—and I am going back some 12 to 15 years— that if Bermuda was going to stand without strife, that these things had to be done. This, which was absolutely right, has been done in a most remarkable way. I give full credit to the people of Bermuda, both black and white, for what has been done, and the way it has been done.

—Sir Richard Sharples, in an interview with CJCH-TV, Halifax, Nova Scotia, January 29, 1973, just weeks before his assassination

TONY CORDEIRO FOR GUARDS MAGAZINE

Murdered: Governor Sir Richard Sharples and aide Captain Hugh Sayers

sensationalism Bermudians had never imagined could be applied to their community.

Certainly the episode marked the shock intrusion of the worst kind of 20th-Century coming-of-age. After so many years spent as a microcosm consumed by introspection, Bermuda had, indeed, joined the larger world. If nothing else, the incident underscored the blatant presence of guns on the island, along with the hatred to use them. To a population living in a time still not inured to the graphic violence that would later saturate the globe, it represented a rude awakening. There was no doubt the impact of deep social upheavals in the United States during the 1960s and '70s had been felt on the island, where racial militancy had sparked several insurrections since the 1968 Floral Day Parade Riot. Indeed, America's Black Power revolt had come to Bermuda in a smaller form: local activists had formed the Black Beret Cadre, a group of young black males who modelled themselves on the paramilitary Black Panther Party in the US. Wearing black leather jackets and caps reminiscent of French resistance fighters, Cadre members described their goal as a political one, publically decrying the island's white power structure and what they called Bermuda's long history of black suppression.

Bermudians in the early 1970s had felt largely shielded from severe politically-, socially- and racially-motivated violence, buffered, perhaps, by the island's small-town quality. The Sharples tragedy changed that, plunging horrified locals, particularly whites, into something of an identity crisis. Suddenly Bermuda seemed as vulnerable as any other society. Was the island not a peace-loving place where everyone knew their neighbour and could count on a safe and prosperous future for their children? Was this quaint, fragile society, long shaped by lucky circumstance and responsible

Public view

Prayer *We shall hold prayer sessions in memory of the five men who lost their lives as a result of being assassinated by the two men who presently stand to lose their lives after being convicted of the offences. How can those five men be forgotten at this time?*

Contempt *Six-thousand signatures of Bermudians have been ignored. Two lives are at stake. How can we show contempt for the wishes of people not to hang these men in our civilised society?*

Civilised *We have worked hard to make our country a civilised one. If a hanging takes place, then we have taken a step in the wrong direction. Such a step will be detrimental to our future. The Governor has the right to reprieve them. Stop the hangings.*

Slaughtered *If you think we will be committing legalised murder on Friday, December 2, spare a thought for the five just and innocent men who were brutally slaughtered in cold blood by these two callous men.*

No shame *There is no shame attached to justice!*

—*Letters to the editor,* The Royal Gazette, *December 1, 1977*

citizenry, now self-destructing? The rest of the decade would be spent analysing questions such as these. The strong post-war confidence could no longer be taken for granted. Instead, the future was uncertain. For the crimes and their outcome—whether politically motivated or not—were symptomatic of a traumatised country, a place torn by bitter racial, labour and economic frustrations that would plunge Bermuda into a period of more frightening violence and social unease.

The Sharples slaying was not the first such attack: just six months earlier, on September 9, 1972, in eerily similar circumstances, Police Commissioner George Duckett had been shot by a .32-calibre revolver on a Saturday night in the kitchen of his North Shore, Devonshire home, the unfortunately-named "Bleak House." Scotland Yard detectives, working with local officers, had failed to find his killer despite a $25,000 reward. Now authorities believed the two crimes might be linked. Some observers suggested the murders could be the work of Black Beret Cadre members, whose confrontations with the island's mostly white police force were frequent. No firm link, however, was ever proven.

Deputy Governor Ian Kinnear was appointed Acting Governor while Sharples's successor was sought. Meanwhile, the slain governor and his aide were buried at St. Peter's Church in St. George's, and a grieving island pondered the future.

But the wave of violence was not over. A month later, in April 1973, the co-owner of Hamilton's Shopping Centre supermarket, Victor Rego, and his bookkeeper Mark Doe, were shot dead during an armed robbery in which the killers stole more than $12,000. Official reaction was swift. On April 14, Parliament passed emergency legislation banning all firearms and police announced a 10-day amnesty for the surrender of all firearms, licensed or not. The call saw a total of 1,440 guns surrendered. The investigation continued. In June, authorities set a reward of $300,000 for information on the murders of Duckett, Sharples, Sayers, Rego and Doe.

By July, Sir Edwin Leather was sworn in as Bermuda's new governor, but the spree of violence had not abated. Gunshots were reported in various incidents around the island and armed robberies took place at the Bank of Bermuda on Church Street and the Piggly Wiggly supermarket in Hamilton Parish.

Later that year, in October, police arrested their prime suspect, Erskine Durrant "Buck" Burrows, a Bermudian janitor whose jobs had included cleaning up at police headquarters. Burrows was named as Commissioner Duckett's killer in a June 1975 inquest. A November inquest the same year into the Government House assassinations, named Burrows and another Bermudian, Larry Tacklyn, as the culprits, with other persons unknown.

As 100 tall ships brought the youthful exuberance of America's bicentennnial celebrations to the island in June 1976, the murder saga continued. At his trial, Burrows was found guilty after confessing to the

Slain Police Commissioner George Duckett

BERMUDA POLICE SERVICE

BERMUDA POLICE SERVICE

Erskine "Buck" Burrows and (above left) Larry Tacklyn

In their own words

■ Erskine "Buck" Burrows

I, Erskine Durrant Burrows, as former Commander in Chief of all anti-colonialist forces in the island of Bermuda, wish to willingly reveal the part I played in the assassination and murder of the former Governor of Bermuda Mr. Richard Sharples and his ADC, Captain Hugh Sayers.

I wish to state, not forgetting that killing is wrong and sinful, that it was upon my direct orders and inspired efforts and determination, that what was done was done, performed with a Magnum .357 six-shot handgun. I was not alone when I went up to Government House to kill the Governor but I shall never reveal who or how many others were with me...

We arrived up at Government House at about 10:15 at night and waited just to the right of the steps leading down to the grounds of Government House. After we had been waiting for some time, we saw some people come out of Government House and begin to leave in cars that were parked outside. After they had gone, it was suggested to me that maybe the Governor wasn't going to come out and that we should leave. But I insisted that we continue to wait a bit longer.

Now, soon after this short conversation, we heard some noise coming from the front of the house. I looked through the opening in the balcony and saw someone walking towards the steps in our direction. Before he reached the steps, someone else came out and hurried to catch up with the first person. When they both reached the top of the steps, they stopped and I heard them quietly conversing together.

Now right about this time, the dog came down the steps and came right around to where we were. I was minded to shoot him then, although I was not the one who eventually killed the dog, for I realised that to have done so then would have given undue warning to our victims. So I ignored the dog, cocked the gun I had in my right hand, aimed and began to fire at the two persons who were standing at the top of the steps.

They both fell to the ground right away. One of them didn't make any sound at all, but I heard a groaning sound coming from the other person. I commenced shooting at them from between the openings that were in the wall. The dog was shot immediately

after this as it was blocking our path of escape. It is sufficient for me to say that we came on foot and left on foot...

The motive for killing the Governor was to seek to make the people, black people in particular, become aware of the evilness and wickedness of the colonialist system in this island. It clearly can be seen that there is no strong backbone in the people so that they may stand strong and united against this evil...

Secondly, the motive was to show that these colonialists were just ordinary people like ourselves who eat, sleep and die just like anybody else and that we need not stand in fear and awe of them.

—Letter of confession by Erskine "Buck" Burrows to the murders of Governor Sir Richard Sharples and Captain Hugh Sayers

A blazing car separates armed police and rioters on Court Street, Hamilton, at the height of the December 1977 unrest

AP/WIDE WORLD PHOTOS

Resolve *Although my stay on this island has been so violently cut short, I personally shall be leaving with many memories of happiness that I have experienced here. This is*

BERMUDA SUN

the Bermuda which in so short a time my husband and I came to love so deeply; the hospitality, generosity and kindness of its people; the beauty and changing moods of its maritime setting. This is your island and your way of life which I prefer to remember and which I pray will be preserved. But only you—the people of Bermuda—can keep it this way and I am confident that you can be successful. If the assassination of my husband has in any way strengthened your resolve against those who would wish it otherwise, then perhaps his death has not altogether been in vain.

—*Lady Pamela Sharples, 1973*

Duckett murder, and sentenced to death. The same month, Burrows and Tacklyn went on trial for murdering the governor and his aide; Burrows was again convicted of the capital offence, while Tacklyn was acquitted. Later that year, the pair were found guilty in the Shopping Centre murders and this time, both received death sentences.

In 1977, the National Committee Against Capital Punishment (NCACP), whose 13,000-signature petition had won support from MPs on both sides of the House of Assembly, lost a last-ditch campaign to both the Court of Appeal and the Privy Council for both men's reprieve. The British foreign secretary in London reported to the Bermuda government that he was "unable to advise the Queen to intervene."

At dawn on Friday, December 2, 1977, Burrows and Tacklyn were hanged within 30 minutes of each other at Casemates Prison in Sandys. While it may have seemed to some that an ugly chapter in Bermuda's history had finally closed, their deaths only triggered a fresh outpouring of violence. The hangings proved the flashpoint for all Bermuda's social frustrations of the time, splitting the island largely down racial lines. While many Bermudians felt justice had been served, many more considered the hangings the proverbial last straw in a catalogue of unequal treatment of black Bermudians by the island's white leaders—not just in its judicial system, but in education, politics and general social reform. Moreover, many blacks, particularly the younger generation, felt a growing sense of exclusion, shut out of Bermuda's increasingly prosperous economy. Like its counterpart in cities across the US where urban race riots had laid open a maelstrom of repressed anger and frustration, black Bermuda was a tinderbox waiting to explode.

The backlash, when it came, was swift and catastrophic. Beginning on the eve of the hangings, the night of December 1, riots swept through the streets, ransacking the island for the next 48 hours. A state of emergency was declared as more than 20 businesses, most of them white-owned, were attacked by arsonists, and police riot squads clashed with crowds of black youths on the back streets of Hamilton. A fire set by arsonists at the Southampton Princess Hotel killed two American tourists and a Bermudian employee. On December 4, after a slew of fire-bombing despite the dusk-to-dawn curfew, 250 British soldiers of the Royal Regiment of Fusiliers, hardened by riot and terrorism control in Northern Ireland, were flown in by the Bermuda government to restore order. With their arrival, the riots subsided and the island began counting the physical and social cost.

Bermuda's national crisis had taken a deep toll—on the country's consciousness, as well as physically and fiscally. Several businesses, including the Shelly Bay Piggly Wiggly supermarket and a Gosling Brothers liquor warehouse, were gutted; many others were wrecked and looted, causing an estimated $17.5-million in lost revenue and damage. Tourists fled the island and hundreds more cancelled holiday reservations. Far more devastating in the long-term was the effect on Bermudians themselves. The island's sense of trust and community had been shattered. What was happening to their island home? Would life as they had known it ever return? As residents began to pick up the pieces, Premier Sir David Gibbons and Governor Sir Peter Ramsbotham called for calm.

Sir David Gibbons

"Our country is passing through a time of deep anxiety," Sir Peter noted, "a time when people are clearly apprehensive about what might happen, and perhaps fearful that malign influences could be let loose among us to spread bitterness and division. Were that to happen, all that has been achieved these past years in promoting prosperity and racial harmony could be lost. We cannot afford to let that happen."

Nor could Bermuda afford to ignore the weight of public emotion. The riots pointed to the need for an immediate evaluation of a racially-divided country's fundamental problems. Britain's Labour government appointed a royal commission of inquiry, and chose as its chairman Lord Pitt, a Grenada-born physician from London. Two months of hearings began in April 1978, in which the Pitt Commission heard evidence from the whole community, some 250 witnesses, from the premier down even to some of the rioters.

And as promises to listen and make amends were made, the island's deep social wounds slowly began to heal.

Published in July 1978, the commission's 196-page report pointed to unequal opportunities in Bermuda's economy as one of the key causes of the riots. It found a lack of support for small businesses, particularly black-run enterprises, and a concentration of the island's economic power in Front Street and the banks. Poor housing and a general lack of national unity were also underlined. The report concluded Bermuda's parliamentary process did not properly represent the island's citizens, either. It suggested a constitutional conference between the UK and Bermuda—including PLP representation—be held to discuss everything from the island's

---

'Them and us' *In the midst of one of the highest standards of living in the world there are those who feel so aggrieved, so deprived and so frustrated that they would attempt to destroy their home. No commission can solve a problem that deep. What is needed is a national concern so great and so sustained that Bermudians get together and stay together until they reach a mutual understanding which will cure at the root rather than simply provide a cosmetic. Bermuda must also develop a sense of national togetherness so that there will no longer be a divisive feeling of 'them and us.' There is no room in so small a country for polarisation.*

—*Editorial in* The Royal Gazette, *December 5, 1977*

Racism *Institutional racism occurs throughout Bermuda Society—in government, business, banks, churches, schools, unions, political parties, clubs and courts— and generally seems to be committed in the name of preserving business traditions and maintaining standards. It is a serious problem.*

—*The Archibald Royal Commission on drug abuse, October 1984*

In their own words
■ Rick Richardson

Journalists are always looking for a story of some magnitude, a story that will ultimately define who we are, what we're all about, what we do. We're not looking for a riot, but the riots of '77 certainly defined who I was as a journalist.

People during those times weighed up every word. They examined exactly how we portrayed events. I was mindful of that. How was I going to describe the next fire, the next Molotov cocktail explosion? Leading up to the riots, there was an eerie feeling that something big was going to happen. The court cases, the press conferences, the petitions, the failed attempts by the legal team headed up by Mrs. Lois Browne Evans MP, the heightened awareness in the community—it all led us to believe something was about to explode.

I lived near the South Shore in Warwick, and one night that December, I remember hearing sirens. I followed the noise to the Southampton Princess Hotel. I was probably the lone journalist on location after the fire broke out. I remember watching hotel guests being helped out of second- and third-floor windows, sheets being tied together and people clutching them as they scrambled to the ground.

There was an awareness that this was something huge. It went beyond the average court case, beyond the average fracas. This was touching Bermudian families, touching our lives. I tried to make sense of it. At first, I felt angry. Then I felt a sense of duty—to get the story. Then there was fear. Fear, not simply for me, but for all those folk whose lives were at risk. This was no longer a demonstration or rally; this had erupted into what appeared to me to be all-out war. At some point, I started to describe it that way. It felt like being on the front lines. And I was caught between Rick the citizen and Rick the journalist. Sometimes, I didn't know exactly when I was on this side or that.

As a Bermudian, I felt someone should have stopped this. Who, I don't know. But how could we have not had the wherewithall to resolve it? I felt angry. As a so-called literate and affluent society, why were we not able to avoid it? Later,

Rick Richardson at work in the 1970s

analysing what happened, I thought perhaps this *had* to happen, as sad as it was. Perhaps we had to, not physically, but certainly psychologically, vent and express emotion. Maybe this was a period of our history that was inevitable. I began to see it as something that paved the way for a period of growth towards maturity. Today I view it as a necessary evil, painful as it was at the time. I don't think anyone would have wished for violence, but in hindsight I think if it hadn't happened then, it would have happened at some point. There's always pain before we grow.

What set off the emotions? A feeling of impotence, of powerlessness, a feeling that, at the end of the day, there were still racial barriers no matter what you did. Those of us who expressed ourselves in a different manner would never have advocated violence, but 500 or so angry young men were expressing the feelings of thousands of black Bermudians who were saying not just "Stop the hangings!" but "Stop the injustices! Truly bring us into the mainstream. Take down all the barriers." I was no different. In my field, I was covering sports when I could have been writing and doing so much more. Blacks were saying, "We have the ability—let us go. And pay us." Within the environment I was working, I had to hold my tongue. I saw things were not being done correctly, that we were not fully serving the community as a communications medium. But I had to work within the rules. I think many black Bermudians felt the same way.

When the curfew was called, most people in the media stayed inside. Often I was the only reporter out there. I felt this was a time when we had to be out reflecting what was going on. Things were already at fever pitch. At the station, we kept up continuous coverage. I advocated that we stay on the air, and we did all night.

There were too many stories, too many angles. I felt overwhelmed by the magnitude of the damage, the human side, the injuries to people who just happened to be caught in the crossfire. I remember anticipating via two-way radio the movement of rioters and positioning myself, telling the cameraman, "We need to go to this location, I believe there's going to be a firebombing there." Arriving somewhere, we would see the perpetrators about to firebomb a building. I remember thinking, this is just not a good position, this is not a place I want to be right now. Are we to alert someone? Are we to record what happens? What is my responsibility right now? I knew the rioters were cognisant of the fact we were filming and some were very angry. People were calling me by name. I could hear people behind a clump of trees, for example, and they would say, "Don't shoot there!" At one point I shouted back, "I'm simply here to do my job. I'm not working for the police." I felt guilty saying that, because, after all, whose side was I on? I had to keep remembering I was there as a journalist.

When I returned from the streets to the studio, foreign media were waiting on the telephones. Coming back with nothing but pictures of destruction, fire, carnage, I would describe for our own anchors what we were seeing. Once, I came off the air and there was a call for me. A woman, a white Bermudian, was on the line. She said, "Take those confounded fires off the air. Why must we continue to watch Bermuda in flames?" I took a deep breath and said, "Lady, I'm simply doing my job in the best way I know how. And my job is to reflect and report on what's going on." That kind of call was the exception rather than the rule. While people cringed, they really wanted to know the extent of the damage, to know if this was going to subside or gain momentum. I was their barometer.

I think blacks and whites shared a feeling of shock about the overall impact on the island's economy and reputation. However, whites were shocked not only by the level of destruction, but by the level of anger. They had no idea of the pent-up emotions and frustrations felt by a large segment of the community. Of course, white Bermudians also had more to lose materially. They owned those huge buildings and Front Street stores.

It all lasted 48 hours, and I was up through the whole ordeal. I realised at the time that this was going to change us. A lot of legislation, a lot of our social policies and social norms would be shaped by the events of that time. It was not dissimilar to some of the things I had experienced in the US when I was a student reporter in New Jersey and New York. I followed [civil rights leader] Jesse Jackson through Brooklyn and saw the urban tensions. Here it was closer to home. I could detach myself when I was in the US. Here, I could not. I felt the emotions; it was this welling up within. I lamented it, and it made covering the story very difficult.

—Rick Richardson, a ZBM reporter and correspondent for ABC News, on the December 1977 riots. He later became Bermuda Broadcasting Company CEO

Troubled waters: tall ships arrive in Bermuda in 1976

independence from Britain to revamping electoral boundaries.

The Pitt Commission's findings mirrored some of the same issues highlighted in an earlier March 1978 report by an American consulting firm, Clark, Phipps, Clark & Harris, Inc., hired by the government to help identify ways to ease racial tensions. Headed by black sociologist Dr. Kenneth Clark, that report recommended the government create a public-housing programme, maintain education standards in public schools, hire more black Bermudians as police officers, and increase the number of blacks in policy-making positions.

Both reports revealed in blatant terms what many Bermudians already suspected or knew from first-hand experience, but what was rarely discussed in any kind of public forum. Not since the push for desegregation in the 1950s and '60s had the chasm between Bermuda's two races been so overtly portrayed. Now there could be no avoiding the fact of substantial problems in Bermuda. It was time for candid debate between blacks and whites, along with a firm resolve by the government and all Bermudians to work together.

Out of the horror of the tumultuous 1970s came Bermuda's gradual evolution into a more democratic, inclusive society. As such, the post mortem on the riots was not really an ending, but rather the start of a thorough look at the country's social ills, a process that would continue. It began with small steps. The government and private sector pledged to help small businesses. The premier urged companies to increase black representation on boards of directors. Scholarship fees were increased and a hotel-training college created.

The bubble of complacency had been burst, the island's 'dirty laundry' aired and the voices of all Bermudians finally heard. In hindsight, the troubled 1970s promised to be a positive catalyst, a wake-up call for the island that would have a dramatic impact on Bermuda's political, social and economic climate until the end of the century.

Rejected *The most frequently discussed problem by all Bermudians, and particularly black Bermudians of all economic levels, is the problem of the need for a "more equitable distribution of the wealth" of Bermuda. While all respondents agreed that Bermuda enjoyed a comparatively high standard of living, and that unemployment was by no means a major problem, black Bermudians described a number of specific forms of economic and employment disparities which are perceived, and resented, as forms of pervasive racial discrimination…*

Young black Bermudians insist that they are discriminated against when they apply for white-collar managerial and supervisory jobs in banks, insurance companies and hotels. Some of these young people state that in spite of their seeking higher education and training abroad, when they return to Bermuda and apply for positions consistent with their training, they are rejected, and these positions are given to white non-Bermudians. It is important to note that the intensity of these complaints increased around the days immediately following the early December disturbances, and were being expressed by middle-class or upwardly mobile black Bermudian youth who did not participate in the actual violence or arson, were not arrested for curfew violations, but seemed sympathetic to those who actually participated in the disturbances.

—From The Clark Report, "A Proposal for a Comprehensive Programme Toward Racial Integration and Economic Equity," March 1978

Bermuda Industrial Union members on the march

BIU chief Ottiwell Simmons in the 1970s

Labour strife during the 1970s also had its roots in racial disparity, given that most of the island's largest employers were white and its unionised workers black. It was a decade punctuated by contract disputes, walkouts and sympathy strikes that sometimes crippled the island's economy for weeks. Bermudians in these years became accustomed to having their daily lives disrupted by shutdowns in essential services of all kinds; carpools, grocery shortages and the perennial stench of rotting garbage were normal headaches as locals weathered the fallout of labour feuds.

The first year of the decade set the scene, with strikes by dockworkers, airport employees and postal workers over the course of several months, along with mini-riots connected to some of those disputes. The next few years saw similar action by marine pilots, stevedores, telephone company workers, bus drivers, garbage collectors, pilots and ferry captains. Such economic discord would continue throughout the turmoil of the late 1970s and into the next decade.

The biggest labour faceoff took place on April 11, 1981, when the BIU called a 21-day general strike. The unprecedented industrial crisis grew out of a double-headed dispute—over wage hikes and cost-of-living adjustments—between government and 'blue-collar' workers, and the hospital and its unionised staff. After six months of talks, both disputes were stalled, prompting BIU president Ottiwell Simmons, a PLP MP, to raise the ante by calling out thousands of workers across the island to support their colleagues. Buses and ferries ground to a halt; taxis followed suit; trash collection stopped; hospitals had to limit admissions and discharge many patients; hotels, haemorrhaging staff and tourists, were forced to shut their doors; airlines cut flights, and cruise ships abandoned their schedules to the island.

Crowds cheer Bermudian Gina Swainson on "Gina Day," a special public holiday declared to celebrate her return after winning the Miss World crown in 1979

Bermudians suddenly found themselves living in a virtual war zone. The government embodied the Bermuda Regiment and Reserve Constabulary to head off violence and looting. Stores and businesses boarded up their windows and many operated with skeleton staffs and shortened opening hours. Emergency trash-dumping sites were organised. Mail service was sporadic. Volunteers manned the hospital and some other essential services. Secondary-school attendance plummeted. At the airport, baggage-handlers walked off the job, causing traffic hold-ups in the area lasting hours.

Faced with such widespread chaos, the government capitulated, and by May 7, a deal had been struck. The union won increases averaging 20 percent, and celebrated its victory with a rally attended by thousands at BIU headquarters in Hamilton. But at what cost? By the time the strike was over, many Bermudians' nerves were frayed, resentments lingered, the economy had lost millions of dollars, and just 1,200 tourists remained in Bermuda. The island had struggled through dark days, but once again, it was a time for healing.

Decimal dollars

Bermuda made the change to decimal dollars on February 6, 1970. The old British system of pounds, shillings and pence, adopted in 1841 as the island's legal tender, was dropped and replaced with Bermuda's first currency of its own. The transition was orchestrated by the newly-formed Bermuda Monetary Authority, in charge of issuing or calling in the island's currency.

Still they came...

Despite troubled times, Bermuda continued to be a magnet for the famous and the not-so-famous. Clockwise from above: like flies on the beach during College Weeks, 1970s; US civil-rights activist Jesse Jackson; Queen Elizabeth in 1975; Roots *author Alex Haley, and former US president Richard Nixon*

CHAPTER TWENTY

Into the Future

TERRORISM, TRAFFIC AND THE DOWNTURN OF TOURISM

I've got to go

*Oh my God! The second
half of the building just
fell. I've got to go.*

—*Yvonne Morgan, at the
Bermuda Department of
Tourism office in midtown
Manhattan, during a phone
interview with* The Royal
Gazette, *September 11, 2001*

*Ruins surrounding the
World Trade Center after
the twin towers fell*

A s Bermuda residents sipped their morning coffee, delivered
children to school or checked email in Hamilton offices on
September 11, 2001, anyone near a television screen or
computer terminal suddenly was riveted. Like citizens
around the world with access to live news coverage,
islanders watched in disbelief as a tragedy of enormous proportions gripped
America. At 8:45 a.m. (Eastern Time), on what began as a balmy, late-summer
Tuesday in Manhattan, an American Airlines flight hijacked by Islamic
terrorists crashed into the north tower of the World Trade Center. A quarter
of an hour later, at 9:03 a.m., a second 767 passenger
jet was slammed into the New York landmark's south
skyscraper. Witnessed from neighbouring downtown
streets and captured on global TV, the disaster unfolded
like a grotesque replay of a Hollywood blockbuster.
Giant fireballs engulfed the twin 110-storey towers,
trapping thousands in a deadly inferno before both
buildings imploded over the next 90 minutes, and
crumbled to the ground.

The attacks—"acts of war," in the words of US
President George W. Bush—were part of a devastating
onslaught that morning. In Washington DC, another
airliner was plunged into the Pentagon, while in a
failed fourth attack, a passenger jet crashed into a
field outside Pittsburgh, Pennsylvania. Within a few
hours, nearly 3,000 people would be listed as dead or
missing—including two Bermudians, Rhondelle
Tankard and Boyd Gatton, who worked at the World
Trade Center. The seemingly impenetrable Pentagon,
the concrete embodiment of American military might,
lay torn open and on fire, while lower Manhattan's
skyline was irrevocably altered. For islanders, like

*Bermudians
Rhondelle Tankard
and Boyd Gatton
died in the 9/11
terrorist attack*

In their own words

■ Nichole Tatem, *2001*

It was a normal Tuesday morning. I had lived in New York since 1992. I worked in Manhattan as a reception supervisor for a health and fitness management company. We had opened a state-of-the-art facility for Merrill Lynch employees at the World Financial Center. We'd been there for about six months.

That morning, I prepared paperwork and helped clients. I was taking classes at Hunter College up at 68th Street twice a week; I'd get to work about 7 a.m., then leave for class around 8:30 a.m. to catch the train at the World Trade Center. I was running 10 minutes late this day. I was rushing. My class was experimental psychology and we were due to have a test.

I went through the Winter Garden of the Financial Center, through a glass bridge into the World Trade Center, to get the R Train uptown. I went towards the escalator. As soon as my foot touched the escalator, that's when all hell broke loose. I never got on it. Thank God.

All of a sudden, I heard loud noises. I froze. I went into a state of shock. I heard screaming and felt stuff falling from the sky. Something had happened to the building and it wasn't safe. When I saw grown businessmen running, I knew I needed to get out of there. I ran back towards the glass doors. I looked towards the World Financial Center, and I could easily have run back there, but big boulders were falling on the ground and I was afraid of being hit by something from the sky. The Trade Center had a balcony that led to a pedestrian bridge that crossed Vesey Street. If I ran around the balcony, maybe I could get out.

I began to run. It was a beautiful day, and I had on four-inch platform wedge-heel shoes—my favourites. I had my big black leather pocketbook. There were about 10 people running with me. We hit the corner and saw a wall blocking the way. I looked down. Everyone was telling me I'd kill myself if I jumped. I heard some saying the building was on fire.

A short caddie-corner jump away, there was a pedestrian bridge over to the next building. The only thing I could think of was getting home to Brooklyn to my kids—my son Taaj, who was nine, and my daughter Nasyah, just two. I was frantic. I was crying. My worst fear had always been that if something ever happened to those buildings, the whole of lower Manhattan would be crushed.

I knew the Trade Center complex very well because I did everything there: I banked there, I

Nichole Tatem

studied there, I hung out with friends there, I ate breakfast, lunch and dinner there, I shopped there. I kicked off my shoes and left them on the balcony and decided I would jump. I straddled the rail and made the leap over, at least five feet, from one balcony to the next. Now I was barefoot. As I began to run, I realised there was lots of broken glass all over the ground. I stupidly thought, "They're probably doing construction." It never occurred to me the glass was from the building itself.

I ran to Seven World Trade Center. Some workmen opened the locked door. Suddenly, I felt like I was in *The Twilight Zone*, because people were just standing around. They were taking orders from security people, who said, "Go back to work, it's just a fire. Do not leave the building." I ran around screaming like a lunatic: "How do you get downstairs?" I wanted to get out to the street. No-one was paying attention. Finally I got to the ground floor. I tried five doors, and the last one opened and I got out. Outside, I saw a woman on the ground. I couldn't imagine she was dead, but someone was helping her, so I kept running.

I ran down Greenwich Street, running for my life. I was amazed people were coming towards the Trade Center, taking pictures and talking on their cell phones, giving play-by-play action. Then I looked up and saw fire. It was just a big chunk of building on fire. I couldn't contain my tears. I kept running, barefoot, as I cried. My feet were bleeding. I started screaming at people, "You guys need to run the other way!" It was surreal. Not just the fact the building was on fire, but that people were trying to get closer.

Emergency units were racing in, and had an ugly feeling they weren't coming out alive. They were sacrificing their lives to save others. When I looked up, I didn't want to believe I saw people jumping out of windows. To this day I have a mental block. I saw stuff, but I don't believe it.

My cell phone didn't work, so I went into our SoHo centre. The first person I called was my Granny Lambert in Bermuda. I wanted to let her know I was okay because she always worries about me. She doesn't like the fact I live in New York. She had been watching it all on TV.

There was a grand exodus uptown. Everyone was walking. I decided to go towards the East Side, to the river. I figured if all else failed, I could swim to safety. Being near the water made me feel comfortable. Maybe it had to do with being Bermudian. I stopped when I heard someone say, "They're gone." They were talking about the World Trade Center towers. I walked into a nearby security office. "Is it true?" I asked. They told me to look at the TV. And there was nothing there. Just smoke. The very spot where I had jumped, where I was told not to go— it was gone.

—Bermudian Nichole Tatem, 29, describes her escape from the World Trade Center in New York City on Tuesday, September 11, 2001

AIDS takes its tragic toll

"Churches have to recognise that dead people cannot go to church," raged an editorial in *The Royal Gazette* on October 25, 1993. "Educators must face the fact they may be educating young people and wasting the education by letting them die for want of a condom. Bermuda needs to get over stigmatising this dreadful disease. It is not confined to gays or Haitians or even to cockroaches."

AIDS (acquired immunodeficiency syndrome) was an acronym which, from the 1980s, opened a Pandora's box of social, political and moral complexities which Bermuda grappled with like the rest of the world. Contracted through bodily fluids, usually via sexual contact, the pandemic would change not only healthcare protocol, but the very nature of relationships, catapulting once-private issues—the rules of dating, fidelity in marriage, sex education—into the arena of public debate.

The disease was eventually found to affect all races, backgrounds and genders, but in the '80s, science first believed it confined to certain parts of the population: gays and lesbians, Haitians and Africans, intravenous drug-users and prostitutes. Mis-information, moralising, and bias against the gay community resulted. Bermuda's human-rights activists lobbied against old laws criminalising homosexuality, and worked to protect AIDS/HIV (human immunodeficiency virus) sufferers from denial of jobs and housing because of their disease.

By the 2000s, an AIDS support group was running, a palliative care centre was open, and drugs helped infected people live longer lives. But 387 Bermudians had died, and over 600 were reported with HIV/AIDS, along with some 13-million worldwide.

Americans, it was the day the world changed. "9/11," as it would be remembered, marked an awful milestone in our progress to the post-modern era, as scarring to western psyches as it was to the physical architecture of American soil. With its unprecedented scale and political fallout, the tragedy questioned the very nature of freedom and brought home the stark uncertainty of the 21st Century with shuddering impact.

New York's horror was especially meaningful to Bermudians, given the city's strong geographic, social and corporate connections to the island. A 90-minute flight away, New York was a favourite destination for thousands of islanders every year. Bermudians had friends and relatives in the city, and during the weeks that followed, they waited anxiously for news of their survival. Like thousands of other victims, Tankard and Gatton were declared casualities although their bodies were never found. Staff at the Bermuda Tourism Department's office in midtown Manhattan had witnessed the World Trade Center attacks and experienced the chaotic aftermath. And the island's business community was sorely affected, since the twin towers, crowning symbols of western capitalism, housed insurance and financial companies affiliated with Bermuda-based operations.

The impact of 9/11 on Bermuda was immediate in practical terms. As a state of emergency was called and American airports shut down that day, international flights were diverted to the island. More than 1,000 travellers from grounded aircraft filled Bermuda hotels overnight as they waited to be re-routed. Bermuda residents offered rooms in their homes for the stranded. Armed police officers and Bermuda Regiment soldiers patrolled Bermuda International Airport and guarded key 'targets' such as Government House and the US Consul General's headquarters. In the ensuing months and years, as US-led wars were raged against terrorist-linked regimes in Afghanistan, and later Iraq, such precautions were as routine a practice in Bermuda as any other part of the world. Heightened alerts and safety procedures became an accepted new ingredient of daily life.

Bermuda Regiment: on alert

Bio-terrorism, chemical warfare, even the threat of naturally-spreading diseases such as the SARS (sudden acute respiratory syndrome) pandemic—the dramatic elements of the 21st Century all served to underscore Bermuda's undeniably close connection to the rest of humanity. Insularity, the navel-gazing affliction of islanders anywhere, was no longer our privilege. Gone were the days of playing a sheltered "fairyland" for visitors or boasting itself "another world," as extolled in the island's unofficial national anthem of the 1970s. For better and worse, Bermuda had joined the 'real world,' its miniscule size, mid-Atlantic position and British dependency no longer factors keeping islanders at arm's length from the alternatively ugly and empowering machinations of the new millennium.

Bermudians had always felt intimately tied to the world, but throughout the 1990s and into the 2000s, they found themselves true global citizens, sharing both the era's triumphs and tragedies. Through happy circumstance,

In their own words
■ **Noel Chiappa,** *2003*

In the 1970s I'd realised two of the most important technological events of the last 100 years have been communications (the telegraph and telephone), and computers. Put the two together and you'd have tremendous synergy.

The first Internet working group meetings I attended were in the fall of 1977 at Hanscomb Field, a US Air Force base outside Boston. There were about a dozen people there…and that was it—the entire Internet community of the whole world. There weren't any users because it wasn't in service. I was 21 and ready to make an impact.

I began to specialise in boxes we call 'routers,' which are the telephone exchanges of the Internet. I began writing what's called a multi-protocol router, or 'MPR,' in 1979. It allowed you to hook together a group of networks and use any protocol over the entire collection, just as a telephone network handles different languages.

I didn't invent the concept of a router; I invented a particular kind, the MPR. It was a passing phase of technology, as it turned out, but at the time, it was critical to networking. Not too many people are given the opportunity to change the world that extensively in their lifetime. It's an extraordinary feeling, to be a relatively young person and already be looking back on that.

—Bermudian Noel Chiappa, 47, an MIT computer scientist, on his pioneering work during the birth of the Internet

Construction seemed to be everywhere in the 1990s and early 2000s

coupled with entrepreneurial zeal, Bermudians' standard of living rose to one of the highest anywhere, enabling islanders to fully participate in the global economy and all it offered. They travelled to exotic destinations, educated their children at overseas universities, derived all the benefits of medical advances, both on the island and at renowned foreign hospitals, and enjoyed every consumer comfort, from cell phones to cabriolets.

But it was the phenomenon of galloping technology, the celebrated "Digital Revolution," which altered the fabric of island life most radically. From the mid-'90s onward, Bermuda residents found themselves able to live a virtual existence as well as a real one. "Cyberspace" made for a parallel universe, a borderless, electronic world whose only passkey was a computer. The Information Age changed the way they shopped, interacted and gleaned news. Now islanders could e-mail faraway friends and buy and sell in an international, and increasingly wireless, marketplace. By 'surfing' the Internet, a Bermudian mother could order a toy or piece of furniture from an online retailer and have it delivered to her Warwick doorstep as easily as the farmer in Iowa or the Paris executive. High-schoolers could browse the web to research class projects—or the latest Nintendo offering—or share chat-room jokes with peers from another culture. Foreigners could read *The Royal Gazette* and *Bermuda Sun* online. Even the timeless power of nature was different now: during the fury of Hurricane Fabian in September 2003, Bermudians used battery-powered laptops to describe the sound of 150 mile-per-hour winds to friends overseas, or order generators to ease them through the inevitable aftermath until electricity was restored.

'Distance-learning' allowed university degrees to be earned from island living rooms. And thanks to e-commerce, a merchant on Front Street or King's Square was no longer restricted to physical customers; a shopper unaware even of where Bermuda was, might click his mouse to order a watercolour or rum cake.

Bermudians studied and established careers overseas. They fought in global conflicts such as the Gulf War in 1991 and 9/11's fallout, the 2003 War on Iraq. They brought expertise home—or took it abroad. As the world

In their own words
■ Shaun Goater, 2003

Growing up in Bermuda, I used to think [Diego] Maradona was a top-class player, because I read that 10 or 11 people had named their babies after him in Argentina. The biggest compliment I've ever had was a fan who actually tattooed my name on his back.

It was a Saturday afternoon home game at Maine Road [stadium]. I parked the car and walked into the dressing room. You always have a minimum of about 20 fans waiting when you arrive, and more tag along as you're walking inside. The average fan can't get enough in terms of conversation and photos. And never mind the booklet or piece of paper for autographs—they want you to sign their boots, their shirt, their shorts, their arm… When we come out after the game, the fans are there again waiting in the dark and cold. For a photo. For an autograph. For you to sign a birthday card for someone. Because it's for their daughter, their cousin, their friend, it would "make their day." I always have time for it, because it comes with the job. I believe when they stop asking, then you should get worried.

On this particular day, a guy came up to me as I went in. I recognised him, because I'd encountered him several times before over the previous year. He sometimes asked for an autograph or for me to pose for a photo with him.

Shaun Goater

THE ROYAL GAZETTE

His name was Gareth. He was about 24 with bright ginger hair.

He said, "Hey, Shaun, look at this. Look what I've had done."

He already had two tattoos on his arm. One was a Man City crest, and another was something else related to City. I thought he had added another crest or something. Then he lifted his shirt and showed me. It stretched right across his whole back! My name and team number in Man City's sky blue, each letter four or five inches high: "GOATER 10."

At first it was scary to me—I thought he was crazy. But he was just a truly fanatical fan who loves City, and anyone who does well for City, he loves them, too. It's nice to have fans like that. They just appreciate what you do.

—Soccer star Shaun Goater, 32, in his fifth season as Manchester City striker, in February 2003

Don't rock the boat

Since the 1960s the atmosphere in Bermuda has been generally one of affluence, high consumption and don't-rock-the-boat conservatism. Conservation of resources has not been a concern to most residents except for fresh water. Business was booming and scarcity was unknown to most people.

—Bermuda's Delicate Balance: People and the Environment, 1981

In Iraq *The food's getting better but it's nothing like home-cooked. Pretty soon, I'm going to have to bring out my winter gear.*

—Sergeant Jason DiGiacomo, 22-year-old Bermudian soldier with the US Army's 25th Field Artillery Batallion in northern Iraq, in a letter to his parents, September 2003

shrank, or at least our sense of it did, Bermudian heroes also became international stars. Soccer's Shaun Goater, singer-songwriter Heather Nova, surgeon Malcolm Brock, solo sailor Alan Paris—many of Bermuda's young men and women made names for themselves far beyond the island's borders.

Bermuda's geographical isolation had not changed, just the means to overcome it. With distance no longer a factor in communication, diminutive size and relative political insignificance could seem, after 500 years of history, suddenly inconsequential. Yet were Bermudians better for it? Were their lives more enriched? Was the community more united? Did the stimulating pace of progress also promise children brighter futures? As islanders, Bermudians still asked the same fundamental questions their ancestors pondered: "Who are we?" And, perhaps more urgently, "Where are we going?"

The island's evolution into a stable and prosperous global participant was steady, but gradual. Bermuda's reinvention followed the troubled years of the 1970s and early '80s, when great social strides were made, yet not without a painful coming of age. Through the second half of the 1980s, Bermuda finally entered a settling-down period that heralded the wealth and opportunities of modern times. While tourism boomed, and then waned, international business only increased, injecting the island with thousands of new jobs and creating a second economic pillar that would strengthen and surpass the visitor industry over the next 20 years. A sea-change of development —commercial, technological, socio-economic—happened largely as a result, but also thanks to the sweep of fast-forward progress touching the world at large.

Tourism's rise lasted through the mid-'80s, when it hit a record peak of 650,000 arrivals per year—more than 10 times the local population. Retailers were kept busy supplying visitors' needs, and banks prospered by servicing merchants. The Bank of Bermuda—acquired for $1.3 billion in 2004 by behemoth HSBC Group—and Bank of Butterfield became powerful institutions, opening offices in overseas markets like Europe and the Far East. Bermuda Commercial Bank, which originated as a retail institution, later refocussed to cater solely to international business. A fourth bank, Capital G, run by the Gibbons Company group, opened in the 1990s.

With prosperity came a new responsibility towards Bermuda's heritage and the arts. The Bermuda National Trust, set up in 1970 to safeguard open spaces and the island's unique architecture, solidified its role as protector of environmental treasures. The Bermuda Festival of the Arts became a strong winter draw for locals and visitors to the island. The Biological Station for Research attracted top scientists to study climate, the ocean and marine pharmaceuticals. The Bermuda National Gallery, opened at Hamilton City Hall in 1992, showcased an impressive permanent collection and encouraged new artistic talent. The Masterworks Foundation succeeded in repatriating Bermuda artworks by luminaries such as Georgia O'Keeffe and Winslow Homer. The Bermuda International Film Festival made headlines in Hollywood, while helping Bermudian moviemakers hone their celluloid dreams. In the East End, the Bermudian Heritage Museum told the struggle of black Bermudians, while at Dockyard, the Bermuda Maritime Museum restored the 175-year-old Commissioner's House as a grand space to celebrate the island's cultural diversity. And on the eve of the new millennium, in December 2000, a campaign by the St. George's Foundation won Bermuda's first town prestigious status as a UNESCO World Heritage Site—an honour that would stoke cultural appreciation and eco-tourism along with restoration in St. George's and other parishes through the following decade.

Tourism's slide, when it began in the second half of the '80s, was precipitious, prompted by both foreign competition—more and cheaper destinations—and waning interest and soaring costs at home. Fewer young Bermudians were choosing the tourist trade as a career. Who wanted to be a waiter or chambermaid, many questioned, when a well-paid office job promised better security? Investment in hotels and guest properties on the island slumped. By the late 1990s and early 2000s, several large hotels had closed, including the Castle Harbour Marriott, the Belmont, Newstead, Lantana and the Palmetto Bay Hotel. Bermudian men and women were joining international business, as accountants, secretaries, lawyers, actuaries, underwriters, marketers and media consultants. The trickle-down success of the business sector fuelled widespread economic growth and strengthened the commercial infrastructure for which Bermuda's jurisdiction was envied by competing offshore markets. Its impact was felt on everything from

Corporate partnerships benefit island schools, charities and cultural groups. XL Capital chief Brian O'Hara, right, gets a digital demonstration from students

BERMUMDA SUN

Death throes *Let's face it, tourism has declined so far that if it were not for business visitors and relatives of guest workers, it would be in its final death throes.*
—Letter from Smith's Parish resident to The Royal Gazette, *October 28, 2003*

Struggle *Race relations issues are worldwide issues. Bermuda is no different from any other country as it struggles with race issues.*
—Myra Virgil, director of CURE (Commission for Unity & Racial Equality), Bermuda Sun, *November 5, 2003*

A controversial late-1990s Bermuda tourism ad

Sold our souls *Greed seems to have consumed this beautiful island which I love and have called home all of my life. Having sold our souls for the sake of a dollar, looking at Bermuda today in comparison to the Bermuda of 20 years ago, are we really better off?*
— *Letter to* The Royal Gazette, *May 17, 2003*

Business impact

■ *12,567 international companies were registered in Bermuda at the end of December, an increase of 9.5 percent on the previous year (1999)*
■ *International companies spent $967.3 million and their visitors a further $58 million*
■ *$405 million was paid as wages, salaries and benefits in Bermuda*
■ *1,825 Bermudian employees and 1,399 non-Bermudians worked for international companies*
— *Findings of the Archer Report of the Impact of International Business 2000*

Pivotal *If one place can be singled out as being pivotal to the growth and expansion of the reinsurance industry in the past 20 years, it is Bermuda.*
— Reactions *magazine, April 2002*

bustling restaurants to non-stop construction, while the largesse of cash-rich corporations fed art galleries, education initiatives and social-welfare projects.

Between 1995 and 1996, a benchmark was reached: international business finally eclipsed tourism in terms of foreign-exchange earnings. In that budget year, international-company spending generated a total of $154.3 million, compared to $126.3 million contributed by the visitor industry. The trend would only continue and the island's whole economy benefitted as a result; by 2003, Bermuda's total gross domestic product, the value of all its goods and services, totalled more than $3 billion. Jobs multiplied as more companies flocked to the island. Between 2002–3, the business sector created 236 new posts—twice the number generated by Bermuda's health, education or social services sectors.

The saturation of international business in Bermudians' daily lives—its vital importance to their well-being as individuals—was evident on the most fundamental levels. Where else might so many teenagers aspire to become actuaries? How many small-town newspapers would carry as much ink on the arcana of 'D&O' (directors and officers liability), 'ART' (alternative risk transfer), or 'RIMS' (Risk and Insurance Management Society)? And how many residents of a tiny community would be as familiar with them? Efforts to revive tourism continued, but it appeared there was no turning back. Bermuda's economic fortunes had forged a new path—one that would deliver sweeping benefits, but also pose uniquely daunting challenges.

Brian O'Hara remembers his first days, in the mid-1980s, at a new Bermuda company called EXEL—a title prescient of its unbridled fortunes over the next two decades. "I came here," he says, "attracted to the opportunities I saw in Bermuda becoming a truly international centre." An erstwhile California resident, O'Hara would appreciate that he was riding a symbolic wave, one that would generate millions of dollars for shareholders of companies like EXEL (later XL Capital Ltd., of which he was president and CEO), and for the island in which such corporations chose to put down stakes. It was the beginning, in many ways, for although international business, and more specifically the insurance industry, had discovered Bermuda's benefits as early as the 1940s, it was not until the '80s that the sheer volume of success would begin to be realised.

The Bermuda market, which averaged 13-percent annual growth in total assets between 1984 and 2003, gained a reputation for its lack of onerous regulations, its relatively sophisticated infrastructure, and innovation. Some of that new thinking created companies like XL, and ACE Ltd., excess liability

TIMELINE 1945–2005

BERMUDA

1946 Law is changed to allow motor cars for public use in Bermuda

1951 The Royal Naval Dockyard closes

1955 Islanders tune in to first TV station broadcasting from US base

1959 Cinema boycott spurs desegregation in churches, hotels, restaurants

1968 UBP wins first general election contested by political parties

1970 Currency goes decimal, replacing pounds and shillings with dollars and cents

WORLD

1946 Nazi leaders on trial for war crimes in Nuremburg, Germany

1947 UN agrees to split Palestine into Arab and Jewish states, a move fought by Arabs

1953 Edmund Hillary and Sherpa Tensing conquer the top of the world, Mount Everest

1955 Europe's Communist states sign military treaty, the Warsaw Pact

1962 Jamaica, Trinidad and Tobago become independent; Barbados follows four years later

1969 US astronaut Neil Armstrong takes first steps on moon; 600 million watch via live TV

Too much traffic?

Bermuda's general affluence has spawned ugly side effects, such as traffic congestion and resulting noise pollution and safety worries. Overcrowding on the roads has been a theme of concern among lawmakers and the public from as early as the 1960s, prompting much discussion of inducements and solutions ranging from improved pedestrian routes to micro-cars. Yet Bermudians have been reluctant to forego the convenience of their private vehicles in favour of public transport, car-pooling, ownership limits or other restrictive measures.

BERMUDA SUN

Couch potatoes

Bermuda can pat itself on the back following a recent survey that showed the island is among the most technologically advanced in the world when it comes to telephone lines, Internet usage and personal computer ownership. But one statistic in the World Economic Forum survey should be cause more for embarrassment than pride. It showed there are 108 televisions on the island for every 100 persons— the highest rate in the world. Television-watching, unlike using the Internet, is an essentially passive activity. Are we such couch potatoes that we need (by some estimates) three TVs in every household?

—*Editorial,* The Royal Gazette,
January 15, 2004

insurers whose mandate was to ease a worldwide shortage of capacity for coverage in the late '80s. Both would evolve their scope and also play a role in the development of the reinsurance market during subsequent decades.

The island saw a gradual convergence of the financial and insurance industries, drawing ever more newcomers to Hamilton's expanding borders. Centre Re, Commercial Risk, Stockton Re—these and several other key players followed ACE and XL, and the credibility of the Bermuda market grew. In turn, international business brought demand for legal, accounting and banking services, along with supporting industries such as travel agencies and communications firms, driving the local economy. Self-regulating industry bodies such as the Insurance Advisory Committee were established, working with the Bermuda Monetary Authority to vet new incorporations—an example of the close private-sector-government partnership dubbed "Bermuda Inc." by the business media.

Bermuda's status as a leading business centre was confirmed in the 1990s after the ravages of California's Northridge Earthquake and Hurricane Andrew in southern Florida. A slew of so-called "big cat" catastrophe insurers arrived—Renaissance Re, PartnerRe, Tempest Re—bringing with them billions of dollars of capital. Throughout the '90s the market expanded and diversified, with key players acquiring companies and adding new lines of business. Over time, a mature market emerged, rivalling established centres such as Lloyd's of London.

1973 Governor Sir Richard Sharples and aide Hugh Sayers are assassinated at Government House	**1977** Street riots protest the hangings of killers Larry Tacklyn and Erskine Burrows	**1987** Tourism reaches an all-time record of almost 630,000 visitors a year	**1998** First PLP government wins landslide election victory	**2001** Bermudians killed in New York's 9/11 attack; security tightened around island	**2004** HSBC, the world's second-largest bank, buys Bank of Bermuda for $1.3 billion
1970 First "jumbo" jet flies from New York to London	**1978** Louise Brown, the world's first test-tube baby, conceived by in vitro fertilisation, is born in UK	**1982** Scientists identify the AIDS virus, and discover a hole in the ozone layer over Antarctica	**1990** Apartheid ends in South Africa and jailed black leader Nelson Mandela goes free	**1991** The World Wide Web, created by British scientist Tim Berners-Lee, makes its public debut	**2003** US captures Iraq dictator Saddam Hussein, who denies building 'weapons of mass destruction'

BERMUDA

WORLD

A long haul

Bermuda's unusual fish-hook shape has caused transport problems for as long as there have been tracks or roads. Today's daily commute to Hamilton from the outer parishes is a long haul at the best of times and over the years there have been many proposed schemes to ease the problem, from a bridge over the Great Sound to a traffic tunnel beneath it. Current thinking favours the new fast ferries (below) to tempt motorists from behind the wheel.

BERMUDA MEDIA

Benefits *If [machinery manufacturer] Ingersoll actually wants to leave the United States and set up shop in Bermuda, so be it. Lovely golf courses, and all that. But Ingersoll-Rand doesn't want to leave. Its executive offices are in Woodcliff Lake, New Jersey. Its CEO and all its top officers live here in the States. It wants the benefits of US citizenship; it just doesn't want to pay for them.*
—Article headlined "Tax Cheat, Inc.,"
The New Yorker, *April 22, 2002*

Unpatriotic *I'm tired of seeing chief executives permitted to take their millions or billions to Bermuda and leave the average American here at home stuck with the tax bill. You know what I call that? Unpatriotic.*
—US Democratic presidential
candidate, Massachusetts Senator
John Kerry, in a campaign speech
before winning the New Hampshire
primary, January 27, 2004

Another wave of insurers hit Bermuda after September 11, 2001, creating a veritable "global insurance community," according to *Forbes* magazine in December 2002, estimating Bermuda's insurance sector would pay $5 billion of the $24-billion tragedy. But with companies such as Endurance Speciality, Montpelier Re, AXIS and DaVinci Reinsurance, 9/11 also brought a $20-billion injection of new capital—or $275,000 for every man, woman and child of the 63,500 population. By the close of 2001, some 1,600 international insurers and reinsurers were based on the island, with a total of $172.7 billion in assets. None could now argue the Bermuda market's success was beginner's luck; instead, its tiny business laboratory was the envy of the world.

Such progress happened against the backdrop of the "New Economy." Rapidly developing technology allowed business to be speedier and more efficient. Small firms found the power to compete with well-established entities without spending on traditional overhead. And rare was the company, or, increasingly, the home, which did not have a computer to carry out a transaction or tap into 'Net-based resources. Online shopping, chat rooms, day-trading, e-commerce—in the second half of the 1990s, Bermuda morphed along with the rest of the world into a "wired" society. Aside from the way it changed private lives, electronic business also was touted as a potentially vast new economic sector that might draw a slew of "dot-com" start-up companies to the island. That prediction turned out to be short-lived, particularly after disenchanted stock markets turned the worldwide dot-com boom to bust in 2000. But there was no turning back. The Digital Revolution had changed the world forever, and the island was no exception.

Did it buy us more leisure time, as promised in the halcyon days of science fiction, when trend-predictors envisioned gadgets making our lives easier? No, in fact we had less free time once cell phones could track us down at the beach on Sundays, and e-mail beckoned 24 hours from work and home. Technology's toys, while enabling us to connect with each other, had somehow brought more stress, not less. Information overload was the world's new headache. Change was the only certainty. Against such a frenetic outlook, past rhythms of life seemed almost laughably archaic. Had islanders really rushed down to Front Street in the 1890s to welcome the weekly mail steamer? What of those long Thursday afternoons of the 1950s and '60s, when Hamilton believed in shutting down so citizens could play golf or go swimming instead? It wasn't just a song anymore; Bermuda *was* another world.

Although the island was largely sheltered from shifting economic conditions by its business boom, Bermuda remained frighteningly dependent on the whims of the world.

After September 11, 2001, an outpouring of nationalistic fervour by America saw a backlash against US companies that chose to use Bermuda as headquarters for tax and other reasons. American lawmakers and consumers branded Bermuda-based US corporations as anti-patriotic tax-dodgers, and launched a major campaign to force them home. When it made plans to reincorporate in Bermuda after 9/11 while keeping its physical base in the US, manufacturing giant Ingersoll-Rand Co. was singled out as symbolising the flight of capital, and corporate taxes, from US shores. Though the company carried through with its plan, saving an estimated $40 million a year, and America's hand-wringing eventually ebbed, the case underscored Bermuda's economic fragility. Perennial threats of higher tax levies or

The quest for nationhood

The question of sovereignty—should Bermuda end its colonial status and become an independent nation?—has been a perennial political football, as well as an emotional and financial puzzle for islanders.

Such a move would necessitate opening foreign embassies, bolstering island security and defence, and signing treaties with mainland neighbours, among other things. Over the years, many Bermudians argued cutting colonial ties was just a matter of time. The island's royalists, however, felt that time should never come.

The Pitt Commission into the 1977 riots recommended independence as a salve for the island's social turbulence: "Only with independence can national unity be forged and pride in being Bermudian fully develop," it opined.

UBP Premier Sir John Swan's push for sovereignty forced him to resign after a 1995 referendum found most Bermudians were against cutting ties with Britain. The PLP, which had long advocated nationhood, urged a boycott; it felt independence should be decided via a general election.

In 1999, Britain's white paper on remaining overseas dependent territories stated Westminister would back sovereignty "when independence is the clear and constitutionally expressed wish of the people."

In 2004, Premier Alex Scott again opened the door to nation-building, calling for a full independence debate.

"The subject of independence does not belong to any one political party," noted Chamber of Commerce president Charles Gosling. "It belongs to the people of Bermuda. We have to ensure this is not something that is going to be divisive and ultimately destroy the island."

COURTESY OF PETER WOOLCOCK

Premier Jennifer Smith takes aim at US tax-haven opponents in cartoon

work-permit restrictions led to similar corporate jitters, and put Bermuda on notice that competing offshore centres such as Dublin or Cayman were waiting in the wings should the island falter.

The closure of military bases in Bermuda in the final decade of the 20th Century was another example of the price of our dependence on foreign capital. The Canadian base closed in 1994, followed the next year by HMS *Malabar* when the Royal Navy completed its withdrawal from Bermuda, recalling its handful of remaining liaison officers. The US Naval facility in the East End was also shut down in 1995 following a sweep of cost-cutting closures by America's military throughout the world. Thousands of American servicemen pulled out, leaving the airport and baselands once again in Bermudian hands—a full 10 percent of Bermuda's landmass.

How to use the windfall was just one of the many questions facing islanders in the ensuing years. Some land was used for subsidised housing and recreational facilities, but with property at such a premium, decisions were lengthy and difficult given the long-term economic ramifications.

With no significant manufacturing base or natural resources, Bermuda could sell only its physical beauty and tax-friendly status. But as the first decade of the new century unfolded, lawmakers and laymen alike began to call for economic diversification and more thoughtful long-term planning to avoid mistakes of the past. Bermudians had a talent for seizing shifting opportunities; but more than once, islanders had made the fatal error of risking all their economic eggs in a single basket.

As voters went to the polls on November 9, 1998, they held in their ballot the political fate of two party leaders: Pamela Gordon and Jennifer Smith. Both could claim evocative life stories. One was the daughter of strident 1950s activist and MP, Dr. E. F. Gordon, who, perhaps surprisingly given her father's career of black-rights campaigns, had chosen the historically white, conservative United Bermuda Party in which to make her political mark. Her counterpart was a St. George's artist, journalist and Senator who had risen through Progressive Labour Party ranks to embody its black-rights struggle and grassroots support. The election was to be a

*A PLP supporter celebrates after
the 1998 election victory*

The expat issue

*It is time for a government of
Bermudians, meaning people that
were born on this island, to take a
stand. There is going to come a
time, and we are headed there soon,
that our island home will be over-
thrown by foreigners. You wonder
why we have a housing crisis in
Bermuda, why our roads are overcrowded?*
—*Letter to* The Royal Gazette *from a
Paget resident, November 5, 2003*

*I find it very disheartening to have
to read and listen to unacceptable,
non-progressive, biased attitudes
when all we are doing is bringing
our skills and experience, choosing
to have a temporary lifestyle change
and going about our business quietly
and lawfully.*
—*Letter to* The Royal Gazette *from
an expatriate, responding to
Bermudian criticism of foreign
workers, November 4, 2003*

watershed in the island's political history, but perhaps even more significant than the result, was the fact both leaders were not only black, but female. Bermuda had come a long way from the days of Gladys Morrell and the fight for universal suffrage.

As pundits predicted, it was Smith and the PLP who scored an unprecedented victory that day—throwing the UBP into the role of government opposition for the first time in its 35-year history. The ballot was an undeniable landslide: 26 seats to 14, with 54 percent of the national vote (including a new wave of younger voters, since the age limit had been lowered to 18 in 1989). The outcome galvanised black Bermudians, many of whom felt it was a long-deserved chance at more inclusive democracy. The PLP had also won support from white voters. Some felt annoyed by UBP dalliances with political hot potatoes such as independence from Britain and the attempted lifting of a franchise ban for McDonald's. Others felt having a government rooted in black activism would perhaps help to heal racial frictions.

Yet no-one could deny Bermuda had made substantial political and social strides over nearly four decades. The school leaving age was raised to 16 and schools were finally integrated. In 1974, existing post-secondary institutes and the Sixth Form Centre were amalgamated as the Bermuda College, which opened at Prospect before moving to the Stonington Campus in Paget. Education got a further revamp in the early 1990s, when the system was restructured into primary and middle schools and two senior secondary schools—Berkeley Institute and CedarBridge Academy. Scholarships abounded for high-school graduates hoping to pursue university degrees from fine art to engineering. The island's healthcare was also upgraded, with massive spending at the King Edward VII Memorial Hospital, which added new operating rooms, breast cancer-screening and CT scan systems, an MRI machine, and a recompression chamber for divers. Partnership with top American hospitals allowed patients to be flown overseas for complex procedures such as heart operations.

Business had flourished, and with it, the job market, offering more and better opportunities for Bermudians. Notably, by the turn of the 21st Century, half of the island's 35,000 jobs were held by women. But Bermuda's unavoidable labour shortage created a gap that was filled by qualified expatriate workers, mostly from the UK, the US and Canada, fuelling a sense of alienation among many Bermudians, particularly young black men, who felt shut out of the island's success story. Many blamed entrenched racism, a persistent problem, though islanders black and white were at last talking openly about prejudice and ways to end it.

The first four years of PLP government could not heal such deep-rooted wounds any more than UBP efforts had done. By the first election of the new century, on July 24, 2003, one of the most notable changes had been a contentious campaign to redraw constituency boundaries for a one-man, one-vote electoral process, reducing the number of parliamentary seats from 40 to 36. The government argued such a system was fairer and brought Bermuda in line with modern universal suffrage. Vindicated by voters, the PLP again secured a majority, this time of 22 to 14 seats, though Premier Smith was promptly replaced by her peers the following day with party stalwart Alex Scott.

The social challenges facing his government, and all Bermudians, were

Culture club Bermuda has long been a melting pot of cultures and never more so than in the 21st Century. In addition to the colourful traditions of gombeys and Portuguese (above), the island now includes growing overseas communities such as Filipinos and East Indians, each enthusiastically adding to the diversity and palette of this small island nation.

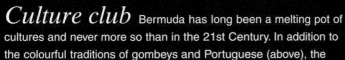

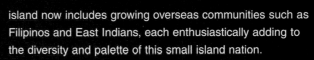

Laughable *The salaries which my husband and I bring home put us (according to the latest census data) in the well-off income bracket. This was quite laughable to us, because where else in the world but in Bermuda would someone whose income categorises them in this way still not be able to afford to purchase their own home?*

—*Letter to* The Royal Gazette,
May 17, 2003

By its wits *This is an island that has always had to live by its wits and has had to overcome greater challenges than it faces now. It has done so in spite of internal differences and through a recognition that everyone who lives on this island, black and white, rich and poor, young and old, rises and falls together. Bermuda is too small, and Bermudians have too much in common, for it to be any other way.*

—*Editorial,* The Royal Gazette,
December 31, 2003

crucial to solve. Ironically, some of the biggest pressures were fruits of Bermuda's runaway success: building development threatened open space and biodiversity, including fragile species like the whistling tree frog and endemic skink; the influx of foreign workers pushed affordable housing beyond the reach of many locals (the average home price stood at about $1 million by 2004); traffic snarls (caused by 44,000 cars and motorcycles), noise pollution and waste disposal challenges were the nasty by-products of North American-style consumerism, while drug abuse, rising crime, even gang warfare, threatened the traditional island way of life.

What would Juan de Bermúdez make of modern Bermuda? Or Sir George Somers? Or Mary Prince, or the first Portuguese? How would they judge us as inhabitants who hold the future of this island they once knew? Perhaps in the core of our consciousness, we are not that different. Our strength as Bermudians has been an ability to overcome incredible odds. Over 500 years, we have made one single achievement above all others: survival. And with it won democracy, freedom and wealth. Century after century, islanders have managed to turn adversity into opportunity, find silver linings, weather unknowns and forge successes big enough to span generations. If we have one characteristic symbolic of who we are, something which defines us as Bermudians, it is probably this.

The story of Bermuda is the story of its people—resilient, pragmatic, big-hearted in the face of threats, be they hurricanes or terrorism. We are comforted by what we can count on in each other, islanders' traits like neighbourliness, humour amid tragedy, a tell-it-like-it-is brand of stoicism towards the world's uncertainties. For all our self-absorption and perennial complacency, Bermudians cannot escape the powerfully unifying force of a shared legacy. Whether we have a generations-old birthright, British parents, West Indian roots or an Azorean name, we are bound by the tales of pioneers and pirates, and inspired by faith in the future, wherever it leads us.

Bibliography

GENERAL REFERENCE

Articles & Essays

Granatstein, J. L., and Hillmer, Norman, "Canada's Century, The 25 Events That Shaped the Country," *Maclean's*, July 1, 1999

Hitchens, Christopher, "Why Americans Are Not Taught History," *Harper's*, November 1998

Kirn, Walter, "Lewis and Clark, The Journey That Changed America Forever," *Time*, July 8, 2002

Books

Bernard, Bruce, *Century, One Hundred Years of Human Progress, Regression, Suffering and Hope* (London, Phaidon Press, 2000)

Bryans, Robin, *Azores* (London, Faber & Faber, 1963)

Chisholm, Jane, *Timelines of World History* (Usborne, 2002)

Evans, Harold, *The American Century* (New York, Alfred A. Knopf, 1998)

Farndon, John, *Concise Encyclopedia* (New York, DK Publishing, 1999)

Garner, Joe, *We Interrupt This Broadcast, The Events That Stopped Our Lives...from the Hindenburg Explosion to the Death of John F. Kennedy Jr.* (Illinois, Sourcebooks, Inc., second edition, 2000)

Jennings, Peter and Brewster, Todd, *Century* (New York, Doubleday, 1998)

The New American Desk Encyclopedia (New York, Meridian, 1987)

The Norton Anthology of English Literature, third edition (New York, W. W. Norton & Company, 1975)

The Random House Timetables of History (New York, Random House, 1991)

The Riverside Shakespeare (Boston, Houghton Mifflin, 1974)

Schama, Simon, *A History of Britain, At the Edge of the World? 3500 B.C.–1603 A.D.* (New York, Hyperion/talk miramax books, 2000)

BERMUDA REFERENCE

Newspapers, Periodicals & Journals

Bermuda Journal of Archaeology and Maritime History, Volumes 1–13, 1989–2003

Bermuda Historical Quarterly, Volumes 1–39, 1944–83

Henderson, Dwight Franklin (ed.), *The Private Journal of Georgiana Gholson Walker 1862–1865, With Selections from the Post-War Years, 1865–1876* (Confederate Publishing Company, 1963)

Market Solutions 2003, Bermuda: The World's Risk Capital, Insurance Advisory Committee (Bermuda, 2003)

The Royal Gazette, Bermuda Sun, The Mid-Ocean News, The Workers Voice, The Bermudian, Bermudian Business, Bermuda, RG magazine, MARITimes (various issues)

Film

Bermuda: Five Centuries, six-part series, Panatel VDS Ltd. for the Bermuda Millennium Committee, 1999

Williams, Errol, *When Voices Rise...*, 2002

Articles & Essays

Allen, Frederick Lewis, "Bermuda, 1938," *Harper's Monthly*, No. 1055, April 1938

The Association of Bermuda Affairs, "An Analysis of Bermuda's Social Problems (the limited franchise, segregation and discrimination)," 1953

Barreiro-Meiro, Roberto, "Las Islas Bermudas y Juan Bermúdez," Instituto Histórico de Marina, Madrid, 1970

Forster, Tony, "The Day the Captive Was Born," The Fred Reiss Foundation, 2002

Higginbottom, Dennis J., "The Development of the Bermuda Reinsurance Market," *Journal of Reinsurance*, Spring 2002

Jarvis, Michael J., "Cedars, Sloops and Slaves: The Development of the Bermuda Shipbuilding Industry 1680–1750," thesis presented to the Faculty of the Department of History, The College of William & Mary, 1992

Lavela, Bean Jolene, "West Indians in Our Midst, A Brief Study of Our West Indian-Bermudian Heritage," *The Bermudian*, May 1992

Mardis, Allen, "Richard Moore, Carpenter," *Virginia Magazine of History & Biography*, October 1984

Maxwell, Clarence V. H., "Race and Servitude: The Birth of a Social and Political Order in Bermuda, 1619–1669," *BJAMH*, Volume 11, 1999

McCombe, Leonard and Skadding, George (photogs.), "Bermuda Makes Modern History," *Life*, Volume 35, No. 24, December 14, 1953

Strock, George (photog.), "Old Bermuda, Honeymoon Isles Become US Defense Bastion," *Life*, August 18, 1941

Surowiecki, James, "Tax Cheat, Inc.," *The New Yorker*, April 22 & 29, 2002

Taft, William Howard, "The Islands of Bermuda, A British Colony with a Unique Record in Popular Government," *National Geographic*, Volume 41, January–June 1922

Ziral, James, "The Seduction of Black America," *The Bermudian*, May 1997

Books

Aspinall, Algernon, *The Pocket Guide to the West Indies* (London, Sifton, Praed & Co., 1923)

Beebe, William, *Adventuring with Beebe, Selections from the Writings of William Beebe*, (New York/Boston/Toronto, Duell, Sloan and Pearce/Little Brown, 1955)

Bell, Frank R., *Beautiful Bermuda: The Standard Guide to Bermuda* (New York, Beautiful Bermuda Publishing Co., Inc., ninth edition, 1946)

Benbow, Colin H., *Gladys Morrell and the Women's Suffrage Movement in Bermuda* (Bermuda, The Writers' Machine, 1994)

Benbow, Colin H., *Boer Prisoners of War in Bermuda* (Bermuda, Bermuda Historical Society, third edition, 1994)

Bermuda Islands Guide: The Complete Map and Information Guide to Bermuda (Bermuda, Clarion Enterprises, 1982)

Bermuda National Trust, *Bermuda's Architectural Heritage: Devonshire* (Bermuda, 1995)

Bermuda National Trust, *Bermuda's Architectural Heritage: St. George's* (Bermuda, 1998)

Bermuda National Trust, *Bermuda's Architectural Heritage: Sandys* (Bermuda, 1999)

Bermuda Trade Development Board, *Residence in Bermuda*, 1936

Bernhard, Virginia, *Slaves and Slaveholders in Bermuda, 1616–1782* (Columbia, Missouri, University of Missouri Press, 1999)

Blagg, G. Daniel, *Bermuda Atlas & Gazetteer* (Dover, Delaware, Dover Litho Publishing Company, 1997)

Boyle, Peter G. (ed.), *The Churchill-Eisenhower Correspondence 1953–1955* (Chapel Hill, North Carolina, The University of North Carolina Press, 1990)

Britton, Nathaniel Lord, *Flora of Bermuda* (New York, Scribner & Sons, 1918)

Butler, Dale (ed.), *L. Frederick Wade: His Legacy* (Bermuda, The Writers' Machine, 1997)

Calnan, Patricia, *The Masterworks Bermudiana Collection* (Bermuda, The Bermudian Publishing Company, 1994)

Cox, John (ed.), *Life in Old Bermuda* (Bermuda, John Cox, 1998)

Crombie, Roger, *Conyers Dill & Pearman: A*

History (Bermuda, Walsingham Press, 1998)

Darrell, Owen H., *Sir George Somers: Links Bermuda With Lyme Regis* (Bermuda, Owen H. Darrell, 1997)

Deichmann, Catherine Lynch, *Rogues & Runners: Bermuda and the American Civil War* (Bermuda, Bermuda National Trust, 2002)

Dorr, Julia C. R., *Bermuda: An Idyl of the Summer Islands* (New York, Charles Scribner's Sons, 1884)

Gates, Henry Louis, Jr. (ed.), *The Classic Slave Narratives* (New York, Mentor, 1987)

Godet, Nan and Harris, Edward C., *Pillars of the Bridge: The establishment of the United States bases on Bermuda during the Second World War,* (Bermuda, Bermuda Maritime Museum Press, 1991)

Hallett, A. C. Hollis, *Bermuda Under the Somers Islands Company, Civil Records 1612–1684* (Volume 1, 1612–1669) (Bermuda, Bermuda Maritime Museum Press, 2004)

Harris, Edward C., *Bermuda Forts, 1612–1957* (Bermuda, Bermuda Maritime Museum Press, 1997)

Harris, Edward C., *Great Guns of Bermuda, A Guide to the Principal Forts of the Bermuda Islands* (Bermuda, Bermuda Maritime Museum Press, second printing, 1992)

Hayward, Stuart J., Gomez, Vicki Holt and Sterrer, Wolfgang, *Bermuda's Delicate Balance* (Bermuda, Bermuda National Trust, 1982)

Hayward, Walter B., *Bermuda Past and Present* (New York, Dodd, Mead & Company, 1910)

Heyl, Edith Stowe Godfrey (ed.), *Bermuda Through the Camera of James B. Heyl 1868–1897* (Glasgow, Robert MacLehose and Company, 1951)

Hodgson, Eva N., *Second Class Citizens, First Class Men* (Bermuda, The Writers' Machine, third edition, 1997)

Hunter, Barbara Harries, *The People of Bermuda: Beyond the Crossroads* (Bermuda, Barbara Harries Hunter, 1993)

Ingham, Jennifer M., *Defence Not Defiance: A History of the Bermuda Volunteer Rifle Corps* (Bermuda, Jennifer M. Ingham, 1992)

Ives, Vernon (ed.), *The Rich Papers, Letters From Bermuda, 1615–1646* (Bermuda, Bermuda National Trust, 1984)

Jones, John Matthew, *The Naturalist in Bermuda. A Sketch of the Geology, Zoology and Botany* (London, Reeves & Turner, 1859)

Jourdan, Silvanus, *The Discovery of the Barmudas* (London, 1610) (facsimile edition)

Kennedy, Jean, *Isle of Devils, Bermuda Under the Somers Island Company 1609–1685* (Glasgow, William Collins Sons & Co., 1971)

Kerr, Wilfred Brenton, *Bermuda and the American Revolution: 1760–1783* (Bermuda, Bermuda Maritime Museum Press, 1995) (facsimile edition)

Klein, Herbert S., *The Atlantic Slave Trade* (New York, Cambridge University Press, 1999)

Lefroy, Major General Sir John Henry, *Memorials of the Discovery and Early Settlement of the Bermudas or Somers Islands (1511–1687)* (Volumes I and II) (Bermuda, reprinted by the Bermuda Historical Society and the Bermuda National Trust, 1981)

McCallan, E. A., *Life on Old St. David's, Bermuda* (Bermuda, Bermuda Historical Society, second edition, 1986)

McDowall, Duncan, *Another World: Bermuda and the Rise of Modern Tourism* (London, MacMillan Education Ltd., 1999)

Mudd, Patricia Marirea, *Portuguese Bermudians, Early History and Reference Guide 1849–1949* (Louisville, Kentucky, Historical Research Publishers, 1991)

Packwood, Cyril Outerbridge, *Chained on the Rock* (Bermuda, The Island Press, 1975)

Philip, Ira, *Freedom Fighters: From Monk to Mazumbo* (London, Akira Press, 1987)

Plowman, Piers and Card, Stephen J., *Queen of Bermuda and the Furness Bermuda Line* (Bermuda, Bermuda Maritime Museum Press, 2002)

Raymond, Jocelyn Motyer, *Saturday's Children: A Journey from Darkness into Light, Bermuda, 1850* (Bermuda, Arrowroot Press, 1994)

Robinson, Kenneth E., *Heritage, Including an Account of Bermudian Builders, Pilots and Petitioners of the Early Post-Abolition Period 1834–1849* (London, MacMillan Education Ltd., The Berkeley Educational Society, 1979)

Rushe, George, *Bermuda: As a Matter of Fact* (Bermuda, George Rushe, fifth edition, 1988)

Simons, Tamell (photog.), *Date With Destiny, A Photographic History* (Bermuda, Baobab Publishing, 1999)

Smith, James E., *Slavery in Bermuda* (New York, Vantage Press, 1976)

Stark, James H., *Stark's Illustrated Bermuda Guide* (Boston, James H. Stark, 1902)

Stranack, Ian, *The Andrew and the Onions, The Story of the Royal Navy in Bermuda 1795–1975* (Bermuda, Bermuda Maritime Museum Press, 1990)

Strode, Hudson, *The Story of Bermuda* (New York, Harrison Smith & Robert Haas, 1932)

Thomas, Martin J., *The Natural History of Bermuda* (Bermuda, Bermuda Zoological Society, 2004)

Trimingham, R.W., *Under the Calabash Tree: 150 Years of the Royal Bermuda Yacht Club* (Bermuda, The Bermudian Publishing Company, 1996)

Tucker, Terry, *Bermuda's Story* (Bermuda, Bermuda Bookstores, 1959)

Tucker, Terry, *Bermuda: Unintended Destination 1609–1610* (Bermuda, The Island Press, second printing, 1982)

Verrill, Addison E., *The Bermuda Islands* (New York, Addison Verrill, 1902)

Wells, Carveth, *Bermuda in Three Colours*, (New York, Robert M. McBride & Company, 1935)

Wilkinson, Henry C., *The Adventurers of Bermuda* (London, Oxford University Press, 1933)

Wilkinson, Henry C., *Bermuda in the Old Empire* (London, Oxford University Press, 1950)

Wilkinson, Henry C., *Bermuda From Sail to Steam, A History of the Island From 1784 to 1901* (Volumes I & II) (London, Oxford University Press, 1973)

Williams, Malcolm E., Sousa, Peter T. and Harris, Edward C., *Coins of Bermuda* (Bermuda, Bermuda Monetary Authority, 1997)

Williams, Ronald John, *Bermudiana* (New York/Toronto, Rinehart & Company, 1946)

Winchester, Simon, *Outposts: Journeys to the surviving relics of the British Empire* (Great Britain, Sceptre, 1988)

Woolcock, Peter, *Woppened 14, The Year in Review: 2001–2002, Cartoons for* The Royal Gazette (Bermuda, *The Royal Gazette*, 2002)

Writers' Machine, The, *Mazumbo*, 1994

Zuill, William, *Bermuda Sampler, 1815–1850* (Suffolk, England, Richard Clay & Sons, 1937)

Zuill, William, *Horsewhips in High Places: The Turbulent Decade 1819–29* (Bermuda, The Hamilton Press, 1976)

Zuill, W. S., *The Story of Bermuda and Her People* (London, MacMillan Caribbean, MacMillan Publishers, second edition, 1983)

Index